Snake Hill

An Investigation of a Military Cemetery
from the War of 1812

Edited by Susan Pfeiffer and
Ronald F. Williamson

Dundurn Press
Toronto & Oxford
1991

Design: JAQ
Copy Editor: Martin Ahermaa
Production: Eva Payne
Printing and Binding: Gagné Printing Ltd., Louiseville, Quebec, Canada

Dundurn Press wishes to acknowledge the generous assistance and ongoing support of **The Canada Council, The Book Publishing Industry Development Programme of the Department of Communications, The Ontario Arts Council,** and **The Ontario Heritage Foundation.**
    Care has been taken to trace the ownership of copyright material used in the text, including the illustrations. The editors and publisher welcome any information enabling them to rectify any reference or credit in subsequent editions.
                                                                — J. Kirk Howard, Publisher

Canadian Cataloguing in Publication Data

Snake Hill : an investigation of a military cemetery
        from the War of 1812

ISBN 1-55002-090-0

1. Fort Erie (Fort Erie, Ont.) – Siege, 1814.
2. Canada – History – War of 1812 – Antiquities.*
3. United States – History – War of 1812 –
Antiquities.   4. Fort Erie (Ont.) – Antiquities.
5. Excavations (Archaeology) – Ontario – Fort Erie.
I. Pfeiffer, Susan, 1947–   . II. Williamson,
R. F. (Ronald F.).

FC3099.F67A38 1991   971.03'4   C91-094755-4
F1057.9.S53 1991

Dundurn Press Limited   Dundurn Distribution
2181 Queen Street East   73 Lime Walk
Suite 301   Headington
Toronto, Canada   Oxford, England
M4E 1E5   OX3 7AD

Snake Hill

Published with the assistance of the
Ontario Heritage Foundation,
Ministry of Culture and Communications

CONTENTS

Appendices: The U.S. Military Button Assemblage from Snake Hill

References

LIST OF FIGURES

LIST OF TABLES

ACKNOWLEDGEMENTS

This volume provides a summary of two years of archaeological and biological anthropological research which would not have been possible without the generous support of a number of institutions. We would like to thank the Ontario Ministry of Culture and Communications, Veterans Affairs Canada, the United States Army, the Royal Ontario Museum, the Hannah Institute for the History of Medicine, the Social Sciences and Humanities Research Council, the Canadian Armed Forces, the United States Armed Forces Institute of Pathology and the Town of Fort Erie. In particular, we would like to thank the Town of Fort Erie for having the extraordinary vision to immediately assume leadership once the urgency and complexities of the situation were delineated. The Town, in deliberations with other provincial, national and international agencies, consistently and expertly argued that the first priority was the timely and professional exhumation of the skeletal remains, prior to their destruction by inclement weather. Mr. Bob Smith of the Town of Fort Erie coordinated the logistical support, without which, the project would not have been possible. His efforts, at times, went well beyond that which can be expected. We would like to thank Mr. Harry Rosettani for his warmth, encouragement and generous hospitality to the entire team. We would also like to thank Mr. Ron Rienas, Town Planner, for his invaluable assistance.

We are also indebted to the various field assistants including Mr. Jim Pengelly, Ms. Sue Pengelly, Ms. Penny Young, Ms. Anita Buerle, Mr. Andrew Stewart, Ms. Kathy Mills, Ms. Carol Ramsden and Mr. Ron Yalowika. Special thanks are owed to Mr. Brent Wood of the Niagara Region Health Services Department and Ms. Kathleen Arries. The heavy machinery was operated by Mr. Kevin Beam and Mr. Brian Cloke who were especially sensitive to the needs of the project.

We are also indebted to Mr. William Fox of the Ministry of Culture and Communications for his assistance, to Dr. Peter Storck for arranging access to laboratory facilities at the Royal Ontario Museum, and to the landowners, Mr. Vince Dunn, Mr. Howard Beattie and Ms. Valerie Beattie, who were faced with several difficult months.

Mr. Michael Musick of the National Archives and Record Administration of the United States and Mr. Stephen Everett of the U.S. Army Centre of Military History also provided crucial assistance. All of the field photographs were taken by Sgt. Lawrence Llewellyn of the United States Armed Forces Institute of Pathology and the laboratory photographs by Mr. John Glover. We would like to express our deepest appreciation to Lt. Col. D. W. Prosser, Canadian Armed Forces, Lt. Col. R. Trotter, then with the United States Army and former Fort Erie Deputy Mayor Doug Martin for their understanding and endeavours in securing the funds in order to conduct a comprehensive analysis of the archaeological and skeletal remains.

Finally, we are indebted to Ms. Janice Wiseman, Ms. Catherine Vanderburgh-Kerr, Mr. David Johnston, Mr. Andrew Allan and Ms. Carol Short for their editorial assistance and aid in preparing the volume. Ms. Short, especially, has expended major effort and time in the preparation of this work, and it simply would not have been possible to finish it without her.

Foreword # Recovery and Analysis of Human Remains from Historic Sites

To paraphrase the evolutionary biologist Stephen Jay Gould, medicine and human biology are "sciences with a history." They can only be fully discovered and documented as we come to understand the cultural, historical and social forces which shape human health, disease and illness. However, true field work in the biomedical sciences is becoming all too rare with the decline of "phenomenology" and the growing strength of the assumption that all external reality is indefinitely reducible and accurately reproduced in the laboratory setting. Even outside the laboratory enthusiasm with biostatistical methods sometimes causes numbers to become reified, seeming to take on more significance than the biological phenomena they are meant to represent.

Projects such as Snake Hill demonstrate that health and medical science at a given time and place in human history can be studied through documentary research and through recovery, analysis and interpretation of human remains from historic sites. Our approach was necessarily multi-disciplinary. Our goal was to integrate medical historic information with data generated by the archaeological analyses of the site, and the physical and forensic analyses of the skeletal remains. The results reflect significant methodological advances in the involved disciplines and encourage other broad research initiatives.

Study of the systematic processes of disease, injury and medical therapy that determine the gross morphology of bone, as well as the taphonomic influences on bone postmortem, are becoming better understood as natural sciences. These sciences, which draw upon traditional anatomy, anthropology and archaeology, can provide a basis for historical interpretation. The critical factor, necessary for effective research, is the integration of these approaches.

Thus the recovery and analysis of human remains from historic sites like Snake Hill, plus the continuing development of medical history, traditional anatomy and anthropometry, is providing an increasing role for the modern field scientist in helping to understand human life and health. Forging a new role for the medical historian on site in the course of archaeological excavations is changing the manner in which both medical historical scholarship and anthropological analyses of skeletal remains are conducted. Skeletal remains allow the historian of medicine to test documentary evidence against material reality. The historian also helps the archaeologist understand burial positions by a reading of the history of burial practices, and helps the physical anthropologist understand human remains by a reading of the history of medical practices.

The power of medical history in the anthropological analysis of human remains is achieved through the ability to read the thoughts and intentions of medical therapists and compare these with the material results of medical therapy. The traditional "prehistoric" archaeologist may attempt to understand the belief systems of ancient societies through analysis of their material culture and "symbolic archaeology." However, human health beliefs, behaviors and practices though time cannot ultimately be tested by archaeology and physical anthropology alone. The addition of medical historical analysis adds an important dimension to the study of human health systems in diachronic perspective. Another critical dimension is added to the medical historical analysis by the expertise of contemporary physicians and pathologists whose understanding of physiology and disease processes set biological parameters within which historic inferences may be drawn.

We are coming to realize that the causes and prevention of the modern "diseases of civilization," lie not entirely within the realm of the contemporary medical system. It therefore becomes increasingly important to sample human health experiences from past times and places to achieve a better understanding of what constitutes a healthful human physical and social environment. By permitting us to examine human populations prior to modern medical therapy, such information offers us a broader understanding of human biology and the natural history of disease. For example, assumptions about which injuries and diseases are considered either fatal, or alternatively, survivable in modern medical practice do not always hold up to historical analysis. A better understanding of cultural and social responses to disease and debilitation throughout history is helpful, too, when modern medical technology begins to outdistance the contemporary ethical and legal systems in considering matters of human life, health and death. Thus, recovery and analysis of human remains from historic sites provide important and unique information regarding the fundamental character of human health and medical practice.

PART ONE:
The Historical Setting

One   Introduction

RONALD F. WILLIAMSON

This book conveys a story of suffering and carnage, as documented by the human remains found in a military cemetery from the War of 1812. It was a time in which complex wounds were made simple, through the use of amputation, with neither anaesthetics nor an understanding of microbiology. Indeed, the physical remains of 28 soldiers, encountered in the course of archaeological investigation of the Snake Hill cemetery, substantiate vividly the horrible picture described in writings of the period. In a history of Jefferson County, New York, written in 1854, there is a biographical sketch of a Dr. Amasa Troubridge, who served on the Niagara Frontier and at Fort Erie during the summer and fall of 1814. The author commented on "the continued scenes of carnage which came under the professional observation of a Doctor Troubridge; he was faced with every kind and degree of wound to treat, made by musket balls, cannon balls, grape and shrapnel shot, fragments of shells, congrave rockets — in fact, all the missiles used in modern warfare." It should not seem too surprising then, that this site yielded evidence of eight amputations and death by severe battle trauma.

The site was discovered in April 1987, when human skeletal remains were reportedly encountered during excavation of a basement foundation on a lakefront lot situated approximately 700 metres west of Old Fort Erie, now a regional park (Figure 1.1). While possession of this land had been bitterly contested in the latter part of 1814, it had remained virtually undeveloped until the 1940s when summer cottages were erected along the lakeshore. Only recently, however, with the construction of permanent homes, has the land yielded evidence of its distant past.

Once human remains had been professionally verified, it was recommended to the Town of Fort Erie by the Cemeteries Branch of the Ontario Ministry of Consumer and Commercial Relations that no further development on the subject property occur until the extent of the cemetery was defined. Archaeological Services Inc., a consulting firm in Toronto, Ontario, was initially retained by the Town of Fort Erie to determine whether the cemetery extended onto adjacent lots and then, once human remains had been encountered, to delineate the complete nature and extent of the cemetery. With the discovery of War of 1812 American military paraphernalia, Archaeological Services Inc. was asked to direct an international team of scholars and scientists in the process of exhuming all of the skeletal remains, identifying their former nationalities and reporting the team findings to a number of Canadian agencies. This was to be followed by a ceremony at which the appropriate individuals would be repatriated to the United States with full military honours.

The initial objective of identifying the nationalities of the deceased soldiers involved the integration of historical information with data generated by the archaeological excavation and analyses of the site and the biological analyses of the skeletal remains. This apparently simple objective held implications for the advancement of knowledge in all of the disciplines involved. With respect to military history, the project necessitated collating both Canadian and American historical data. It has resulted in the enhancement of our understanding of events before, during and after the 1814 siege of Fort Erie. It has also provided information concerning military clothing, personal gear and other details of the day-to-day life of a soldier during the War of 1812. Medical history was also investigated, especially details of medical intervention and mortuary practice under conditions of war. Archaeology served to link historical records with the physical remains of the site. Their biological interpretation contributed information concerning the age, stature and details of pathological conditions observed on the interred individuals.

Indeed, the skeletal remains and artifacts which were recovered from the site have been subjected to intense analysis over the past two years. The skeletal analyses were conducted by a number of biological anthropologists, each of whom was responsible for a different aspect of study, all of which contributed to the goal of identifying the individual characteristics of the remains. These included elements of age at death, sex, race, stature, possible battle injuries, other related or unrelated pathological elements, any peculiarities in growth and development and chemical and isotopic characteristics.

At the same time, the importance of ascertaining nationality and, if possible, regimental unit affiliation for each burial, signified that spatial and metric analyses of the military and civilian artifactual remains, especially buttons, were very important to the archaeological inquiry.

The spatial patterning of buttons suggested that in some cases clothing was partially or completely removed to facilitate access to wounds for medical treatment. Not all wounds appear to have left traces in the hard tissue, especially in the case of abdominal wounds. The partial removal of the high-waisted military overalls may constitute circumstantial evidence for such wounds. Alternatively, it is likely that garments were loosened for ease of breathing in any case of serious injury. The state of dress may also provide other trauma-related inferences. It has been suggested that upon hospitalization, a soldier's outer garments would have been removed. Therefore, full removal of military clothing might be one indication of extensive or prolonged medical attention. Partial removal, however, especially in an area of demonstrable trauma, might be an indication of death soon after field treatment. A fully dressed individual with little clothing disturbance may have died instantly or soon after wounding before medical treatment was administered.

The results of these analyses are presented herein and will provide the reader with a rare glimpse of life and death during the War of 1812. The volume begins with a section detailing the results of an exhaustive search for archival and documentary information relating to the Niagara campaign and more specifically, the American occupation of Fort Erie during the summer and fall of 1814. This is followed by the archaeological data. The second part presents the results of analyses of the physical remains. Finally, interpretations and conclusions are provided. Appended to this volume is extensive information concerning the U.S. military button assemblage which includes a complete catalogue.

Figure 1.1: The Niagara Frontier in 1814

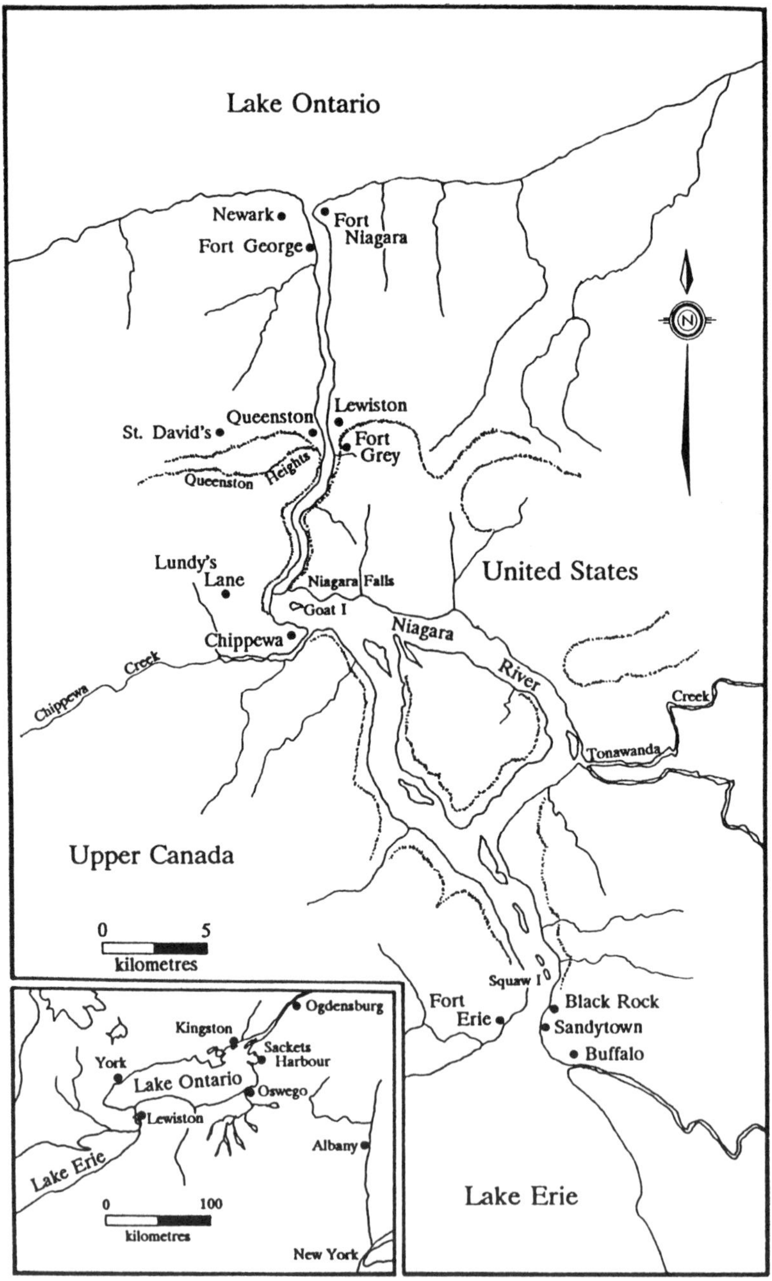

Lake Ontario

Newark
Fort Niagara
Fort George

Lewiston
St. David's Queenston
Fort Grey
Queenston Heights

United States

Lundy's Lane
Niagara Falls
Goat I
Chippewa

Chippewa Creek

Niagara River

Creek

Tonawanda

Upper Canada

0   5
kilometres

Squaw I
Fort Erie
Black Rock
Sandytown
Buffalo

Lake Erie

Ogdensburg
Kingston
Sackets Harbour
York
Lake Ontario
Oswego
Lewiston
Albany
Lake Erie

0   100
kilometres

New York

Two | **Fort Erie and U.S. Operations on the Niagara Frontier, 1814**

JOSEPH WHITEHORNE

Introduction

Hostilities between the United States and Great Britain had erupted for a second time in June 1812. The clash resulted from a series of tensions building up over several years as a result of Napoleon's struggle for supremacy in Europe and Britain's struggle against him. American maritime interests were caught between the equally high-handed policies of the two belligerents. The Royal Navy was in a better position to enforce Britain's policies, however, it became the focus of much American ire. Affronts to American sovereignty such as the impressment of suspected British deserters from U.S. flag ships brought howls of rage from many political leaders.

The image of perfidious Albion persisted also in the western part of the U.S. because of continued British reluctance to end all support for former Indian allies now living in the American Great Lakes region. Every act of Indian hostility was attributed to British treachery rather than judged on its own merits. Thus western politicians felt that war with England would end the Indian threat in the Old Northwest. Perhaps more importantly, it seemed to provide a golden opportunity to pluck the Canadas from the Crown and add vast amounts of land to the New Republic. The Administration of President James Madison was unable to control these pressures and, ironically, declared war at about the same time British Orders in Council ended most of the abuses that were upsetting so many Americans.

The American military was not ready for war. The U.S. Navy was efficient but small. After several preliminary successes, it was suppressed by the Royal Navy, which then proceeded to blockade the U.S. coast. Significant naval action shifted thereafter to the Great Lakes. There the U.S. army was woefully inadequate in size and mobilization planning, and thus was forced to rely on levies of untrained volunteers and militia. The British were most vulnerable at Montreal; its capture would cause all positions further inland to wither. Unfortunately for the American campaign, the most willing and largest number of volunteers came from the Midwestern states. Consequently, the first campaign of 1812 was launched against Fort Malden, opposite Detroit. Led by an elderly veteran of the Revolution, William Hull, the U.S. forces were handled quickly by the British General Sir Isaac Brock, who captured Detroit as well as Hull's army. A few months later Brock repulsed an American probe against Queenston on the Niagara River, losing his life in the process.

This set the pattern of the war along the border thereafter. The Americans enjoyed no strategic direction of any value from the War Department while their forces continued to nibble timidly along the edges of Quebec and Upper Canada. In 1813, a potentially promising thrust up the Champlain Valley toward Montreal was turned back at Chateauguay while modest success was experienced with the capture of Fort George on the Niagara Frontier. The one salutary effect of this poor military performance was the culling of the old veterans initially in command and their replacement by younger, abler, more vigorous men. This change meant that at least in 1814 the fighting would be harder and the American forces more efficient, although their direction by the War Department remained inadequate to the end.

Overview

On 3 July 1814, a force of about 4,000 Americans under the command of Major General Jacob Brown (see Plate 2.3) crossed the Niagara River from points near Buffalo and quickly captured the British fort and garrison at Fort Erie, Upper Canada (see Plate 2.1). This move marked the opening of the hardest fought campaign of the War of 1812. About 1,800 Americans and 2,400 British were killed or wounded over the next four months in a series of battles that were to be prominent in the U.S. military memory for many generations. The campaign ranged the length of the Niagara frontier with battles at Chippawa and Lundy's Lane and numerous other skirmishes. Despite some tactical success, the Americans were forced back into Fort Erie by the end of July. There they underwent an arduous siege throughout August and September characterized by heavy casualties on both sides. The U.S. forces lingered on at Fort Erie until October, finally abandoning the fort in early November.

Fort Erie had been a military site since 1764, when Captain John Montresor of the Royal Engineers built a small fort there to protect the ferry site from Black Rock and the road west along the lake shore to Detroit. It was used as a depot for troops in transit to the western garrisons in the aftermath of Pontiac's Rebellion. Montresor's effort was replaced by new construction in 1779 and again in 1791, each on slightly different sites. The locations chosen continued to be unsatisfactory because of winter damage caused by proximity to the lake shore. Consequently, another fort was begun a bit more inland in 1805. Construction on this facility continued intermittently until 1813. At that time, it consisted of two stone barracks and two bastions facing eastward to the lake shore. It was fronted on that side by an earthen parapet. A stockade and ditch were added to the incomplete western side after war was declared in 1812.

The Americans had been repulsed in an attack on Fort Erie soon after hostilities began in 1812 and the British successfully held them off for the remainder of the year. However, American operations against Fort George in 1813 at the mouth of the Niagara forced a British withdrawal from the Niagara Frontier to include Fort Erie, which was evacuated in May. The post was reoccupied in December 1813 as part of a successful British counterattack that not only recaptured Fort George but also gained Fort Niagara on the American side. American farms and villages as far south as Buffalo were burned in retaliation for similar U.S. atrocities committed on the Canadian side. By early January 1814, the British had pulled back to Fort Niagara while occupying the entire Canadian Niagara shore. A force of New York Militia took up positions around Fort Niagara and along the U.S. banks of the Niagara River. Under their dubious protection, the devastated village of Buffalo began to make a remarkable revival. By May, it contained three taverns, four stores, 12 shops, 23 houses, and 30 to 40 other commercial and farm structures. There was collaterally a thriving timber and brickmaking business, which were significant to the later support of U.S. military activity in the area.

The British activities in western New York caused Secretary of War John Armstrong in January to direct Major General Jacob Brown to move his Left Division of the 9th Military District from French Mills to reinforce its defences at Sackets Harbor. In February, the two men considered a movement over the ice against the British naval base at Kingston. However, the strength of Kingston's defences and ice conditions militated against the plan. Consequently, General Brown decided to follow through on a suggested option and in March moved his division to the Niagara Frontier. His objectives were the recapture of Fort Niagara and the clearing of British forces from the whole area. His move took the Secretary of War by surprise, as it had not been considered seriously until Brown reported his actions on 20 March. Confronted with a *fait accompli,* the Secretary immediately began to make plans to take advantage of the situation.

Ultimately, he directed that while Brown operated in the Niagara area, Colonel George Croghan was to seize British posts on the upper Great Lakes at Mackinac and St. Joseph. At the same time, the Right Division of the 9th Military District led by Major General George Izard (see Plate 2.5) was to move up the Lake Champlain Valley and threaten British communications along the St. Lawrence River at a point between Kingston and Montreal. The plan of campaign was to take advantage of U.S. naval control of Lake Erie by concentrating troops from around its shores into Brown's division in the Buffalo area. Doing so would avoid having to contest control of Lake Ontario, partially negating the effect of British naval strength there, while thrusting toward Burlington Heights. This move would sever British western bases from their lifeline and put a U.S. ground force in position to move overland east toward Kingston. Capture of that city would destroy British naval capabilities on Lake Ontario as effectively as if done so by the Navy in a lake battle. It would further limit British control to the St. Lawrence Valley.

At a minimum, Secretary Armstrong hoped that Brown could ensconce himself securely at York. This would clear the Niagara Peninsula and set things up for a later move on Kingston. To do this, Brown counted on a fairly quick link with the U.S. Navy on Lake Ontario. He recognized that otherwise he could not sustain his force for a prolonged campaign, as Buffalo was too remote and there was insufficient ground transport. He later decided to cross the Niagara river at Fort Erie to open the campaign because at that point he could be assured of getting over sufficient forces and heavy equipment quickly despite the relative scarcity of boats. He intended to follow the river north to Queenston Heights, then move against either Fort George or Burlington as the situation allowed. Secretary Armstrong favored making the first move against Fort Erie for the more prosaic reason that it promised an easy victory.

U.S. Preparations

Command of the Buffalo troops was taken over by Brigadier General Winfield Scott (see Plate 2.6) while General Brown was absent from the Buffalo area from 20 April to 7 June, attending to the defence of Sackets

Harbor and coordinating support for his forthcoming campaign. Scott created vigorous training programs which were to transform the force into the best fielded by the U.S. during the war and shaped the character of the little army that crossed the Niagara and later came under siege at Fort Erie. As late as 1814, there was no standard training period for recruits, nor was there any policy for unit training, which was due in part to the lack of initiative by many commanders. More serious was the absence of any standard drill manuals. Those which were available, William Duane's *Handbook for Infantry* (1813) and Alexander Smyth's *Regulations for the Field Exercises...of the Infantry* (1813), were confusing and incomplete. The 9th Military District tried to compensate for this by declaring Steuben's *Bluebook*, first published in 1778, as the standard. Smyth's and Steuben's works were of some value in standardizing camp activities. However, Scott preferred the use of a French system available in translation, *Rules and Regulations for the Field Exercises of the French Infantry* (1803). In his memoirs, Scott says he trained first his officers, then had them train the men.

General Scott initiated an increasingly vigorous training program as soon as the troops settled into camp in the Flint Hill area north of Buffalo. Each Sunday he conducted a full field inspection of the entire force. Daily battalion and company drills began to be required, General Scott personally conducting some. By early May, the entire duty day was devoted to drill. Regimental commanders were expected to supervise a minimum of four hours of squad and platoon drill each morning. Emphasis was placed on mass movements and instinctively developing the desired pace and cadence. Scott made it clear that he expected all persons to participate in the drills regardless of special duties or commitments, such as those of quartermaster and paymaster.

An inspection on 8 May by the Assistant Division Inspector General, Major Azor Orne, indicated improvements in the capabilities of the regiments. Individual weapons were in excellent condition and the men were slowly being issued haversacks as General Scott had directed in early April. The big problem, especially in the 9th and 11th Infantry Regiments, was the condition of the men's clothing. The situation was so bad that General Scott announced to the troops on 8 May that he was making "every exertion" to procure sufficient cloth to have uniforms made for all the men who needed them. He encouraged the units to make up in drill and discipline what they lacked in appearance.

Supply procedures continued to be tightened throughout May and June. Units were directed to use the system outlined in Smyth's regulations as a guide for marking and numbering clothing and unit equipment. Scott desired the system to be standard throughout the division. At the end of May, he was compelled to prohibit the use of hospital tents in headquarters and by guard details. Surgeons' requirements for medicines, hospital furniture and surgical equipment also were monitored to assure that necessities were being met. The Inspector General had discovered doctors had only been reporting what was on hand to the Apothecary General, not stating their needs.

The drill schedule was even more demanding by early June while becoming increasingly sophisticated. More attention was given to drill in firing motions using three ranks. The schedule was expanded further. Reveille was at sunrise. At that time, troops were expected to turn out under arms to perform squad and company drill for about two hours until breakfast. Following a short break, the same routine continued until dinner at about 1200. There followed a slightly longer break; then at 1500 the entire division fell out for battalion drill that lasted to about 1900. The men then had supper and free time until lights out at 2100. General Scott alone determined if weather conditions merited any amendments to this schedule. Volunteer units were subjected to the same regimen after they joined the command.

On about 20 June, Scott organized his brigade for training into standard size units for these afternoon drills. Ten uniform companies were formed from the 11th Infantry (four companies), and the 9th and 25th Infantries (three companies each). Once gathered in their regimental areas, the companies were formed into a drill battalion organized by the date of rank of their captains, regardless of regiment. This composite battalion then was wheeled into columns of companies, the companies made roughly equal in size and then divided into two platoons each. Scott and the field officers then took turns, hour after hour, drilling this nearly perfectly sized regiment. The officers gained considerably more experience conducting such large unit drill. The men, in turn, became accustomed to taking orders from officers outside their own units. These were developments that proved most valuable in the forthcoming campaign. Scott was pleased with the progress made. "They began to perceive why they had been made to fag so long at the drill of the soldier, the company, and the battalion. Confidence, the dawn of victory, inspired the whole line." As training continued, General Scott and his fellow brigadier, Brigadier General Eleazer W. Ripley, continued to press the regimental leaders to enforce division policies, frequently insisting on full participation at drills and on the officers' presence at reveille.

Each infantry company had been required on 29 May to designate one of its better privates as a pioneer. Each regiment had to name a corporal to be in charge of the group so selected whenever they were away from their companies. These men were exempted from their companies' extra duties so they could train. General orders specified that they would carry "proper tools" such as saws, spades and axes. These were "handsomely cased" in leather and carried in leather slings over the shoulder. All pioneers wore a linen apron that extended from neck to knee. At regimental drills the corporals positioned themselves with the regimental staff while the privates stood to the centre rear of their companies. When the force became besieged in Fort Erie in August and September, the improvements in the fortifications were made by infantry work parties under the direction of these same pioneers, supervised by the few engineer officers. Their authority extended over any soldiers assigned to them, regardless of regimental affiliation.

Scott intuitively connected the health of the men with the sanitation of the camp. Smyth's regulations were cited again as a guide for the proper police of the encampments. The men were required to bathe three times a week, "in the lake, not in the creek." Tents were expected to be struck the first fair day after every rain. Special stress was placed on the quality and cleanliness of food preparation. An officer was required to inspect the food before every meal prior to allowing the men to eat. Even salted meats were expected to be cooked.

Equipment issue was accelerated by the last week of June, most units receiving everything necessary. Orphan units were attached to one of the regiments to assure proper supply support. For example, when the companies of the 22d Infantry under Captain Sampson L. King arrived on 30 June, they were attached to the 9th Infantry. There, Major Henry Leavenworth of the 9th Infantry supervised the new units' proper supply and equipping so that by 3 July they were at the same levels as earlier arriving units, with no serious shortages. These incoming units posed a major supply problem for Scott's quartermaster. Colonel James Fenton of the 5th Pennsylvania Volunteers, for instance, wrote ahead from Erie, Pennsylvania to warn General Scott that the quality and quantity of his men's firearms and flints was inadequate for a campaign. He wanted Scott to know that the Pennsylvanians would have to draw additional weapons. He announced further that his regiment lacked a rations contractor and consequently would have to impose itself on the resources available at Buffalo. Fenton's 3 May letter, by the way, was Scott's first inkling that the 5th Pennsylvania Volunteers was being assigned to Brown's Division.

The clothing promised earlier by General Scott arrived on 23 June. The uniforms were made of grey cloth due to a shortage of the standard blue color. Final requisitions were based on a series of intensive inspections conducted by the division Inspectors General. All personnel regardless of rank turned out in as complete a uniform as possible to include the new knapsacks. These were expected to contain one shirt, one pair of summer pantaloons, one pair of shoes, one pair of socks or stockings, one fatigue frock, one pair of trousers and one blanket. A hairbrush and handkerchief were the only authorized optional additional items. The inspectors noted the deficiencies on the turn out, provided requirements to the quartermaster, and directed the units to get what they needed.

The troops were issued woolen roundabouts, close-fitting jackets with sleeves, to wear in the summer heat in lieu of the heavier woolen coats. Companies which already had been issued new uniform coats were told to box them and turn them in, each marked with the owner's name, as soon as the roundabouts were available. All other clothing items not authorized similarly were to be boxed and stored. Every man was required to have a haversack and the officers were encouraged to conform. The haversack was to contain three days' bread and meat. The last items issued just before crossing to Fort Erie were gun slings and worm screws. There can be no doubt that under Scott's direction, Brown's force was as close to the ideal in training, discipline, and equipment of any organization fielded by the U.S. during the war. It is reasonable to assume that the men carried and wore in practice what in other units was only theory.

The condition of the volunteers accompanying the force was understandably not the same quality. The 5th Pennsylvania Volunteers (see Plate 2.4), already mentioned, were in the best shape. This unit had been on active service since March. It had been at Erie, Pennsylvania, where elements participated in several raids on Canadian targets. During its stay in the Erie garrison, the men were fully equipped and clothed. Everyone except the field officers drew the regular army enlisted soldier's uniform. The field officers continued to wear their state militia uniforms. The Pennsylvanians were disciplined and toughened further by their road march along the lake shore from Erie to Buffalo. On arrival at the latter place, they were fully integrated into Scott's training program. By the time their rear party approached Buffalo on 22 June, the growing militia portion of Brown's force had been augmented by upwards of 250 Indians, mostly Iroquois. This number was to reach about 500 by the time of the opening of operations. The Indians dressed as they pleased, most going into battle painted and with minimum clothing.

The New York Militia called up for the campaign were much slower in reporting. A portion of Major General Amos Hall's Division had already been serving rotating tours along the Niagara Frontier, hence interest in further, more dangerous, duty was quite low. Thus, the response to Governor Daniel D. Tompkins' 3 May call for militia was minimal. Deploying the militia was further impeded by a lack of equipment. Stocks had been depleted at the state armories by earlier call-ups and had not been replenished because of controversy over financial responsibilities between New York State and the federal government. The commander of the militia brigade, Brigadier General Peter B. Porter, had hoped to have 1,000 men under arms at the rendezvous point at Canandaigua by 20 May. The men drifted in, but not the equipment. Consequently, he was forced to leave his infantry at Batavia under the command of Colonel Philetus Swift while they awaited supplies throughout June. As the time for the invasion approached, Porter hurried ahead to Buffalo with about 150 mounted men. There, he took command of the Pennsylvanians and Indians already on hand. The New York Militia present along the Niagara Frontier from earlier call-ups continued under Porter's loose control to conduct security and support missions on the American side of the river. Porter and his mixed brigade crossed the Niagara on the night of 4 July, joining General Brown's force on the banks of the Chippawa River at noon 5 July. By 1500 they had begun their advance on the British pickets to open the Battle of Chippawa.

The Invasion

The hours of "fagging" imposed on the soldiers by Scott paid off in this hard fought battle as the U.S. troops manoeuvered professionally against the British, forcing them to withdraw from Chippawa. Heavy casualties were sustained by both sides. This is not the place to describe the engagement. However, it should be noted that 6 July was devoted to burying the dead on the battlefield and treating and evacuating the wounded by boat to the U.S. shore. The U.S. dead were buried in a mass grave and a sermon was delivered by the chaplain.

After the battle, there seems to have been a decline in discipline. Gordon's Company of Pennsylvanians refused to go beyond the Chippawa River and its members tried to persuade others to do likewise. General Brown ordered Captain Gordon to take his men back to Fort Erie to work on the fortifications. Despite this incident, Brown still considered the militia generally sound. By 11 July, General Scott had resumed the series of drills and inspections in a program much as it had been before the opening of the campaign: every day at 1600 all those not on an operational mission were required to stand full equipment inspections. Shaves and haircuts were expected and Scott insisted that unit officers enforce his standards of cleanliness and appearance. Otherwise, he threatened action against them for failure to exercise proper supervision.

Meanwhile, Brown's Division pressed the British northward into Fort George. Brown decided to invest the fort; however, he did not have the heavy artillery necessary to achieve a decision. The opposing forces skirmished with each other for several days, inflicting light casualties. The ferocity of the Chippawa fight combined with the lack of excitement in the ensuing Fort George operations persuaded most of the Indians on both sides to withdraw. By 20 July, they had left both forces except for small groups. Each side's Indians seem to have agreed to avoid further involvement so long as the other did so.

General Brown learned on 23 July that the Navy would be unable to bring him the heavy ordnance he required, and that it could not interdict the flow of British reinforcements arriving from Kingston. Consequently, he directed a withdrawal from positions before Fort George and on Queenston Heights back to the Chippawa River. At the same time, he directed the shipment of as much heavy artillery as possible from locations in western New York. Four 12-pounders with solid, shrapnel, and canister rounds and 25 barrels of gunpowder were shipped from Batavia. Nearly all of the ammunition, rifles and sabers in stock at Fort Schlosser on the east bank of the Niagara were sent over, along with its only ten pounder mortar. Five 18-pounders at Oswego and 600 solid shot, sent there from Sackets Harbor, were shipped as well. This heterogeneous collection was added to the siege train on arrival and later became part of the heavy defenses of Fort Erie and Black Rock.

General Brown required all the units "to be rendered light as possible," once he decided to pull back from Queenston Heights. All officers' personal baggage was ordered returned to Buffalo, as were all "subjects for general hospital." These and the baggage crossed the river at Fort Schlosser. Brown also ordered all women attached to the army to return to Buffalo where they were to work at the hospital. At that time two women were serving as hospital matrons and one as laundress in each regiment. Intervention by the surgeons from the 9th and 23d Regiments led General Brown to modify this part of his order. A matron and a laundress were allowed to remain with each regimental hospital. All other surplus persons and material were shipped across the river under the supervision of Major William A. Trimble, 19th Infantry, who was directed to manage this part of the retrograde.

The reinforced British now under the overall command of Major General Sir Gordon Drummond quickly pressed forward. While a column advanced from the direction of Burlington Heights, a second came from Fort George. From the latter area, a feint was sent from Fort Niagara toward Fort Schlosser, threatening its depot and hospital. Hearing of the feint from Swift's New York Militia stationed there, General Brown assumed that it was the main British effort. Accordingly, on the afternoon of 25 July, he dispatched General Scott and his brigade from Chippawa to counter that threat. By coincidence, the British columns on the west side of the Niagara were approaching the same point from the opposite direction. The result was a bitter engagement starting at about 1800 at Bridgewater Mills, or Lundy's Lane as it is known today. The struggle continued after midnight, with both sides firing at close range in the darkness as they fought over possession of a low ridge and the guns on it. Casualties on both sides exceeded 1,500 men each, with the losses particularly high among the U.S. senior officers.

The American Lundy's Lane casualties were removed back to Chippawa. From there on the 26th they went by boat first to Tonawanda then to Buffalo. Militia were used as boatmen. Those wounded who died on the night of the 26th were buried at Tonawanda. Medical facilities were taxed heavily handling the casualties brought in after the battle. One surgeon said mortality would have been considerably higher were it not for the care given the men by the wives and other camp followers attached to the hospitals during the crisis. Left in possession of the battlefield, the British were forced to dispose of the slain. Several large pyres were built and most of the Americans' remains were cremated; only a few were buried.

Generals Brown and Scott were among those injured. Prior to his evacuation Brown told the surviving senior officer, Brigadier General Ripley, to pull the troops back to the Chippawa campground. He wanted the men to regroup there, then return to the battlefield. At the same time all of the wounded who could be found were to be evacuated. When Ripley later marched his force back to Lundy's Lane, he found the British in possession of the battlefield and he decided to pull back to Fort Erie. Ripley correctly assessed his force to be in no condition to resume the fight. He had been able to collect approximately 1500 men. Major Henry Leavenworth of the 9th Regiment had 64 men, while Scott's entire brigade could muster less than 600. The 11th Infantry could only muster about 125 men. Typical was the case of Lieutenant Samuel Tappan's Company, the 23d Infantry. Forty-five men had gone into battle, but on the morning of 26 July only nine men were on hand. Another 19 straggled in over the next few days while 17 were found to have been killed or wounded. This attrition, especially the loss of key leaders, severely impaired the cohesion and effectiveness of the organizations that had survived.

Fort Erie Positions

General Ripley led his battered forces back to a point opposite Black Rock on the afternoon of 26 July. The next day, he continued the withdrawal into Fort Erie. The U.S. forces had done some work on the original facility while the fighting was going on to the north. Most of this, however, had been limited to repairs to the old fort itself with little thought being given to developing the surrounding area. This changed with the arrival of the troops on 27 July. Battery positions were laid out between 28 and 31 July and work begun under the supervision of Lieutenant David B. Douglass along with the help of unit pioneers. Douglass' own company built a small battery to the right of the original fort while he oversaw the efforts of several hundred men at Snake Hill. Unit fatigue parties worked in eight-hour shifts around the clock on the ditches and breastworks linking the old fort with the flanking batteries. The old fort quickly became a segment of a larger system of parapets and traverses, all edged by a ditch and abatis.

The fortified area encompassed about 12 ha (Figure 2.1; Plate 2.1). The so-called Douglass Battery, on the north or right, was connected to the old fort with a 2 m high parapet bounded by the exterior ditch. Left of the fort a longer parapet with a double ditch ran about 750 m nearly parallel to Lake Erie's shore. It terminated at Snake Hill. This was a low sand mound that was built up by about 7.5 m. The stockade on the west side of the old fort itself was replaced by bastioned earthworks. A British patrol on 30 July attacked the U.S. outpost at the ferry crossing opposite Black Rock, seizing some of the boats the Americans were guarding there, giving urgency to the American efforts. On 2 August, Douglass' Battery was sufficiently complete to get its guns in position. Snake Hill received part of its armament the next day and responsibility for its further development passed to the battery commander, Captain Nathan Towson (see Plate 2.2). Its location on Snake Hill may be plotted with reasonable accuracy by combining the information provided in the papers of Lieutenant David B. Douglass with other contemporary maps and modern terrain analysis. Douglass describes the parapet as extending 275 m westerly from old Fort Erie to a point where it angled 310 m southerly to another point, then 70 m further around Towson's Battery to the shore. The battery was on Snake Hill. The scale map he provides allows the angles he cites to be calculated, thus permitting some precision. It may be concluded that Snake Hill is the area on Lakeshore Road in the vicinity of its intersection with Albert Road, adjacent to the burial site.

The British main body arrived on 2 August on the heights opposite Black Rock. Camps were set up about 3 km above the fort in the vicinity of the modern day racetrack, and General Drummond decided to take the place by siege. His engineers began building battery positions north of the fort on the river's edge. The enfilading capability of these positions caused the Americans to build large traverses throughout their area. At the same time, animal parks and hospital tents were installed in what Lieutenant Douglass called the "most secluded places." Large numbers of soldiers participated in the work parties necessary to this effort. The incessant labor was trying to the men on both sides.

The Americans continued to develop their fortifications throughout the siege. The engineers dealt directly with the quartermaster in Buffalo, Captain John B. Hogan, to get what they needed. It became routine for orders for as many as 400 shovels or 200 axes to be sent to the harried supply officers. A junior quartermaster officer was engaged full time at Fort Erie just keeping track of the construction materials being sent. By the end of August, this officer also supervised the use of eight yoke of oxen that had been sent to aid in heavy hauling at the request of the senior engineer, Lieutenant Colonel William MacRee. By that time, the American positions had been thoroughly developed. A total of 27 guns lined the works. Overhead cover had been created for all the artillery positions and Snake Hill had been formed into a fully enclosed redoubt. Most of the troops were housed in tents throughout the siege. These soon became shredded by British shell fragments. When General Brown resumed command on 2 September, effort was increased to provide shelter for the troops. A great deal of timber was sent across the Niagara to make tent flooring. All canvas in use on the U.S. side was sent over for the use of the besieged troops. Brown directed that all wounded be moved into permanent buildings so every tent possible could be available. Quantities of "2 ft. or 3 ft." plank were sent over. By 13 September, all loose boards in the Buffalo area had been transferred and General Brown was demanding another 10,000 feet.

The Americans were able to sustain the large force at Fort Erie because of their nearly complete control of the water route from Buffalo. Several vessels from the Lake Erie Squadron arrived in late July with reinforcements from the west. They were retained to secure the water route and to provide fire power on Fort Erie's water flank. The loss of two of these ships to a brilliant British raid on 12 August had little effect on the movement of goods and men between Buffalo and the fort. On 1 August, Captain Hogan reported that he had 13 boats of all types on hand. Four of these were under repair and another two were set aside for the exclusive use of the Ordnance Department and the rations contractor. Thirty light batteaux, each capable of hauling 30 men, were under construction while all the necessary oars were on hand already.

These small craft plied between Black Rock and the fort or from Sandytown to the fort. Sandytown was an area at the foot of Porter Avenue, now eroded away, which was later marked by the entrance of the Erie Canal into Black Rock Harbor. It was due east of the fort across the river. The first British battery set up opposite Black Rock could in part interdict the water route between Black Rock and the fort. At least one boatman lost his arm to British fire while ferrying reinforcements to Fort Erie. Since the Americans depended on daily contact with the Buffalo area depots for provisions, resupply and the transfer of personnel, a great deal of movement was undertaken at night with boats crossing and recrossing in the darkness. A U.S. battery under Lieutenant Colonel George McFeely was established at Black Rock to suppress British fire on U.S. shipping. Daytime crossings were made more often from Sandytown to a point near Snake Hill. After 15 August many people crossed to this area to sell produce to the troops. General Brown allowed this so that the consumption of fresh vegetables by his men would increase.

Medical System

This concern for health raises the issue of medical support and the condition of the command. Regimental surgeons reported relatively little illness or disease during the training period prior to the invasion. Smallpox and what Dr. Troubridge of the 21st Infantry called "intermittent fevers" posed a modest health problem during May and June. All such patients were referred to his hospital at Flint Hill. The influx of reinforcements and militiamen in late June saw an increase in the incidence of typhus. Dr. Joseph Mann reported that "intermittent, acute rheumatism" became a major complaint in the course of the campaign caused, no doubt, by the men's prolonged exposure to the elements. The arrival of more militia in September marked an increase in diarrhea and what Dr. Mann called "idiopathic dysentery." Certificates of disability issued after the war indicate that many of those who survived the siege of Fort Erie had serious physical problems undoubtedly shared by those killed there. Hernias and piles, so severe as to make any labor impossible, were common complaints as was the virulent, long-term diarrhea cited by Dr. Mann. Compensation given for debilitating rheumatism contracted while on fatigue duties at the fort also support Dr. Mann's observations.

The men were pushed to their physical and emotional limits in the course of the siege, performing heavy labor for extended periods under dangerous conditions. Although rarely without food, the men's diet did little to improve their condition. The basic ration consisted of salt pork and hard bread. Spirits, vinegar, salt and soap were available occasionally, but the issue of soap and vinegar proved particularly difficult.

The rations were issued directly to units by contractors on the signature of their commanders. The Inspector General assured that prisoners of war were fed properly while surgeons signed for rations in their hospitals. The hospital ration differed substantially from that given to the troops in their regiments. Hospitals were authorized to procure a variety of vegetables and dairy products outside the basic ration. Further, the surgeons were allowed to draw only those component parts of the rations they needed. They could sell their surpluses and use the money derived therefrom to procure additional specialty items.

Food preparation sometimes was done by people other than the soldiers themselves. In several cases the quartermaster hired local women or the wives of soldiers to cook for a group. This was especially the case for fatigue parties or groups of teamsters or carpenters who were not as well structured as the line units. The items purchased from civilian entrepreneurs who dared to cross to the fort included butter, onions, and potatoes and a few prepared items such as pies and cooked meat. The prices charged for these items, as can be imagined, were exorbitant. Consequently, the continued scarcity of antiscorbutics in the soldiers' diet was an increasing concern. Finally, on 25 August, the quartermaster, Captain Hogan, was directed by the commanding general to procure potatoes at any price "to save my men from the ravages of sickness which is making rapid approaches toward paralyzing my strength." This marginal diet was sometimes made worse when bad weather impeded the flow of goods. In short, the men were not well fed, were subjected to hard physical labor, had little sleep and were under considerable tension from the British bombardment.

Before the invasion, General Scott had paid periodic visits to the various regimental hospitals, warning the physicians that the campaign would bring busy times for them. His predictions were to prove tragically true. These field hospitals were supported by an existing hospital system. By

1814 there were general hospitals already established in Burlington, Vermont, and Plattsburgh, Malone and Greenbush, New York. The threat to facilities at Fort Schlosser led to the decision in late July to erect a permanent general hospital at Williamsville, about 19 km east of Buffalo. The site was picked on 29 July on the recommendation of the senior surgeon, Dr. Ezekiah Bull. Thus, 37 ha and the stables of Raphael Cook's farm were leased for the construction of a general hospital. Ironically, the contract specified "no burying place in the premises." Despite this, a well cared for series of mass graves remain as the last vestige of this hospital. These further provide evidence that having a burying ground adjacent to a medical facility was an accepted practice. The Williamsville cemetery contains the remains of both U.S. and British personnel in a series of mass graves. The British remains are set apart on one edge of the plot. This segregation of enemy and friendly dead seems to have been a common, if not official, practice on both sides. For example, after Lundy's Lane, the British buried their dead while cremating American remains on the field. Likewise, the Americans report after the battles at Chippawa and Cook's Mills, and Drummond's 15 August attack that the British dead were buried separately from the Americans. The separation of enemy dead from friendly is a custom that has endured to the present.

As soon as it was decided to concentrate patients at Williamsville, a vigorous building project was begun. At first, a large tent city was erected as indicated by the use of 3,000 board feet of timber for flooring 100 hospital tents and 12 loads of hay for bed ticking. Each tent could hold 16 to 18 men. Captain John Larkin was named supervisory quartermaster for the construction of the Williamsville Hospital. He brought in skilled workmen from as far away as Rochester and Utica. Huge quantities of locally produced brick were purchased in Buffalo and hauled to Williamsville to be used for construction of the hospital barracks. The permanent nature of the structures may be seen in the later purchase of glass and shingles needed to complete them. Patients began being moved to the Williamsville site on 30 July.

An additional general hospital was opened at Buffalo in July to accommodate the surge of wounded men from the Battle of Chippawa. This was located at Sandytown about 300 m from Buffalo Creek. The wounded were brought to it by boat, then carried by litter the last few hundred metres. By 1 August it held nearly 1,100 patients. A British raid a few miles north at Scajaquada Creek on 3 August demonstrated the hospital's vulnerability. Consequently, as many men as possible were removed to the growing

Williamsville facility. Surgeon Bull with Surgeon's Mates William Thomas and Joseph Lovell supervised the Williamsville facility. Surgeon's Mate William E. Horner remained at Buffalo caring for the small numbers of patients who could not be moved. Thereafter, the Buffalo Hospital served as the clearing center for casualties from Fort Erie, sending patients to Williamsville as quickly as it could. Naturally, not all men survived, and a graveyard was opened adjacent to it, as evidenced by the periodic surfacing of human remains for many years thereafter.

There were several smaller regimental hospitals in the Buffalo and Black Rock areas that had come in with their units. Despite their regimental affiliation, they were expected to provide support to whatever troops were in their area. Buildings were leased to house these. Additionally, rooms in private houses were rented for the use of convalescent officers. These smaller facilities were concentrated beginning in late October. The sick and wounded at Williamsville who could travel were sent in a series of convoys to the hospital at Greenbush. Once they were cleared out, beginning on 8 November, everyone possible was moved to Williamsville. Most officers and about 80 critical patients remained in private houses around Buffalo. It should be noted that the unprecedented casualty rate experienced throughout the campaign, combined with that at Plattsburgh and elsewhere, placed heavy demands on the medical supply system. Apothecary General Francis LeBaron at Albany advised his superiors in Philadelphia that the Williamsville Hospital "devoured" reserve stocks "like cormorants" so that by November nothing was left on hand.

The Siege

Active patrolling began almost as soon as the opponents regained contact on 2 August and the activities consonant with the siege of the fort promised even more business for the medical personnel. The next day a sizeable British force was repulsed in an attack on the newly arrived 1st U.S. Rifles at Scajaquada Creek. This was the action which caused the hospital adjustments in Buffalo. General Drummond ordered siegeworks to begin at the same time and for a few days both sides gave their full attention to engineer work. During this time, Brigadier General Edward L. Gaines, believed by the convalescing General Brown to be more aggressive than Brigadier General Ripley, was brought in from Sackets Harbor to assume command of the besieged garrison. He immediately increased the tempo of combat patrols in the hope that General Drummond could be lured into a decisive engagement. In one of these on 12 August, Major Lodowick Morgan, 1st Rifles, a hero of the earlier fighting at Scajaquada Creek, was killed. There was sharp fighting beginning on 6 August and nearly every day thereafter, but the British persisted in developing their siege lines.

British Battery Number One was on the shore about 1,000 yards from the fort. It contained three 24-pounder guns and one 18-pounder to which later were added two large mortars. It opened fire at sunrise of 7 August, inaugurating the weeks of pounding the Americans were to receive. The battery proved only marginally effective as it was set too far back from Fort Erie to cause any breaching. Accordingly, work began immediately on a second battery about 185 m from the river and 685 m from the fort. It eventually held two 18-pounders, one 24-pounder and an 8-inch howitzer. The British line ultimately stretched about 900 m from the shore to a point about 410 m from the U.S. positions. Infantry casualties were incurred during skirmishing which cleared the woods to protect the working parties building the batteries. Attrition was particularly bad among the British during the unmasking phase when there was little chance to be discreet; for example, one work party of 120 lost six men and had 30 wounded. However, the American practice with solid shot was not too effective compared with the devastation caused by the British use of grapeshot. The combined casualties from these brawls in the swamps and brush of no man's land posed a serious loss to both sides. Few prisoners were taken, and only the fortunate wounded were dragged to safety and treatment by their comrades.

The U.S. fleet had arrived finally off the mouth of the Niagara River on 4 August. It could no longer abet General Brown's original concept of operations. However, it was able to establish a sufficiently tight blockade to cause growing logistical and personnel problems for General Drummond, who decided he had to attack the fort rather than to rely on the slow strangulation characteristic of a typical siege. The presence of the U.S. fleet and his proven inability to interdict the American water routes to Buffalo sufficiently to starve out the U.S. garrison were factors which influenced his decision. He was persuaded further by his false assumption that the U.S. garrison at Fort Erie numbered less than 1,500 men, when it really was nearly double that.

The Americans covered every part of their line with men and guns. On the north, or right side, Douglass' Battery was supported by a force under the general supervision of Lieutenant Colonel William MacRee, the chief engineer. Starting at the lake edge were about 100 dismounted New York cavalrymen led by Captain Claudius V. Boughton. Next in line were the 50 men of Douglass' Company, manning a 6-pounder and a 12-pounder. To

Douglass' left were the remaining 165 men of the 9th Infantry led by Captain Edmund Foster. Between the 9th Infantry and the fort were 120 men equally from the New York Militia and the 5th Pennsylvania Volunteers, all under the command of Captain Micajah Harding of New York. A reserve of elements of the 11th and 22d Infantry Regiments under the command of Lieutenant Colonel Thomas Aspinwall was held at a point roughly equidistant from the fort and from Douglass' Battery.

Fort Erie itself was defended by two companies of 118 men from the 19th Infantry and by about 60 artillerymen under the command of Captain Alexander J. Williams. The artillery in the fort consisted of a 24-pounder, an 18-pounder and a 12-pounder. The American line stretched about 730 m southward to the lake shore near Snake Hill. Captain John J. Fontaine's Battery of two 6-pounders was adjacent to the fort itself. Two hundred and thirty metres further south along the breastworks was Captain Thomas Biddle's Battery of three 6-pounders. A combined force of companies from the 1st and 4th Rifle Regiments under the command of Captain Benjamin Birdsall manned the line from Fontaine's Battery southward to a point where it joined with Swift's New York Militia Regiment and the 5th Pennsylvania Volunteers. These units, all under the command of Brigadier General Peter B. Porter, in turn linked with Brigadier General Ripley's Brigade at Snake Hill.

The focus of the Snake Hill defences was Captain Nathan Towson's Battery of six 6-pounder guns. Four companies of the 21st Infantry, 250 men, under the command of Major Eleazer D. Wood, were on the extreme left. Two companies were in reserve behind the battery. Under command of Captain Benjamin Ropes, their mission was to protect the battery from any attacks coming from the direction of the shore. Three companies from the 23d and one from the 17th Infantry were in position between the battery and the militia. The units were reasonably well dug in by 13 August and the entire line was protected by the abatis.

British artillery fire commenced with a shower of hot shot and explosive shells at first light on 13 August. It continued and it was increasingly heavy throughout the entire day, night and on into the 14th. Just at retreat on 14 August, a stray British shot hit a small magazine, creating quite an explosion. This incident convinced the British that more damage was done than actually had been. The artillery fire slackened at about half past midnight and ceased entirely about an hour later, indicating to the garrison the imminent possibility of an assault. Generals Gaines and Ripley put their men on full alert. At about 0200, General Ripley was riding with his aide toward Snake Hill when the British attack there commenced. This lasted for about 20 minutes with an incredible display of defensive fire that made the night as bright as day.

The British, led by Lieutenant Victor Fischer with the DeWatteville Regiment, made five valiant tries to get into the American position. They were stymied by the fires of Towson's Battery and the 21st Infantry companies to its left. The two companies in reserve successfully repulsed a British effort to wade into the lake, out around the abatis, and back onto the beach. An estimated 190 British were captured while many others were swept away by the current. According to General Gaines, the first British rush against Snake Hill was not checked until it got to the abatis, three metres away from the American earthworks. Gaines started to send some riflemen to support the Snake Hill defenders but held them back when he determined that resistance had been successful. A few of the men from the 4th Rifles attached themselves to the 17th Infantry company on Towson's right.

The British attack was a three column converging movement. In the darkness it inevitably could not be as precisely timed as General Drummond had intended. It appears that the Snake Hill fighting had ended before there was any contact with the other British columns. Some of the more nervous U.S. pickets forward of Douglass' Battery had to be ordered back to their positions as they withdrew prematurely on hearing the uproar at Snake Hill. The left British column consisting of the 103d Regiment under Colonel Hercules Scott finally made its appearance at about 0230. It made two gallant efforts to close with the Americans. But it was blown back by the fire from Douglass' guns and another piece rushed up by Lieutenant MacRee, plus fire from the defending infantrymen. Colonel Scott was killed and the 103d remnants were forced to withdraw, pursued by Harding's militia. A few of them joined the third British column.

This force, led by Lieutenant Colonel William Drummond, a nephew of the British Commander, made three tries against Fort Erie proper. On the third try it wrested, in desperate fighting, the northeast bastion from the defenders. The American defence was led at first by Captain Alexander Williams and First Lieutenant Patrick McDonough. Both officers were killed as Drummond's men piled in. After the British secured the bastion, Major Jacob Hindman, the overall artillery commander, and Major William Trimble with the 19th Infantry troops led unsuccessful counterattacks. The American success at the adjacent Snake Hill site allowed General Ripley to send three companies from the 23d Infantry and the 17th Infantry company to the fort's aid. Earlier, its defenders had been joined by a detachment from the 4th Rifles and later a larger force of 11th and 22d Infantry men from the reserve were led into the fray by Captain William Foster, 11th Infantry, and one of the assistant inspectors, Major Nathan Hall. None of these efforts were successful because of the limited approaches into the fort. Then, just as it seemed as if British victory was inevitable, the bastion was rocked by a tremendous explosion.

A magazine in the northeast bastion had exploded from some unknown cause. It completely shattered British resolve, killing or wounding nearly 400 men and dazing hundreds of others. Bits of flesh and debris were hurled throughout the area, causing even American casualties. British survivors not captured broke contact and withdrew to their own lines as best they could. General Drummond prepared for an American counterattack. However, there were only a few tentative probes as General Gaines seemed happy to settle for a defensive victory. He also was faced with repairing the damage and caring for the casualties caused by this tragic event. The British had suffered an estimated 1,000 casualties, compared to fewer then 90 Americans.

Field Medicine

Fortunately, the American field medical system was established sufficiently to cope with the medical disaster represented by the British defeat. One field hospital under Dr. Amasa Troubridge, 21st Infantry, was set up in tents in the middle of the encampment, just in front of a permanent building occupied by General Gaines as quarters and sometimes used as a surgery. This hospital cared for the British wounded and coordinated their evacuation to the American shore. Most of them were sent to the hospital at Sandytown within a few days. It was another four days for the last of them to be moved from there to Williamsville. Civilians who recalled seeing them passing by in wagons remembered that many of them appeared to be badly burned. Healthy prisoners of war were evacuated directly to Williamsville.

Casualties were cleared as quickly as possible from the northeast bastion so it could be repaired. Lieutenant Douglass reported "more than 100 bodies were removed" as well as partial remains. The British dead were passed over the embankment in front of the Douglass Battery and were buried with honors in mass graves of 40 to 50 each. It took several hours to get all the "wounded and burnt" out of the ruins. Nearly two days were consumed in burying the dead. An estimated 200 British dead near Snake Hill were allowed to float down river, presumably without honors.

A second field hospital had been set up near Snake Hill under the auspices of the 23d Infantry. It was to stay there until American withdrawal. Adjacent to it, or nearby, was a burial place described by Benson Lossing as "just back of Towson's Battery." This appears to have been used to bury soldiers who died of disease or injury before they could be sent to Sandytown and may be the one that generated this study. Officers' remains, on the other hand, seem to have been returned to the U.S. for burial as a matter of routine. When Major Lodowick Morgan lost his life, for example, his body was sent the same day from Fort Erie to Buffalo where it was buried the next day at Park Meadow. In other cases, the quartermaster contracted with teamsters to carry officers' remains to locations outside the battle area, apparently at the request of families.

The Snake Hill area hospital came to be known unofficially as the Fort Erie General Hospital, or words to that effect. Rations drawn for the "sick and attendants" over the month of August show as many as 200 men and five women staff or patients. This indicates, along with pay vouchers, that the matrons requested by the surgeons to remain with their hospitals served throughout the siege at Fort Erie with their units well into October.

One of the duties of these matrons was to remove the personal effects of the deceased for return to next of kin or the government as appropriate. First Sergeants or adjutants performed the same duties in the field. This regulatory requirement, especially in the hospital, explains the absence of such effects in most burials. In any case, those wounded who could be evacuated first went to Sandytown. Many of the sick, however, went directly to Williamsville.

Other civilians in addition to the matrons occasionally could be found in Fort Erie during the siege. Entries on the vouchers submitted by rations contractors indicate the periodic presence of persons classed as "indigent families" and "refugees." In one case, two people classified as "Canadian women" were issued flour. These groups were encountered most commonly in July and again in October, times when it was probably most convenient for American loyalists living in Canada to pass through the fort to the U.S. shore. Occasionally the families of deceased soldiers came to Fort Erie to settle the dead man's accounts. In one case, for example, the wife of a 23d Infantry soldier killed at Lundy's Lane was at the fort on 17 October. She drew her late husband's back pay and retained bounty from the regimental paymaster and collected her husband's property from his old company. Her visit from West Point, New York, was not viewed as unusual. The presence of these civilians and local produce sellers in such a dangerous place raises the possibility of civilian casualties being incurred during the siege.

A third medical facility was established in September, during the latter part of the siege. A separate hospital was established for the 1,500 New York Militia under the direction of Hospital Surgeon Eli Hill, a veteran of several earlier militia call-ups. This appears to have been located west of Snake Hill but worked closely with the hospital there, almost certainly sharing the same graveyard. Surgeon Hill's operation remained at Fort Erie until the second week of October. Following the surge of patients resulting from the 15 August attack, the hospitals remained busy thereafter.

Combat actions continued at a fairly high rate after the abortive British attack. These added to the random casualties inflicted by the incessant British artillery fire. The worst day for artillery deaths was 27 August when Lieutenant Sylvanus Felton of the New York Militia was killed and 20 others were injured or later died. There were severe skirmishes almost every day. One of the most celebrated of these was on 5 September. A sortie of 100 men led by Lieutenant Colonel Joseph Willcocks of the Canadian Volunteers followed up on a successful skirmish begun by a patrol from the 21st Infantry. Willcocks and Lieutenant Thomas W. Roosevelt of the New York Militia were killed in the ensuing fracas. A few days later, a British raid on American picket number four resulted in fifteen U.S. killed and seven captured at the cost of two British casualties. The situation meant that the field hospitals were treating both small arms and artillery casualties as well as men in increasingly poor health.

Militia medical operations often were distinct from their federal counterparts although they were similar in structure. Problems lay in matters of accountability for material and equipment and in requisitioning procedures. The reason for this lay in the definition of what the federal government's responsibilities were for reimbursing the state when this property was used in federal service. A standardized central issue system was developing in federal medical forces, but not among the militia. Militia surgeons ordered and used items in quantities based only on their own judgment and training. Consequently, it often was simpler to keep militia medical facilities separate from their federal counterparts even when working in close association with each other.

Military Business/Supplies

The Americans continued to work on their defences and to patrol beyond their lines. Both undertakings proved to be extremely hazardous. Lieutenant Douglass stated that daily losses during this phase of the siege averaged about one in every 16 men in the garrison. Especially hard hit were the fatigue parties laboring on the fortifications. The British fired about 300 rounds a day into the American positions. They used mostly solid shot, but shells and rockets also contributed to the damage. Battery Number Two pounded the works to try to effect a breach, while Number One harassed personnel. The 30 days after the 15 August attack were remembered by the Americans as being the hardest of the whole siege. The continual attrition, hard work and poor conditions proved too much for 70 men who deserted.

No one was immune from the rain of shells. General Gaines was severely injured on 28 August. Brigadier General James Miller, newly promoted, assumed command briefly until the convalescent General Brown could resume command on 2 September. Brown had not been idle while he was recovering. As early as 1 August he had written New York Governor Daniel D. Tompkins requesting an additional militia call-up. In the interim, he asked the regional militia commander, Major General Amos Hall, for men. Hall produced fewer than 300 as of 19 August, because of financial support questions similar to those mentioned above in connection with hospitals. Brigadier General Porter worked with state officials to clear up issues of pay, supply and contracting. As a result, a second call for militia on 21 August drew a much more favorable response from the men of Cayuga, Seneca, Ontario, Steuben and Genessee Counties. What grew to a total of 4,000 men began converging on the rendezvous point at Batavia, thanks largely to Porter's efforts and those of the Governor's representative, Colonel John B. Yates. It proved easier to get the men organized into regiments and companies and properly mustered than it did to get them supplied and equipped.

There were supply deficiencies in every category. The federal and state arsenals already had been depleted by earlier requirements imposed by the unprecedented attrition of the campaign. The state arsenal at Onondaga exhausted its small arms stock on 31 August, issuing "70 English and three French muskets with bayonets" and 20 bayonets with scabbards. The previous day it had shipped to Batavia 122 British and four French muskets with bayonets and a miscellaneous collection of accoutrements to include 38 "unserviceable" cartridge boxes and belts. There was such a variety of weapons that standard ammunition and bayonets could not be issued. The countryside was scoured for weapons not turned in previously by militia already mustered out from earlier calls. The armories at Whitesborough and Canandaigua, as well as that at Onondaga, were emptied. Captured British weapons and equipment also were issued. A limited supply of flints was available; knapsacks and blankets, however, were very hard to procure.

This, in part, explains General Brown's insistence that the men be given tents when they arrived at Fort Erie.

The militia were not alone in experiencing supply problems as the siege progressed. The engineers' demand for tools and building materials was voracious. For example, in the first week of September Lieutenant Colonel MacRee demanded 610 broadaxes "without delay." It was apparent from his requisitions that work on the fortifications was still going at a furious pace. The supply system began to feel the strain. The 9th Military District usually drew its ordnance and quartermaster supplies up the Hudson River directly from Philadelphia. However, operations in the Lake Champlain Valley were consuming equally vast resources. Further, the transportation net west of Utica was so underdeveloped that it placed a severe strain on the pipeline. The flow of goods to Buffalo therefore was shifted in part to cross Pennsylvania instead. Thus, by the end of July, cartridges and gunpowder were coming from Pittsburgh overland to Erie and then to Buffalo by boat.

Perishables and regionally produced items were received from the contractors by the public store keeper, Ezra St. John, at Buffalo. They were held there, then sent to Buffalo Creek where they were loaded into open boats for the trip across to Fort Erie. There was only one small storehouse at the fort; consequently, most goods had to be held in open storage. As a result, there was a high degree of damage and waste. Bad weather could also impede the steady flow of fresh rations. Hence the diet became increasingly monotonous as the siege continued. Salt meat and hard bread became the staple.

It is interesting to note the volume of quartermaster business conducted in the Buffalo area in support of actions beyond the scope of General Brown's campaign. Contracts for lake vessels indicate a steady movement of troops from points in the east to Detroit. Throughout August, for example, elements of the 3d and 5th Infantry Regiments — bag, baggage, and families — embarked for the western posts through Buffalo.

The increasingly uneven status of supplies was reflected in inspectors' comments. Colonel Josiah Snelling cited the deteriorating condition of the livestock due to the lack of balanced forage. Even more serious were his comments reflecting the declining condition of individual equipment and clothing. On 30 August, for example, he reported that more than 100 men in the Rifle Regiment were without shoes. Their condition, he said, was similar to that of the entire command. The clothing situation worsened throughout September and October. By the end of the campaign, General Brown said it was approaching desperation. The remaining stocks in local depots as far east as Auburn had been absorbed by the reinforcements coming to

Buffalo. He predicted a serious health crisis unless adequate clothing and footwear were made available immediately.

The Sortie

General Brown resumed command when the situation appeared critical to him. The British completed a third battery with a supporting blockhouse to its rear on 4 September. It was located 460 m from the U.S. positions and contained three 24-pounders, an 8-inch howitzer and a mortar. It could not be allowed to function unchallenged; otherwise the continued slow pounding represented by such British tactics would doom the fort. Brown began bringing over as many troops as possible to increase the offensive power of the garrison. At the same time, he embarked upon the program to house them as comfortably as possible in the increasingly rainy weather. A few veteran units returned after resting in Buffalo. Also a steady trickle of newly arrived regular units were moved from the U.S. shore as they arrived from places as distant as Detroit, Sandusky, and Rutland, Vermont.

Brown also directed General Porter to select his most reliable militia regiments and bring them over. Five regiments in addition to Dobbin's, already deployed, were chosen. There were a few men who hesitated to cross over because of their understanding that under law they could be used only defensively. After a harangue from Porter, they fell in with their more enthusiastic colleagues. None of the New York Militia were in uniform. Porter consequently ordered them to wear red cloths around their necks or heads so they would be recognized as members of his brigade. General Brown directed that the movement of this large force take place in the darkness of the night of 9–10 September. He wanted to conceal the deployment in order not to alert the British to the possibility of an American attack. The movement of Porter's Brigade was helped greatly by the fortuitous arrival of four vessels from Erie bringing reinforcements. They provided security while the load carrying capacity was added to by their small boats. Most of the militia crossed that night without incident and set up a camp protected by rude breastworks west of Snake Hill in a cleared forest along the Lake Erie shore. The remainder of the New Yorkers crossed the next night along with Major Thomas S. Jesup's 25th Infantry. Fifteen hundred New York Militia remained on the American shore performing various security and support duties.

General Brown may have sensed a subtle shift in the situation. British fire was slackening because of a growing ammunition supply problem. General Drummond, as a matter of fact, was reporting to his superiors that the ammunition shortage was so acute he no longer felt his fire was having any effect on the American situation. Additionally, the British did not have tents and were living in whatever temporary shelters they could manage. None were adequate with the advent of rainy weather, as shown by the rapid growth of the sick list. General Brown, on the other hand, had pressed successfully to get his troops under shelter, either in floored tents or dugouts. Thus the bad weather did not have the same adverse effects on the Americans.

Continued British aggressiveness and their growing vulnerability led General Brown to decide to risk a sortie to gain the initiative. He began making his plan in consultation with a few trusted officers but did not reveal his full scheme until the evening of 16 September, the day before the attack. In the meantime however, American artillery fire beginning on 13 September increased considerably and there was a rise in picket skirmishing as the Americans probed the British positions. They also were protecting bands of pioneers clearing access routes to the British west flank. On the morning of 17 September heavy artillery fire became "incessant," in the words of one British soldier, as the Americans moved to their attack positions.

The American attack consisted of two converging columns massed against British Batteries Three and Two. The American thrust under General Porter was divided into three columns. The first target was Battery Three, which was to be followed by Battery Two. All the militia troops were in Porter's force along with about 500 regulars. A supporting force under General James Miller positioned itself to help Porter and also to threaten Battery Two. Both forces were later to descend on Battery One after destroying the other batteries. General Ripley commanded a general reserve that held itself in the garrison area. Major Jesup with the 150 men remaining in his regiment, the artiller and a number of convalescents comprised the rear area defenders in Fort Erie itself.

The attacking units formed at about 1200 on 17 September and advanced close to the British line undetected in blustery, rainy conditions. At 1430 they attacked the batteries and the one British brigade protecting them. Batteries Three and Two were taken in fierce fighting and largely destroyed. All three of Porter's column commanders were killed. Battery Number One was occupied briefly. At about 1630, Drummond's other two brigades counterattacked and the increasingly disorganized Americans were forced back into Fort Erie, bringing many of their wounded with them. General Ripley was seriously wounded when the reserves were committed to cover the American withdrawal. The U.S. forces sustained over 500 casualties and were especially hard hit by officer losses. The British had perhaps as many as 650 casualties. An estimated 400 British prisoners were brought into the fort as well. Bad weather prevented shipping them to Buffalo until the afternoon of 19 September. Even then the waters were rough. Those Americans who died on the British lines were buried there in the British trenches.

The sortie combined with General Drummond's logistical and personnel problems served to convince him the time had come to raise the siege.

End of Operations

On the 18th of September the British began moving their heavy equipment and stores back to the Chippawa River. The British infantry broke camp at 2000 on 21 September, left their campfires burning, and trudged back to Chippawa. British pickets remained opposite Black Rock, then skirmished northward the morning of the 22nd as the U.S. Rifles and Dragoons discovered the withdrawal and probed forward. The siege of Fort Erie was lifted but the drama was not ended as another American force closed into the area.

Major General George Izard's Division was moving slowly into the region as a result of an earlier call for help from General Brown. A British courier riding between Kingston and York had been captured about 7 September by a naval landing party from Sackets Harbor. The contents of the papers he was carrying revealed that two more regiments were enroute to reinforce General Drummond. This was the information which prompted General Brown on 10 September to solicit General Izard's aid and may have influenced his decision to make the sortie as quickly as possible.

General Izard's force of 4,300 men left Sackets Harbor on 21 September and slowly moved westward. He and General Brown conferred at Batavia on 27 September and decided that General Izard should first attack Fort Niagara while Brown held Drummond and his force at the Chippawa. Both men considered Fort Erie to be no longer threatened. Accordingly, General Izard's men headed for Niagara, reaching Lewiston on 5 October. There Generals Izard, Brown and Porter conferred and concluded that it would be better for all U.S. forces to consolidate in Canada and operate together there. General Izard moved to Fort Schlosser on 8 October intending to cross the Niagara River at that spot; however, there were not enough boats available. Consequently, on 9 October he moved his entire force to Black Rock and his army crossed into Canada on 10 and 11 October where it camped two miles north of Fort Erie. On 13 October, he left a garrison under Major Hindman at the fort and took the rest of his force northward. He camped at Black Creek, then moved to Street's Creek the next day. He deployed from there in battle order on the 15th and confronted General Drummond's force arrayed on the opposite bank of the Chippawa. An artillery duel ensued in which four Americans were killed and one wounded. The dead, all artillerymen, were buried near where they fell.

General Izard then tried to flank the well defended British position by sending Brigadier General Daniel Bissell's reinforced brigade to Cook's Mills on Lyon's Creek. General Drummond countered the move by sending a force of about 750 men. A heavy skirmish developed on 19 October near the mills in which the Americans lost 13 men and 53 wounded, to one British death and 35 wounded. Bissell's Brigade was reinforced with another two regiments. His troops burned the mills, buried the enemy and friendly dead, then withdrew on the afternoon of 20 October. The next day the U.S. units again appeared opposite General Drummond's Chippawa positions. However, General Izard declined to attack what he judged to be too strong a position, and at noon on 21 October he pulled all of his forces back to Fort Erie.

Two days earlier, General Brown had asked permission to leave for Sackets Harbor. General Brown left on 20 October, followed by his division on 24 October. General Porter's Militia crossed at the same time, going to Batavia for discharge. The militia hospital closed at Fort Erie on 19 October and all sick and wounded were sent to Buffalo. It was the last medical facility at Fort Erie. As late as 24 October, the Americans were still undecided about retaining the fort. General Izard even made tentative plans to establish a winter camp at Black Rock to be in support of the fort. Captain Samuel B. Archer along with nearly 100 men were improving the fort defences while General Izard continued to think that he was outnumbered by the British. Then, on 25 October, continued rough weather convinced General Izard that the oncoming winter would make the fort impossible to secure.

On that day, General Izard directed his chief quartermaster, Major John G. Camp, to gather the necessary men and boats to evacuate the troops and equipment from Fort Erie. The major got 111 experienced boatmen from the units at Buffalo and another 130 hired from among the discharged militiamen. An additional 30 officers and men were assigned to the docks at Buffalo and Black Rock and told to stand by. Also on 25 October, Captain Archer was told to stop what he was doing, destroy the foundation of the blockhouse he was building on Snake Hill and demolish the whole site. His men set to with such zeal that they broke nearly 20 picks and spades that day.

On 1 November, General Bissell's Brigade was the last major tactical unit to leave. It should have returned earlier but progress was hindered by the continuing foul weather. Plans for the destruction of the fort were also completed on the same day. Major Hindman supervised the removal of all heavy equipment and guns. Fifteen guns remained and were gradually removed over the next three days. Then, on 5 November, the last troops, artillerymen and engineers, placed the last charges, boarded their boats and rowed away as the fort was rocked by explosions. General Izard dispersed the force into winter quarters, sent as many hospital patients as possible to Greenbush, and gathered most of the 2,000 remaining at Williamsville. The Niagara Campaign of 1814 was over.

Conclusion

This look at the hard-fought campaign began as an attempt to explain how 28 American soldiers were buried on the Lake Erie shore. That explanation in turn led to a more detailed and novel view of the campaign and the army that fought it. It has been acknowledged by all who knew or know of General Scott that he was one of the U.S. Army's great trainers. However, exactly what he did and what the results of his efforts were at the time were not widely known.

Understanding why there would be a graveyard at Snake Hill has inspired a detailed look at the medical and administrative operations of the 9th Military District. These operations proved to be reasonably efficient and sophisticated. There can be no question that the American officers in charge had learned from bitter experience. They presided over a responsive support system and a well-organized medical structure, fully capable of sustaining a large force in the field as a result of General Scott's vision and Brown's leadership. This force developed into a form surprisingly reminiscent of its modern counterpart. The way it worked, explains why these American soldiers were buried in Canada.

A Note on Sources

The basis for this chapter has been the holdings of the U.S. National Archives at Washington, D.C. Other archives, published documentary collections and memoirs, and secondary sources have been used when appropriate. The primary sources used consisted of personnel records, supply and fiscal documentation, and correspondence among and between commanders, staff officers and War Department officials. These consist for the most part of practical accountability documents for men, equipment and money.

Their perusal in quantity gives an excellent picture of the daily operations of General Brown's command. Since most of them deal directly or indirectly with aspects of pecuniary liability, it is reasonable to presume they are as accurate as possible. Commanders' reports are less detailed and critical but still give a reasonable picture of events. Memoirs are less reliable when dealing with matters outside the immediate experience of the memorialist, but still are useful for documenting personal experiences. The least reliable sources proved to be modern secondary sources. In some cases, these sources repeat errors, while in others the brevity of the treatment leaves an incorrect impression. This study relies on the documentation produced by those responsible for the daily operations of General Brown's forces and attempts to cut through to the level of the most reliable documentation possible. At the same time, it is hoped that the reader can gain something of the perspective of those who were there.

Figure 2.1: Location of Study Area

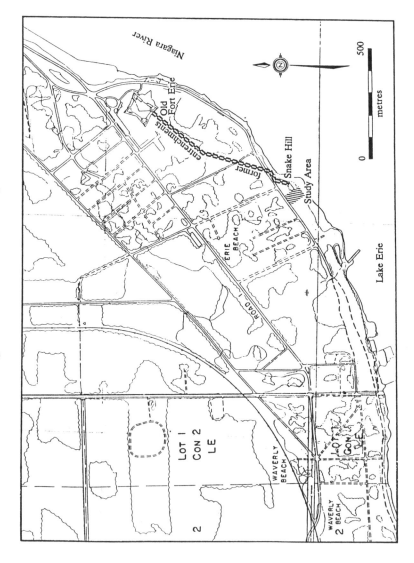

Plate 2.1: Undated Map Detailing the Boundaries of Fort Erie in 1814

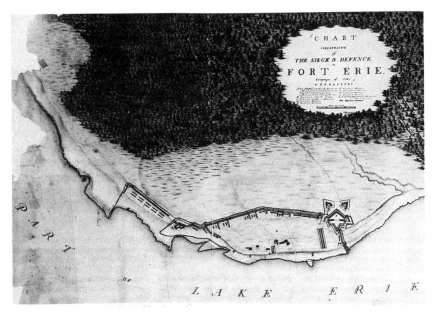

Reproduced from an item in Records of the Chief of Engineers, RG77, National Archives, Washington, D.C.

Plate 2.2:
Captain Nathan Towson

*Courtesy of Division of Armed Forces
History Smithsonian Institution,
Washington, D.C.*

Plate 2.3:
Major General Jacob Brown

*Courtesy of Division of Armed Forces
History Smithsonian Institution,
Washington, D.C.*

Plate 2.4: 1ˢᵗ Pennsylvania Volunteer, 1813

*Watercolour by Mr. Don Troiani. Reproduced, with
permission, from The First Century: A History of the
28ᵗʰ Division. Prepared by Uzal W. Ent. Harrisburg,
Pennsylvania: Stackpole Books. 1979.*

Plate 2.5: Major General George Izard

Reprinted from Benson J. Lossing, The Pictorial Fieldbook of the War of 1812. New York: Harper. 1869

Plate 2.6: Brigadier General Winfield Scott

Engraving by Thomas Gimbrede (1786-1866). Reproduced, by permission, from The National Portrait Gallery. Smithsonian Instiution, Washington, D.C.

Three

Medical History

ADRIANNE NOE

In his 1816 work, *Medical Sketches of the Campaigns of 1812, 13, 14 ...,* Surgeon James Mann complained that medical treatment had not improved since the Revolutionary War; that many surgeons and physicians had not transmitted their experiences and observations from that war. Mann found it significant that the forms of diseases and injuries encountered in the War of 1812 were similar. Nevertheless, many of the medical personnel were unfamiliar with military hospital functions and the nascent system within which they were beginning to work. But for a very few documents such as the observations of Tilton (1813), no American reports of Revolutionary War medicine survived. Physicians were generally unpracticed in contending with maladies peculiar to both travelling and stationary armies.

In a similar vein, Surgeon Amasa Troubridge wrote:

> In the history of the Revolutionary War but little is known in relation to the medical department. During the progress of the late war of 1812 the surgeon who accompanied the various divisions of the armies on the northern and western frontier, was sensible that the country through which he passed and to which he was called for the exercise of his professional duties had before been the theater of war and human distress from disease whose cause was the same that then surrounded him. He witnessed the sudden changes of atmosphere peculiar to countries surrounding large and extensive lakes and the local causes of disease. He witnessed the many fields on which armies had been encamped and on which surgeons had put in all their talents and skill and experience to counteract or mitigate wasting pestilence and disease. (Troubridge n.d.)

This chapter addresses several questions oriented toward supplementing the archaeological, physical anthropological and historical perspectives in the Snake Hill reports. I will explore available historical documentation involving mortuary practices and actual burial activities, medical philosophy and intervention techniques, personal reports of physicians or individuals involved in the medical enterprise, and include a brief note on extant relevant medical instrumentation.

Burial Practices

Documentary evidence of burial activities at Fort Erie are meagre. In his memoirs, Amasa Troubridge, Surgeon with the 21st Infantry, refers to July of 1814, providing one of the few such recorded comments:

> On the 26' the American Army commenced a retreat to Fort Erie and thence began to fortify itself. The enemy followed and in three days after opened a constant and heavy fire upon the fort with cannon and mortar, which was continued with constant picket skirmishing until the 15' of August when a general assault was made upon the fort and encampment by the enemy. They were repulsed with great slaughter and loss. The repulse was decisive [?] by the explosion of a magazine under the east bastion of the fort, killing 300 and wounding 149 with 5 officers prisoners. There was scarcely a wound found by the surgeon that was not exemplified among them. A special order from the General assigned to the care of Dr. Troubridge [*sic*] the wounded of the enemy.
>
> In a few days the greatest part were sent to the Gen'l Hospital, Buffalo . . . Two days were occupied in burying the dead. (Troubridge n.d.)

Although Troubridge does not mention the location of the specific site, burial took place at the front of the fort.

Another memoir of burial-related activity appears in the *Diary of Jarvis Frary Hanks,* written between 1831 and 1842. It includes recollections of the Niagara Campaign. Hanks mentions that for their crimes of desertion, men were made to dig graves with only enough distance between them to allow for kneeling. Hanks, too, makes no mention of grave locations, yet he does allude to the use of coffins.

Coffin remnants at the Snake Hill site appear to be those of six-sided, shallow, unlined, softwood, flat boxes, typical in style of those produced and used in the Northeast region at the time. Metal nails were used in their manufacture; again, typical of the time and place. In specific form, size and shape, these hand-wrought nails are logically expected to vary, as the United States government had not as yet established an embalmer's office. Civilian undertakers were contracted for soldiers' burials, although it seems more likely that individuals with carpentry skills from within the military units were pressed into service for coffin production. For example, nineteenth century historian Ernest Cruikshank records in his extract from a letter of Dr. Young, Surgeon to the 103d Regiment, 18 August 1814:

> Your brother was wounded in the fort. He was carried off the field by a sergeant of the grenadiers and one of the men.
>
> His remains were interred on the evening of the day on which he fell. We had a coffin made by the regimental carpenters, who have since enclosed his grave with a wooden paling. (Mann 1816)

Most of the soldiers were buried in the remnants of their uniforms, yet on or near some of the remains were found metal straight pins, some with heads. These may have been used to secure bandages or winding shrouds of sheets or strips of fabric. Anthropologist T. Dale Stewart (1979) reports that such pins or evidence of their use, such as characteristically colored or shaped stains from the pin, represent the common practice of securing together the upper ends of the fabric. In addition to the use of shrouds, it appears a number of the bodies were bound at hand and foot, although this could have been done to facilitate conveyance to the burial site or to aid in the physical management of the corpse.

Parenthetically, the fabric was likely to have been wool. In addition to its availability, wool in a felted or woven form would have been the material of choice for reasons established as early as 1666. In that year, a formal Act of the British Parliament established that all persons should be buried in a shroud composed of English woolen material in place of the previously used linen. This Act was firmly embraced by the Anglican church and it remained formally unrepealed until 1815.

In addition to the use of wool in a broad shroud, the Act stipulated that the feet and hands (in cruciform configuration for members of the Roman Catholic church) were to be tightly bound, again with English woolen.

Funerary practice historian Bertram Puckle (1926) records the practice of loosening the foot and ankle binding immediately prior to burial, in order to allow speedy egress in the event of premature burial.

Physical orientation of the corpse within the grave is a matter of some interest. Centuries of Roman Catholic and Protestant burial practices have established a "feet in the east" orientation unless the burial takes place in or near a church. In that case, the placement of the feet toward the altar takes precedence over other orientations. Puckle has also reported on the issue of physical placement and orientation in European cemeteries. For example, of the 70 gravesites studied at the Iron age cemetery at Chervaise, 67 were oriented with feet to the east. A face downward posturing indicated a victim of cholera—a position it was hoped would stay the plague.

Burial practices apparent at the Fort Erie site are generally consistent with American practices. However, in relevant matters of military tradition, American regulation or informal habit was probably informed, if not dictated, by previously established British action. Thus, the findings are consistent with expected British behavior as well.

Medical Practices

Medical activities at the Siege of Fort Erie are reasonably well represented in the literature. However, it should be remembered that the medical activities significant enough to be recorded are often those which are more remarkable for the survival of patients than for their demise.

The health of the American troops near the Niagara frontier reportedly varied throughout the spring, summer and fall of 1814. High rates of illness were prevalent during the early months, with some diseases reaching epidemic proportion. Pneumonia, disabling rheumatism, intermittent fever, "Lake Fever," cholera, typhus, syphilis, small pox, dysentery and non-specific diarrhea were all reported among the men (Roland 1983). Health improved toward the beginning of the summer (Gillett 1981) and then-Hospital Surgeon Lovell reported only two deaths due to disease when crossing the Niagara on 3 July (Mann 1816). However, soon after the start of the siege of Fort Erie, the "rainy season" began, claiming growing numbers to disease, particularly the quickly dehydrating and debilitating diarrhea and dysentery. Typhus was particularly severe among the militia, whose members were seldom sent to a general hospital until the third day of fever, by which time no general treatment was available (Mann 1816).

The nearest General Hospital was located at Williamsville, eleven miles from Buffalo. It had opened on 1 August, as the Buffalo General Hospital was crowded with casualties from the recent Battle of Lundy's Lane (25 July). Apart from the regular Medical Department staff, each regiment assigned to Fort Erie had its own surgeon. He in turn had two mates. Archival records reveal that some buildings were leased for hospitals; other materials indicate tents were erected for medical activities (Troubridge).

The list of these activities is short. Trepanning (or trephining, opening one or more small holes in the skull to relieve pressure), probing, draining and suturing describe a great deal of it. Surgeries were limited; the chest and abdomen were not opened. Except for those in his operating kit, the surgeon relied on very few tools. When time permitted, postmortem examinations were performed, although in limited number.

Amputation, however, was "the prototypical act of nineteenth century military surgery" (Roland 1980). As a medical management practice, it made a ragged, irregular, complicated wound into a relatively clean and uncomplicated one, and was a technique better represented than most in the medical literature. Mann and the Canadian surgeon John Douglas both noted that, when called for, it should be performed as quickly as possible— on the battlefield, if necessary, to avoid the consecutive (later) amputation (Mann 1816; Douglas 1985). The relative need, timing, and environment for amputation later became the subject of much debate. Although associated mortality rates range from 10 to 90% (Roland 1980), surgeons of the early nineteenth century followed English and continental amputation practices and employed them often. Mann himself was convinced that every individual could survive the amputation when in good health, and preferred the risk of the procedure to the risk of lengthy transportation to a general hospital and a concomitantly long stay there.

Fort Erie Battle Medicine

Amasa Troubridge, Surgeon at Fort Erie, trained with and assisted James Mann in a number of these operations. Mann (1816) relates Troubridge's first such procedure, included here to describe the technique and to help identify some of the markings on the amputated bone ends found at the site.

> Jacob Blunt, a private in CAPT. VAN VECHTEN'S company, 23d regiment, 24 years old, in the action at Sackett's Harbour, 29th May 1813, received a grapeshot in his leg, which shattered the tibia and fibula. It soon inflamed and became much swollen. Cloths wet with diluted spirits were continually applied. By the fourth day the limb was so much swollen as to induce DOCTOR TROWBRIDGE [*sic*]

to make several incisions through the integuments, from just below the knee to the ankle. At this time mortification had considerable progressed. The leg assumed a mixed colour of yellow and purple; the cuticula was raised in small blisters. The leg and thigh were continually wet with cold rum and water, until the tenth of June, when the mortification ceased. Inflammation had disappeared from both the leg and thigh so much that an amputation was determined upon. Upon the 11th of June I performed the amputation in the following manner just above the knee. I gave the patient, 30 minutes before the operation was commenced, two grains of opium, when he was placed on a high table. After the application of the tourniquet, DOCTOR TROWBRIDGE [*sic*], my operative assistant, grasped the thigh with both hands, and kept the integuments steady, while the first incision was made down to the fascia; after which he retracted the integuments as much as possible, while I dissected them up from the muscles with a scalpel. Having dissected the skin with the cellular substance about an inch and half up, and turned them back on the thigh, at this point, I made a second incision with a steady and firm stroke of the knife around the thigh down to the bone. [Note. It requires considerable strength and firmness to carry the knife through the thick muscles and firm tendons, at one stroke. If we are not aware of this, we shall fail in our first attempt. At the moment the incision is made, the venous and arterial blood gushes out in such torrents, as to alarm the young surgeon, performing his first amputation, fearful that the tourniquet was not sufficiently secure. But soon I found the blood issued from the veins and arteries below the incision, when apprehension of danger ceased.]

The muscles being divided down to the bone, the operative assistant applied the retractor, made of strong linen, (preferable to leather,) and drew back the divided muscles, while I dissected the muscles from the bone one inch or more, when the bone was divided with the saw, and arteries taken up with the tenaculum. In this case they were five; more in number than usual. After sponging the stump with warm water to clear away the clotted blood to search for other bleeding vessels, and finding none, I turned down the integuments over the stump, and secured them in apposition, with strips of adhesive plaster, and dressed in the usual method. (Mann 1816)

This technique would anticipate evidence of nicks or cut marks near the amputated bone ends (made when cutting through the fascia), striations on the bone ends, and a tab of bone left when the bone was snapped from its attachment. Bilateral amputation, such as that found among the unassociated skeletal material at Snake Hill is also documented. Jarvis Hanks recalled in his diary seeing a corporal cooking meat in open camp ground and taking a shot to both arms. They were immediately amputated above the elbows and Hanks reports that the corporal lived.

Evidence of trauma caused by gunshot is also present among the remains (see Owsley et al., this volume). Roland (1980) reports an associated mortality of 10 to 50%. Disease, which is said to have generally accounted for more deaths that trauma, must also be considered as a cause of death. Many of the relevant diseases caused rapid dehydration and debilitation such that there would be no trace on the skeleton. Finally, drug overdoses may account for some of the deaths. The wide use of calomel, acetite of lead for dysentery, and tartrite of ammonia for diarrhea were common. In overdose, these remedies could have caused death.

Conclusions

The medicohistorical evidence is consistent with these remains being American. Burial and mortuary evidence is consistent with American practice. Medical philosophy and medical intervention technique are consistent with American practice. However, it is imperative to note that the American medical enterprise at this point was almost entirely formed by European thought and practice. The relatively poor quantity and quality of American medical literature forced the reliance upon the texts and manuals of respected members of the European medical community. Many Americans took their training and purchased their instruments in Europe.

In one respect, however, American medicine was beginning to diverge, as exemplified by this telling comment from James Tilton (1813), then Physician and Surgeon General, and later organizer of military hospital systems:

> In Britain, a high degree of civilization and luxury have divided the practice of physic and surgery; and that after the fashion of their country, the British are, in some measure, obliged to put these professions into different hands, in their military hospitals. It is, however, very different in our country, where every medical character practices both professions, and it is found, by experience, in our Army, to be impracticable to separate these duties. (Tilton 1813)

These conclusions are based on a survey of the archival, bibliographic and documentary materials at a variety of locations, including the regular and historical collections at the National Library of Medicine in Bethesda, Maryland, the book and manuscript collections at the Library of Congress, the National Museum of Health and Medicine of the Armed Forces Institute of Pathology, and the National Archives and Records Service in Washington, D.C. Surveyed materials are of American, British, Canadian and French origins. In addition, several trips to the site and the Fort Erie/Buffalo area provided opportunities for direct observation and access to documentary material at the Buffalo and Erie County Historical Society, Buffalo, New York.

Comment: Medical Instrumentation

No medical instruments that were certainly used at the Snake Hill site have been located to date. However, instruments that date to this chronological period are extant in the United States, Canada and abroad. Their careful study may be of use in interpreting information relating to medical intervention techniques such as autopsy and fracture management. In conjunction with the written and graphic records, the recovered skeletal material may in fact shed light on operative procedures and the tools necessary to perform them.

A careful study of the wear on bone saws, for example, may now become informed by amputated bone-end evidence (striations from saw motions and break tabs, for instance) and may help us understand such issues as how much stress these amputations placed on the patient, the instrument and its wielder. Care of the tools is an issue little represented in the medical technological and historical literature. Although it is the surgeon's mate who was responsible for the medicines and instruments, new light may be shed on what that entailed. It may become more nearly possible to determine how dull a saw might become before it was deemed unusable and discarded or resharpened—a significant finding for medical and technological history.

In his *A System of Operative Surgery, Founded on the Basis of Anatomy* (1812), Sir Charles Bell suggests a list of instruments necessary for practice of military surgery. It includes the following items: crane bill forceps, levers, tenacula, lancets, catheters, probes, bougies, knives, scalpels, saws, forceps and gorgets. Examples of these instruments may be found in various museums with major medical technology collections, including the following: National Museum of Health and Medicine, Armed Forces Institute of

Pathology, Washington, D.C.; The Hartford Medical Society, Hartford, Connecticut; Howard Dittrick Museum of Historical Medicine, Cleveland Heights, Ohio; Museum of the History of Medicine, Academy of Medicine, Toronto, Ontario; Medical Science Division, National Museum of American History, Smithsonian Institution, Washington, D.C.; and The Wellcome Museum of Medical History, Royal Science Museum, London, England.

Four   # Archaeological Investigations

STEPHEN C. THOMAS
RONALD F. WILLIAMSON

Field Methodology

Lots 1 and 2, Plan 59R-4235, Town of Fort Erie, constituted our principal area of investigation. Each lot was systematically stripped of both topsoil (A horizon) and subsoil (B horizon) until underlying sterile sediments (C horizon) were encountered. This procedure was necessary, since relic topsoils, overlain by windblown sands, were often found below the modern subsoil. The removal of soils was accomplished in shallow increments by an experienced gradall operator under the constant supervision of archaeological personnel.

Twenty-eight primary inhumations, three medical waste pits and an ox burial, all dating to the War of 1812 period, were documented. All of these features, with the exception of the ox burial and Burial 24, were situated within two spatial components (Figure 4.1). While all of the graves discussed below were discovered within the confines of the two lots, it is likely that additional individuals had been interred on the lot to the west.

The graves were first recognized through a slight discoloration in the subsoil, formed at the time of their excavation and use by the in-filling, which was comprised of both subsoil and topsoil. Once the initial grave shafts were recognized, only enough of the burial was exposed to document that an articulated body was to be found within. Once most of the grave shafts had been found, Canadian military tents were assembled over the burial areas to protect exhumation activities from inclement weather. The Town of Fort Erie also provided full logistical support for the excavations, including electric lighting and propane heating. In addition, a trailer was installed on the site and equipped with a telephone. This allowed communication between the field and the temporary laboratory and office at Old Fort Erie. Using these facilities, all of the defined historic features were recorded and excavated.

Once the outline of the grave shaft was delineated, a 30 cm pedestal of earth was created around the skeletal remains of each burial. The graves appear to have been originally excavated both in haste and leisure. Some are shared, some are too small and still others appear to have been larger than necessary (Table 4.1). Once the stain had been mapped in reference to a five metre grid system, the exacting work of carefully exposing each skeletal el ement and associated artifact(s) began. The remains were then fully exposed, drawn (Plate 4.1), and photographed in black and white, colour negative, and colour slides. Approximately 10 hours of VHS video tape was recorded in order to document the various activities involved in such a complex project. Each skeleton was reviewed by a professional physical anthropologist in order to record significant field observations concerning age, trauma and pathology. This was a precautionary move, since some very fragile elements might have been destroyed during transportation of the remains to the laboratory. Only after exhaustive field documentation of each individual did the process of exhumation commence. Each skeletal element was removed separately, carefully wrapped, and placed in a paper bag within a steel-reinforced cardboard container for shipment to laboratories in Toronto.

Laboratory Analysis

While samples of bone were subjected to detailed analyses elsewhere, the skeletal remains were, for the most part, examined at the Royal Ontario Museum and at Archaeological Services Inc. The methodologies for these examinations and analyses are described below in their respective chapters.

Alternatively, all of the artifacts were analysed at Archaeological Services Inc. although preliminary conservation activities were conducted at the Canadian Conservation Institute, the Royal Ontario Museum and the Ontario Ministry of Culture and Communications. These activities were necessary for several buttons, since corrosion and encrustation limited our ability to accurately measure their diameters and to discern their motif patterns.

Of those that were discernible, four major U. S. Army button motifs were identified including:

> Script "I"   140
> Eagle   29

> "US"   23
> Script "RA"   2
> Other American   1

In addition, twelve buttons were found with other motif types, including five British Army motifs and five civilian floral motifs.

Wherever possible, the recognizable motifs on buttons were compared and identified to a type specified in Albert's *Record of American Uniform and Historical Buttons with Supplement* (see Appendix A). Also, clear descriptions and illustrations of period military uniforms may be found in *Military Uniforms in America,* (Volume 2, The Company of Military Historians, John K. Elting, ed., 'Presidio Press, San Rafael, California, 1977). In the descriptions of button patterns for each burial, the terminology for outer torso garments includes coatee, roundabout, or vest, and for "pants," uniform overalls and civilian trousers. While military issue garments might be expected for most regulars, members of some militia units can be expected to have used civilian equivalents which wouldn't necessarily have the same button patterns.

Twenty-four buttons were found of the perforated, four-hole, pewter type. These can also be considered American in origin since they are largely, if not completely, absent from British collections. It would appear that flat, shanked, pewter buttons with a "US" motif, as well as these common four-hole, depressed-centre pewter buttons were restricted to military issue trousers or overalls. This garment was high waisted and suspender attachment buttons might be expected to appear in the lower thorax area. The garment also had three flaps which could be opened for medical treatment of abdominal and leg wounds. This may have resulted in the deposition of buttons anywhere from below the hips to the lower forearms.

A distinctive large type of one-hole bone button appears to have been associated with civilian trousers in the cases of Burials 19 and 24. This type ranges from 15.5 to 17.7 mm in diameter. Small one-hole buttons are apparently shirt buttons. Neck closure buttons were found with Burials 07, 08, 11, 14, and 23. Bone shirt-cuff buttons were identified in association with Burials 2 and 28, and represented the only recovered buttons in those cases. This may indicate that these two individuals were buried wearing only undershirts and that they may have been admitted to the field hospital prior to their demise.

Thirty-six buttons are described as having an "Obsured Motif." These buttons have motifs rendered unidentifiable by corrosion, but which might be revealed by restorative work. "U/I" designates a button which deteriorated to the point where it is difficult to determine whether the button was plain or decorated. Beside the overall motif, some buttons have unit designation areas (e.g., the ovals in the lower portions of buttons in Appendix B, Plate 11, 16 and 23). These fifty-one buttons appear to have intact unit designation areas, but the design within the area is obscured by corrosion.

Therefore, three arbitrary categories of preservation were used. Buttons in "excellent condition" refer to those that can generally be measured, and are probably restorable. Nine of the "Obscured Motif" buttons are considered to be in excellent condition. Specimens judged to be in "good condition" are more corroded or damaged; typically, the disk has developed severe cracks or the surface has exfoliated. At least some motif characteristics may be discerned, and some diameters measured. Items in "poor condition" are more fragmentary, and may have been reduced to granules. Motif characteristics could be discerned in very few of these cases.

In order to better represent the information potential of most of the buttons, their percentage completeness has also been documented. "Intact" specimens are at least 90% complete. They include the area of attachment (shank or perforations), and can furnish a diameter measurement. "Deteriorated" specimens are those judged to be less than 30% complete and therefore cannot be measured.

The majority of the buttons were made from pewter. With respect to buttons manufactured from other metals, analysts were rarely able to differentiate between copper and brass, although some of the copper and silver buttons were indentified. All of these evaluations are provided in the button catalogue in Appendix D.

With respect to button locations relative to the skeleton, precise positions are provided in the catalogue, within the anatomically oriented Location Information Number column. Diagrams illustrating button locations are provided for those burials which contained complex button patterns. No buttons were found on Burials 5, 30 and 31. In the case-by-case descriptions, the buttons are often described in terms of functionally related area groupings. Indeed, it was not always possible to be precise with respect to the association of buttons to body area. The skeletons typically had their hands crossed over the thorax, waist or pelvis. This overlapping frequently caused difficulty in our assignment of buttons to specific parts of the body.

This is especially true in the mid-body area: the lower chest, hips and forearms. This is where patterns of upper garment front buttons converge with tail buttons, pocket buttons and contents, overalls or suspender attachment buttons and closure buttons of overalls. The overalls can be closed, or can separate into three divergent flaps. Moreover, the mid-body is the general location of cuff buttons, which are typically situated in line with, and parallel to, the forearm. For those buttons which were situated near to, at the side of, or underneath an arm, the orientation of the shank toward the forearm bones was considered important. Nevertheless, it is improbable that all of the cuff buttons were identified.

Some emphasis has been placed on the diameters of buttons. Button measurements in certain burials offer clues about types of garments, since different garments tend to have different sized buttons. Assuming that different garments would have been produced with buttons from different manufacturing lots, or even different manufacturers, this size clustering effect would be expected. Factors leading to a lack of uniformity in measured button size include the soldiers' periodic replacement of lost or broken buttons and our measurement error, caused by the variable effects of corrosion and encrustation. Even in the case of severe corrosion, it was possible to differentiate some button fragments into size classes by observing the curvature of the remaining circumference, the distance from centre to rim, shank size, and proportional size of motif elements. It was possible to assign most buttons to one of two size classes (see Figure 4.2). Button diameters were measured with dial calipers to the nearest tenth of a millimetre.

Our interpretations regarding button association may have been affected by many factors. For example, the shank orientation of buttons overlying hard tissue, such as the rib cage, may have remained more stable than the orientation of buttons overlying soft tissue, such as the abdomen. In yet other cases, it was noted that battle trauma may have prompted the removal of clothing, presumably to facilitate access to the wound for medical intervention. Of course, many wounds would not leave traces in the hard tissue, especially abdominal wounds. The partial removal of the high-waisted military overalls may constitute circumstantial evidence for such a wound. Alternatively, it is also possible that garments were loosened to ease the injured man's breathing in any case of serious injury. The state of dress may also provide other trauma-related inferences. If the complete or partial removal of military clothing is taken to be evidence of hospitalization or, at least, field treatment, a fully dressed individual with little clothing disturbance may have died instantly or soon after wounding, before the administration of medical treatment. Thus, the archaeological analysis of the Snake Hill site represents a combination of cautious, carefully documented excavation and deductive interpretation, conducted within the context of historical information.

The remainder of this chapter presents summaries of the archaeological data associated with each of the burials and descriptions of the recovered items.

BURIAL 1

Burial 1 had been placed within an excavated grave shaft in an extended and supine position with the head to the west (Figure 4.3). While the right arm had been severely disturbed, the right hand lay pronate across the sacrum and right ilium. The left arm appeared to have been placed at the side of the body, since the humerus and ulna were visible but the radius was not. There appeared to be no bending or twisting of the arm. One phalanx was found next to the femur.

The skull and the hip bones were badly fractured and the pubic symphyses were missing altogether. The femora were also badly fragmented with considerable damage to the heads and the midshafts. The distal femora, the patellae, and the tibiae were present and well articulated with the fibulae and tarsals. The feet rested on the heels, slightly apart, and were rotated laterally.

A rib fragment from a different individual was recovered from within the same graveshaft. One end of this rib had been cut.

Twenty-three buttons were also recovered, although generally, their preservation was poor. This preservation problem, as well as the apparent pattern of multiple, short, linear series in the central torso area, made the interpretive association of these buttons with garments difficult.

The principal identifiable button type was the large, flat, round, shanked pewter button with a script "I" motif, although Button 03, located in the torso midline series, was a convex, eagle motif button with an even larger diameter. There was a range of 1.1 mm in the diameters of the flat buttons, which suggests that the garment may have been refitted with new buttons on one or more occasions.

The individual was probably buried in a coatee and overalls. The presence and patterning of two collar buttons and one shoulder button (02A, 02B and 09) are consistent with the American Army coatee which had, on each side of the neck, two collar buttons and one epaulet or shoulder strap button. In a number of other Snake Hill burials, clusters of three buttons occurred in the neck area, usually separated by a small distance. In this case, however, it would appear that only the right half of the collar-shoulder series survived.

Moreover, an aligned series of five buttons (03, 06, 04, 07 and 16) was found in the central torso region. If the coatee hypothesis is correct, this group would logically represent the lower end of the front row of buttons. Two buttons, 14 and 15, were found close to the midline in the lower left thorax, aligned vertically. These may represent a portion of the other linear front series of the coatee or alternatively, they may represent a torn and inferiorly displaced group of upper jacket buttons. It may be that buttons 10 and 11 were coatee cuff buttons since button 10 was located above the left wrist and button 11 above the right wrist.

This burial, like others, had an isolated button between the left arm and thorax, even with, or slightly caudal to, the distal left humerus. This is a common location for an isolated button. It seems unlikely that it represents a randomly deposited detached button. The most likely functional explanation would appear to be a suspender attachment or overall flap. Similarly, three buttons (08A, 12 and 13) were found between the torso and the right arm.

Moreover, buttons 05A and 05B were found parallel with the vertebral column in the upper right waist area. While the pair could conceivably have been a laterally displaced lower extension of the coatee front button series, it seems more logical to attribute them to overalls.

Therefore, while it is probable that this individual was interred wearing a coatee and overalls, both patterns were incomplete. Indeed, the coatee would appear to have been in poor repair at the time of death. Only the lower half of the front row and only two of the regulation six to eight cuff buttons were in place. It would also appear that the coatee had been refitted with new buttons at least once. The cuff button complement had been reduced to one on each side, suggesting hard use. There is no reason to suppose that the observed reduction of buttons on the coatee would not have been paralleled by a similar reduction on the overalls.

Alternatively, the overall button pattern is similar, especially across the central thorax region, to that described for Burial 29. In that case, it is very likely that the individual was not wearing the garments, but that they had been laid over the body. Yet, the discovery of a cluster of three buttons in the collar area and one over each wrist with this individual represents good evidence that he had been interred wearing the garment.

BURIAL 2

Burial 2 had been placed within an excavated grave shaft in an extended and supine position with his head to the west (Plate 4.2).

His skull appeared to have rotated forward slightly, probably due to postmortem shifting. The body was well aligned with no obvious twisting or disarticulation. The arms were gently flexed such that the right forearm lay across the lumbar region and the left forearm lay over the right. The feet, which may have been bound, were close together resting on the heels with the toes pointing distally and upwards.

The skeleton was in generally good condition, although the ribs had deteriorated and were very fragile. There was also damage to the anterior surfaces of the vertebrae and the outer surface of many of the long bones was flaky. The hip bones were also cracked.

A fragment of a copper pin was recovered from underneath the right scapula (Plate 4.3 - middle). The pin measured 1.9 mm in width at the head (round) and 1.24 mm in width at its widest point along the shaft. It appears to have been attached to a piece of wood and other organic material.

Two small one-hole buttons were found associated with this individual, located in positions other than the usual neck area. Button 1 was found overlying the left wrist, while button 2 was found beneath the fourth lumbar vertebra, almost directly below button 1. Since shirt-cuffs were sometimes fastened with bone buttons, it is possible that button 2 had been displaced downwards during decomposition of the body. Alternatively, they may represent suspender attachments or front closure buttons for civilian trousers. The fact that both hands were found beneath button 1 does not preclude the latter explanation. It is possible that the hands or forearms of a casualty might have been placed inside the trouser flaps or waist band to maintain their position while the body was carried to the cemetery and lowered into the grave shaft. However, the small size of the buttons makes cuff fasteners seem more likely.

The possible binding of the feet and the discovery of the copper pin, perhaps a bandage pin, suggest the individual may have been hospitalized prior to death.

BURIAL 3

Burial 3 had been placed within an excavated grave shaft in an extended and supine position with the head to the west and facing north (Figure 4.4).

While the skull had sustained limited damage on the right side, the rest of the skeleton was in extremely poor condition. The clavicles were only partially preserved and very fragile. The proximal end of the left humerus was damaged and the distal end was only partially present. The distal and proximal ends of both the left ulna and the left radius were damaged or missing. Portions of the right humerus, ulna, and radius were entirely missing. The ribs were displaced and many were also missing. The femora were in poor condition with the proximal ends missing, the distal ends only partially present, and the outer surface deteriorating. Almost no elements of the feet remained. Nevertheless, it was possible to determine that the legs had been placed slightly apart and parallel. Due to the fragile condition of this skeleton, some of the bones were removed from the burial encased in plaster to transport them to the laboratory.

Similarly, all that remained of half of the numerous buttons was powder, granules, or small fragments. Therefore, some of the perceived gaps in the button patterns were likely due to poor preservation rather than predepositional damage.

Seven buttons were recovered from the neck region, three of which (12, 21 and 22) were found in a tight cluster near the base of the skull. Three others were taken from a block of soil from beneath the skull (27, 28 and 29). The latter group could not be mapped precisely. Each of the two neck clusters had at least one large convex button, and the group from beneath the skull had at least one small convex button. This pattern, while incomplete, is very similar to that documented in the Burial 27 neck area. Burial 27 had what may have been a complete coatee collar/shoulder strap series, consisting of two clusters of one small and two large buttons each. The seventh button (26) was of the large convex type and was found beside the right side of the jaw, near the neck midline. It may represent a continuation of one of the two vertical linear series on the torso or it may have been a shirt button.

The left torso series of buttons consisted of buttons 05, 06, 07, 08 and 24, while the right torso series consisted of buttons 14, 15 and 16. There may have been a few additional buttons at the ends of either series but they have been lost, likely due to preservation problems and/or the disturbance in the thoracic area.

Three large convex buttons (09, 11 and 23) and one small flat button (10) were found between the torso and the left arm. The three medial to the humerus were found at a level slightly above the body, while the button lateral to the humerus was at the side of, and level with, the body. All of the shanks were up. The triangular shape of the group suggests an open lapel.

Buttons 13, 19 and 20 were found between the torso and the right arm and appeared to mirror those found on the other side of the body. No size or shape data were available for these three poorly preserved buttons.

Three large convex buttons (01, 03 and 04) were found on the left forearm. They were probably cuff buttons, rather than part of a left torso vertical linear series of pants buttons, since their locational associations were all well documented. Button 01 was found over the left forearm and button 03 was found on the medial side of the left radius, shank touching the radius. Button 04 was also found on the medial side of the left radius, although it could not positively be attributed to the series. Two other pairs of copper or brass buttons were documented in the region of the hands or wrists. Buttons 25A and 25B were discovered near the distal right forearm with their faces touching while buttons 31 and 32 were found in close proximity beneath the left hand, over the right ilium, with their shanks up. Alternatively, it is remotely possible that these copper or brass buttons were associated with a lower garment.

Buttons 02, 17, 18 and 30 were all found in a context suggesting an association with either the forearms or lower torso. Unfortunately, only one of the four buttons had a measurable diameter and two were reported as convex. Buttons 02 and 17 had shanks down, which in combination with their location, suggested pants buttons. If present, the lower garment had a severely depleted button complement.

There is significant variation in the diameters (21.8 to 23.4 mm) of the large convex pewter buttons recovered from this burial. This may be due to either manufacturing or preservation factors although it is more likely that the uniform underwent extensive refurbishing using buttons scavenged from several sources.

Indeed, the torso garment conforms to descriptions of a double-breasted 1808-model uniform and buttons 01 and 24 have tentatively been identified as an old type, predating the War of 1812. Moreover, the pattern of three buttons in the left forearm or wrist area which seemed to characterize a horizontal cuff pattern would conform to the pre-1814 style. Unfortunately, there was no definite cuff button pattern in the right forearm area. Since some militia units are known to have been provisioned with old-style uniforms, it is likely that this individual was enlisted in a militia rather than a regular unit.

BURIAL 4

A hexagonal pattern of iron nails that tapered toward the head and feet (Figure 4.5) indicates that this individual was buried in a coffin. The body had been placed within the coffin in an extended and supine position (Figure 4.6) and, unlike most of the other burials, the head was to the east and facing north. It appeared he had been turned very slightly to the right as the transverse processes of the vertebrae were visible. Also, the right clavicle was tightly wedged between the right side of the mandible and the acromion process of the right scapula. Both arms were properly articulated and were medially rotated such that the hands were resting on the femoral necks of their respective sides. The skeleton of this individual was generally in good condition although the skull and right femur had suffered considerable post-mortem damage. The ribs were fragmented and quite fragile and although the femora were correctly articulated, the distal right femur was fractured. There was a great deal of wood intermixed with the bones of the feet, which were badly disturbed and scattered toward the north or right side of the body, perhaps due to rodent disturbance.

This individual appears to have been wearing an intact and possibly new uniform. Postdepositional button movement seems to have been mini-mized and most of the buttons are in excellent condition. The close correla-tion between series and button diameter (see Appendix A), as well as the tight clustering within button types, suggest that the uniform was relatively new at the time of interment, with minimal button replacement. It therefore represents one of the most complete Snake Hill button assemblages with its spatial relationships nearly intact (Figure 4.6; Plate 4.4). In addition, the placement of the arms at the sides simplified the separation of possible cuff buttons from possible overalls buttons. Most of the latter were either of the four-hole, depressed-centre type or of the round, flat, shanked, pewter vari-ety bearing a "US" motif.

No buttons manufactured from bone or any other material were noted in the neck area that could be attributed to a shirt. Given the relative complete-ness of the button assemblage, if shirt buttons were originally present, it is possible that they were made of wood and did not survive burial.

Buttons 01 through 07, and 11 constitute a series on the right side of the torso. All buttons in this series except for 07 were of the small, round, flat, shanked, script "I" type. The variation between largest and smallest buttons was 0.4 mm, which is small for a group of seven specimens. This series be-gan in the upper right torso with button 01, ending in the waist area with 07 and appears to have shifted to the right. This shift around the axis of the torso was also apparent in the trouser buttons and is consistent with the placement of the body as indicated above. Button 01, the top button, was out of line with the main group, perhaps due to random postdepositional move-ment or to the fact that the top button was left unfastened at the time of burial. Alternatively, it may have resulted from slightly hunched shoulders, which may have caused the garment to fold in the upper chest area.

It is also possible that the lowest of the group, button 07, did not belong to this vertical linear series. It had been displaced laterally out of line with the main group. It was so severely deteriorated that neither motif, size nor attachment-type attributes could be observed.

Two vertical linear series of three four-hole buttons (15a, 15b and 16; 8, 9 and 10) were found, one on each side of the waist. The top two buttons in each series partly overlapped, as if a fold in the overalls front had traversed the upper waist. The middle button in the left series was a flat shanked button in such poor condition that size and motif could not be ascertained. All were found at a level above the body. Another vertical linear series of four buttons (12, 13, 14 and 20) extended from the first to the fifth lumbar vertebra. At the top and bottom were large, flat, shanked "US" motif buttons. The two central buttons were of the four-hole type. This series probably joined the left and right flaps of the overalls.

Moreover, it has been tentatively concluded that buttons 18 and 21 were back suspender buttons and that 17 and 19 were front suspender buttons. Buttons 18 and 21 were of the four-hole pewter type and were found opposite each other and at the same level. Buttons 17 and 19 were the only small, round, flat, shanked pewter buttons with a "US" motif. They, too, were found approximately even with each other, slightly above the level of the skeleton. Although suspender attachment buttons would have been located on the waist band, which would have extended up to the lower rib cage, the rear suspender buttons were found somewhat higher. There was also considerable lateral displacement of the suspender support buttons and the front flap buttons. It is likely that these locations may have been partly affected by decomposition of the abdomen.

The single row of small, round, flat, shanked pewter buttons, without collar or cuff buttons, conforms to the button pattern of the American roundabout and suggests that this individual was probably an infantryman belonging to a regular unit.

BURIAL 5

Burial 5 had been placed within a fairly wide excavated grave shaft that was square at the head and became much narrower at the feet. The grave appeared to have been made deeper at the foot than at the head and shovel marks were visible at the bottom of the shaft.

Situated on the north side of the grave was a contemporaneous feature which has been interpreted as a medical waste pit. Although this feature was badly disturbed, it was possible to determine that it was approximately rectangular in shape. The bottom of the feature was 25 cm below the top of the left tibia. A fragment of a human femur which showed sharp spiral fractures was found in this feature, along with three other fragments of human bone.

Evidently the grave shaft had intruded upon deposits from an earlier culture. Several prehistoric Amerindian artifacts were encountered both in the grave fill and in the remains of the intersected historic feature. A stone flaking tool was found in the grave shaft adjacent to the left innominate and a chert biface was found under the midshaft of the right tibia. A small amount of calcined animal bone as well as some charcoal and chert were also encountered throughout the graveshaft.

Two small deposits of carbonized nutshell were found, one below the right foot and the other below the right hip bone. A copper pin was discovered on the superior surface of the sternum (Plate 4.3). This pin was complete and measured 26 mm in length, 0.8 mm in thickness along the shaft and 1.82 mm at the head. This may have been used during the application of a bandage to a wound. A greenish staining was also noted on the zygomatic process of the left temporal bone.

There is indirect evidence that this individual had suffered a traumatic death. An iron grapeshot and an irregularly-shaped brick fragment were found lodged against the inferior surface of the right scapula and the inferior surfaces of the seventh and eighth thoracic vertebrae respectively (Plate 4.5). The brick fragment measures 23 mm in length, 19.5 mm in width, and 10.8 mm in thickness. The iron ball measures approximately 21.4 mm in diameter and weighs 29 g. These projectiles may have entered the body as a result of the explosion of a structure. Damage to the right 10th rib confirms that the individual sustained a traumatic injury.

No buttons were found associated with this individual.

Most noteworthy, however, was the discovery of an amputated hand and distal forearm, lying supine, adjacent to and below the right elbow of the primary individual (Plate 4.6). No other elements of a second individual were recovered.

BURIAL 6

Burial 6 was found at the west property line of the site. Unfortunately, it had been truncated during excavation of the adjacent construction trench. Although the upper thorax and the entire skull were missing, it was quite clear that this individual had been placed extended and supine with the head to the west (Figure 4.7). As both arms were slightly flexed, the right hand lay over the right pubic bone and the left lay over the head of the left femur. The left femur and tibia were completely extended while the femur and tibia of the right leg were slightly flexed. The left tibia and foot appear to have been laterally rotated and the position of the right leg indicated that the right foot may have been medially rotated. The only elements of the feet which remained were the talus and calcaneus of the left foot.

The overall condition of the skeleton was fair to poor. The left scapula was missing and the right scapula very fragmentary. The proximal ends of both humeri were missing with only the distal third of the left humerus remaining. None of the cervical vertebrae were present and thoracic vertebrae had sustained heavy postmortem damage.

Despite the postdepositional damage, 41 buttons were recovered, representing one of the larger assemblages on the site.

Buttons 18, 19, 20, 22, 36 and 37 were all large and convex with iron shanks. Those with unobscured motifs had an eagle design.The large size of the buttons, the identification of probable cuff buttons, and the identification of a probable vest front-row pattern suggest that this vertical linear series was probably the front row of a coatee. There is significant variation in the diameters of these buttons (20.6 to 22.5), especially when compared with the front row of the roundabout buttons recovered from Burial 4 to indicate this may be one or more episodes of button replacement, and hence, that the garment was not new. Button 19 had a "21" in its regimental oval.

Alternatively, buttons 14, 15, 16 and 17 were small, flat, shanked buttons. Button 15 had an eagle motif with a "US" in the regimental oval. This series conformed in location and size to descriptions of a "vest" front button series although it appears to have been truncated on the cranial end. An examination of the range of diameters (14.4 to 15.5) suggests a discontinuity comparable to that observed in the torso left series, although the sample size is small.

Buttons 28 and 29 were in the left cuff area. Both were located over the body, 28 with shank up and 29 with shank towards the radius. Both were large convex buttons, with an eagle motif and a "21R" in the regimental oval. Similarly, four large convex buttons (01A, 02, 03 and 05) were documented along and transverse to the right forearm. All were located on a level above the body and manufactured from pewter except for button 03 which was copper or brass with an obscured motif. While the location of button 03 could suggest an overall function, it was found above the level of the body and its shank was oriented towards the ulna. It was therefore attributed to the cuff. Buttons 01A, 02 and 05 all had eagle motifs, and button 05 had "21" inscribed inside the regimental oval.

Button 04, a flat button with copper staining on its shank, was located close to this cuff group. However, its flat shape, differentiated it from the other convex buttons. The morphological difference and its location in the waist area suggested an overalls function.

An apparent cluster of seven buttons (24, 25, 26, 30 and 35) occurred between the left elbow and waist, all at a level above the body. Buttons 25, 26 and 30 had eagle motifs, and the first two had "21R" in the regimental oval. An even tighter cluster of six, large, convex buttons (06, 07, 08, 09, 11 and 33) was found in the area between the distal right humerus and rib cage. All these buttons were also found at a level slightly above the body. Two buttons in the right series (07 and 09) also have a "21" inscribed in the regimental device oval. Based on the similarity of design, motif and diameter with the vertical linear series on the left side of the torso, these buttons belonged to the coatee and the clusters represent open lapels or side rows. It is also remotely possible that these buttons represent two badly worn garments, or parts of a garment(s) used as a wound dressing(s) or discarded with the body. Four other buttons, one pair found within each cluster, are of the four-hole depressed-centre variety (27 and 34; 10 and 13) and were different from the other large, convex, iron-shanked buttons in the groupings. Indeed, a total of six four-hole pewter buttons were recovered with this individual. Buttons of this type have been securely identified in Burials 4 and 16 as belonging to overalls or trousers. In this case, they occurred in a diffuse pattern across and to the sides of the upper waist/lower thorax region. Their locations were consistent with suspender attachments or with undone overalls side flaps. Two other flat, shanked, pewter buttons were too poorly preserved to provide diameter measurements or motif data, although their locations and their dissimilarity with other series suggest that they were overalls buttons as well.

Button 21, which was in line with the middle torso left series, was probably not a part of the same series, since it was a different size. It is suggested that it was a front suspender attachment because it was situated opposite button 13 and because there is no other obvious choice for a front suspender attachment on the left side. Alternatively, it may have been a laterally displaced component of the torso mid-line vest series. It has an eagle motif with a "US" in the regimental oval. This button style is uncommon in the Snake Hill assemblage and is found in only one other case—buttons 02 and 03 of Burial 18.

A number of isolated buttons were also recovered. Button 38, found overlying and touching the 11th thoracic vertebra, appears to have been a round button with red staining on its shank. Two large, round convex buttons were not mapped. Button 40 was located under the body and suggests either a rear suspender attachment button or a flipped-up coat-tail button. Button 39 was found beside and under the right ribs suggesting either a coatee tail or suspender attachment button.

Button 12, a large, convex, iron-shanked pewter button of the British 104th regiment, appeared to be close to the path of the torso midline series. However, there was a wide gap between it and the other torso midline buttons, and it was much larger. In other Snake Hill burials, artifacts were found in the lower right and left thorax areas, consistent with the locations of pockets in these regions. Therefore, button 12 is likely a memento rather than a functional button.

The soldier in Burial 6 appears to have been wearing both a coatee, fitted with large convex buttons, and a vest, which had small flat buttons. There were no collar/epaulet buttons, obviously due to the disturbance of the grave. Possible tail buttons include 01b, 39 and 40. As the American cuff button pattern changed from transverse to parallel with the forearm after 1814, this uniform is consistent with the older style since these cuff buttons appear to have had a transverse orientation. If the inference of a pre-1814 uniform is correct, there may be a link between convex buttons and old-style uniforms. Moreover, the button diameters in the torso garment series seem to be discontinuous. This again may indicate one or more episodes of button replacement, employing buttons from different manufacturing lot sources. The eagle motif was the only one noted in the analysis with the exception of the British 104th Regiment button (button 12).

This individual also appears to have been wearing military overalls. A group of six four-hole, depressed-centre buttons in the lower torso or waist area indicated that the overalls were in place. A large flat round button touching the 11th thoracic vertebra may also have been part of the overalls pattern. It would have been situated consistently with the topmost button of the upper central abdominal series of military overalls. Buttons 13 and 21 may have been front suspender buttons, and buttons 39 and 40 may have been rear suspender buttons. While the presence and general location of these buttons would suggest that the individual had been interred with trousers, the apparent absence of the classic overalls pattern, as recognized in Burial 4, suggests that the front of the overalls had been opened, probably for medical attention. A critical abdominal wound might explain the opening of the overalls and the death of the individual prior to hospitalization.

Finally, the recovery of nine buttons with a "21" identified in the regimental oval suggests that this individual may have indeed belonged to the 21st Regiment of Infantry or alternatively, he may have been enlisted in a militia unit and outfitted in an old uniform from that regiment.

BURIAL 7

This individual had been interred in a common grave with Burials 12 and 13 (Plate 4.7) in an extended and supine position with the head to the west (Figure 4.8). He was the southernmost of the three bodies and as the right elbow of Burial 12 lay over his left, it is probable that he had been placed into the grave shaft before the others. The shoulder joints were slightly abducted and the elbows were flexed. The right hand and lower right arm were medially rotated slightly, perhaps due to postmortem disturbance. The right forearm was lying across the lower abdomen with the hand over the left hip bone. The right hand may have been clenched because the metacarpals were lying flat while the phalanges were extended back and toward the vertebral column. The left arm was abducted more than the right and the left forearm was pronate. The hand was lying immediately adjacent and slightly inferior to the left ilium with the fifth digit extended up toward the palm and the thumb flexed under the other four digits. The spine was relatively straight with a slight lateral curvature to the left in the cervical region, probably because of the downward flexion of the head. There was also a slight curvature toward the right in the lumbar region. The femora and tibiae were slightly rotated laterally as were the feet, which were approximately three centimetres apart (measured at the ankles) and inverted. The calcaneus and the talus of the right foot had been pushed forward (superiorly), although the metatarsals were correctly articulated. The phalanges were jumbled.

Portions of the skull were intact, including the zygomatic processes and the maxilla; however, much of the superior portion of the face was missing, including the nasal bones. The clavicles and the scapulae were present, although somewhat damaged. The ribs were badly damaged. The elements of the arms were present except for the proximal end of the right radius. The hip bones were very fragmented. The pubic bones were broken near the acetabula and the pubic symphysis was damaged. The left femur was broken at the proximal end near the greater trochanter and the proximal end of the left fibula was damaged.

Although the largest number of buttons was recovered from this burial, their extremely poor preservation resulted in significant gaps in data concerning shank orientation, motif, and diameter. Indeed, out of 48 metal buttons, only 13 were sufficiently intact to allow measurement of their diameters (19.6 to 22.0 mm) (Figure 4.9). All of these were of the large, flat, shanked, pewter type. As no other type of metal button was identified, it was difficult to distinguish between the various series of buttons.

A single bone button (47) is assumed to have been a shirt button. It was located under the body at the right side of the neck. If this interpretation is correct, either the shirt fastened at the back or the button at the front closure of the shirt was displaced downward during postdepositional decomposition.

Seven metal buttons (13, 14, 15, 16, 17, 18A and 18B) occupied a 5 cm square area directly to the right of the neck. An eighth, button 46, was located under the skull. While these would appear to relate to a collar and shoulder strap or epaulet, eight buttons exceeds the total compliment of collar and shoulder buttons on the U.S. enlisted man's uniform. Therefore, not all of these could have been collar/shoulder buttons. Moreover, the cluster of three buttons (19, 28 and 29) found beneath the upper left thorax may have been left collar/shoulder buttons displaced by damage to the uniform top. Therefore, a collar association for the majority of the larger cluster involves both a displacement of all left collar/shoulder buttons away from their normal positions at the left of the neck and an alternate explanation for the left cluster. Indeed, such a displacement might be due to profound damage to the neck area of the uniform while the left cluster may represent a garment portion used to dress the wound noted in the upper left thorax.

Seven buttons, consisting of two subgroups, were found in the left thorax area. While none of the specimens was measurable, it was possible to determine the size class of five. Of the four buttons in a vertical linear series in the central and lower left thorax (4, 6A, 6B and 8), three were in the small size range. Of the three buttons in a triangular group in the upper left thorax (9, 26 and 39), two are in the large size range. On the basis of size, it would appear that these two sets are not related, despite their apparent vertical relationship. The small buttons may be the remains of a depleted vest front row series while the second set may represent part of a garment used as a field dressing, perhaps as a result of treatment for the wound in the upper left thorax.

A vertical linear series consisting of five buttons was documented close to the torso midline. All are in the large size range and their placement suggests they are the remains of a depleted coatee front row series. Five buttons were also associated with the left forearm. Button 43 was lateral to the left elbow at elbow level and beneath the rib cage of contiguous Burial 12.

Buttons 40A and B, 41 and 42 were clustered around the distal portion of the left forearm overlying the body. It is possible that buttons 40A, 40B, 41 and 42 represent a horizontal cuff which had been pulled up slightly. The horizontal cuff was typical of the pre-1814, double-breasted coatee. Also, button 02 was found on the right ilium and 2 cm lateral of the distal right radius. Since the shank was oriented toward the right arm, this button was tentatively identified as a cuff button. Two other shanked pewter buttons (44 and 45) were found in the right wrist area over the hip bones. One or more of these three could have been cuff buttons as well.

Buttons 38 and 22 were located at opposite lower lateral corners of the thorax (38 under and 22 over the body) and may have been suspender buttons. Button 24 was found in the midline under the body, beneath the third lumbar vertebra and may also have been a back suspender button. Alternatively, both buttons 24 and 38 may have belonged to a coat tail.

A vertical linear series of four buttons (30, 21, 20 and 1) was found at the lateral side of the right ilium. Button 25, located at the lateral edge of the left ilium, may have corresponded with buttons 20 or 21, located at the lateral edge of the right ilium. The largest buttons in the Burial 7 assemblage occurred in this series (buttons 01 and 20 averaging 22.10 mm). It should also be noted that the six largest buttons in the Burial 7 assemblage (01, 20, 30, 31, 32 and 33) occurred between the distal right humerus and the proximal right femur.

Numerous other buttons were found clustered in two groups between the right torso and the right arm, some at a level equal with the body, some from above and below. As Burial 7 seems to have been dressed in shirt, vest, coatee and overalls, it is unlikely that this series represents another garment worn by the individual. Perhaps the lower cluster represents a pulled-up coatee cuff while the upper group represents a discarded garment which may have served as a wound dressing.

Button 30 of this burial, recovered from the vertical series adjacent to the right hip, had a regimental affiliation of the 15th Regiment of Infantry. However, as it was not possible to identify any other affiliations and since the distribution and use of uniforms were inconsistent, the affiliation is tentative at best. Nevertheless, the individual does appear to have been an infantryman.

BURIAL 8

This individual had been interred within an excavated grave shaft in an extended and supine position with the head to the west (Figure 4.10). Although the skull was badly damaged, the orientation of the occipital bone suggested that the face may have been turned slightly toward the north. The clavicles were in good condition and in normal anatomical position. Although the humeri were also in normal anatomical position, they were slightly rotated medially at the shoulders. Both arms were flexed and forearms pronate with the hands crossed over the lower abdomen, left over the right. The fact that the sternum was sitting directly on the thoracic vertebrae suggested that this individual had been placed squarely on his back although the sacrum appeared to have been slightly tilted toward the left. The femora were in anatomical position and the tibiae were parallel to one another and were also oriented anteriorly. It would appear that the knees and ankles of this individual had been bound as the knees were only 3 cm apart and the ankles were approximately 1 cm apart. Such preparation for interment suggests hospitalization prior to burial. The toes appeared to have been pointing upward.

Only fragments of the skull remained, none of which included dentition. The proximal end of the right humerus was damaged, most of the head having been destroyed, and the lower ribs were in poor condition. The bodies of the lower thoracic and the lumbar vertebrae were also in poor condition although the sacrum was in good condition. The iliac crests had been damaged and the pubic symphysis was missing. There was some damage to the distal femora and the proximal tibiae but these elements were in relatively overall good condition.

A cream- or honey-coloured gun flint was recovered from within the right pocket area. It measures 31.7 mm in length, 28.6 mm in width and 7.6 mm in height. It is characterised by retouch on three dorsal margins and ventral retouch on the other.

An excellent assemblage of well-preserved buttons was recovered here (Figure 4.11). Indeed, these buttons may be grouped according to size in relation to garments or possibly even functional parts of garments.

A pair of bone shirt buttons (17 and 18) was located close to the base of the neck, above and beneath the body. This may constitute evidence for front and back closures on at least some shirts worn under the uniform jacket. Alternatively, the location of button 18 beneath the base of the neck, may be due to postdepositional movement.

A vertical series of similar buttons was found along the midline torso (08, 09, 12, 14, 15 and 16). These were all small, flat, pewter buttons with script "I" motifs and all were oriented shank down. The garment was likely a roundabout rather than a coatee since only small buttons appeared in the front row, and there was a lack of collar buttons and no obvious major, bilateral rows of cuff buttons. Button 13, found shank up at the left side of the thorax, may have been laterally displaced from the above front row series since it was a similar button. It was located directly left of a gap between buttons 14 and 12.

The fact that only six of the front series have been identified suggests that the garment was in need of repair and/or that some buttons belonging to this series have not been identified. Button 10, located adjacent to 09 of this series, was excluded because it was a large button that seemed to be part of another grouping of large buttons located over the abdomen.

A series of four large script "I" buttons (01B, 10, 05 and 07), was documented in the waist area. However, the interpretation of their association with garments is complex. For example, the position and shank down orientation of button 05 suggests that it, along with 06, may have been part of a cuff series. On the other hand, there was no similar pair on the opposite cuff, and roundabouts were not usually fitted with large cuff buttons. It is more likely that these buttons are part of a general waist-area grouping of large buttons which belong to overalls.

Button 19 was also found shank down beneath the proximal right forearm, close to the waist. No diameter or motif data were available. The most analogous button on the opposite side of the body was number 06, for which very little information was available. The best interpretation for this button would appear to be an overalls flap or suspender attachment button. Similarly, button 21 was found beneath the body just superior to the left ilium. It appears to have been balanced by button 20, situated beneath the right hip bone with the shank oriented medially. If the torso garment was a coatee, these could have been tail buttons. It seems more likely, however, that these were rear suspender attachment buttons.

Four buttons (01A, 2 ,3 and 4), were situated below the pelvis and between the proximal femurs in an apparently square pattern. In the field they were thought to be a definitive coatee tail series. However upon analysis, it is clear that this series actually represents an overalls flap in a down position. It was noted that the two buttons on the left were of the large variety, giving the square an asymmetrical effect while button 11, another small flat button, was located just laterally of the proximal left femur roughly in line with buttons 02 and 04. Moreover, given the locations of buttons 22 and 23 and the approximate locations of buttons 20 and 21 from under the pelvis, the two vertical series begun by buttons 03 and 04 on the left, and 01A and 02 on the right, could have continued in either direction. The five small buttons in this series (four "US", and one script "I" motif) were remarkably uniform in diameter and would appear to differ in both mean diameter and range from the series of small script "I" buttons along the midline torso. Indeed, six of the seven buttons from below the waist have the "US" motif. This type of button appears to have been restricted to military overalls.

A large civilian button was also recovered from the left shoulder (Figure 4.10; Plate 4.8). It measures 30.3 mm in diameter and is 4 mm thick. It has a bevelled edge of 1 mm and is manufactured of a copper alloy. It is finely engraved with a series of lines and punctates. Its recovery seems to suggest the use of an overcoat, perhaps civilian, despite what appears to be an excellent representation of a military issue uniform. The presence of a large civilian cloak button may indicate a militia affiliation.

It would appear therefore that at least four types of buttons were recovered from these overalls: large and small script "I" motif buttons, and large and small "US" motif buttons. In fact, all of the "US" motif buttons in the Burial 6 assemblage were found in the trousers area. Since most overall buttons would be covered by the torso garment, such a wide variety would not be noticeable. The lack of uniformity of the overall buttons would seem to have been in contrast to the jacket, with its front row of uniformly small script "I" buttons. The variety of overall buttons would suggest prolonged use of this garment, with more than one episode of repair.

MEDICAL WASTE FEATURE 9

This feature, originally Burial 9, was a medical waste pit comprising three groups of post-cranial elements, two of which signalled surgical amputations. These skeletal remains were encountered in the upper 20 cm of the fill of the grave shaft of Burial 8. No feature outline was discerned and the material was disturbed prior to recording. Nevertheless, it is believed that all of the material was recovered.

The first group of elements included bones of the right and left arms, likely from the same individual the subject of a bilateral amputation. In each instance, cuts had been made above the elbow, leaving the distal shaft and end of the humerus and associated forearm bones. The right radius and ulna were complete and the latter showed trauma to the proximal shaft. The hand was also present and appeared complete. Both left forearm bones were fractured at about midshaft, and only the proximal segments were present. There were no wrist or hand bones. These injuries are more fully described in Chapter 8.

The second group included the femur, tibia, fibula, talus and calcaneus of a left leg that had been cut off through the femur shaft below the lesser trochanter. The femur showed a comminuted fracture from about the middle to the distal part of the shaft. The leg belonged to an older person than the individual represented by the arm bones.

The third group consisted of one bone, an adult left tibia, that showed no signs of pathology or surgical intervention.

Descriptions of the buttons found in this medical waste pit can be found in Appendix A. Although there is no explanation, some of the buttons in the finest condition recovered from the site were found in this assemblage, including those of an American officer, an American Rifle Regiment and both American Artillery and British Royal Artillery.

BURIAL 10

This individual had been interred within an excavated grave shaft in an extended and supine position with the head to the east (Figure 4.12). While Burials 8 and 11 were aligned roughly parallel to the lakeshore, Burial 10 was oriented slightly more northeast to southwest. This individual is one of only three who were placed with their heads to the east.

Two large rocks were encountered beside and below the left side of the face. The skull was heavily damaged and the upper face and frontal bone were broken, although the teeth were in fairly good condition. The clavicles were in normal anatomical position as were the humeri, which were also medially rotated and abducted. The arms were slightly flexed and the forearms were pronate with the hands overlapping across the lower abdomen, probably with the left over the right. The spinal column was fairly straight through the cervical region with a slight curvature to the left in the thoracic region and a slight curvature to the right in the upper lumbar region. The individual appeared to have been slightly twisted to the left (north) through the lumbar region. The femora were laterally rotated slightly although the knees appeared to have been pulled close together, suggesting that they had been bound.

A spoon, a musket tool and two gun flints were all found in the pocket areas of this individual (Plate 4.9; Figure 4.12). The spoon was made of pewter, a tablespoon with a bent handle (Plate 4.10). The bowl length is 74.3 mm and the width is 44.7 mm. The musket tool (Plate 4.11) is manufactured from iron and is 105.5 mm in length from crosspiece to tip. The crosspiece is 94.3 mm in length. The diameter of the circular area on the surface of the tool at the junction is 12.3 mm. The maximum and minimum widths of the shaft are 15.7 and 11.1 mm. The end is spatula-shaped and large portions of the tool are fabric impressed. The two gun flints are cream- or honey-coloured. This indicates that they are French in origin. They measure 35.7 by 28.2 by 6.5 and 31.3 by 26.3 by 6.6 mm (in length, width and thickness, respectively). Each exhibits the same retouch pattern as that described for the one recovered in Burial 8.

Twenty-eight, mostly well-preserved buttons were also recovered with this individual (Figure 4.13).

Three buttons were documented between the right shoulder and the neck, and two others to the left of the neck (01, 02, 03, 27 and 28). A total of five buttons is consistent with that expected for collar and shoulder buttons on a coatee.

A torso midline series (04, 05, 06, 07, 08 and 09) had the appearance of a line of vertically paired buttons, a pattern which is unique at Snake Hill. It is possible that button 07, an isolated button slightly to the right of the midline in the upper thorax, may have been displaced and was originally paired with button 04.

Buttons 21, 23 and 24 were of similar size and nature. They occurred in a 5 cm long linear series parallel to, and beneath, the distal right forearm. If these were cuff buttons, then the coatee would have been of 1814 vintage.

All of the above buttons, presumed to belong to a coatee, were of the flat, pewter, script "I" variety. A shanked, pewter, script "I" button was also situated near each elbow. Button 19, on the left, was located under the level of the body with the shank up while button 18, on the right, was located at the level of the body with shank up. Their positions suggest they were probably suspender attachment buttons. Another pair of buttons, closely matched in size, was situated at the lower lateral corner of the thorax, over the body. The shank of button 11 was oriented down, while that of button 12 was oriented up. Since they were in an area that may have had a pocket, one or both may have functioned as pocket buttons. Alternatively, one or both may have been an overalls flap or suspenders attachment buttons. It should also be noted that this pair of buttons was in line with button 17, which was of the same type.

Specimens 15 and 16 were the largest measurable buttons associated with Burial 10. It is suggested that this pair, located near the midline over the fifth lumbar vertebra, served as the central closure for the overall flaps. While they were lower on the body than might be expected, they may have been shifted during medical attention to the abdominal area. The other buttons also did not form a clear overalls pattern.

Buttons 25 and 26 were found in the lower thorax area beneath the body. They were close to the expected locations for rear suspender buttons. However, it is perhaps more likely that these represent a coatee with the tail tucked up.

It is therefore suggested that this individual was buried in a coatee with a tucked-up tail, and probably military overalls. However, coatees were known to have had large buttons in the front row, and the waistcoat and roundabout to have had small, front-row buttons but no collar buttons. The garment in question clearly combines small front buttons with collar buttons and probably cuff buttons. Moreover, in other identified collar/shoulder series in the Snake Hill assemblage, large buttons appear to outnumber small buttons. Therefore, the upper garment worn by this individual has unique features. This may indicate a different uniform pattern, a lack of standardization, or extensive button replacement. On the other hand, the fact that most of the measurable collar and front row buttons had diameters close to 14.5 mm suggests that the uniform had not been extensively refitted with miscellaneous replacement buttons.

Despite the fact that there were a number of buttons found in the waist and adjoining areas which appeared related to overalls, no clear overalls pattern emerged. This may suggest that either the overalls front was undone, or parts of the overalls had been removed in order to facilitate medical attention to an abdominal wound. That buttons 18 and 16 appeared to indicate a downward shift of the central fastening buttons is also consistent with this inference. Although fully dressed, he may have been at least briefly hospitalized as is indicated by the binding of the legs.

BURIAL 11

This individual had been placed within an excavated grave shaft in an extended and supine position with the head to the west (Figure 4.14). However, it was difficult to distinguish the outline of the grave shaft due to a considerable number of rocks and root disturbance throughout the fill. Also, a pipe from a nearby septic tank crossed the end of the grave shaft just east of the feet. Some disturbance was also encountered at the west end of the grave shaft. A bone fragment which appeared to be from a large mammal was found approximately 35 cm west of the cranium and at the same depth. It should also be noted that isolated animal bone fragments were found in the area between Burials 8 and 11, at the same depth as these burials.

The skull faced north and somewhat east. The clavicles were in normal anatomical position, as were the humeri which were also medially rotated.

The arms were slightly flexed such that the hands appeared to have been folded across the upper abdomen. The sternum had fallen slightly to the left and the vertebral column appeared to have been slightly twisted toward the left. While both femora were in anterior position, the right tibia was laterally rotated, probably as a result of disturbance. The left tibia was rotated medially to such an extent that the fibula and the lateral side of the calcaneus were exposed. The left foot was also rotated medially.

The skull was in good condition. However, the left clavicle was badly damaged and the right scapula was very fragmentary. Only the head of the left humerus was extant, although damaged. The proximal end of the right humerus was badly damaged. However, the distal end remained intact. The right ulna and radius were also intact. The lower vertebrae were extremely fragmentary and the bone was in very poor condition. Very little of the hip bones remained and only the upper portion of the sacrum was present. Only the shaft portions of the femora remained. The proximal left tibia was broken and so was the distal left fibula. The proximal right fibula was absent. Some elements of the feet were missing.

Only six buttons were recovered with this individual. Two one-hole, bone buttons were found 2 cm apart, resting on the seventh cervical vertebra. Their presence suggests that the individual was wearing an undershirt. Three flat, round, shanked buttons with "US" motif were also found in a linear series, transverse to the proximal femora. As well, one other flat, round, shanked button with a "US" motif (06) was found in disturbed context to the north of the grave shaft. Buttons 04 and 05 were found below the level of the body with shanks up while button 03 was found at the side of the body with its shank down. These may represent military trousers, as indicated by the "US" motif, common to trousers and overalls. The fact that this individual had sustained a trauma to the left femur would provide a reason for partial removal of the garment.

BURIAL 12

This individual had been interred in a common grave with Burials 7 and 13 as described above (Figure 4.8; Plate 4.7). He had been placed in an extended and supine position with the head to the west. His right elbow lay over the left elbow of Burial 7 indicating that Burial 12 was placed in the grave shaft after Burial 7. The face appeared to have been turned slightly to the right (south). The clavicles were in normal anatomical position, although the shoulders were somewhat medially rotated and slightly abducted. The arms were tightly flexed with the forearms pronate and lying across the abdomen with the left hand over the right hand. The tips of the right fingers extended almost to the left iliac crest and the tips of the left fingers extended almost to the right iliac crest. The vertebral column was fairly straight, although the lumbar vertebrae were turned slightly to the left and the mid-thoracic vertebrae appeared to have been slightly raised. The pelvis was tipped slightly to the left. The entire right leg was laterally rotated.

Much of the upper face was missing. However, the maxilla and the zygomatic bones were present and the teeth were in reasonably good condition. The clavicles were in good condition, although there was some damage to the scapulae and the proximal ends of both humeri. Both of the radii and the ulnae were damaged. The proximal and distal ends of the right femur were damaged as were the distal ends of the right tibia and fibula. There was no trace whatsoever of the left leg.

Two fragmentary copper pins were recovered from the sacrum (Plate 4.12). Their location and probable use as bandage pins suggest medical intervention prior to burial, perhaps relating to surgical removal of the left leg.

A Y-shaped musket tool was recovered from the right pocket area of this individual (Figure 4.9; Plate 4.13). It is manufactured from iron and measures 78 mm by 49 mm. Also recovered in association with this tool was a feather primer, characterized by a concave pewter top measuring 20.8 mm in diameter. The shape of the musket tool is in contrast to the T-shaped American tool in Burial 10. It is thought to be British in origin and attests to the use or collection of enemy tools on occasion. The primer suggests some association with artillery.

The right arm and thorax of Burial 12 overlapped the flexed left arm of Burial 7. For this reason, buttons in the overlap zone were examined closely in order to ascertain their proper provenience. For example buttons 02, 03 and 04 comprised a series of three, round, flat, brass buttons, found at the right edge of the thorax aligned in a fairly evenly-spaced vertical linear series. All were positioned over the level of the body. Buttons 03 and 04 had their shanks up while button 02 had its shank oriented down. All three were covered with fabric and/or leather on the front and back.

However, the diameters of all three differed significantly. The function of these buttons is unclear. A similarly positioned series of three brass buttons with a civilian motif was found with Burial 19. It is possible that these were also front row buttons from a civilian jacket, left open at the time of interment. The size variation may relate to repair and button replacement. Alternatively, the adherence of leather suggests that this series may represent a pack harness or some other type of equipment. Regardless of their function, their position relative to the skeleton, and their alignment with the right edge of the thorax, clearly indicates their association with Burial 12.

Two flat pewter buttons (01A and 01B) were found immediately aside the lateral edge of the right ilium, about 5 cm away from the left wrist of Burial 7. Both buttons were in poor condition with less than 50% remaining. Number 01A was probably a small button and 01B seemed to have an unusual script "I" motif although the identification is tentative.

Another cluster of buttons (40a, 40b, 41 and 42), was located over the forearm of Burial 7, between the waist and right elbow of Burial 12. While this cluster may represent a rolled-up cuff on the left forearm of Burial 7, their similarity with buttons 01a and 01b indicate they might also represent part of the same garment on Burial 12. The identification of the garment relates, in part, to the removal of the left leg by surgery or trauma. It is therefore improbable that the individual would have been interred wearing trousers. It seems more likely that the cluster represents a ruined garment or part of a garment, possibly used as a wound dressing, which had been folded or wadded up and placed in the grave at the time of interment.

BURIAL 13

This individual had been placed in an extended and supine position within the common grave with Burials 7 and 12 (Figure 4.8; Plate 4.7). Burial 13 was the most northerly of the three burials. His head was in the west with the neck extended and the face turned slightly to the left (north). The shoulders were in normal anatomical position with slight medial rotation and very slight abduction. The arms were slightly flexed and medially rotated and the forearms were pronate. The hands were folded over the lower abdomen, probably with the left hand lying over the right. The left carpals had settled into the pelvic cavity. A slight curvature to the left was evident in the lumbar region and the sternum had fallen slightly to the left. The left foot was laterally rotated.

The skull was in reasonably good condition. However, there was some damage to the right temporal bone. There was evidence of damage to both the scapulae and the proximal end of the right humerus. A green stain was encountered approximately one-third of the way up the shaft from the distal end of the left ulna. This appeared to be due to the proximity of copper artifacts. Only the proximal portions of the right ulna and radius remained. The sacrum had been damaged. The left femur had been broken postmortem below the lesser trochanter. The midshaft of the right femur had been shattered and portions of this element were missing (Plate 4.14). The distal end of the femur was turned so that the condyles were pointing upward and the broken shaft was projecting down into the soil with the patella also pointing upward. The foot was lying above the ankle joint with the navicular out of position and the talus pointing upward. The foot appeared to be medially rotated with the tarsals and metatarsals having been disturbed. The left tibia and fibula were intact.

Only seven buttons were recovered with this individual. Buttons 05 and 04 overlay the twelfth thoracic and second lumbar vertebrae, respectively. Button 06 was about even with the ninth thoracic vertebra but was displaced laterally, out of line with buttons 04 and 05. All three were positioned above the body with shanks down. Buttons 04 and 05 had script "I" motifs. Button 07 was located at the right edge of the central thorax, over the body, with shank up. The fact that it was approximately in line with buttons 05 and 06 suggests that it, too, was a laterally displaced front-row button. Button 03, found over the body, appears to have been too high for a front suspenders button or an overalls flap button and may also have been a displaced jacket button.

The oval copper or brass specimens 01 and 02 have been identified as parts of a civilian cuff link which would have been joined with a chain. They were probably used to fasten the cuffs of a shirt.

It is therefore suggested that Burial 13 wore an unidentified military garment which was severely damaged and had few buttons remaining. It is not clear whether the torso garment was a coatee or a roundabout. While the large size of the front buttons (20.5 to 20.6 mm) are consistent with a coatee, the upper part of the garment appears to have been torn away, with displacement of the button row to the right. Therefore, the lack of collar buttons doesn't necessarily rule out a coatee. However, given the lack of identifiable cuff buttons on the undamaged left arm, it would appear that the garment would most likely have been a large buttoned roundabout. Whatever interpretation is correct, it is unlikely that the individual had been interred in overalls. The overalls were likely removed to facilitate attempted medical examination of the traumatized right femur.

The presence of a civilian shirt suggests this individual may have belonged to a militia unit.

BURIAL 14

This individual had been placed in a very shallow grave shaft in an extended and supine position with the head to the west.

The skeletal elements of this burial were generally in good condition. However, the right long bones, cranium and lower left leg bones were missing altogether. Moreover, the hip bones and some vertebrae were somewhat fragmentary. The left humerus and radius were correctly articulated. The right hand lay under the left ulna and radius with the digits adjacent to the left iliac crest. There was no archaeological indication of why skeletal elements were missing.

Only seven buttons were recovered. A single, one-hole, bone button found on the left side of the sternum was probably from a shirt.

Buttons 02, 03 and 04 were suitably placed for overalls buttons. Button 04 was found beneath the left wrist. Because of the design, a "US" motif, it was almost certainly an overalls button rather than a cuff button. Also, button 06, found in the grave shaft, is a four-hole depressed-centre button, of the sort usually associated with military overalls. However, lack of locational data precludes further inference. Button 05, also found within the grave shaft, is a convex iron-shanked button with an eagle motif. This type does not often occur with large flat-shanked buttons, such as 03, and it may be an accidental inclusion. Button 07 was very fragmentary.

It would therefore appear that this individual was interred in a shirt and military overalls. While there is no evidence that the overalls flaps were opened, the small number of buttons may indicate pre-depositional damage to the garment.

BURIAL 15

This individual had been placed in a grave shaft in an extended and supine position with the head to the west. A large rock was found over the left hip bone.

The left side of the skeleton had been badly disturbed. Indeed, most of the left arm and the left upper leg were missing altogether, although the left patella was present. The left ribs and hip bone were fragmentary. The skull and dentition of this burial were also damaged and rather fragmentary.

Unlike the left, the right side of the body was largely intact. The right arm had been flexed so that the hand was resting in the pelvic region. The hand had an abnormal adduction, suggesting either secondary inhumation or pre-mortem damage to the wrist. The phalanges and metacarpals of the right hand had settled around the lower lumbar vertebrae, whereas the left metacarpals were still articulated. This suggests that the left hand had been placed over the right. The vertebral column and pelvis were well aligned with the rest of the body. However, the third, fourth, and fifth lumbar vertebrae were slightly disturbed. The right femur and tibia were laterally rotated slightly and the patella was laterally displaced. The right foot was turned on its lateral side so that the talus was clearly visible on the medial side. The left tibia appeared to be in anatomical position. The left fibula was visible. The tibiae were lying 11 cm apart.

A copper pin was recovered adjacent to the left temporal bone perhaps associated with a bandage as bony lesions were documented on the inner surface of the skull. It was a complete straight pin measuring 30.8 mm in length and 0.8 mm in width. The head has a diameter of 2.0 mm. Fibres of fabric and hair adhered to the pin.

The most obvious cluster of buttons in this burial was a linear series of four situated slightly lateral to the right forearm. Buttons 02 and 03 initially appear to have been cuff buttons. They were in line, parallel to the forearm, near the wrist, located over the forearm, and had shanks oriented downwards. There was, however, no trace of any other button series for torso garments. Therefore, the presence of cuffs is unlikely. It is more likely that the buttons were related to buttons 05, 06, and possibly 07. Buttons 05 and 06 would appear to have been overall buttons, or they may have been associated with buttons 02 and 03 as a garment fragment used to dress a wound. Button 07 was found close to the third lumbar vertebra. This is where one would expect to find the central, upper waist overall buttons. Buttons 05 and 07 had script "I" motifs.

Button 01 was found about 30 cm to the left of the central torso. It would not appear to have had an obvious garment function and may not even be associated with the primary interment. It too, had a script "I" motif. Therefore, these buttons are most likely related to overalls, with many of the normal complement of buttons missing.

BURIAL 16

This individual had been placed within a grave shaft in an extended and supine position with the head to the west (Figure 4.15). The face was turned to the right (south) with a slight twisting to the right of the cervical vertebrae. The arms were crossed over the abdomen with the right hand over the left lower arm and the left hand over the right iliac crest. The right leg was laterally rotated and the left leg was medially rotated so that both of the feet had fallen to the right, indicating that they may have been bound. Buttons 01 through 07 and 19, were four-hole, depressed-centre buttons. Most were distributed across the lower pelvic area. The pattern was consistent with typical trousers or overalls, with the high front shifted down for access to the abdominal area. All the buttons were located over the hip bones, except for 01 and 07. These were located beneath the level of the body, lateral to the hip joints. It is possible that these represent rear suspender attachments. Buttons 08 and 09 occupied a narrow space between the thorax and the left humerus, close to the humeral midshaft, and were approximately 5 cm apart. Only a trace of each remained. It is possible that 09 was a four-hole button with depressed centre. If this impression is correct, this pair of buttons may represent the left overall flap.

The presence of this distinctive type of four-hole pewter button suggests the individual was wearing military issue overalls.

BURIAL 17

This individual had been placed within a grave shaft in an extended and supine position with the head to the west (Figure 4.16). The skeletal remains were generally in fair condition, although the hips, ribs, and vertebrae were very fragile. The cranium was damaged during the initial removal of topsoil and was not documented *in situ.*

The left arm was flexed such that the forearm lay pronate across the body above the hip bones. The left hand was lying over the left hip bone. The right arm was flexed such that the right forearm crossed the abdomen approximately at the level of the second or third lumbar vertebra. The right hand rested on the left forearm and the phalanges were flexed with the appearance of gripping the left forearm. The ribs and the spine were in normal anatomical position with no bending of the spine. The pelvis was in normal anatomical position and the femoral heads were still articulated with the acetabula. The femora and the patellae were in standard anatomical position. The lower legs were positioned horizontally, approximately 7 cm apart. No rotation was evident in the tibiae. The feet were inverted and extended at the ankles and the toes were flexed, indicating that the feet were probably bound.

The limb of another individual had been interred adjacent to, and slightly above the left humerus of the primary interment (Plate 4.15). The intrusive elements included the distal femur, tibia, fibula, and foot bones of a left leg. The limb was medially rotated and the phalanges were somewhat disturbed. There were no other elements of the second individual recovered.

Twelve buttons were recovered. Those found left of the waist area were difficult to interpret because of the overlapping of the right and left forearms and the lower torso. The position of button 03, a script "I" motif button, resembled that of the left rear suspender button in Burial 4. Button 07 was a plain brass or copper button with cloth adhering to each side. Plain brass buttons were sometimes used on the front of overalls. Button 07 could have been an overall button, considering the lateral spread of the overall buttons found with burial 4 and others. Indeed, its position so close to the elbow suggests that, even though the shank faced the ulna, it seemed to be poorly placed for a cuff button. Button 08, represented by only a trace of metal, was the most difficult button to assign. It seemed well placed to be a cuff button on either wrist. However, there were no buttons unequivocally assignable to a jacket. At the same time, there were buttons which fit the normal overall pattern. Therefore, it would appear best to ascribe an overall front function to this button.

Buttons 01, 02 and 06 comprise a vertical linear series that overlay lumbar vertebrae two through four. Orientation information was available only for button 02, which had the shank pointed downward. It is possible that 06 was a cuff button. However, as noted, there is a lack of other buttons assignable to a jacket. Moreover, this series is in the proper position for the closure buttons which would join the two side flaps of overalls. Buttons attributed to the sides of the fall or main flap were not in their functional positions, but neither did they indicate that the flap was open. The best interpretation would seem to be that subsequent to placement in the grave shaft, the flaps of the overalls had been folded into approximate position.

Buttons 09 and 10 were also well placed for overall flap buttons although they might also be considered for cuff buttons, since they were situated more or less parallel to the forearm. There was no information for either button, concerning position relative to the body, or shank orientation. Again, they are best interpreted as overall buttons in the absence of any evidence of a jacket.

Two pewter buttons (04 and 05) were found associated with the extra tibia, fibula, and foot bones. These buttons were discovered above the level of the primary interment. Both were round, flat, and had shank attachments. Button 04, with a diameter of 15.0 mm, was in excellent condition, had an iron shank and an obscured motif. Button 05 was in poor condition. Buttons 11 and 12 were round, convex, iron-shanked buttons with the circled "89" motif of the British 89th Regiment. They were found overlying the area of the left wrist. However, they were documented at a level slightly above the primary interment. It is likely that all four buttons were associated with the intrusive limb.

This individual would appear to have been interred with his feet bound and wearing U.S. military overalls. A fatal wound to the soft tissue of the abdomen, without hard tissue trauma, could explain the disturbance of the overalls closure.

The British buttons appear to have been associated with the intrusive limb.

BURIAL 18

This individual had been placed within a grave shaft in an extended and supine position with the head to the west (Figure 4.17).

The skull was displaced slightly to the left and had sustained considerable damage. The left clavicle and upper left ribs were absent and the remaining ribs were fragile. The right clavicle was present but had been displaced. Both humeri were present, although they, too, had sustained some postmortem damage. Both arms were flexed such that the forearms lay pronate across the lower chest, right over left. The right hand was rotated downward slightly at the wrist. Many roots were intruding along the vertebral column and, although the lumbar vertebrae were in anatomical position, there was some postmortem displacement to the left in the region of the lumbar vertebrae. The hip bones were fragile but still articulated with the sacrum. The proximal left tibia and the left patella were very fragmentary. The femoral heads were articulated with the acetabula. The distance between the knees was 4 cm and the distance between the distal tibiae was approximately 6 cm. The legs lay in standard anterior-posterior orientation. The feet were extended at the ankles and the toes were flexed with the left foot everted approximately 30 degrees. They had clearly been bound.

The buttons recovered with this individual were very poorly preserved. Most were in poor condition and in seven cases, 30% or less of the button remained.

Four buttons, which lay approximately in the midline of the torso, may be attributed to the front row of a roundabout (Figure 4.17). Button 03 was a small, round, flat, button with an eagle motif. Button 02 also had an eagle motif, and while not measurable, was in the same size range. The small size of the front-row buttons, as well as the lack of collar and shoulder buttons, indicated that the garment may have been a roundabout.

Buttons 05 and 06 were found overlying the right forearm between the radius and ulna. As they were represented by only small fragments or granules, there was no shank orientation, motif, or size information available. Buttons 07 and 08, with shanks oriented down and to the right respectively, extended toward the hip bone from Button 06. Although buttons 05 and 06 were well positioned for cuff buttons, none were found in a similar location on the left arm. Alternatively, they may have been overall flap buttons or perhaps a continuation of the front midline torso series. Indeed, some other burials at the site appear to have had their arms fixed into the overalls, perhaps to facilitate transport to the cemetery and placement in the grave shaft. It is possible that the forearms of the individual in Burial 18 were immobilized by wedging them under the roundabout thereby explaining the displacement of buttons 05 and 06 from the alignment of the other front row buttons. Similarly, buttons 07 and 08 may also have been a continuation of the laterally displaced front-button row. While neither could be measured, button 07 was of the small, flat type, similar to front-row buttons 02 and 03. It is also possible that buttons 07 and 08 were overall flap buttons.

Button 09 was found close to the lateral edge of the broken left ilium. Button 10 overlay the sacrum. This would place it in the pelvic midline, close to the level of button 09. Both buttons likely relate to overalls.

In summary, although poor preservation limited interpretation, the upper torso garment is thought to have been a roundabout because of the small, flat, front-row buttons, the lack of collar buttons and the lack of symmetrical cuff buttons. The individual may also have been interred in overalls although few buttons remained.

BURIAL 19

This individual was interred within a coffin as shown by a hexagonal pattern of iron nails that tapered toward the head and feet (Figure 4.18). The body had been placed within the coffin in an extended and supine position (Figure 4.19) and, unlike most of the other burials (but similar to Burial 4), the head was to the east and facing north.

Although the vault of the skull and the facial bones were fragmented, the dentition was intact. The left arm was flexed such that the forearm lay pronate across the abdomen and over the right arm. The right arm was flexed such that the forearm was lying over the lower abdomen. The elements of the hand had settled into the pelvic cavity. The thoracic vertebrae were displaced to the right. The pelvis was in normal anatomical position, but the left hip bone had sustained traumatic fractures as had the left femur, sacrum and lower left ribs resulting in an obvious gap in the mid to lower left abdomen. The feet were hyperextended and the ankles were approximately 5 cm apart and they had obviously been bound.

A large wood fragment, to which three buttons were adhering, was lying immediately west of the skull, in the collar and upper arm area. Buttons 02, 03 and 04, are flat brass or copper buttons with soldered shanks. They are very evenly matched in size, and bear the same non-military motif. The design, in all cases partially obscured by corrosion and encrustation, may depict a basket of flowers, or the capital of a fluted ionic column with flowers. It has also been suggested that the motif depicts a stylized crown. The design is encircled by a raised border, which may include some lettering.

The three buttons were aligned in a vertical linear series on the right side of the thorax. The most likely garment would be a non-military jacket.

Button 01 is the largest bone button in the Snake Hill assemblage. Most bone buttons from this collection would appear to have functioned as shirt buttons. However this one occurred too low on the thorax to be a neck button of a shirt, and it was found so far from either forearm that it is unlikely that it was a shirt cuff button. For these reasons, and because of its large size, it is unlikely that it was a shirt button. Given its location at the lower edge of the thorax, it may be a trouser button, possibly part of the vertical series commonly found in the upper central abdomen. It is very similar to the large bone buttons of Burial 24 which are thought to be civilian trousers, or even gaiter, buttons.

From the scanty evidence at hand, it would appear that this individual was interred wearing a civilian upper garment, jacket or vest, and trousers. If this is true, then this individual is the best example in the Snake Hill assemblage of someone who died violently while dressed in civilian clothing, a probable militia casualty.

BURIAL 20

This individual shared a common grave with Burial 21. He had been placed in an extended and supine position with the head to the west, within the grave shaft directly beside and south of Burial 21 (Figure 4.20).

Although there was some damage to the upper face, the mandible was still articulated with the skull. The ribs were very fragile and had sustained much damage. However, the remainder of the skeleton appeared to be present and in proper anatomical alignment. The arms were flexed such that the left hand lay on the left hip bone and the right hand lay over the right iliac crest. The distal end of the right forearm was approximately 15 cm higher than the distal end of the right humerus. Both forearms were pronate. This pronation was especially pronounced in the left forearm. The femoral heads were articulated with the acetabula and the femora and tibiae exhibited considerable lateral rotation. The knees were approximately 20 cm apart and the ankles were approximately 15 cm apart. The feet were rotated to the extent that they lay on their lateral sides. The elements were correctly articulated with the exception of the phalanges, which had been somewhat disturbed. It is unlikely that the feet or legs had been bound.

The cause of death may have been a gunshot wound to the face. The skull and face were badly fragmented and a musket shot was found inside the skull. The diameter of the shot was 8.2 mm, and its shape was somewhat flattened, suggesting that it had, indeed, been fired.

The button assemblage is similar to Burial 15. What few buttons remained were mostly in ambiguous association with the forearms and the waist. Buttons 01, 02 and 05 were grouped somewhat to the right of the third and fourth lumbar vertebrae, and within 4 cm of the right radius. The ulna and radius of the right forearm diverged by about 9 cm. If the ulna, the distal end of which was associated with elements of the hand, best defines the location of the wrist area, then this group would be more likely to have been associated with the waist rather than the forearm. Therefore, the most likely garment association for this group would be trousers or overalls.

The proximity of buttons 03 and 04 to the left forearm, and their alignment parallel to it, suggest they might be cuff buttons. However, there was no evidence for collar or front row buttons of a torso garment. This being the case, the most appropriate association for this cluster would also seem to be overalls. Button 03 bore a script "I" motif, so the garment represented was probably military overalls.

Therefore, the only garment worn by this individual appears to have been military overalls, with several buttons missing. The buckshot wound which penetrated the front of the skull may have caused death instantly. Therefore, it is likely that this soldier was interred dressed this way when he died. Lack of a uniform top suggests that he may have died while on fatigue, or while off duty.

BURIAL 21

This individual shared a common grave with Burial 20 as described above. He had been placed directly beside and north of Burial 20 in an extended and supine position with the head to the west and the face turned to the south (Figure 4.20). Although the skull had sustained considerable damage, the remainder of the skeleton was in good condition and in correct anatomical position. The arms were flexed such that the left hand lay over the lower left abdomen, aside the second, third, and fourth lumbar vertebrae, while the right hand lay over the 10th, 11th and 12th thoracic vertebrae and extended over the left ribs. The left arm was laterally extended much farther than the right. Both forearms were pronate. The right wrist was at a slightly higher level above the body than the left wrist. The legs were only slightly rotated laterally with the right leg rotated a little more than the left. The knees were lying approximately 12 to 15 cm apart and the distal tibiae were approximately 10 cm apart. The feet were extended at the ankles. The fact that the legs were lying parallel and close together suggests that the knees and ankles were bound.

Fragments of cloth and metal were discovered near the left shoulder of this individual. Despite some similarities, it was concluded upon detailed analysis that this material did not represent the remains of an epaulet, although it is not clear what its function was. Three pieces of coarsely woven fabric, a two-prong strap buckle, a number of small spring-like fragments and a cone-shaped copper piece were recovered.

Two copper pins were also recovered with this individual, one from the left scapula (Plate 4.3) area and the other from the sacrum. Both are straight pins which may have been used to secure bandages. Only the latter one was complete, measuring 21 mm in length and 1.7 mm across the head.

There were two main series of buttons recovered with this individual: one extending from the right shoulder, under the neck, to the left shoulder, and possibly further laterally; the other, located between the rib cage and the right humerus, extending from the right shoulder to a point lateral of the left abdominal margin. The two series blended in the area of the right shoulder. Because of the indistinct boundary between these series, the group affiliation of at least buttons 17 and 18 remains ambiguous. Each button cluster included a wide size range. The relationship between button sizes and body areas is unclear.

The cluster between the right humerus and rib cage may represent an open roundabout or coatee worn by the individual or a garment that had been folded or bunched and placed in the grave beside the body. If he had been wearing a coatee with cuff buttons, the best possibilities for cuff buttons would be button 03 on the left and buttons 10 or 12 on the right. While these may have been part of the larger, side-of-body group, button 10 was over the body and button 12 was under the body. It is assumed that a loose garment laid in the grave beside the torso would have been placed either over or under the forearm. Similarly, the front-button row of an opened jacket worn by the individual would probably come to rest either over or under the forearm. Hence, either button 10 or 12 may have been a cuff button attached to a sleeve of a garment worn by the individual.

The wide range of button sizes (20.7 to 24.9) is noteworthy. There was little regularity and the diameters extend into the extra-large range. If the garment represented by this cluster was a vest or a roundabout, small buttons would predominate. Alternatively, a coatee would have, in addition to large buttons, small buttons in the collar/shoulder group. Indeed, buttons 17 and 18 of the shoulder/neck series were in the small range and were found on either side of the neck. Three of this series had script "I" motifs.

It would appear that the neck and shoulder series began adjacent to the right shoulder, continued left in a tight formation under the neck, fanned out in the left shoulder area (including three or four buttons on the left shoulder), and continued past the left shoulder in a thin scatter (01, 02 and 13). There were 21 buttons in this cluster, close to a total coatee complement. However, if the side-of-body cluster represented the front row of an opened coatee, and if the collar buttons of this garment had survived, they would have blended in with the other buttons in this shoulder and neck group. Collar series were often found in clusters of three, each with two large buttons and one small button. Thus, the two small buttons in the shoulder and neck cluster could be coatee shoulder buttons. On the other hand, more than one garment, or parts of more than one garment, may be involved. The diameters of these buttons ranged from 15.6 to 23.1 mm.

Both series in Burial 21 lacked the relative uniformity of size found in garments in certain other burials. For the shoulder/neck series there were two buttons that fell into the typical small button range (15.6 and 15.8 mm). At the large end of the scale, there was variation between 20.1 and 22.2 mm, with an average of 21.2 mm for thirteen specimens. The size variation could be interpreted in two ways: an old, repaired garment or shreds of several garments may have been used as wound dressings. This would be consistent with the recovery of a bandage pin on the left scapula. Alternately, if we assume that this series represents a single garment, rather than several garment fragments, then it could be either a pair of overalls or a coatee. A roundabout or waistcoat is ruled out on the assumption that small buttons would predominate in the front row. Overalls remain a possibility, and no lower body garment was detected in this burial. On the other hand, the garment could have belonged to another soldier.

The apparent lack of overalls, the binding of the legs and feet and the recovery of bandage pins suggest that this individual had received medical attention and may have been hospitalized. No hard tissue trauma was noted that could have been the cause of death. However, the fact that the individual was associated with uniform garments, and the possibility that he was interred in a torso garment, suggest that death came quickly and that he was only briefly hospitalized.

MEDICAL WASTE FEATURE 22

This feature, originally Burial 22, was identified as a medical waste pit. It contained several artifacts and numerous isolated bone fragments. The bones included a mandible with teeth, a patella, and a right femur shaft fragment which was the product of a surgical amputation. The femur had been cut below the lesser trochanter, apparently in response to a traumatic fracture. Also found in the feature was a cream- or honey- coloured gun flint similar to those found elsewhere on the site. It measured 35 mm in length, 28 mm in width and 9.5 mm in thickness. Eight buttons were also found in the feature including several of the flat, round, pewter type, one of which has a script "I" motif and one of which was of the four-hole depressed centre variety. It is assumed that these buttons represent a number of discarded garment fragments.

BURIAL 23

This individual had been placed within a grave shaft in an extended and supine position with the head to the west (Figure 4.21; Plate 4.16). The head was turned to the left with the face toward the northeast and the mandible resting on the left clavicle. The right side of the cranium had sustained some damage and the right scapula was fragmentary. Otherwise, the individual was in good condition and in normal anatomical position.

The arms were tightly flexed with forearms pronate. The right hand had settled over the area of the left fourth, fifth, and sixth ribs and the left hand was touching the chin. While the carpals were correctly articulated, the second metacarpal was turned under the third. Although the ribs were present, they were quite fragmentary. The upper thoracic vertebrae were slightly twisted toward the left and the lumbar vertebrae were slightly twisted toward the right with a gap between the first and second. This appeared to have been caused by root action. The femora, tibiae and fibulae were not rotated and the tali were approximately 1 cm apart (Plate 4.17). This positioning suggests that the knees and ankles of this individual were bound (Plate 4.18). The bones of the feet were well articulated.

Two plain, one-hole buttons were discovered, about 2 cm apart, just to the right of the base of the neck (Figure 4.21). They were very close in size, having diameters of 11.5 and 11.6 mm, respectively. Their presence suggests that the individual had been interred in a shirt.

Another series of six buttons was situated across the pelvis. Four buttons extended in a roughly linear formation from the lateral edge of the left ilium to the centre of the first sacral segment (06, 05, 04 and 03). Two other buttons (07 and 08) were found inferior to the fifth sacral segment in the same midline axis as button 03. All six were flat, shanked buttons in excellent condition and all but button 06 had a "US" motif. Within these buttons, there seem to have been two size subtypes. Buttons 05, 06 and 07 were each 19.9 mm in diameter, while buttons 03, 04 and 08 ranged from 18.3 to 18.5 mm. Buttons 05 and 06, of the larger subseries, were situated at the lateral edge of the left ilium, while 03 and 04, of the smaller subseries, overlaid the sacrum. The reason for this variation may have been functional, aesthetic, or mere coincidence. Regardless of the reason, other trousers or overalls series in the Snake Hill assemblage also tended to incorporate a variety of size types.

Therefore, this individual appears to have been interred wearing a bone-buttoned shirt and military overalls. The button complement of the latter garment had been depleted. The pattern suggests that the abdominal portion of the garment was turned down, but there was no sideways displacement indicating opened flaps. The absence of a uniform top along with the binding of the legs suggest that the individual had been hospitalized, at least briefly.

BURIAL 24

This individual had been placed within a grave shaft in a extended and supine position with the head to the west (Figure 4.22). Unfortunately, the roots of a large tree, situated approximately 1.5 m to the south of the grave shaft, caused considerable disturbance. The skull was badly damaged and the fragments were scattered westward for a distance of approximately 50 to 60 cm. The arms were gently flexed and were medially rotated so that the hands lay, left-over-right, over the area of the fourth and fifth lumbar vertebrae. Both of the femora were articulated with the hips. However, the right hip bone and femur were laterally displaced slightly and the femur was broken into three pieces at the distal end. This appeared to be the result of three large roots growing along the length of the femur and through the proximal end and the acetabulum. The left tibia and fibula were articulated with each other. However, the whole lower limb had been inferiorly and medially displaced from the distal left femur. The elements of the feet were jumbled. The condition of the feet, together with the presence of nails around the body, suggests that this individual had been buried in a coffin.

A single unfired buckshot was recovered adjacent to the midshaft of the left radius. It measures 7.5 mm in diameter. A cream- or honey- coloured (French) gunflint was also recovered in the vicinity of the right pelvis. It is

35 mm in length, 29 mm in width and 9 mm in thickness. It is characterized by retouch patterns similar to those recovered from other burials.

A loose cluster of six pewter buttons (05, 06B, 07, 08, 09 and 10) was located in the right waist area, adjacent to the right ilium (Figure 4.22). The three which were over one half complete were of the small, flat, shanked, script "I" type. The series appeared to have been positioned over the abdomen and under the right forearm. The lack of buttons in the central and left abdominal area suggests that the cluster did not represent overalls or a torso garment worn at the time of interment but rather part or most of a garment, folded or bunched, which had been placed over the abdomen at the time of burial. The random shank orientations support this suggestion. Because the three measurable buttons were in the small size range, it is possible that the garment was a roundabout or waistcoat.

Another series found below the hips consisted of five flat, unusually large one-hole, bone buttons (01, 02, 03, 04 and 06A). Only one other bone button of this type occurred in the Snake Hill assemblage, in Burial 19. This group was also unique in that it included the only bone buttons to have been found below the waist. Due to a manufacturing error in button 03, there is clear evidence that this type was cut from the flat blank with a small hole saw, which drilled a central hole while it cut the round disk. Of course this technique was not necessarily restricted to this type of button alone.

This series was primarily centred between the distal tibiae, except for one, button 04, situated just medial of the distal right femur. The distinctiveness of these buttons suggests that they were all associated with the same garment. The primary group seemed to be associated with the medial sides of the distal tibiae, one pair on each side. While these may represent gaiters, gaiter buttons would normally have been located on the lateral, rather than the medial sides of the legs. They may also have been trouser buttons. A trouser hypothesis is supported by the location of button 04 between the knees. The only other bone button of this uncommon type, found with Burial 19 at the lower margin of the thorax in the midline, was interpreted as a trouser button.

Therefore, this individual does not appear to have been wearing a torso garment when he was interred although the button cluster in the right waist area may represent his uniform top. If so, the number and size of the buttons would indicate a roundabout or waistcoat rather than a coatee. This would imply the mixing of a military top with civilian trousers. Given that the individual had been interred in a coffin, it is likely then that the individual belonged to a militia unit and that his ruined torso garment had been placed in the coffin with him. The overalls may have been partially removed, perhaps to facilitate medical examination of an abdominal wound.

MEDICAL WASTE FEATURE 25

This medical waste pit contained the amputated left leg of an individual. The recovered elements included: the distal half of the femur, fragments of the patella, the tibia, the fibula and some elements of the foot. The reason for the amputation appears to have been a comminuted fracture of the knee. No buttons were found in this feature.

BURIAL 26

Burial 26 was found at the west property line of the site. Unfortunately, it had been truncated during excavation of the adjacent construction trench. Although a major portion of the body was missing, it was quite clear that this individual had been placed within a grave shaft in an extended and supine position with the head to the west. The cranium, the scapulae, the clavicles, all of the cervical vertebrae, the first through eighth thoracic vertebrae and the upper ribs were all missing. The remaining ribs were very fragmentary, especially those of the left side. The right arm was folded with the wrist resting over the fourth and fifth lumbar vertebrae. The left hand was resting on the left iliac crest. The pelvic girdle was turned slightly to the right and the sacrum was separated from the hip bones. All elements of the right leg and foot were missing. The left leg was rotated laterally to approximately 45 degrees causing the femoral head to have partially come out of the acetabulum. The left foot appeared to have been laterally extended. However, the metatarsals and phalanges of the foot were absent.

The single button found in Burial 26 was flat, with a "US" motif, and measured 14.3 mm in diameter. It was found shank up at the lateral side of the distal right ulna overlying the right wing of the first sacral segment. Given the lack of a corresponding button in the area of the left cuff area, and the lack of other possible uniform top buttons, the association with the right wrist was probably coincidental. As the button was suitably placed for a pair of overalls, and as the "US" motif has been strongly associated with such garments, overalls would appear to have been the most likely association for this button. Most of the buttons from this piece of clothing must have been missing. Alternatively, some buttons may have been lost when the grave was disturbed.

BURIAL 27

This individual had been placed in a grave shaft in an extended and supine position with the head to the west (Figure 4.23). The head was turned to the left (north) and the body was inclined to the left. The distal end of the left clavicle was displaced superiorly, approximately 60 degrees from horizontal. The arms were resting just above the pelvis, with the left over the right. The right forearm was pronate and the left forearm was displaced laterally and superiorly with the left hand flexed. The ribs were fragmentary and the sternum was displaced to the left. The pelvis was in normal anatomical position. However, the sacro-iliac region was open. The left leg was rotated laterally and the femoral head was displaced from the acetabulum. The left patella was displaced laterally. The feet were together and hyperextended with the left foot turned laterally and the right foot turned medially. The ankles appear to have been bound.

Multiple unhealed fractures were indicated for the left side of the skeleton including the humerus, ulna, sacrum and hip bone. Fifteen pieces of buckshot were found in the vicinity of the right pocket area (Plate 4.19). These pieces are all approximately 8 mm in diameter and none appear to have been fired.

Forty-one buttons were recovered with this individual, most of which were in excellent condition.

Button 35 is a finely-machined, four-hole, bone button, which was situated adjacent to the mandible at a level below the skeleton. It may have been a shirt button since it was located in the neck-shoulders area and since, like other identified shirt buttons, it was made of bone. On the other hand, it was situated more than 10 cm from the base of the neck, while all other shirt buttons at the site were found closer. Moreover, the spatial patterning of the other buttons suggests that the vest and coatee collars were intact at the time of interment. Therefore, this button may have been associated with an outer garment.

Two sets of three buttons, each comprising two large and one small script "I" buttons, were found in the neck area. The set on the left (25, 29 and 31) was beneath the neck in a tight cluster while the set on the right (01, 02A and 02B) was very tightly clustered between the base of the skull and the shoulder. This series may be the best example of a complete collar in the Snake Hill assemblage. Descriptions of coatees include a small button on each shoulder for a shoulder strap and two buttons on each side of the collar. It would seem logical that the four large buttons (02A, 02B, 28 and 31) would be collar buttons. The shoulder buttons were probably 01 and 29.

The association of the series of similar-sized buttons (19.9 to 20.8 mm) found in the right torso region (03, 05, 08, 18, 23, 27, 33, 34 and 36) is difficult to assess because of the discontinuity between the top three buttons and the remaining ones. Buttons 03, 05 and 08 were positioned appropriately to be fastened coatee buttons, while the positions of the lower buttons would be appropriate if the jacket had been unbuttoned and opened. Moreover, the upper buttons are overlying the chest while the lower ones are beneath the arm. Most have a script "I" motif.

It was very difficult to identify cuff buttons in the Burial 27 assemblage because of the presence of other buttons associated with overalls. It is very likely that not all cuff buttons were identified. Buttons 14 and 15, both with script "I" motifs, were identified as right cuff buttons on the basis of their position, overlying the right forearm. If this inference is correct, the button row would have been parallel, rather than transverse, to the forearm. Vertical alignment is characteristic of the post-1814 uniform pattern. Buttons 30 and 40 were copper or brass buttons found above the right hand and beneath the left. Copper or gold coloured buttons are known to have distinguished the cuffs of artillery unit uniforms. However, buttons 14 and 15 are of the large, flat, pewter type. It is therefore likely that buttons 30 and 40 have some other association. Other possible left cuff buttons included buttons 20, 21, 22 and 32. The first three were located at the side of the body, while 32 was located beneath the left radius. Buttons 20, 21 and 32 were in the 20 mm range, while 22 had a diameter of 16.2 mm. Possible right cuff buttons included 16 and 17, both located under the right arm and over the torso, and both in the 20 mm range.

A series of buttons situated over the torso midline (04, 06, 07, 09 to 13) appears to represent a vest. They had a mean diameter of 16.8 mm and a range of 16.5 to 17.3 mm and are smaller than those thought to be associated with the coatee.

Four other clusters of buttons are likely attributable to overalls. The front of military overalls covered much of the midriff. If left open following medical attention, the flaps and buttons could come to rest in a variety of locations, often overlapping other garments. Two clusters were found between the torso and the left arm. The first was a tight cluster of three buttons at the lower left corner of the rib cage, under the body (19, 38 and 39). The second was an adjoining loose cluster of four buttons, centred on the left forearm and as described above, possibly associated with the left cuff (20, 21, 22 and 32). Button 20 of this group is the only plain button from the Snake Hill assemblage to have a regimental oval. Inside the oval was a star.

Buttons 24, 25 and 26 were arranged in a short, vertical, linear series just lateral of the right ilium. A similar series was encountered in Burial 7. They may represent the opened right overalls flap. One of the few small script "I" buttons in the Burial 27 assemblage occurred in this series (button 26). Another, button 22, occupied a somewhat analogous position, lateral to the left hip. Button 22 and two other adjacent buttons in the vicinity of the left forearm could represent the left overall flap.

This individual appears to have been interred in a coatee, vest and overalls. Since he was buried fully clothed with his feet bound, he likely died rapidly, perhaps after brief medical attention.

BURIAL 28

This individual had been placed within a grave shaft in an extended and supine position with the head to the west (Plate 4.20). The head was inclined slightly forward and to the right. The skeleton was generally in good condition and was in correct anatomical position. Both arms were flexed, with the forearms pronate and the hands resting on the hips. The right leg lay in anterior-posterior position with the patella in normal anatomical position, while the left leg was rotated laterally somewhat. The medial surfaces of the knees were approximately 3 cm apart and the ankles were approximately 5 cm apart. The feet were very close together, with the right foot extended and slightly inverted, and the left foot lying on its lateral surface. The close positioning of the legs suggests that the knees and ankles had been bound.

The only button found with Burial 28 was a one-hole bone button measuring 10.9 mm in diameter. It was located about 2 cm medial of the central right forearm, and about the same distance from the superior lateral border of the right ilium. It is likely a shirt-cuff button. No shirt-neck buttons were found. This individual may have been a longer-term patient at the field hospital since he lacked military uniform garments.

BURIAL 29

Burial 29 was found at the west property line of the site. Unfortunately, it had been truncated during excavation of the adjacent construction trench (Figure 4.24; Plate 4.21). Although the cranium, the upper cervical vertebrae, and the proximal right humerus were missing, it was quite clear that this individual had been placed extended and supine with the head to the west. The right arm was flexed such that the right hand lay on the right ilium. The left hand was resting over the left iliac crest and the left pubis. The leg bones and patellae were in normal anatomical position. The left knee was slightly raised above the right knee. Both feet were medially rotated with the first digits touching as if the toes had been bound.

A two-prong brass buckle, measuring 26 mm in length by 17.7 mm in width was found inferior to the right shoulder. As well, a fragment of closely-woven fabric was found by the left shoulder.

Although 21 buttons were found in association with this individual, their preservation was extremely poor. It is possible that some button locations may not have been identified and/or that some identified fragments represented more than one button. Furthermore, the spatial patterning was unusual. It appears to have been an amorphous scatter in the central thoracic and central abdominal areas, bounded on the sides by the arms. Most buttons for which positional data were available were located above the body. Button 36, the exception, was found underneath the thorax. Buttons 32 and 35, to the left of the torso, button 24 adjacent to the sternum, and button 21, to the right of the torso, all had shanks facing down. This suggests that a coatee or other garment(s) had been placed over the body rather than worn by the individual. The buttons were too poorly preserved to identify garment type, although it was possible to determine that one had a script "I" motif and another was of the shanked, convex eagle motif type.

BURIAL 30

The grave shaft of Burial 30, located at the west property line, was also truncated by excavation of the adjacent builder's trench. Only the distal half of the right tibia and the elements of the right foot remained, together with the distal two thirds of the left femur as well as the left patella, tibia, fibula, and elements of the left foot. Their positions suggested that this individual had also been buried lying extended and supine with the head to the west.

No buttons were found associated with the remains of this individual.

BURIAL 31

The grave shaft of Burial 31 also had been truncated by the excavation of the adjacent builder's trench at the west property line. The burial had been very heavily damaged and only the articulated knees and a displaced portion of the left fibula remained. The position of the knees suggested that this adult had been buried lying extended and supine with the head to the west. The fibula shaft exhibited an unhealed traumatic fracture.

No buttons were recovered.

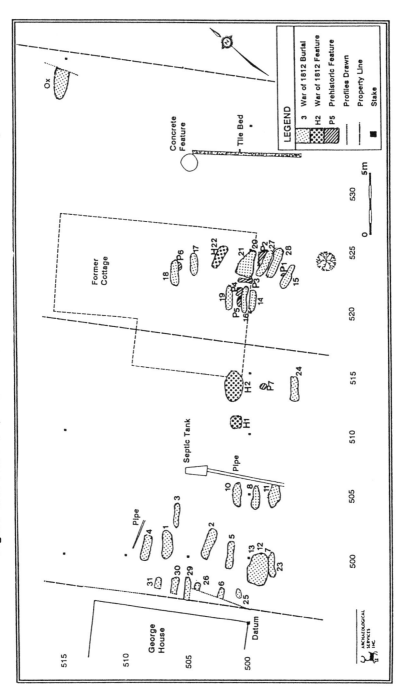

Figure 4.1: Site Plan, The Snake Hill Site: A War of 1812 Cemetery

Figure 4.2: Button Size Distribution

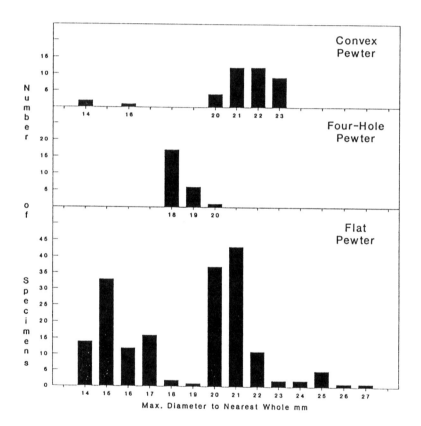

Max. Diameter to Nearest Whole mm

Figure 4.3: Burial 1

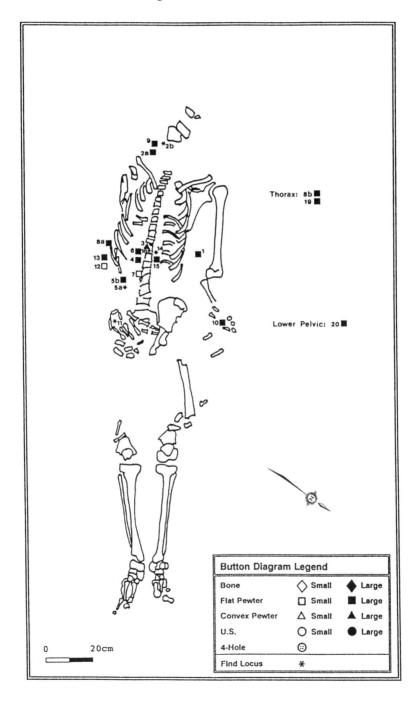

Figure 4.4: Burial 3

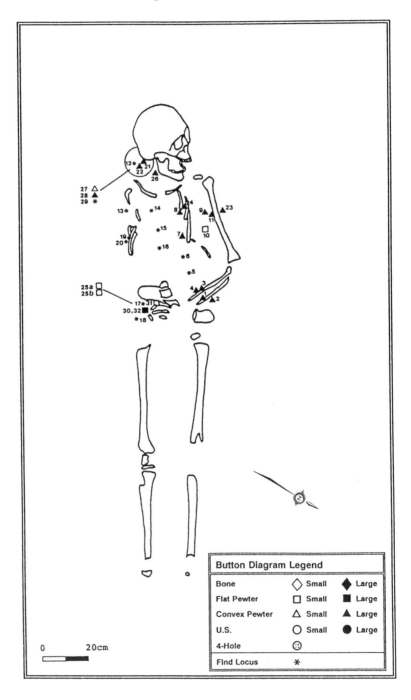

Figure 4.5: Burial 4, Coffin

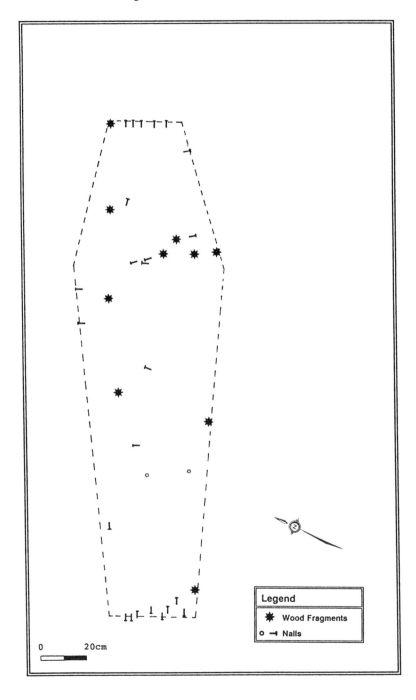

Figure 4.6: Burial 4

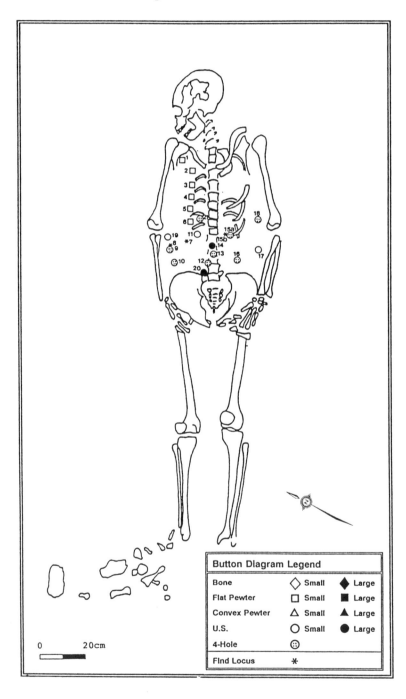

Button Diagram Legend

Bone	◇ Small	◆ Large
Flat Pewter	□ Small	■ Large
Convex Pewter	△ Small	▲ Large
U.S.	○ Small	● Large
4-Hole	⊙	
Find Locus	*	

0   20cm

Figure 4.7: Burial 6

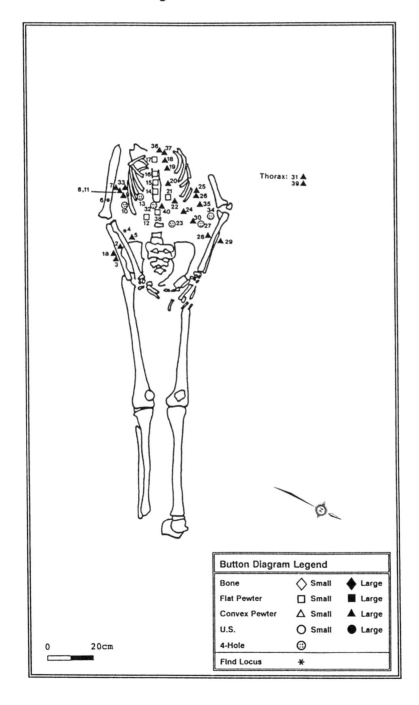

Thorax: 31 ▲
39 ▲

Button Diagram Legend

Bone	◇ Small	◆ Large
Flat Pewter	☐ Small	■ Large
Convex Pewter	△ Small	▲ Large
U.S.	○ Small	● Large
4-Hole	⊙	
Find Locus	✳	

0   20cm

Figure 4.8: Burial 7, 12 and 13, Y-Shaped Musket Tool

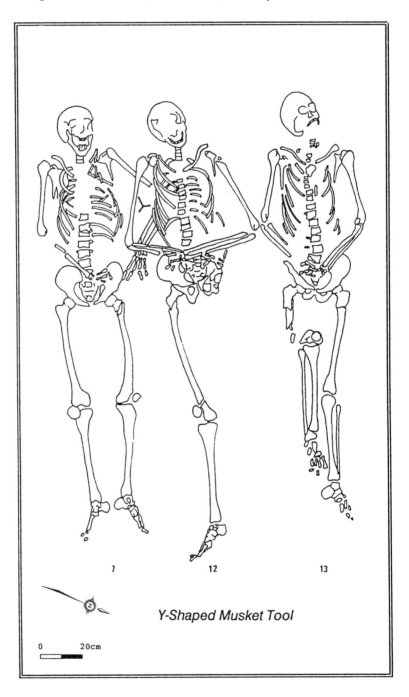

7   12   13

Y-Shaped Musket Tool

0 20cm

Figure 4.9: Burial 7, 12 and 13

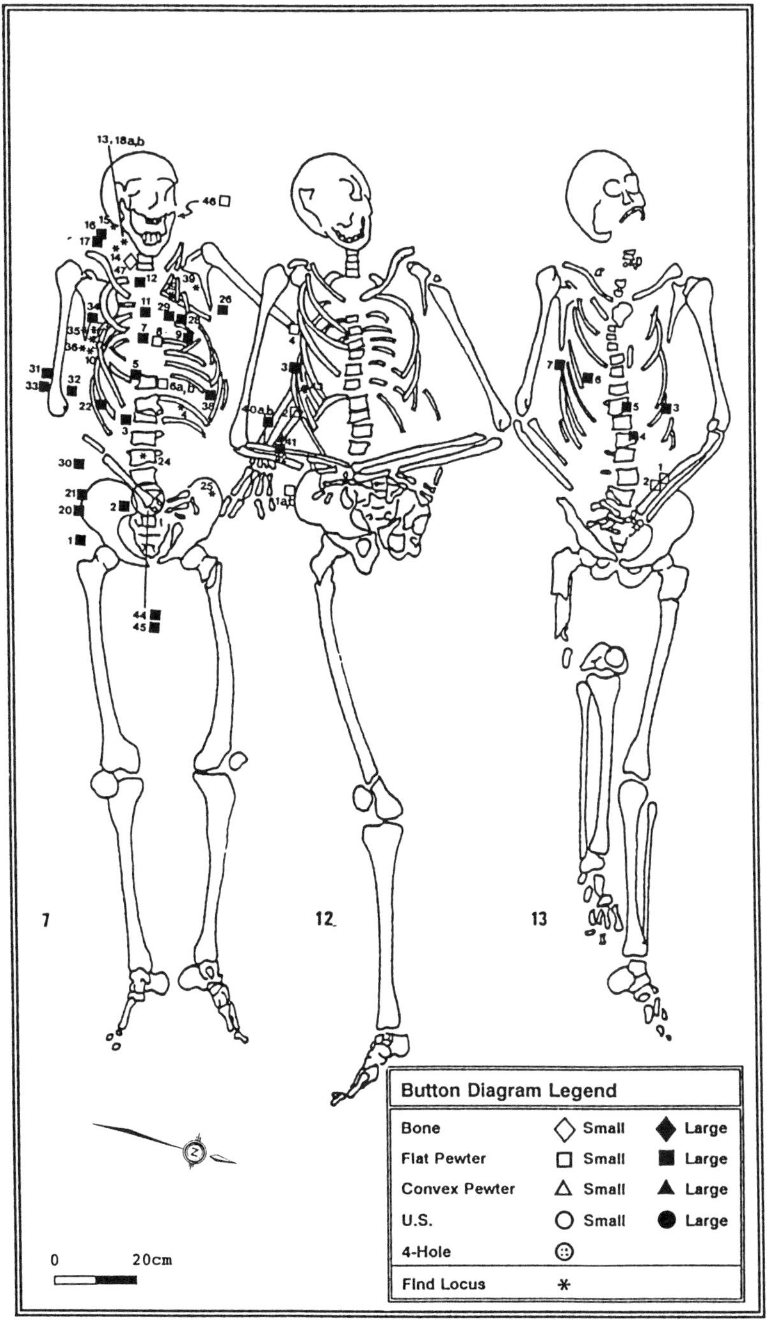

Figure 4.10: Burial 8, Associated Artifacts

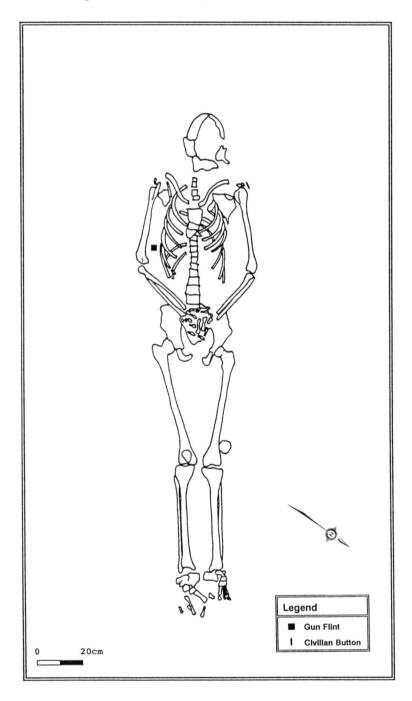

Legend

■ Gun Flint

| Civilian Button

0   20cm

Figure 4.11: Burial 8

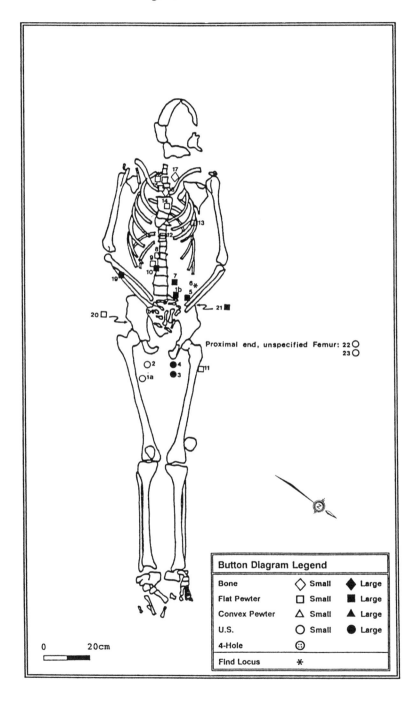

Proximal end, unspecified Femur: 22○
23○

Button Diagram Legend				
Bone	◇ Small	◆ Large
Flat Pewter	□ Small	■ Large
Convex Pewter	△ Small	▲ Large
U.S.	○ Small	● Large
4-Hole	⊙	
Find Locus	*	

0   20cm

Figure 4.12: Burial 10, Associated Artifacts

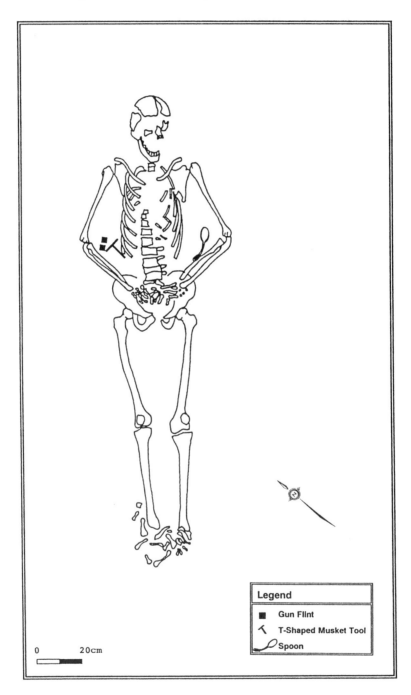

Figure 4.13: Burial 10

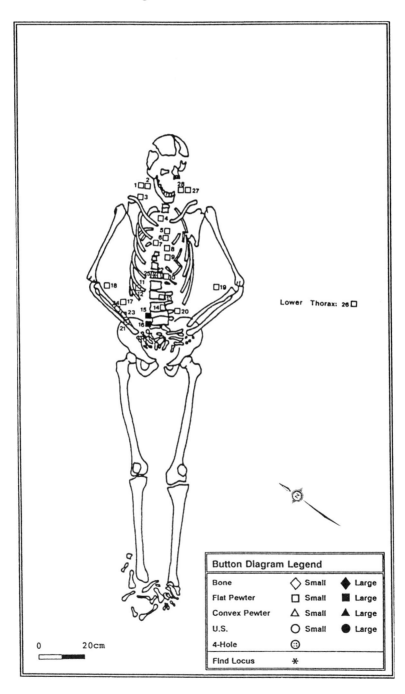

Figure 4.14: Burial 11

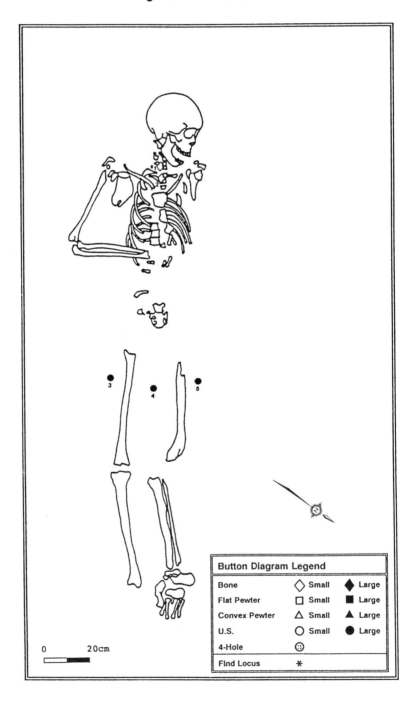

Button Diagram Legend		
Bone	◇ Small	◆ Large
Flat Pewter	☐ Small	■ Large
Convex Pewter	△ Small	▲ Large
U.S.	○ Small	● Large
4-Hole	⊙	
Find Locus	✳	

0   20cm

Figure 4.15: Burial 16

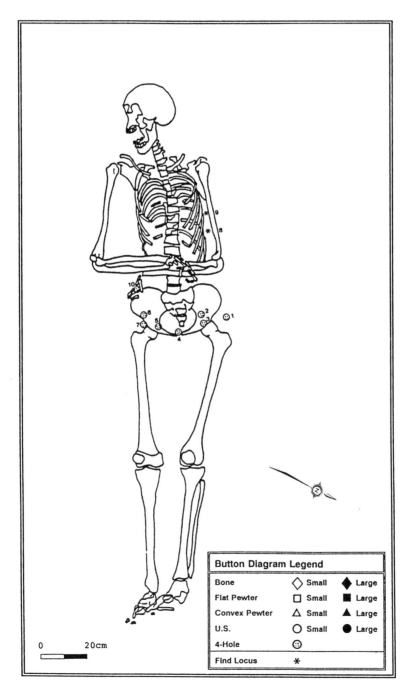

Figure 4.16: Burial 17

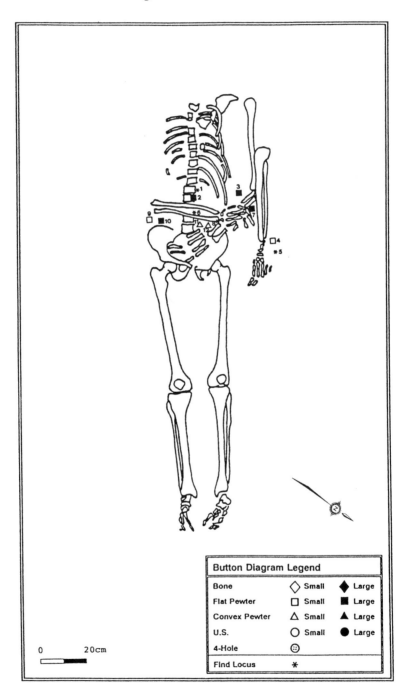

Figure 4.17: Burial 18

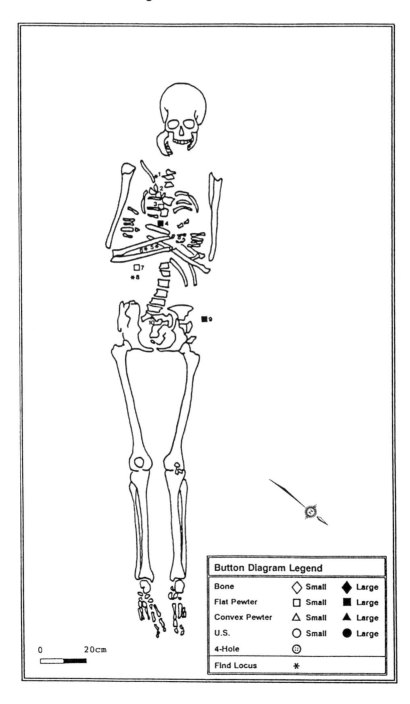

Figure 4.18: Burial 19, Coffin

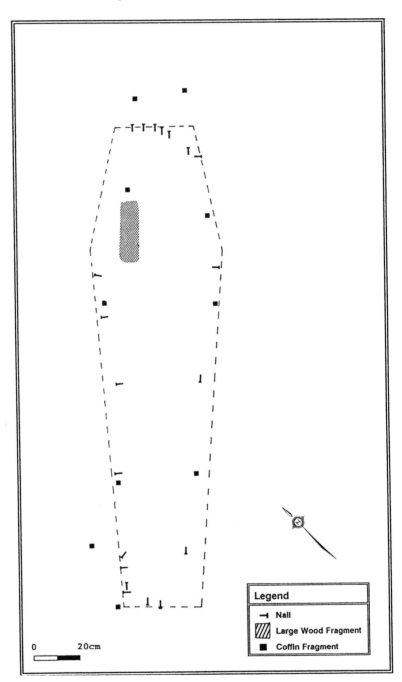

Figure 4.19: Burial 19

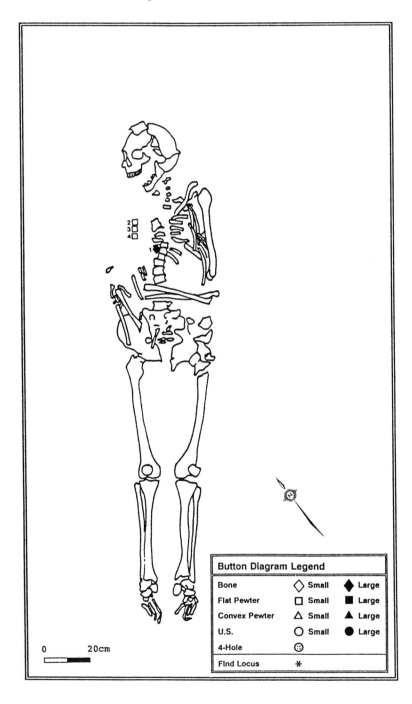

Button Diagram Legend

Bone	◇ Small	◆ Large
Flat Pewter	☐ Small	■ Large
Convex Pewter	△ Small	▲ Large
U.S.	○ Small	● Large
4-Hole	⊙	
Find Locus	✳	

0   20cm

Figure 4.20: Burial 20 and 21

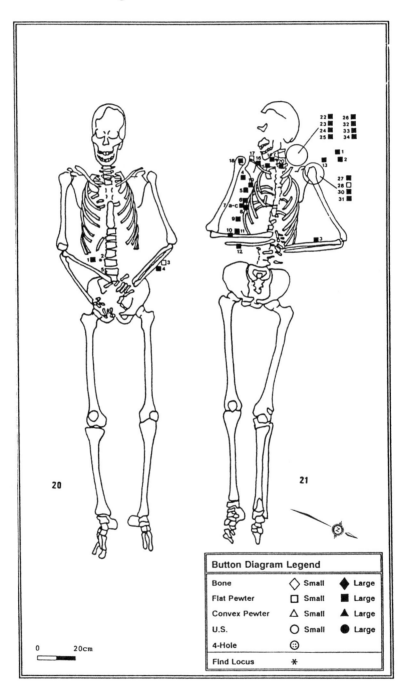

Figure 4.21: Burial 23

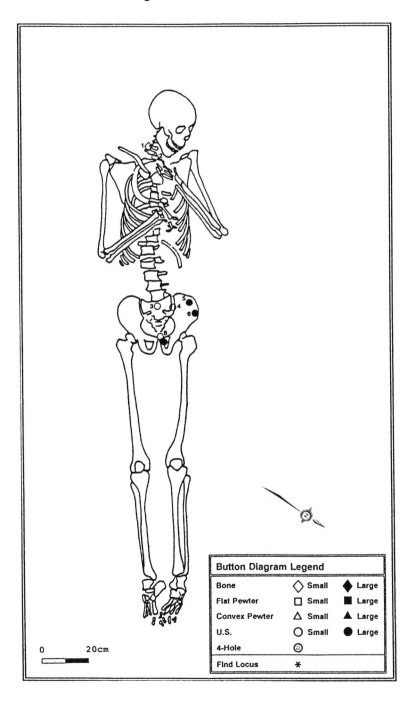

Figure 4.22: Burial 24

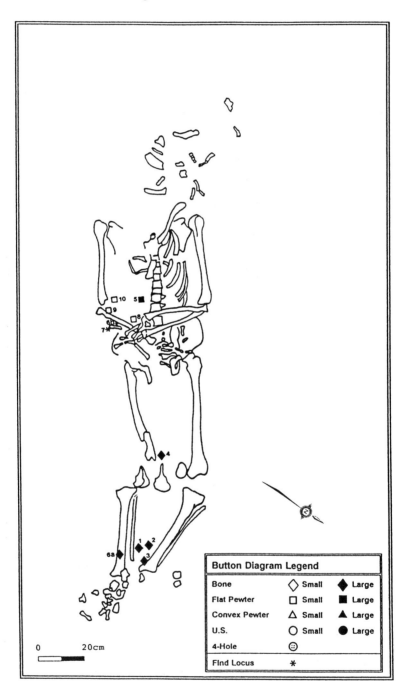

Figure 4.23: Burial 27

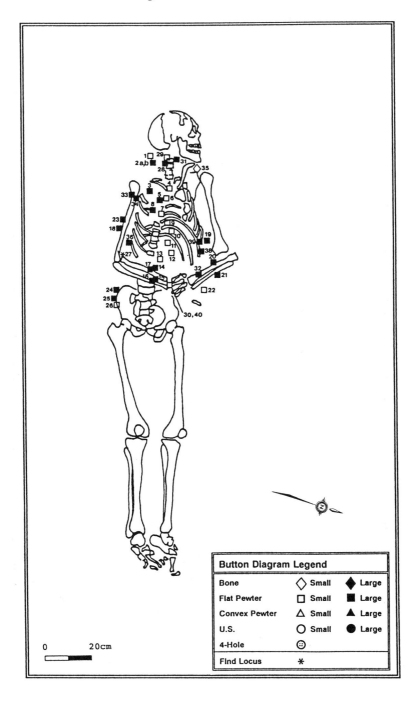

Figure 4.24: Burial 29

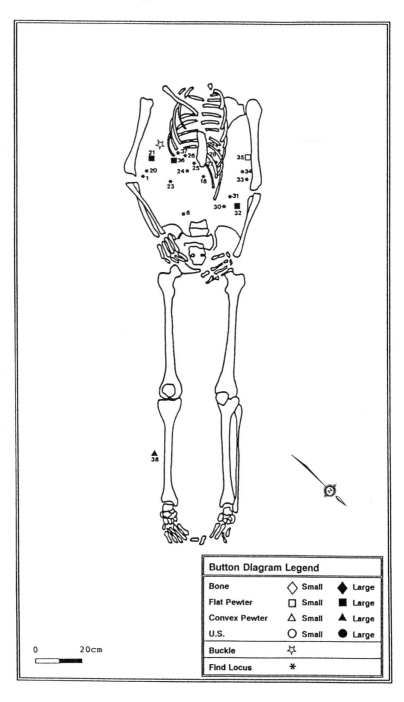

Button Diagram Legend

Bone	◇ Small	◆ Large
Flat Pewter	☐ Small	■ Large
Convex Pewter	△ Small	▲ Large
U.S.	○ Small	● Large
Buckle	✩	
Find Locus	✳	

Table 4.1: Descriptive Data for Graveshafts

Burial/ Feature #	Length (cm)	Width (cm)	Predominant Matrix	Mottling
1	226	90	subsoil	topsoil
2	240	80	subsoil	topsoil
3	205	60	subsoil	topsoil
4	245	70	subsoil	topsoil
5	250	67	subsoil	topsoil
6	ca.160	55	subsoil	
7	255	170*	subsoil	topsoil
8	190	65	subsoil	topsoil
10	195	90	subsoil	topsoil
11	225	80	subsoil	topsoil
12	250	170*	subsoil	topsoil
13	250	170*	subsoil	topsoil
14	190	50	subsoil	topsoil
15	234	70	subsoil	topsoil
16	225	65	subsoil	topsoil
17	170	60	subsoil	topsoil
18	210	70	subsoil	topsoil
19	210	90	subsoil	topsoil
20	220	130**subsoil		
21	220	130**subsoil	topsoil	
23	245	80	subsoil	topsoil
24	190	55	subsoil	topsoil
26	ca.145	60	subsoil	topsoil
27	224	62	subsoil	topsoil
28	230	70	subsoil	topsoil
29	ca.175	55	subsoil	topsoil
30	ca.140	60	subsoil	topsoil
31	ca.75	50	subsoil	topsoil

* 7, 12, 13 shared shaft
** 20, 21 shared shaft
ca. = approximation necessitated by adjacent buider's trench

Plate 4.1: Mapping of Burials

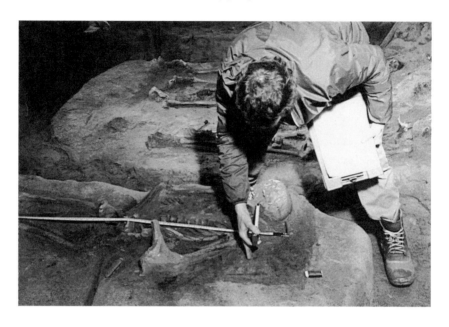

Plate 4.2: Burial 2

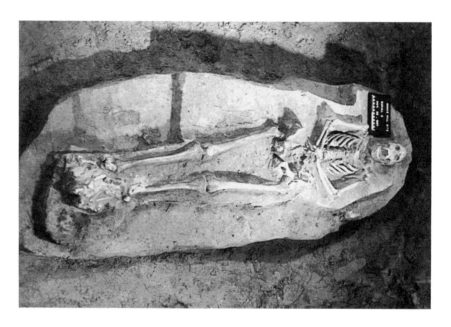

Plate 4.3: Copper Pins

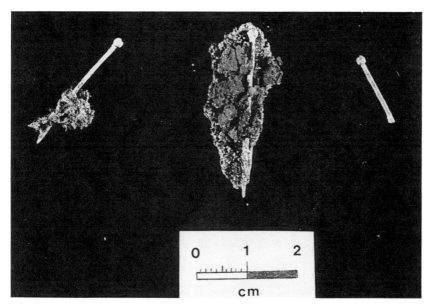

Burial 5 (*left*); Burial 2 (*middle*); Burial 20 (*right*)

Plate 4.4: Burial 4, Thorax

Plate 4.5: Burial 5, Iron Grapeshot and Brick Fragment

Plate 4.6: Burial 5, Thorax

Plate 4.7: Burials 7, 12 and 13

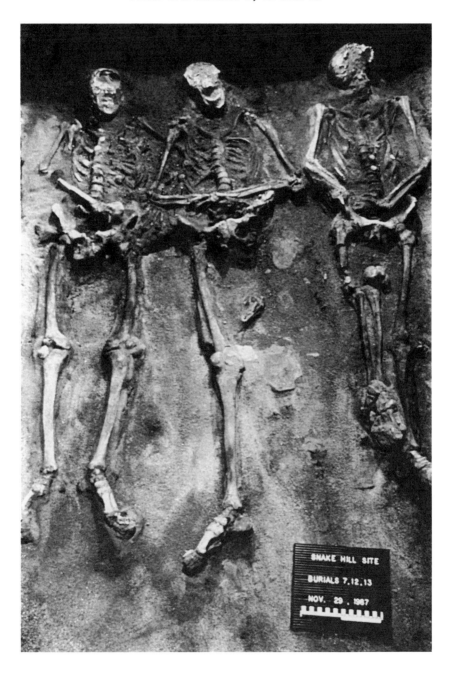

Plate 4.8: Burial 8, Button by Left Shoulder

Plate 4.9: Burial 10, Thorax

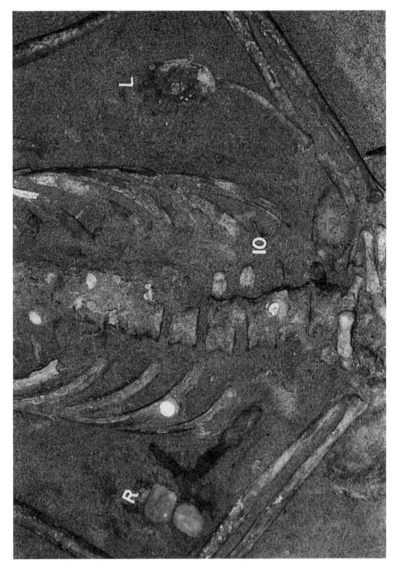

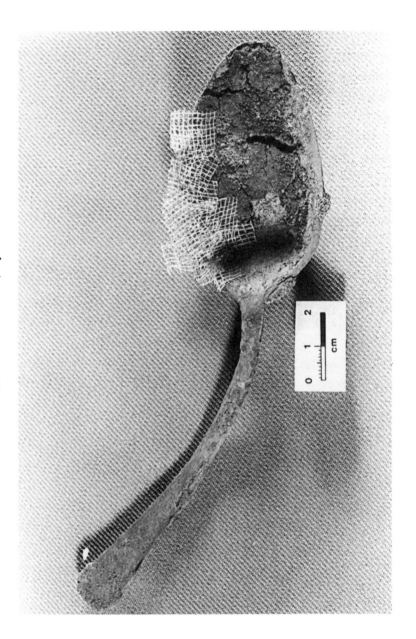

Plate 4.10: Burial 10, Spoon

Plate 4.11: Burial 10, T-shaped Musket Tool

Plate 4.12: Burial 12, Copper Pin

Plate 4.13: Burial 12, Y-shaped Musket Tool and Primer

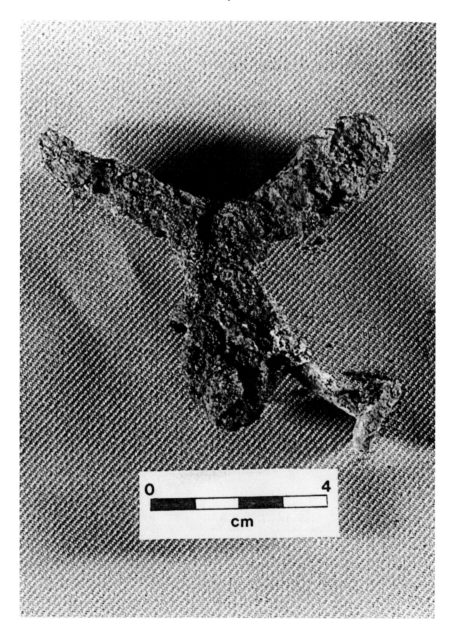

Plate 4.14: Burial 13, Right Femur

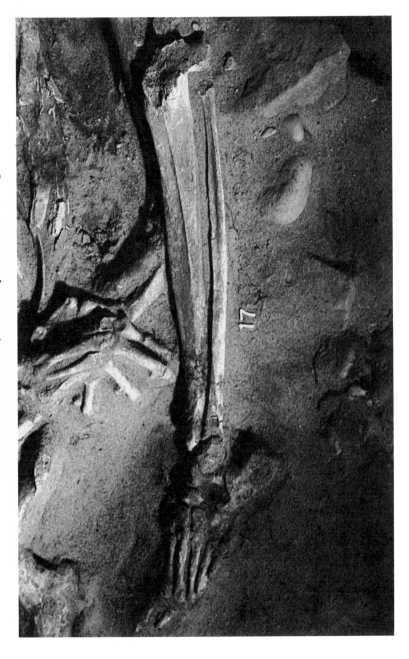

Plate 4.15: Burial 17, Close-up of Intrusive Leg

Plate 4.16: Burial 23

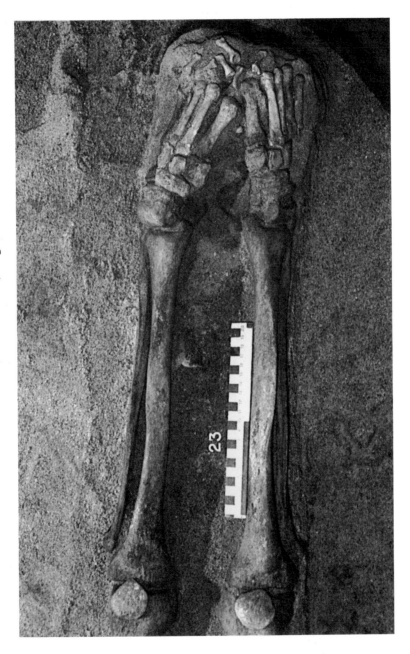

Plate 4.17: Burial 23, Legs

Plate 4.18: Burial 23, Bound Feet

Plate 4.19: Burial 27, Musket Shot

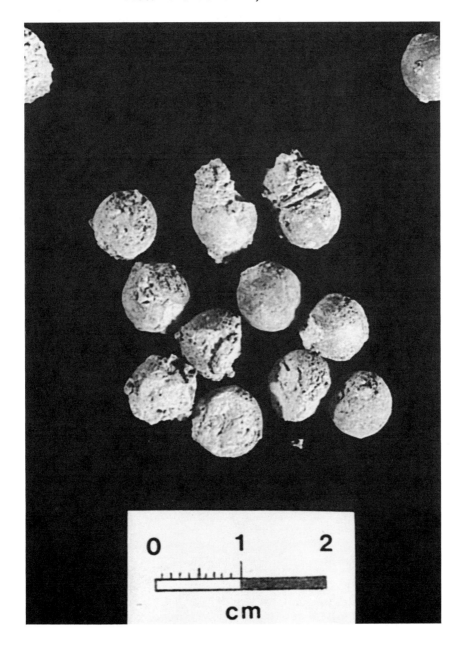

Plate 4.20: Burial 28

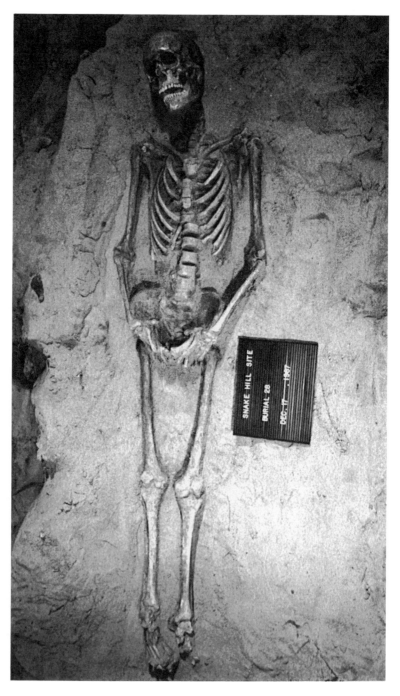

Plate 4.21: Burial 29

PART TWO:
Biological Anthropology

Five

Studying the Bones:
Biological Anthropology

SUSAN PFEIFFER

Introduction

When human skeletal remains are discovered, there is a need to know certain things as soon as possible. Some of the questions asked are, Who were these people? How did they die? How did they live? The archaeological context and associated cultural remains tell part of the story, but some facts can come only from the bones and teeth themselves. The researchers most likely to take on this task of "osteobiographical analysis" are physical anthropologists. These people are trained in a combination of biological and social sciences, with a central interest in human evolution. However, the skills needed to interpret changes in ancestral lineages are highly transferable to situations in which forensic or historical reconstruction is needed.

From the beginning of the Snake Hill project, it was clear that the physical remains of the soldiers would have to be reinterred relatively soon. This meant that a research team needed to be quickly created, so that as much as possible could be learned from the remains. A team of scholars was organized by Dr. R.F. Williamson in consultation with Dr. J.S. Cybulski of the Canadian Museum of Civilization, Dr. D.W. Owsley of the Smithsonian Institution Department of Anthropology, and Dr. M.S. Micozzi of the National Museum of Health and Medicine. The remains also needed to be curated in space that was both appropriate and convenient to visiting scholars. They were temporarily curated in Toronto, at the Royal Ontario Museum and the offices of Archaeological Services Inc., where the various scholars visited and collected information until the remains' preparation for reinterment. The information collected in this volume is thus the result of this extensive co-operation among individuals and institutions.

What Can We Learn?

In order to learn as much as possible from bones and teeth, researchers must be prepared to take an eclectic perspective. The final morphology of bones and teeth is the product of a lifetime's interaction between genetics and environment. Their size, shape and chemical composition can tell us where they have been and what they have done, if we know how to ask the questions. Thus, represented here are authors with primary training in medicine, biochemistry and geology, as well as anthropology. As our perspectives have widened, it has become more important to develop interdisciplinary research networks. No single researcher would have had the skills or resources to pursue the full range of analysis presented here. It is also only fair to acknowledge that there were other research questions that could have been asked but were not. For those future questions, files of data, photographs, casts and tissue samples have been retained.

Each of these chapters focuses on one aspect of the study. Each identifies a specific research goal, a method or approach, and the results gleaned from that approach. The chapters by Pfeiffer and by Saunders focus on the collection of fundamental information such as the determination of age, sex, "race" and stature. Assumptions about age and sex made by subsequent authors are based on this work. Note, too, that here, and throughout the analysis of the bones and teeth, nothing is known with complete certainty. Rather, we make estimates or statements of probability, based on comparison of these remains with those of known individuals or based on our knowledge of human biological processes.

What interests us are features of the bones and teeth that are unusual, that may tell us something about the historical setting. The chapter by Owsley, Mann and Murphy describes the bony evidence for trauma and disease, using the diagnostic approach of palaeopathology. Because of the unique archaeological context, relationships between patterns of "fresh" bone fracture and cause of death can be suggested. The chapter by Sledzik and Moore-Jansen focuses on dental findings, exploring them for evidence of diet and dental hygiene, and comparing the Snake Hill soldiers to other historically relevant populations. The dental study illustrates once again the interactive reliance of the archaeologist, the historian and the anthropologist, as the authors note a possible bias in the sample created by the Army's rejection of recruits who were missing several front teeth!

The next three chapters illustrate the kinds of information that can be derived from the chemical composition of the bones. Rather than examining their size and shape, these researchers explore the remains' composition, as it reflects conditions that pertained to the soldiers' lives. Katzenberg uses stable isotopes to deduce characteristics of the soldiers' diets. In the case of Snake Hill, this leads to deductions about geographic origin and ethnic affiliation. Lalich and Aufderheide continue this approach in their examination of bone lead levels. Here, again, we can look for unusual patterns that may reflect an individual's origin. There is also the added interest of exploring the possible toxic effects of lead. Schwarcz, Gibbs and Knyf introduce the reader to the potential for new developments in this field. Their exploration of oxygen isotopes as markers of geographic origin is novel and innovative.

The final chapter of anthropological analysis focuses not so much on gaining historical insights as on using the Snake Hill remains as a resource. Humans are all different in their size and shape, and today's humans are not necessarily the same size and shape as our ancestors were. Moore-Jansen and Jantz explore the size and shape of the Snake Hill crania from a mathematical perspective, and by comparing them to contemporary crania, derive some surprising results. Please note that a unified bibliography for Part II follows the Appendices.

Considered together, these chapters give a picture of a group of young men, tall and robust, from modest backgrounds, faced with intensely demanding tasks which ultimately took their lives. Some of the more general information about the soldiers is summarized on Table 5.1, with some individuals' unique features noted. The task of the physical anthropologists has been to objectively describe and interpret the physical remains found at Snake Hill. However, as we read these accounts, the humanity of the individuals—their unique features and habits—is also apparent.

Table 5.1: A Summary of the Snake Hill Burials

Burial/ Feature #	Estimated age range (yrs)	Estimated stature (cm)	Special Features	Amputation	Fracture, Projectile Injury	Moderate Inflam.	Spinal Problems sans Schmorl's nodes
1	22-24	170.9	Native American isotopes		X		X
2	24-26	174.1	Pipe wear on teeth				
3	17-19						
4	28-32	175.5			X		
5	19-21	164.8	European isotopes, high lead, enamel hypoplasia		X		
5 - extra hand	14-16			X			
6	14-16						
7	36-38	172.5			X		X
8	19-21	174.1					
9*		177.5 & 185.8		X	X		
10	37-39	169.8	Hapsburg jaw				
11	28-30	184.8			X		
12	21-23	186.2		X			X
13	33-35	173.3			X		
14	34-40	180.6			X		X
15	20-22	183.7			X	X	X
16	17-19	185.0			X		X
17	30-32	175.6			X		X
17 - extra leg	25-35	166.1					
18	24-28	179.0			X		
19	22-24	171.4			X		X
20	22-24	177.2	Native American isotopes, high lead		X		
21	16-18	182.5	European isotopes				
22	33-40						
23	19-21	176.5					
24	27-30	170.1					
25	22-26			X	X		
26	28-30	174.6					
27	21-23	164.8			X		
28	18-20	169.7					
29	25+	176.7					
30	35+	186.2					
31	25+				X	X	

*Burial 9 consisted of several long bones from at least three individuals:
- two amputated arms, almost certainly from the same individual, aged 16-19 yrs;
- portions of two left legs, one quite complete, one represented by a tibia.

Six

Estimation of Age at Death

SUSAN PFEIFFER

It was hoped that precisely estimating the age at death of the Snake Hill soldiers would help establish their identity. While identifying individuals was not possible, the estimated ages at death are still of interest. They corroborate historical accounts of the youth of the soldiers and offer an excellent opportunity to test the accuracy of our age estimation techniques. A variety of techniques were used to estimate the age at death of the 24 relatively complete burials, plus the partial skeletons and medical waste materials. Technically, the term "age at death" is sometimes inappropriate, since the remains included amputated limbs of individuals who presumably survived.

Methods

Estimating the age at death of a skeleton can be done in many different ways. The technique is determined by what parts of the body are available and what maturational stage was reached by the individual. That is, different criteria are used for infants, children and adolescents, and adults. An excellent criterion is one in which all individuals go through the same biological stages, everyone reaches the same end point and where environmental factors have little effect. Thus, the development of most tooth crowns in a growing child can offer an excellent indication of age at death: teeth develop similarly in everyone, virtually everyone ends up with the same number of teeth (third molars excepted), and environmental factors have little impact on the timing of development (although they may affect dental quality). Even with a fine indicator like dental development, however, the estimation of age must be expressed as an age *range*, since no two people grow at exactly the same pace.

As people mature and their skeletons begin to show the changes of aging, estimation techniques become less accurate. Post-maturational criteria rely on changes that are either related to deterioration or are "neutral": that is, not tied to bodily functioning. The process of aging is much more variable than that of growth, and during adulthood environmental factors have many years to make their impact. All skeletal and dental tissue is not moving toward the same end point, as they were prior to maturation. For example, dental development and emergence is predictable. You can see when it is complete. Dental wear is dependent on the person's diet and will continue until the tooth is lost, which can happen any time for many different reasons.

Since post-maturity age indicators are less accurate, as many techniques as possible were applied to the remains from Snake Hill, with the results incorporated into a single age range. The task was made easier by the sample's homogeneity of sex and racial background: all were white males. When alternate criteria were available for a technique, criteria for white males were used. Casts were made of all extant pubic symphyses and auricular surfaces, and midshaft sections were removed from all femora since all material was destined to be reburied.

Age estimation techniques required the evaluation of epiphyseal closure, cranial suture closure, and remodeling of the following: pubic symphyses, sternal rib ends, and iliac auricular surfaces (the latter being the area of subchondral bone forming the iliac portion of the sacroiliac joint). The Suchey-Brooks criteria were applied to the pubic symphyses (Katz and Suchey 1986). Iscan, Loth and Wright's (1984) criteria were applied to the ribs, and the criteria proposed by Lovejoy et al. (1985) were applied to the auricular surfaces. Guidelines for epiphyseal closure were taken generally from Gray's Anatomy (1959) and Bass (1971). Criteria for ectocranial suture closure were from Meindl and Lovejoy (1985). In each instance, these criteria were chosen because they were based on the largest, most representative reference sample and/or they offered the lowest standard error.

The application of the histological techniques of Thompson and Kerley using femoral cortical bone was attempted. However, decomposition of the cortical tissue is common and internally pervasive. Thus far very few individuals have yielded clear and easily evaluated bone thin sections. The nature of the tissue decomposition was subsequently explored (Pfeiffer 1989), but will not be discussed further here.

Results

A. Ages of the Snake Hill Soldiers

The five gross criteria frequently agreed such that a relatively narrow range of age at death could be estimated (Table 6.1). The estimated ages agree well with the historically documented age distribution of a representative company of the regular infantry (Figure 6.1). The estimated skeletal ages range from very young adolescent to middle-aged adult, approximately 40-45 years.

The youngest age listed is 14–16 years for Burial 6 and the extra hand included with Burial 5. Based upon the lack of fusion between any epiphyses and diaphyses, the extra hand could be even younger, perhaps as young as 12 years. However, recruitment of "men" younger than 14 years was illegal and the maturity of the hand is consistent with an age of 14 years as well. The presence of such fragmentary material is not sufficient to suggest the presence of under-age soldiers. The oldest individuals appear to be Burials 14, 22 and 30, with possible ages of 40 years or slightly more. Two of these features (22 and 30) were quite fragmentary.

Using the central point of each age range (N=30) the estimated mean age of the Snake Hill sample is 25.0 years (s.d.=6.9). This compares quite favorably with the average age of Bradford's company (24.7 years) and McFarland's company (25.4 years) (Whitehorne, personal communication).

B. Internal Consistency of Age Estimation Techniques

Analysis of an historically documented sample like Snake Hill allows us to address the relative utility of the various age-estimation techniques. While the techniques' accuracy cannot be addressed directly, since individuals' chronological ages remain unknown, the internal consistency of the various techniques offers us valuable indications of their stability and utility.

Epiphyseal closure was very useful in this sample, since many skeletons showed incomplete fusion of late elements, such as the medial clavicle and vertebral body rings. In the 18 features where they were present, the pubic symphyses followed Suchey and Brooks' stages clearly, and were consistent with most other criteria. Cranial suture closure, on the other hand, was not as useful. The age ranges offered by Meindl and Lovejoy are very broad (e.g.,"under 43"), so that little information was added to that available from epiphyses and pubic symphyses. Using the means of the age ranges, ectocranial suture closure would tend to over-age this sample. While rib age ranges are also sometimes broad, the rib ages tended to agree more closely with those from epiphyses and pubic symphyses. This was somewhat surprising. The Iscan technique is based upon evaluation of the sternal end of the fourth rib only. The costochondral junction generally changes from a smooth, rounded rim with a billowy articular surface to a sharp, uneven rim surrounding a deep pit, but the pace of change is thought to vary within the thorax. Of the 17 instances in which the rib-change criteria could be applied, known fourth ribs were only available in four instances. When other ribs or rib ends of unknown position were available, the age stages of all of them were recorded. They appeared to be relatively consistent in their pattern, and even the first rib could be evaluated in a manner consistent with other techniques' results.

The auricular surface of the ilium was more problematic. Evaluation of this surface as a means of estimating age was first proposed by Kobayashi (1967). However, the system proposed by Lovejoy et al. (1985) is the first to be commonly known and broadly applied (cf., Moore-Jansen and Jantz 1989). Changes to this surface, concomitant with cartilaginous changes, are said to offer estimates "equally accurate to pubic symphyseal aging" (Lovejoy et al. 1985:15), with the added advantage that this skeletal element is not as delicate and is therefore more regularly preserved. Briefly, the surface changes in grain and density, with morphology changing with regard to billowing and striations. It is not an easy system to apply. Auricular surfaces were available from 22 Snake Hill individuals. Generally, estimated ages agreed with the other techniques applied. They were slightly too old in three instances. In three other instances, at least one auricular surface could not be assessed because it showed morphological changes inconsistent with any of the stages. Specifically, the demifaces were concave, the surfaces almost uniformly granular, with no billows or striae present, and the apical borders were discontinuous. Some of these features are expected in late adulthood, others seemed to be anomalous.

As a working hypothesis, it was reasoned that these problematical surfaces could have been caused by traumatic damage to the joint. The traumatic changes to the fibrous cartilage could have thus mimicked age changes. The breaks in the apical border would have been caused by damage to the synovium. Such an hypothesis is consistent with the nature of this sample of soldiers. There was generally a high frequency of traumatically caused changes to the spine, as well as indications of very vigorous muscle use. Whether obtained through warfare or through heaving rocks in work details, chronic damage to the sacroiliac joint seemed quite plausible.

To explore this idea further, casts were prepared from the 18 individuals with relatively complete auricular surfaces. They were distributed to four colleagues without any information regarding the sample's origin. The casts were evaluated by an author of the age estimation technique and a very experienced colleague with whom he works. They were also independently evaluated by two biological anthropologist colleagues in Ontario who were less experienced with the technique, one of whom had access to a sample of known-age skeletons from an historic cemetery from which he could calibrate his estimates.

A comparison of the five sets of age estimates (the four colleagues' and my own) indicates confusion. In no instance was there agreement within a five-year range among all five investigators. Using a non-parametric comparison, (Wilcoxon's signed-ranks test), each set of age estimates is significantly different from all others. In six cases (of 18), there was agreement within a five-year range of the four outside investigators. The two experienced investigators agreed in 5/18 cases. The two novices agreed in 8/18 cases. In all cases, my age estimates were lower than those of the outside investigators. This may be because the fine granular texture of the dental stone, from which the casts were made, caused the auricular surfaces to look older. It may also be a reflection of an intrinsic bias, since I knew that the sample was likely to be comprised of young adults. Note that the estimates of the outside observers consistently follow an approximately normal distribution (Figure 6.2). While the investigators surely were not consciously biasing their estimates, this appears to be an example of unconscious bias. The distribution of their estimates does not mimic that of the reference population (as per Bocquet-Appel and Masset 1982), but rather seems to approximate adult mortality in a prehistoric skeletal population.

One of the putatively pathological auricular surfaces (Burial 11) was, indeed, grossly over-aged by most outside investigators. However, another of them (Burial 15) was not so grossly over-aged and in fact yielded a remarkably consistent range of estimates. The third of the pathological surfaces yielded relatively consistent ages as well, although these may have been influenced by the presence of a more normal auricular surface from the contralateral side.

Conclusions

The soldiers buried at Snake Hill were quite young, some barely old enough to enlist. None were much over age 40, an observation consistent with the conclusion that none were officers. Both the age range and the mean age at death estimated from the skeletal remains are consistent with what would be expected from the analysis of historical information. Table 5.1 provides a summary of information on the Snake Hill burials (i.e., age, stature and characteristics of bony elements).

Tentative conclusions from the methodological exploration are that, for young adult white males, pubic symphysis age estimates and estimates based on epiphyseal closure are internally consistent and in close agreement. Age estimates based on sternal rib ends show promise. The system should be expanded beyond the fourth rib. Ectocranial suture closure patterns contribute minimal information, though they continue to usefully differentiate very young, middle and old adult categories. Auricular surface patterns are problematical. Their application shows great interobserver error with regard to both apparent accuracy and bias. They may not be assessable from casts and they may be influenced by pathological changes to the joint. Much more work needs to be done to develop this system. Historical samples, like that from Snake Hill, will be important to the professional development of more accurate age estimation techniques.

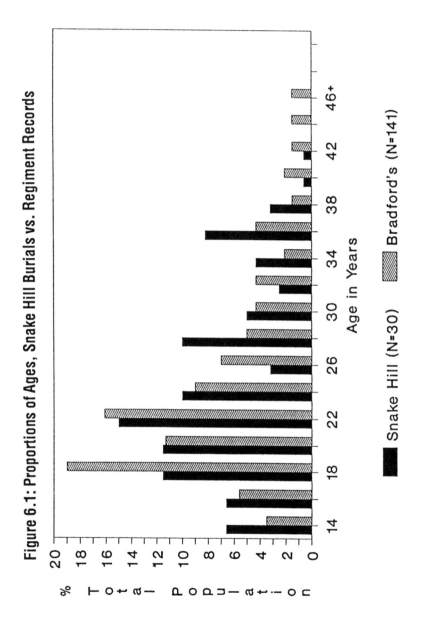

Figure 6.1: Proportions of Ages, Snake Hill Burials vs. Regiment Records

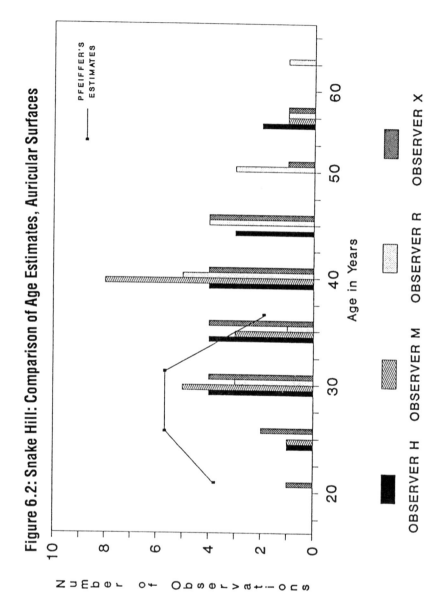

Figure 6.2: Snake Hill: Comparison of Age Estimates, Auricular Surfaces

Table 6.1: Summary of Five Gross Criteria Used to Determine Age at Death

Burial #	E	P	R	A	C	Age range (yrs)
1	x	x	x	x	x	22-24
2	x	x	x	x	x	24-26
3	x					17-19
4	x	x		x	x	28-32
5	x		x	x	x	19-21
5 extra hand	x					14-16
6	x	x				14-16
7	x	x		x	x	36-38
8	x				x	19-21
9*						
10	x	x	x	x	x	37-39
11	x		x	x	x	28-30
12	x	x		x	x	21-23
13	x	x	x	x	x	33-35
14	x		x	x		34-40
15	x	x	x		x	20-22
16	x	x	x	x	x	17-19
17	x	x	x	x		30-32
17 extra leg	x					25-35
18	x	x			x	24-28
19	x		x	x	x	22-24
20	x	x	x	x	x	22-24
21	x	x	x	x	x	16-18
22	x					33-40
23	x	x	x	x	x	19-21
24	x	x	x	x	x	27-30
25	x					22-26
26	x	x	x	x		28-30
27	x		x	x	x	21-23
28	x	x	x	x	x	18-20
29	x					25+
30	x					35+

Key: E = epiphyseal fusion, obliteration
        P = pubic symphysis remodeling
        R = rib end remodeling
        A = iliac auricular surface remodeling
        C = cranial suture closure, obliteration

*   Burial 9 consisted of several long bones from at least three individuals:
     -two amputated arms, almost certainly from the same individual, aged 16-19 yrs;
     -portions of two left legs, one quite complete, one represented by a tibia;
      Both are from fully mature adults. No more specific estimation is possible.

Seven

Sex Determination, Stature and Size and Shape Variation of the Limb Bones

SHELLEY R. SAUNDERS

Introduction

This study examines the morphological and metrical features of the Snake Hill sample related to sex determination and sexual dimorphism in the infracranial skeleton. It also considers stature as estimated from bone lengths, as well as actual bone lengths in comparison to those of other eighteenth to twentieth century North American male samples. Finally, there is an evaluation of lower limb bone robusticity and shape with a discussion of the implications for assessing behavioral traits from bone shape.

Like other aspects of the Snake Hill study, the value of this investigation is two-fold. On the one hand, it can confirm or expand our understanding of the historical events that created the archaeological site. This is illustrated by the confirmation of probable male sex and the determination of surprisingly tall stature. On the other hand, it can offer a test of our usual battery of techniques and observations, illustrating variability and dynamic temporal changes in the size and shape of skeletal samples.

Sex Determination and Sex-Related Skeletal Characteristics

An investigation of unidentified skeletal material normally includes the determination of sex, based mainly on features of the skull and the hips. The visual and metrical methods of sex determination for human skeletal remains each possess their own problems of application. The visual method can be too subjective and dependent upon "experience," while the metrical method requires complete, undamaged bones and relies upon limited reference samples. In the interests of thoroughness, both the visual and metrical methods were applied to the Snake Hill sample, although not the more advanced discriminant function standards for the skull, mandible or pelvis that require multiple measurements used in concert (usually unavailable for this sample).

Accuracy of the visual technique (which utilizes the presence or absence of sex-related features, or the qualitative size and robusticity of bones) is reported to be 94–100% for the complete skeleton, 90–95% for pelvis alone and 77–92% for the skull alone (Krogman and Iscan 1987). However, true accuracy levels are probably lower by 5–10% because of the preponderance of male cadavera used in the accuracy tests and because of the bias for male-like features in most of the visual criteria (Krogman and Iscan 1987). The bones of the pelvis are known to be the most useful for visual skeletal sex determination; one particular method relies on three easily identified female-like features on the pubic symphysis and is claimed to have a 96% accuracy or better (Phenice 1969).

Although it may be reasonable to expect only males in the Snake Hill skeletal sample, this expectation should not be allowed to influence the visual assessments of sex from the skeleton. There is historical evidence for a few women living at or near the fort (Whitehorne, this volume). It is clear that some of the smaller skulls could have been identified as female if their hip bones had been missing and there were five cases lacking both preserved hip bones and skulls. The presence of buttons representing military garments in various graves represents important archaeological information but again, should not be used as a criterion for skeletal sex determination. Certainly, the investigative exercise in this section is as relevant to the theoretical development of methods of skeletal sex determination as it is to the investigation of the Snake Hill skeletal sample itself.

Figure 7.1 illustrates the number of Snake Hill skeletons containing bones useful for visual sexing criteria in descending order, by criterion accuracy and skeletal completeness. For example, 12 of the 31 individuals had pubic symphyses complete enough that the three traits of Phenice were preserved in addition to other pelvic criteria, a skull and long bones. One individual did not have preserved hip bones and five individuals did not have hip bones or skulls, just long bones. Of those with available Phenice criteria, all were identified as males.

A recent test of Phenice's visual method found the mean accuracy level to be only 83%, although there was no difference in accuracy based on the level of the observer's experience (Lovell 1989). The lower level of accuracy was attributed to the effect of advanced age on the cadaver sample used in the study, one which would not be expected for the Snake Hill sample. In the rest of the Snake Hill skeletons with portions of their hip bones preserved, the next most reliable criteria were the presence or absence of the following: a raised auricular surface, a deep, post-auricular groove and a pre-auricular sulcus. The size of the greater sciatic notch, though the best preserved part of the hip bone, was the least reliable indicator when compared to all other criteria that identified these skeletons as male.

Subsequently, a metrical method of sex determination was also employed that examined dimorphism of long bone measures compared to a reference standard. This method is often helpful in evaluating poorly preserved skeletons. Figures 7.2 to 7.4 present the relative distances of the Snake Hill sample means for various long bone measurements from the white male and female means of the University of Tennessee Forensic Data Base (FDB). This is a sample of several hundred personally identified individuals born in the twentieth century (Jantz and Moore-Jansen 1988). Since it was likely that the Snake Hill sample represented War of 1812 soldiers and it is known that blacks and Indians were not recruited into the regular U.S. army at that time (Coffman 1986), whites are considered the most appropriate reference standard, providing data for a variety of long bone measurements (see Table 7.1 for the definitions of the measurements).

The deviations of the Snake Hill means from the FDB male and female means are expressed in *standard deviation units*. It is clear that, for these long bone measures, the Snake Hill sample is consistently and substantially closer to the FDB males than to the females. This proximity also indicates that there are relatively few outliers in the archaeological sample and that these individuals tend to be relatively large in bone length and size. Only two cases, Burial 5 and Burial 27, demonstrate more than one measurement that would fall into the FDB female range. These are the two shortest individuals in the Snake Hill sample. Both have portions of hip bones and skulls preserved, with anatomical features that confirm their male sex assignment. Based on the metric data, none of the incomplete skeletons, represented by long bones alone, would be skeletally identified as female.

Stature Estimates

By the beginning of the War of 1812, all soldiers in the American army, with the exception of musicians, were expected to be at least 168 cm in height, although the minimum varied from 168 cm to 174 cm at different times (Coffman 1986). Enlistment papers in the U.S. National Archives report that 1,656 men recruited from 1810–1819 had an average age of 26.6

years and an average height of 173 cm (Coffman 1986). Nevertheless, the gap between requirements and reality could be substantial and there was often considerable pressure placed on the recruiters. Accounts of drunkeness, disorder and desertion on the part of recruits suggest that officers and civilian recruiting agents, who were paid for each man brought in, may have lowered their enlistment standards (Caldwell 1955). Recorded military statures typically depart from the general population because of military minimum height standards. On the other hand, it has been shown from British infantry regiment data from the late eighteenth century, that shorter men were not under-represented in times of war, owing to the difficulties of mustering sufficient numbers of men (Steegmann 1985).

The Bradford Company data (Figure 7.5) illustrate this leeway in recruiting since individuals are listed as less than 18 years of age and 11 percent of 18 year olds or over were less than 168 cm.

Recently, it has also been shown that there is a correlation between temperature (mean January temperature of the state of origin) and stature and that during the eighteenth century taller men were found in the most physically demanding occupations (Steegmann and Haseley 1988). Greater stature in the eighteenth and nineteenth centuries is also correlated with rural birth. Those regiments that took part in the Fort Erie siege were all mustered from northern states (Fredricksen 1985) and as the records for Bradford's company illustrate, most identified themselves as farmers or rural craftsmen. Further selection during the siege for the largest and hardiest men to defend the fort may have occurred. However, the predominance of tall men represented by the skeletal sample is still somewhat unexpected.

Estimates of stature of the Snake Hill individuals were calculated from regression formulae derived from a sample of Korean war dead, or American white males, studied by Trotter and Gleser (1958). These authors found that the maximum lengths of the femur and fibula together yield a stature estimate with the lowest standard error of all long bones. Consequently, these bones were always selected first, if available. In all cases, only lower limb bones were used to derive the stature estimates (see Table 7.2).

It is fortunate that documented statures of Bradford's Company of the 21st Regiment of Infantry were available to compare to the Snake Hill sample. Table 7.3 summarizes the basic statistics of the two samples. The data for Bradford's Company include only those individuals reported as 18 years and over, most of whom would have been expected to have completed skeletal growth.

Figure 7.5 illustrates a comparison of the percentage frequency distributions of the two samples. It can be seen from the summary statistics and the figure that the statures of the Snake Hill sample, because of smaller sample size, are slightly less variable than those reported for Bradford's Company. However, the Snake Hill statures are estimates from bones. The full range of stature estimates for Snake Hill would be 161–190 cm if the standard errors for the estimates were taken into account. On the other hand, early documented statures such as those for Bradford's Company are noted for their potential sources of error including less than rigorous measuring procedures, false reporting and rounding of numbers (Wachter and Trussell 1982). It is somewhat surprising that the two sets of data are as similar as they are. Though relatively heterogeneous for its sample size, the Snake Hill group contains proportionately more tall individuals (30% are estimated 180 cm or over) and consequently a higher mean stature than that for Bradford's Company.

Previous research has demonstrated that there is a difference in stature between Colonial-born and foreign-born (i.e., European) eighteenth century individuals, reflecting classic anthropological studies of the differences between migrants and native born populations. Table 7.4 provides some examples of mean male statures from the eighteenth to twentieth centuries. It is evident that males born in the Colonies were taller than their Old World counterparts. However, the Colonial-born Americans are shorter than Americans measured in the 1970s by several centimetres. The Snake Hill sample appears to be closest to the modern Americans and taller than even the Civil War recruits of the 1860s. Two groups in Table 7.4 are of particular interest: the Fort William Henry sample and the Quebec City samples from Courtine St. Louis and Bastion des Ursulines. The Fort William Henry sample is a group of very tall soldiers buried at a mid-eighteenth century British fort on Lake George, New York and associated with the French and Indian Wars. The explanation given for their great stature is that they represent a select group of American provincial grenadiers, heavy infantry units who traditionally received the tallest men (Steegmann 1986). The Courtine/Bastion group is part of a sample of human skeletons recovered from the fortification walls of old Quebec City in 1986. These individuals appear to have been Protestant prisoners of war who died between 1746 and 1747, identified partly on the basis of their greater stature, as compared to that of the French colonists (Cybulski, n.d.).

The stature estimates from the Snake Hill sample, Bradford's Company, the Courtine/Bastion sample and the Forensic Data Bank were examined for statistically significant differences. Table 7.5 reports an analysis of variance comparing the statures of these four groups. In this case, individuals without recorded or estimated ages were removed from the samples. It is apparent that there are significant differences between the groups and that the source of the distinctiveness is between Bradford's Company and the Courtine/Bastion means as opposed to the modern forensic sample and Snake Hill. That is, the Snake Hill sample is close to the modern forensic sample but distinct from the Courtine/Bastion sample and the Bradford's Company data because of its high proportion of tall individuals. This indicates that the Snake Hill sample is selectively biased. It is even different from the documented statures of individuals known to have taken part in the siege. In fact, if Bradford's Company is used as a normally distributed reference sample, only 20% of Snake Hill individuals should be expected to be 180 cm or over. This suggests that the lack of randomness of statures of the Snake Hill sample is not due to chance.

Bone Size and External Dimensions

Since documented statures and statures estimated from long bones contain intrinsic error, it would be useful to examine the actual bone lengths from the Snake Hill sample and compare them to other samples. In addition, external bone dimensions can be approached as indicators of robusticity and shape. Thus, they may provide information on the relationships between environmental forces and long bone shape. Ratios of long bone shaft breadths measured in perpendicular planes are correlated with the bones' properties of relative bending strength (Ruff and Hayes 1983). Consequently, the amount of bone and its cross-sectional distribution reflect some of the mechanical properties of bones.

Recently, Jantz and Moore-Jansen (1988) have compared lower limb skeletal dimensions of white males, noting differences between cadaveral samples of men born in the late 1800s (the Terry collection, which includes skeletons prepared from cadavers dissected at Washington University, St. Louis from 1900 to 1965) and the Forensic Data Base, which represents individuals born in the early and mid-1900s. The more recent sample has larger bone lengths and transverse dimensions of robusticity, particularly for the distal and proximal tibia. The modern sample was also observed to have more elliptical bone shafts compared to the preponderance of rounded bone shafts in the Terry collection. Noting that anatomical or cadaveral collections differ from modern forensic skeletons in a number of ways, these authors suggest that differences in length could be due to a secular increase in height in modern times and that shape differences in femoral and tibial shafts may represent biomechanical and/or nutritional differences.

To explore the issue of sample differences in infracranial dimensions further, the Snake Hill sample was compared to published means for two samples as well as the raw data for other archaeological, anatomical and recent samples. Table 7.6 lists the Snake Hill sample means for several femoral and tibial dimensions, including length. The next two columns in the table summarize the absolute differences between the Snake Hill means and the means for the Forensic Data Bank and the Terry collection. The numbers in the two middle columns of the table and the assignment of affinity in the last column illustrate that Snake Hill is closer to the forensic sample for almost all dimensions, particularly for maximum bone lengths and joint widths of the tibia. This would suggest again, that the Snake Hill sample is selectively biased since it more closely resembles the modern Americans who presumably have undergone the effects of a secular trend in height. However, it is also possible that the anatomical collection is not a random representation of the population from which it was drawn. It contains many poor, nutritionally deprived individuals, some of whom may have suffered lengthy illnesses prior to death.

It was also possible to obtain raw data for bone dimensions from the Forensic Data Base, the 1746 Protestant prisoner or Courtine/Bastion sample from Quebec City and a twentieth century anatomical collection, the Grant collection from the University of Toronto. The Grant collection dates from the 1930s to the 1950s. A subsample of males aged 20–45 years, whose birth dates cluster around the turn of the century, was compared to the Snake Hill sample.

Analyses of variance were calculated for a series of lower limb bone dimensions. These included three indices representing determinations of long bone shaft flattening (tendency to ellipsoid shape) at the proximal end and midshaft of the femur and at the proximal end of the tibia. Table 7.7 summarizes the results. The Quebec City and Grant collection tend to have the shortest femora and tibiae of the four samples but the differences are not statistically significant. There are no significant differences in transverse joint dimensions nor even any implication of smaller size in the Grant Collection or Quebec City samples.

Two indices of bone shaft shape, the midshaft index of the femur and the platymeric index of the femur were found to be significantly different between the samples, while the platycnemic index of the tibia was not. The Grant collection has the lowest pilasteric index (i.e., the most rounded shafts) and is significantly different from the other three samples. Results for the platymeric index at the proximal end of the femur indicate that the

Grant collection and the Quebec City sample are relatively more platymeric (i.e., the most medio-laterally flattened shafts) and are significantly different from the other two samples. Although none of the samples are significantly different in cnemial indices, the Forensic Data Base has the most medio-laterally flattened shafts.

Studies of sex differences in the cross-sectional shape of lower limb bones show that males normally have relatively greater antero-posterior bending loads (and therefore antero-posteriorly distributed bone) than females, particularly around the knee. These differences thus involve dimensions at the midshaft femur and proximal tibia (Ruff 1987). At the level of the proximal femur, females have higher values for shaft flattening or elliptically-shaped cross sections than males, but in the medio-lateral direction (Ruff 1987). Expressed in terms of external breadth ratios, females are usually more platymeric than males.

Temporal trends in cross-sectional shape of the lower limb bones in populations have been noted previously (Lovejoy et al. 1976; Ruff and Hayes 1983). These authors have observed a temporal increase in diaphyseal circularity (a decrease in elliptical shafts) from hunting-gathering through agricultural and industrial subsistence technologies. In addition, the degree of sexual dimorphism in bone shaft shape has been decreasing through time. This decrease appears to reflect losses in bone robusticity and less antero-posterior bending strength in male lower limb bones (Ruff 1987). Consequently, the eighteenth to twentieth century samples of males may reflect broader temporal trends in limb mobility and mechanical behavior.

Values for the three shape indices indicate that all four samples fall within reported ranges for agricultural and industrial peoples rather than hunter-gatherers. The significantly different femoral indices show that the Grant Collection sample has the most rounded femoral midshafts and proximal femora which are closer to the female platymeric condition than to males. Although not statistically significant, the values for the cnemial index show the Forensic Data Base to have the least circular shafts. The Grant Collection is the second lowest value. These observations point to the distinctiveness of the Grant collection as having bone shapes which reflect lower antero-posterior bending loads, at least in the femur. These results are independent of age since the Grant sample was restricted to individuals under 45 years but are not independent of perimortem conditions such as prolonged inactivity due to illness. It should be emphasized that altered biomechanical loadings can produce substantial bone mass and shape changes over relatively short time periods (Lanyon et al. 1975). The shapes of bones from skeletons reflect perimortem behaviorial patterns which may differ substantially from earlier periods in their life history. Anatomical collections may therefore represent very biased collections for a variety of reasons, including their age distributions, their health histories and perimortem behaviors.

The Snake Hill sample is closest to the modern Forensic Data Base with respect to lower limb bone dimensions and shapes. This reflects its greater similarity to a more active and, for the most part, probably healthier group of individuals.

Summary

Based only on visual criteria, those Snake Hill skeletons with preserved pelvic bones were all identified as male. A comparison was made of external long bone dimensions of the entire Snake Hill sample to the twentieth century Forensic Data Base in order to evaluate sex-related size dimorphism and to identify fragmentary skeletons without pelvic remains. The Snake Hill sample is closest to the forensic sample males; only two individuals would fall into the size demarking ranges for females because of their small overall body size and these two were identified as male, based on pelvic criteria.

The Snake Hill skeletal sample contains an unexpectedly high proportion of tall individuals (over 180 cm); this is more than would be expected by chance even when estimated statures are compared to those historically reported for one of the Fort Erie regiments. A consideration of documented male statures in the eighteenth through twentieth centuries suggests that there may have been selection for taller men, both before and during the siege, which resulted in this skeletal sample. Nevertheless, the skeletal sample is sufficiently variable in stature to reflect the expected heterogeneity of War of 1812 regiments.

An examination of external lower limb bone dimensions for Snake Hill, the Quebec City eighteenth century Protestant prisoners, the Forensic Data Base and the twentieth century Grant collection, show that while the Quebec City and Grant collections have somewhat shorter leg bones, there are no apparent differences in bone joint and shaft size. However, the Grant collection tends to more circularity at femoral midshaft and more medio-lateral flattening in the proximal femur, features that have been associated with reduced activity levels, particularly less running and antero-posterior bending at the knee. These observations emphasize that anatomical skeletal collections have their own biases and do not serve well as reference samples for archaeological and forensic cases. Snake Hill most closely resembles the modern forensic sample in bone length, bone size and bone shape and this is a reflection of its special nature as a military battle sample.

Figure 7.1: Availability of Visual Criteria for Sex Determination of the Snake Hill Sample

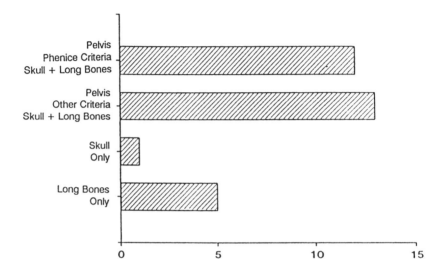

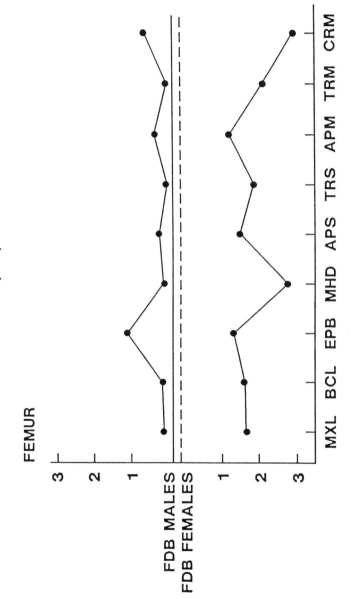

Figure 7.2: Comparison of Snake Hill Femur Dimensions to University of Tennessee Forensic Data Base (FDB) Males and Females

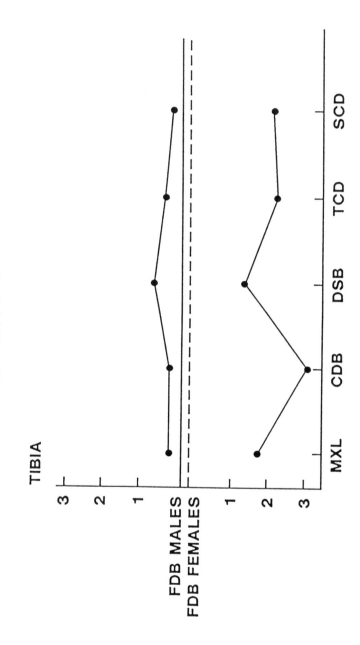

Figure 7.3: Comparison of Snake Hill Tibia Dimensions to FDB Males and Females

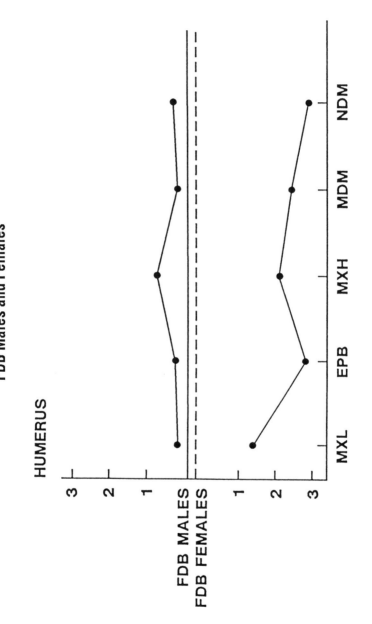

Figure 7.4: Comparison of Snake Hill Humerus Dimensions to FDB Males and Females

Figure 7.5: Comparison of Statures: Bradford's Company and the Snake Hill Sample

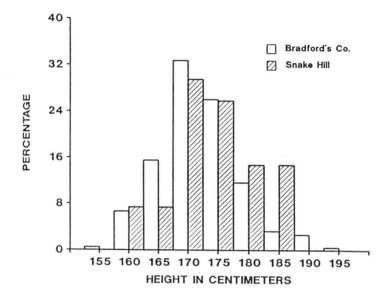

Table 7.1: List of Measurements Used in Sex Dimorphism Comparisons

Humerus

    Maximum Length
    Epicondylar Breadth
    Maximum Head Diameter
    Maximum Diameter at Midshaft
    Minimum Diameter at Midshaft

Femur

    Maximum Length
    Bicondylar Length
    Epicondylar Breadth
    Maximum Head Diameter
    Proximal Sagittal Diameter
    Proximal Transverse Diameter
    Midshaft Antero-Posterior Diameter
    Midshaft Transverse Diameter
    Midshaft Circumference

Tibia

    Maximum Length
    Condylar Breadth
    Distal Breadth
    Transverse Cnemic Diameter
    Sagittal Cnemic Diameter

Table 7.2: Snake Hill Sample Maximum
Bone Lengths and Stature Estimates

Burial/ Feature #	Measure (mm)			Stature Estimates (cm)			
	Femur	Tibia	Fibula	Fem/Fib	Fem/Tib	Fem	Tib
1	463	360			170.91		
2	466	382	380	174.07			
3							
4	474	396	386	175.51			
5	437	351	340	164.84			
6							
7	447	389			172.49		
8	470	376			174.06		
9a		395					177.52
9b		429					185.75
10	458	373	360	169.75			
11		425					184.78
12		431					186.23
13	465	377			173.31		
14	496					180.60	
15	508	422			183.70		
16	513						185.01
17	467	392	(375)		175.64		
18		401					178.97
19	464	374	363	171.45			
20	482	407	391	177.22			
21	507					182.46	
22							
23	479	397	388	176.5			
24	457	357			170.10		
25							
26	(465)	391	381	174.56(fib.)			
27	427	354	349	164.84			
28	445	373			169.72		
29	486	394	386	176.69			
30		431					186.23
31							

Table 7.3: A Comparison of Stature, Bradford's Company Versus Snake Hill

Bradford's Company N = 180		Snake Hill Sample N = 27	
Mean	173.93 cm	Mean	176.31 cm
Median	173.00 cm	Median	175.64 cm
S.D.	6.89	S.D.	6.37
Minimum	158.75 cm	Minimum	164.84 cm
Maximum	197.00 cm	Maximum	186.23 cm

Table 7.4: Eighteenth to Twentieth Century Male Statures

	Date	Series	Sample Size	Mean	S.D.
*	1752	French Isle Royale garrison (1)	938	166.5	5.66
*	1755-1763	British military in America (2)			
		- foreign born	1,647	167.4	6.38
		- Colonial born	1,745	171.6	6.45
+	1675-1879	U.S. Colonials (3)	21	173.4	--
+	1746-1747	Quebec City (1) Courtine/Bastion	30	173.3	6.09
+	1755-1757	Fort William Henry, New York (4)	14	177.3	3.93
+	1814	Snake Hill sample (5)	27	176.3	6.37
*	1812-1814	Bradford's Company (6) 21st Regiment of Infantry, Mass.	180	173.9	6.89
*	1864	U.S. Army, enlisted (4)	150,000	171.4	--
*	1971-1974	U.S. white males, all ages (4)	-	175.5	--

*	documented statures
+	estimated statures from long bones
1	Cybulski, n.d.
2	Steegmann and Haseley, 1988
3	Angel, 1976
4	Steegmann, 1986
5	this study
6	Williamson, 1988

Table 7.5: Stature Estimate Comparison
Using Analysis of Variance

GROUP	CELL N	MEAN
Snake Hill	25	176.3
Quebec City	35	173.3
Forensic Data Base	53	177.1
Bradford's Company	132	173.9

ANOVA

VARIATION	D.F.	SUM OF SQUARES	MEAN SQUARE	F RATION	P
Between Groups	3	865.45	288.48	6.99	<00.05
Within Groups	241	9948.50	41.28		

significance p < .001

Table 7.6: Comparison of Bone Dimensions
from Published Means

Measurement	Snake Hill mean (mm)	Differ. from forensic		Differ. from Terry		Closer to
Femur						
Maximum length	472.35	+	1.15	+	20.74	forensic
Head diameter	48.86	+	0.25	+	0.66	forensic
Distal breadth	82.57	-	2.28	+	0.39	anatomical
Anterior/post. midshaft diam.	30.30	-	0.38	-	1.32	forensic
Transverse midshaft diam.	28.16	+	0.53	-	1.13	forensic
Tibia						
Maximum length	386.00	-	2.75	+	14.97	forensic
Proximal breadth	78.50	-	0.86	+	3.00	forensic
Distal breadth	51.48	-	1.81	+	3.68	forensic
Anterior/post. sagittal diam.	35.81	-	0.19	+	1.21	forensic
Transverse sagittal diam.	25.96	+	0.54	-	0.67	forensic

Table 7.7: Comparison of Long Bone Dimensions Using Analysis of Variance

N Measure	Snake Hill (27)	Quebec City (27)	Forensic Data Base (132)	Grant Collect. (34)	
Femur					
Max. lgth.	472.35	461.00	471.20	458.81	
Head diam.	48.86	48.47	48.61	48.94	
Distal brdth.	82.57	-	84.85	84.79	
Midshaft index	108.39	109.42	110.31	102.44	*
Platymeric index	89.94	83.76	89.17	85.71	*
Tibia					
Max. lgth.	386.00	379.17	388.75	376.29	
Prox. brdth.	78.50	-	79.38	78.77	
Distal brdth.	51.48	-	53.29	53.19	
Platycnemic index	73.75	73.81	70.16	71.24	

* significantly different at the 0.05 level or lower

Eight   # Injuries, Surgical Care and Disease

DOUGLAS W. OWSLEY
ROBERT W. MANN
SEAN P. MURPHY

Introduction

The significance of the Snake Hill skeletal collection is that it represents a different kind of population sample, compared to those encountered in most burial sites. Comprised of military personnel, this demographic sample must be viewed as a special subset of the general population. Because health and other selective factors (e.g., age, sex and body size) determined fitness for induction into military service and influenced subsequent military assignments, the sample of the troops who fought at Snake Hill is not necessarily representative of typical New Englanders. Moreover, the demographic window offered at Snake Hill encompasses the narrow time period of the War of 1812, in contrast with most civilian cemeteries, which reflect an accumulation of deaths, spanning decades. Thus, from a demographic perspective, this population sample is unusual in that it more accurately represents a true age cohort. Such skeletal series are rare in bioarchaeological and paleodemographic research. The demographic composition of this sample is also unusual in that young adults are only occasionally represented in most burial populations.

Ages were assigned to 28 individuals found at Snake Hill, as well as isolated bones from amputated limbs (Pfeiffer, this volume). The demographic composition is comprised primarily of young men aged 15–29 years. Only seven soldiers were identified as being older than 30 years at the time of death. The presence of young adults clearly reflects the adverse circumstances associated with battlefield conditions.

This paper summarizes the analysis of the pathology data, more specifically, traumatic injuries, medical intervention, bone remodeling, skeletal indicators of physical or occupational stress and nutritional status. The objective is to provide a detailed synthesis of the skeletal pathology data. The organizational format includes both observations about each soldier and observations of the group collectively, through summaries based on the total skeletal collection. Tabular presentations provide percentages based on bone inventories (i.e., bone counts) as well as the number of individuals. Where appropriate, observations for specific individuals are listed.

Methods

A. Bone Inventories

Complete skeletons as well as isolated bone fragments and whole limb bones were recovered at the site. The incomplete skeletons were the result of the disposal of amputated limbs and miscellaneous body parts in medical waste pits during the siege. Also, subsequent construction activities had disturbed some of the burials. Because of differential bone preservation and recovery, it was essential to tally specific elements present in the total collection. Bone inventories were obtained for each individual. The coding format used during this examination was designed for computer analysis. Skeletal elements were scored as complete or partial. This method provided precise bone counts by left and right side, including separate tabulation of the numbers of proximal and distal joint surfaces of all major long bones. These inventories were necessary for pathology data analysis.

B. Bone Lesions

The scoring system for pathological conditions followed a detailed coding format allowing computer frequency tabulation of pathological features. In addition, descriptions of any unique observations, useful to differential diagnoses and interpretation, were recorded. Pathological changes were scored, using a hierarchical approach that coded lesions descriptively according to the predominant osteoclastic or osteoblastic response, as: 1) bone loss, 2) bone increase, or 3) loss and increase (resorption and formation).

This classification distinguishes the major changes possible in living bone. Following this determination, a second more precise designation was recorded using descriptors that defined the nature of the lesion:

General	Specific
1. Bone Loss	Resorptive lesion—lytic
	Loss of density—porosity
	Loss of density—cortical thinning

2. Bone Increase   Periostitis

Osteomyelitis

Tumor

Ossified connective tissue

(enthesopathy, myositis ossificans,

ectopic bone)

3. Bone Resorption and Formation

Each lesion was coded for: 1) severity (i.e., mild, moderate, severe); 2) state (i.e., active, healing); 3) extent of involvement (i.e., localized, widespread); and 4) specific location on the bone.

Changes due to degenerative joint disease (osteoarthritis) were scored according to the severity of hypertrophic bone development (marginal lipping of the joint surface—osteophytes), porosity (porous erosion of the joint surface), and eburnation (polishing resulting from bone on bone contact following destruction of the articular cartilage) (Ortner and Putschar 1985; Steinbock 1976).

The skeletons were examined for evidence of trauma and surgical intervention. Each bone fracture was classified as battle related (no healing or actively healing) or non-battle related (healed). Healed fractures represented injuries incurred before the siege.

Results and Discussion

A. Traumatic Injuries and Surgical care

A minimum of 30 individuals are represented, as determined by the single highest bone count (i.e., 30 left tibiae). Twenty-six burials contained relatively complete skeletons. In addition, some surgically amputated or traumatically avulsed bones were recovered as inclusions in other burials and bone waste pits. For example, an articulated amputated left forearm and hand (Spec. No. 5B) was found beneath the right elbow of Burial 5. Medical Waste Feature 9 contained the infracranial bones of three individuals, two of which clearly represented surgical amputations. One group of elements included the right and left arm bones from the same 14- to 17-year-old male, with bilateral (synchronous) amputation of the humeri. A second group of bones included a left femur, tibia, fibula, talus, and calcaneus of a leg that had been amputated through the femur below the lesser trochanter.

Table 8.1 lists the soldiers with perimortem and healed fractures of the skeleton, evidence of surgical amputations and projectile injuries. Of the 26 men with complete or nearly complete skeletons, 13 (50.0%) sustained traumatic injuries resulting in broken bones. Examples are illustrated in Plates 8.1 and 8.2. In many cases (n = 13 in the total collection), the fracture pattern indicated projectile-induced injuries. Many wounds were fatal, although surgical intervention by amputation was applied in several cases when the extremities were involved. In the total sample (including amputated limbs), seven soldiers (7 of 25 individuals with ribs present, 28.0%) have fractured ribs, seven (7/28, 25.0%) have fractured femora, and two (2/22, 9.1%) sustained fatal wounds to the head. Three individuals had fractured ulnae. Of these, one was bilateral with injuries to both forearms.

The total number of perimortem fractured bones observed in the Snake Hill collection was 53. The ribs (16/53, 30.2%) showed the highest percentage of fractures. Other fractures involved the femora (7/53, 13.2%), ulnae (4/53, 7.5%), clavicles, vertebrae, and fibulae (3/53, 5.7%). The distribution of perimortem fractures by body region was 69.8% above, and 30.2% below the waist respectively. More than twice as many fractures were sustained to the left side of the body (30/53, 54.7%) than to the right side (14/53, 26.4%), excluding the skull, spine, and sacrum (9/53, 17.0%). While this asymmetry may be due to chance, it also may indicate something about handedness or the postures taken during battle.

A number of the soldiers revealed osseous or material evidence of battle-related trauma and subsequent death. For example, Burial 1 is a 20- to 24-year-old male with a wound to the head. The projectile entered the posterior left parietal and exited the cranium through the anterior right parietal. His skull also showed an indentation caused by a previous injury. A depressed and nonpenetrating healed wound measuring 26 mm wide was present in the right parietal bone immediately above the temporal squamous.

The soldier from Burial 20, aged 22 to 24 years, died of a gunshot wound to the face. The skull and face were badly fragmented and a musket shot was found loose within the brain case. The shot entered the skull in or near the nasal aperture. The bone in this area is badly fragmented, missing in places, and consistent with a gunshot wound to the face. There are no entry or exit wounds in the frontal, parietals, or occipital.

Burial 5A presents direct evidence that he suffered a battle-related death. Iron grapeshot and a brick fragment were found beneath the right scapula and the seventh and eighth thoracic vertebrae respectively. The right 10th rib (lower back) exhibits a penetrating wound and subsequent loss of 16 mm of bone.

An interesting and important aspect of this skeletal series is the evidence of immediate surgical care for the wounded (Table 8.1; Plate 8.3). Eight surgically amputated limbs were recovered, the product of surgery on seven individuals. One soldier underwent bilateral amputation of the humerus near the midshaft (Plate 8.4); a second individual had an amputation of the distal radius and ulna. From four additional individuals came three left and one right amputated femora.

One of the most interesting burials was number 12, which was in a common grave with Burials 7 and 13. The central male (Burial 12) had a disarticulation amputation of the left femur at the hip socket. Such drastic measures suggest that injury was sustained to the proximal femur, necessitating removal of the leg at the acetabulum. No evidence of cuts or trauma was noted in or around the left hip bone. The soldier (Burial 13) buried to the left sustained a comminuted segmental fracture (massive breakage) of the right femur and also exhibited osseous trauma to the left shoulder and right forearm (Table 8.1).

According to most medical field records, the chest cavity was seldom, if ever, opened surgically (Gillett 1981). If this statement is true, a 6 cm rib fragment found in association with Burial 1 serves as a rare example of either thoracic surgery or autopsy, although the latter is unlikely. One end of the rib exhibited a distinct cut with a terminal snap (protruding bone "tag"). The angle and placement of the cut in relation to the body, as well as the lack of fracturing, suggest that the chest was opened surgically.

B. Bone Inflammation

The incidence of bone inflammation in the Snake Hill sample was low. Inflammation, reflected by increased bone formation and vascularity (blood supply), may have many causes including venous insufficiency, infection, scurvy and trauma.

When the inflammatory response is present on the outer surface of bone, it results from acute or chronic stress (trauma) to the periosteum, the tight outer sheath of connective tissue covering all long bone surfaces other than the articular surfaces. The periosteum consists of two layers: the outer portion is composed of collagenoblasts; the inner layer, which is in contact with the cortex, is capable of producing bone (osteogenesis) and is responsible for the osseous response, commonly referred to as periostitis (i.e., inflammation of the periosteum). Periostitis is a nonspecific inflammatory response where, in most cases, newly formed bone is produced in the same manner regardless of the insult. Hence, the process is nonspecific. When bone is damaged, such as from a blow to the shin, the periosteum is elevated. This stimulates the inner layer of the periosteum to produce new bone at the site of trauma.

When compared to many other military samples (e.g., Civil War), the Snake Hill series has a low incidence of periostitis in either the active or healed stages. For example, the highest frequencies of periostitis (Table 8.2) are seen in the tibia (8/55, 14.5%), fibula (4/55, 7.3%) and scapula (1/50, 2.0%). It is not possible to determine, with any degree of certainty, when or at what age the soldiers developed the healed forms of periostitis. Some cases could reflect trauma or conditions incurred years before the siege.

There is one case, however, where the general time frame associated with the development of periostitis can be ascertained. Burial 15 exhibits an area of actively remodeling periostitis (possibly reflecting infection) in his right scapula. The amount of periosteal new bone formation suggests that he received trauma to his shoulder a minimum of four to six weeks before his death. In other words, it is probable that the soldier received trauma to his right shoulder during the siege and survived, possibly, in a hospital or treatment facility for at least four weeks before succumbing to infection or some other fatal agent. As the individual had been interred in overalls alone (Thomas and Williamson, this volume), it would appear that he died while receiving medical care.

Burial 15 is the only individual to show evidence of infection. The skull of this soldier had three active lytic lesions; two were in the frontal bone abutting the right half of the coronal suture and the third lesion was in the occipital bone. The lesions originated in the inner table of the skull without involving the outer table. The lesions are roughly circular, with bony spicules, pitting, and eroded margins. The gross appearance of the lesions is consistent with tuberculosis and with eosinophilic granuloma of bone. It is not possible to determine whether or not the active periostitis in his right shoulder (mentioned earlier) was related to the cranial lesions. The spine and ribs appeared normal.

C. Physical and Nutritional Stress

Historical documentation for the Niagara campaign and the Fort Erie garrison records the fact that the troops were frequently engaged in heavy physical labor, both in preparation for the campaign and during the siege. The rigorous training program instituted by Brigadier General Winfield Scott transformed the American troops into the finest U.S. force fielded during the War of 1812 (Whitehorne, this volume). Most of the men had backgrounds as laborers or farmers; as soldiers, they were disciplined and efficient. As summarized by Whitehorne, the advanced training schedule was arduous and included daily drills of up to 10 hours with weapons, packs, and equipment weighing about 20 kg. Following the British surrender of the fort on July 3, 1814, and after the decision was made later in the month to strengthen and expand the American garrison to withstand siege conditions, the men were continuously engaged in engineering projects designed to improve the fortifications. Strenuous duties included the construction of extensive breastworks and external ditches, bastions, epaulements, redoubts, a log blockhouse, abatis, traverses within the interior of the fortifications, and placement of batteries. Unit fatigue parties worked in eight-hour shifts around the clock, frequently under conditions of inclement weather and bombardment by the Royal Artillery. "The men were pushed to their physical and emotional limits in the course of the siege, performing heavy labor for extended periods under dangerous conditions (Whitehorne 1988:27)." Certificates of disability issued after the war listed rheumatism, hernias, and hemorrhoids as common complaints of survivors. The physical toll exacted by the field conditions and demanding schedules are also reflected in skeletal anomalies and pathological conditions.

The diet of the soldiers while under siege did little to improve their condition (Whitehorne, this volume). The basic ration was salt pork and hard bread, occasionally supplemented by spirits, vinegar, and vegetables. Fresh produce and vinegar were frequently unavailable or too expensive, and the men experienced shortages that contributed to poor nutrition. The officers were particularly concerned about the lack of antiscorbutics. As the siege continued, these shortages were exacerbated by health problems (e.g., cholera, typhus, dysentery, and diarrhea) associated with poor sanitation and crowded living conditions.

Physical stress can be defined as acute or chronic excessive biomechanical strain on the body. Some of the indicators in the skeleton that reflect physical or mechanical stress include enthesophytes (lesions of muscle and tendon attachment sites), osteoarthritis, and fatigue fractures. Due to the nonspecific nature of these indicators, etiological determinations of unique or individual observations are difficult to make. However, the patterning of bone involvement is important and may reveal the character of the lifestyle of the group; the Fort Erie military series provides such an opportunity. Collectively, several observations — osteoarthritis, Schmorl's depressions, and benign cortical defects in the proximal humerus — suggest skeletal response to excessive physical strain.

Because little osteological research has focused on the effects of occupational or behavioral stress on the human skeleton (e.g., Angel 1985; Kelley and Angel 1983; Kennedy 1989; Owsley et al. 1988), causal factors or inference of physical strain for some of the Snake Hill observations are tentative. Certain lesions, due to their high frequencies, are noteworthy. Detailed information concerning frequencies of occurrence will contribute to future research. Perhaps that future work will determine whether, and how, this skeletal collection reflects an atypical (or high level) pattern of physical stress.

Nearly all of the soldiers were young when they died and few arthritic changes were noted in the spine or the appendicular skeleton. Mild vertebral osteophytosis and osteoarthritis (lipping of the vertebral bodies and margins of the apophyseal joints) of the lower thoracolumbar region were present in a few individuals (Table 8.3). The incidence of polyarticular (multiple joints) osteoarthritis was very low. Only one individual (Burial 17) presented mild periarticular osteophyte development on all of the major long bones including the glenoid fossae of the scapulae. Four soldiers had minor arthritic changes (i.e., periarticular osteophyte development) evident in one or more joints of the arms. Eight men, including three of the above, showed slight marginal lipping of the joints of the legs. The numbers of proximal and distal joint surfaces with arthritic changes, and corresponding base counts used to determine percentages of bones with degenerative changes due to osteoarthritis, are given in Table 8.4. The most frequently affected joints in the sample were the distal femora (12.0 to 13.3%) and the acetabula (12.0 to 15.0%) of the pelvis (hip bones). The levels of degenerative change were mild in most cases. Joint surface changes evident in the acetabula of Burial 24 were classified as moderate to severe in expression, as indicated by surface porosity, and to a lesser degree, by periarticular osteophyte development.

a. Schmorl's Depressions
A high frequency of vertebral end-plate lesions (Schmorl's depressions) in the soldiers' spines suggest the effects of heavy physical strain. Cartilaginous nodes are caused by herniation and displacement of intervertebral disc tissue into the adjacent vertebral bodies. Depressions in the bone result. The cartilaginous discs of the vertebral column are each composed of an outer fibrous ring of tough fibrocartilage (the annulus fibrosus), and an inner pulpy, highly elastic structure (the nucleus pulposus). Thus structured, the vertebral discs and the surrounding

ligaments form strong joints which absorb vertical shock and loading and allow mobility of the spine. With end-plate prolapse, tissue may be displaced from the disc space in any direction. When prolapse occurs, the nucleus pulposus ruptures through the annulus fibrosis and herniates. A posterior prolapse of disc material frequently results in neurological symptoms due to impingement of the spinal cord or nerves. Anterior or lateral displacement often induces hypertrophic spur formation of spondylosis deformans (osteophytes). Superior or inferior prolapse of disc tissue will encroach and erode into the cartilaginous end plate of the vertebral body causing osseous defects referred to as Schmorl's depressions.

The occurrence of Schmorl's depressions in dry bone is recognized by one or more depressions in the superior and/or inferior surfaces of the vertebral bodies. The lesions appear as smooth-walled pits or furrows, usually located near the middle of the body (Plate 8.5). While the depth of the lesion is usually a few millimeters, in rare cases disc material may erode a substantial portion of the body.

Schmorl's depressions are most common in areas of greatest biomechanical strain, specifically the lower thoracic and upper lumbar vertebrae.

> The prolapse of disc tissue ('intervertebral disc hernia', according to Geipel) is a result of the expansive pressure of the nucleus pulposus and especially of the pressure produced by the constant elastic tension of the weight-bearing spine. At first, through the resorption of small, fine trabeculae, a small cavity is created into which more and more of the disc tissue is pressed. Gradually the continued and repeated pressure stimuli produce reactive changes in the surrounding osseous trabeculae which at first produce a cartilaginous and later an osseous casing in the surrounding of the prolapse disc tissue. (Schmorl and Junghanns 1971:159)

The displacement of disc tissue signifies a decrease in efficiency of the disc. Schmorl's nodes tend to be subclinical, or symptomless, unless displacement of disc substance is so great that it produces a narrowing of disc space with subsequent reduction of spinal movements. In severe cases where substantial loss of disc material has occurred, anterior (forward) tilting of vertebral bodies may produce abnormal stresses on the bone leading to arthropathies such as marginal osteophytes, ankylosis (fusion) of adjacent vertebrae, and osteoarthritis of the apophyseal joints (Collins 1949). It has also been observed that the development of Schmorl's nodes in children and adolescents predisposes the dorsolumbar spine to disc degeneration in later life (Hilton et al. 1976).

In some cases, the presence of Schmorl's depressions is considered to be idiopathic, that is, of unknown origin. Their development has been linked to certain diseases and congenital factors that produce a weakening of the subchondral bone and a disruption of the cartilaginous end-plate, as well as degenerative changes associated with ordinary stress on the vertebral column (Schmorl and Junghanns 1971). "The origin, progression, and symptoms of vertebral disc prolapse ... are influenced decisively by everyday demands of life. Fatigue damage, similar to fatigue fractures in the bone, can be produced in disc tissue when the demand surpassed the functional ability" (Schmorl and Junghanns 1971:175). In addition, strong compression caused by traumatic injury can produce Schmorl's depressions. Node development most commonly occurs in the late teens and early adult years and the frequency does not seem to increase dramatically with age (Hilton et al. 1976; Schmorl and Junghanns 1971). The nucleus pulposus reaches turgor during the early years and exerts its greatest pressure on the surrounding tissue. Strain such as excessive vertical loading to the lower back results in increased pressure, which raises the tendency for node development. With increasing age, there is a gradual loss of fluid and a decrease in disc pressure. The risk of node formation is also reduced.

Table 8.5 presents the numbers and percentages of Schmorl's depressions observed in the Fort Erie soldiers. These statistics were tabulated using the total counts of thoracic and lumbar vertebrae, as well as the number of individuals with vertebral elements present for examination. The number of individuals and numbers of affected vertebrae seem quite remarkable with thirteen (13/27, 48.0%) individuals having vertebral end-plate lesions. This high incidence is particularly dramatic when examined on a per individual basis. Six individuals have five or more affected vertebrae. One soldier had pronounced Schmorl's depressions in 11 vertebrae while another had nine. Most of the lesions were located in the lower thoracic (19.0%) vertebrae although 9.7% of lumbars showed evidence of vertebral depressions (Figure 8.1).

Few comparative statistics are available, although there is evidence that different groups vary considerably in the incidence and severity of Schmorl's depressions. The Snake Hill counts are higher than has been reported in a modern (contemporary) cadaveric sample from Germany (males 39.9%; females 34.3%) (Schmorl and Junghanns 1971). Batts (1939) found an even lower incidence, 20%, in a dissecting-room sample from Great Britain reportedly having high frequencies of end-plate lesions (Hilton et al. 1976; Saluja et al. 1986). Saluja and co-workers (1986) found a rate of 71% among thirteenth to sixteenth century skeletons from Aberdeen, Scotland, and an incidence of 49% in an eighteenth to nineteenth century London sample. While there are caveats to this interpretation, it appears that the Snake Hill soldiers' moderately high frequency of Schmorl's nodes indicates a physically stressful routine.

Several other spinal conditions were noted, including compression fractures of vertebral bodies (Burial 14), wedge-shaped vertebrae (Burials 1, 7, 15, and 19; Plate 8.6), intervertebral osteochondrosis of four lumbar vertebrae (Burials 12, 16, and 19), spina bifida of one first cervical vertebra (Burial 1) and spondylolysis (separate neural arch) of one fourth lumbar vertebra (Burial 17A) (see Figure 8.1).

b. Benign cortical defects

Another frequent observation in this skeletal collection that may be attributable to physical stress were benign cortical defects at the insertions of the pectoralis major and teres major muscles in the proximal humerus (Brower 1977). The lesions appear as elongated depressions with smooth cortical margins and an irregular, often porous floor (Plates 8.7 and 8.8).

The pectoralis major muscle has its origin on the clavicle, sternum, and cartilage of the second through the sixth ribs. Its insertion is on the crest of the lesser tubercle of the humerus. This muscle extends and draws the arm down and assists in adduction and medial rotation (for example, the action used in shoveling).

Benign cortical defects, resembling cortical excavations of the humerus, are frequently observed on the posterior surface of the distal femur as well. This location is the attachment site of the medial head of the gastrocnemius muscle. The presence of cortical defects is believed to be related to intense mechanical stress (Bufkin 1971; Resnick and Greenway 1982). This type of lesion has been observed in the humerus, radius, tibia, fibula, metacarpal, metatarsal, and distal phalanx, and always at the site of attachment of a strong muscle (Bufkin 1971). For example, a recent case involved a 29-year-old male who presented with chronic pain in his right shoulder following a strenuous tennis match. Radiography and biopsy of a radiolucent cortical defect in the proximal humerus revealed normal ligamentous tissue at the insertion of the pectoralis major tendon (Brower 1977). With time, the pain resolved and was thought to have been secondary to muscle strain. According to Dr. Jeno Sebes (1989), most radiologists agree that benign cortical defects of the humerus are stress induced, and almost certainly are the result of repeated chronic stress, not acute stress. These lesions are resorptive because of an inflammatory response with increased blood supply and hyperemia (increased blood velocity).

In the Snake Hill soldiers, benign cortical defects in the proximal humerus were found in 16 humeri; 10 (62.5%) are right and six (37.5%) are left. They were generally consistent in shape, but varied in depth both within and between individuals. Bilateral differences were often present. For example, some individuals exhibited large defects at the insertion of the pectoralis muscle and teres muscle in the right humerus, yet only small, shallow defects in the left humerus. If related to muscular exertion, this asymmetry may reflect use differences associated with handedness or other activities performed by the soldiers.

Population data for comparison with the Snake Hill collection are not readily available. Civil War specimens and two American Indian collections — late prehistoric and early historic, from Oregon and South Dakota — were examined in order to provide a preliminary contrast that gives perspective to interpretation of the Snake Hill data (Table 8.6). Subsistence economies for the native American sample emphasized fishing, hunting and foraging in the Northwest, and farming and bison hunting in the Northern Plains.

The totals given in Table 8.6 are based on two tabulation systems as determined by the nature of the skeletal collections. The Snake Hill and Northern Plains counts identify numbers of individuals examined. The Civil War collection is comprised of amputated limbs from battlefield injuries; thus, the total count is based on the total number of left and right humeri available for study. The collection from the Pacific Northwest is from an ossuary-type burial with all remains commingled. Again, the base count was determined by the total number of left and right humeri.

The percentage (40.0%) of Snake Hill soldiers is nearly double the number observed in the Civil War series (22.0%), while the Civil War series is higher than either North American Indian sample. As evaluated using a chi square statistic ($\chi^2 = 10.81$, d.f. = 3, p = 0.013), there are population differences in the frequency of benign cortical defects.

Additional research will help to evaluate the usefulness of benign cortical defects as indicators of activity patterns. Work on comparative studies of populations with different genetic, temporal and geographical origins may help to identify factors involved in the formation of cartilaginous nodes and benign cortical defects. Archaeologically derived samples are of considerable value in this regard, especially if historic or ethnographic information is available concerning activity patterns and lifestyle.

c. Malnutrition

Evidence for malnutrition was noted in cranial bone changes. There was a high frequency of outer table (ectocranial) porosity without concomitant vault thickening. This porosity was characterized by small sieve-like pits, particularly around bregma, the sagittal suture, and the squama of the occipital bone (generally, the top of the vault). These tiny pits resembled the texture and appearance of an orange peel (Mann and Murphy 1990). Among the soldiers at Fort Erie, 23% of the occipital bones exhibit this condition (Table 8.7). All examples were classified as "mild" in severity.

The age distribution of this series rules out the possibility of the condition being an aspect of osteoporosis accompanying old age. Cranial porosity has been reported in some American soldiers who died as prisoners of war during the Korean conflict (McKern and Stewart 1957). There, this condition was attributed to extreme and prolonged nutritional deprivation. According to Angel (1978), outer cranial surface porosity generally indicates nutritional deficiencies, such as scurvy. None of the Snake Hill cases resemble the more pronounced cranial vault changes often associated with conditions like cribra orbitalia or porotic hyperostosis. Such conditions, expressed as outer lamina porosity and hypertrophy of the diploic marrow space, are associated with the hemolytic or iron-deficiency anemias (Angel 1966; El-Najjar et al. 1975; Lallo et al. 1977; Mensforth et al. 1978; Stuart-Macadam 1985).

Conclusions

The discovery and forensic examination of the Snake Hill skeletal collection provided a rare opportunity to address many questions concerning health and nutrition, battlefield injuries, causes of death, and medical intervention affecting military personnel during the first quarter of the nineteenth century. There is very little comparable bioarchaeological information available for early historic period American populations. Hence, the biological and pathological information collected for Snake Hill serves as an important data base for future historical, demographic and osteological research. This investigation benefited from the availability of extensive historical research and from interdisciplinary research that focused on the medical intervention associated with the treatment of battle-related wounds.

Note

Special thanks are extended to Dr. Ronald Williamson, project director, for allowing us to participate in the investigation of the Snake Hill archaeological site. Mr. Paul S. Sledzik and Dr. Peer H. Moore-Jansen assisted in the examination of the skeletal remains. Ms. Susan M. T. Myster furnished data on humeral cortical defects in native Americans from Oregon. Research support was provided by the Research Opportunities Fund, National Museum of Natural History, Smithsonian Institution; the National Museum of Health and Medicine of the Armed Forces Institute of Pathology; and the United States Armed Services Casualty Affairs Division. Administrative arrangements for this funding were coordinated by Dr. Marc S. Micozzi, Director of the National Museum of Health and Medicine, and Lieutenant Colonel Robert Trotter, United States Army. Dr. Milton Jacobs and Ms. Bertita Compton provided valuable editorial assistance.

Figure 8.1: Relative Frequency Histogram of Schmorl's Nodes

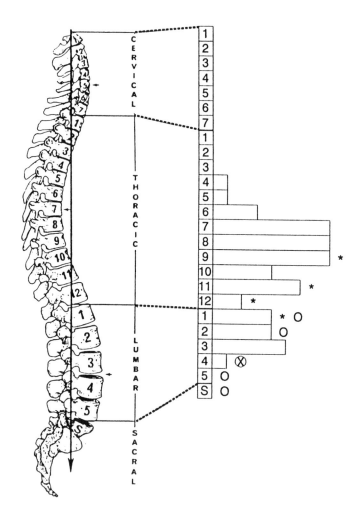

Histogram illustrates the relative frequency of cartilaginous (Schmorl's) nodes. An open square indicates one vertebra affected. Other possible products of chronic trauma include:

*   marked wedge shape or compression fracture of a vertebral body

⊗   spondylolysis

O   osteochondrosis

(Figure modified from Merbs 1983)

Table 8.1: Fractures, Surgical Intervention, Projectile Injuries and Traumatic Death by Individual

Individual	Fracture	Amputation	Projectile Injury	Trauma Death
1	Parietal L		+	+
	Parietal R			
	Parietal R (H)			
4	L rib 11		+	+
5A	Clavicle R			
	R rib 10		+	+
5B		Radius L	+	
		Ulna L		
7	Scapula L		+	+
	Clavicle L			
	Two thoracic			
	L rib 1			
9A	Radius L	Humerus L	+	
	Ulna L	Humerus R		
	Ulna R			
9B	Femur L	Femur L	+	
11	Femur L		+	+
12		Femur L		+
13	Radius R			
	Femur R		+	+
	Fibula R			
14	One thoracic (H)			
	L rib 1 (H)			
	L rib 5, 6			
	R rib 4, 10 (H)			
15	One thoracic			+
	R rib 8, 9			
16	Clavicle L			+
	Scapula L			
	L rib 1, 2, 3, 4			
17A	Fibula L (H)			
	Fibula R (H)			
18	Femur R			
19	Ulna R			+
	One thoracic			
	Left rib 8, 9 (H)			
	Left rib 7, 8, 9, 10, 11			
	Innominate L			
	Sacrum			
	Femur L			
	Hand phalanx R			
20	Maxilla		+	+
25	Femur L	Femur L	+	
	Patella L			
	Tibia L			
	Fibula L			
27	Frontal (H)		+	+
	Humerus L			
	Ulna L			
	Innominate L			
	Sacrum			
31	Fibula R			
Bag O1	Humerus R	Humerus R	+	
Feature 22	Femur R	Femur R		

+ = trait present
H = healed fracture

Table 8.2: Individuals with Long Bone Periostitis and Frequency

Individual	Bone	Severity	State of Remodeling
7	Tibia L	S	Healed
	Tibia R	S	Healed
11	Tibia L	S	Healed
12	Fibula R	S	Healed
13	Patella L	S	Healed
15	Scapula R	M	Active
18	Fibula R	S	Healed
20	Ulna R	S	Healed
	Tibia L	S	Healed
	Tibia R	S	Healed
	Fibula L	S	Healed
24	Thoracic 10	S	Active
	Thoracic 11	S	Active
	Tibia L	S	Active
	Tibia R	S	Active
28	Frontal	S	Active
31	Fibula R	M	Active

S = slight (mild)

M = moderate

Humerus		Ulna		Radius		Scapula		Femur		Tibia		Fibula	
N=53		N=52		N=54		N=50		N=54		N=55		N=55	
Lt	Rt	Lt	Rt	Lt	Rt	Lt	Rt	Lt	Rt	Lt	Rt	Lt	Rt
0	0	0	1	0	0	1	0	0	1	5	3	1	3
n	0	1		0		1		1		8		4	
%	0.0	1.9		0.0		2.0		1.8		14.5		7.3	

(N = Total bones present)

Table 8.3: Individuals with Osteophytosis of the Spine

Individual	Cervical	Thoracic	Lumbar	Sacrum
2	S			
7		M	M	S
10		S	S	S
14		S	M	
18			S	
n	1	3	4	2
%	5.0	12.0	14.8	8.3
Individuals with vertebrae:	20	25	27	24

S = slight (mild)

M = moderate

Table 8.4: Osteoarthritis of Joint Surfaces

Bone	OA Present Left (L)	OA Present Right (R)	OA Present Left P	OA Present Left D	OA Present Right P	OA Present Right D	Left (N) P	Left (N)	Left (N) D	Right (N) P	Right (N)	Right (N) D	Percent LP	Percent LD	Percent RP	Percent RD	Percent Single Bone L	Percent Single Bone R
Glenoid	1	2	-	-	-	-	-	22	-	-	23	-	-	-	-	-	4.5	8.6
Humerus	-	-	1	1	1	1	19	-	21	19	-	23	5.2	4.3	5.2	4.3	-	-
Ulna	-	-	1	0	2	0	23	-	15	23	-	19	4.3	0.0	8.6	0.0	-	-
Radius	-	-	1	1	1	2	20	-	18	21	-	20	5.0	5.5	4.7	1.0	-	-
Innominate	4	3	-	-	-	-	-	26	-	-	25	-	-	-	-	-	15.3	12.0
Femur	-	-	0	4	0	3	23	-	30	21	-	25	0.0	13.3	0.0	12.0	-	-
Tibia	-	-	1	2	0	2	29	-	28	25	-	25	3.4	7.1	0.0	8.0	-	-
Patella	3	0	-	-	-	-	-	24	-	-	22	-	-	-	-	-	12.5	0.0

P = proximal joint
D = distal joint
L = left
R = right

Table 8.5: Individuals with Schmorl's Depressions of the Thoracic and Lumbar Vertebrae

Individual	Thoracic (N=263) (No. affected)	Lumbar (N=123) (No. affected)
1		1
2	5	
4	6	
5A	6	
7	3	
14	1	
15	2	
16	6	3
20	8	3
23	3	
24	6	2
26		3
28	2	
n	50	12
%	19.0	9.7
Individuals with vertebrae	25	27
Individuals affected (%)	44.0	18.5

Table 8.6: Number and Percentage of Benign Cortical Defects in the Proximal Humerus of Four Population Samples

Snake Hill[1]			Civil War[2]			Pacific Northwest[2]			Northern Plains[1]		
N	Cortical Defects	%	N	Cortical Defects	%	N	Cortical Defects	%	N	Cortical Defects	%
25	10	40.0	50	11	22.0	95	15	15.8	132	18	13.6

1) Counts based on numbers of individuals
2) Counts based on total number of humeri examined, lefts and rights combined

Table 8.7: Presence of Ectocranial Porosis by Individual

Individual	Frontal N=22	Left Parietal N=21	Right Parietal N=21	Occipital N=21
1		+	+	+
2	+	+	+	+
10		+	+	+
11				+
15				+
17A	+	+	+	
20	+	+	+	+
21		+	+	+
23	+	+	+	+
27	+	+	+	+
n	5	8	8	9
%	22.7	38.0	38.0	42.8

Plate 8.1: Medical Waste Feature 9, Fracture

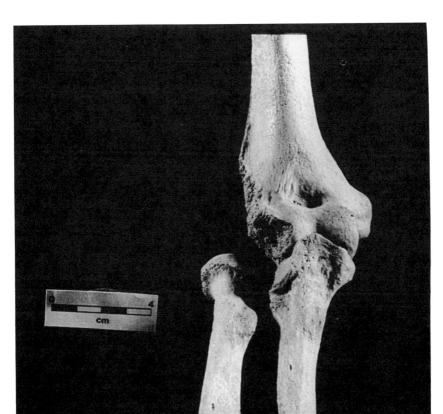

Shot fracture of the lateral epicondyle and capitulum of the right humerus. The corresponding proximal radius and ulna were also fractured.

Plate 8.2: Burial 25, Fracture and Amputation

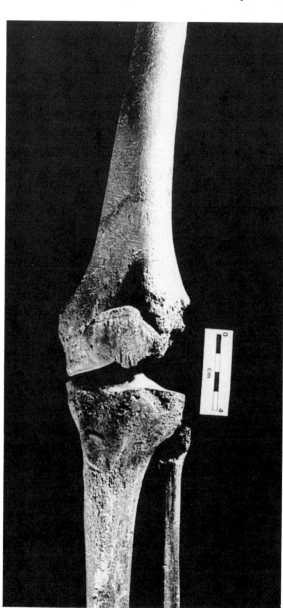

Shot fracture of the left knee involving the femur, patella, tibia, fibula. Amputation of the leg was completed at the midshaft of the femur.

Plate 8.3: Medical Waste Feature 9, Surgical Amputation

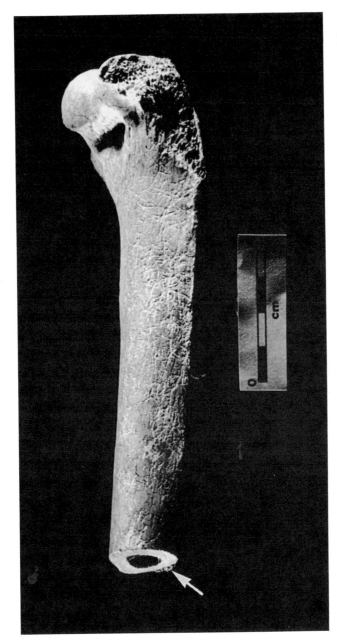

Surgical amputation at the humeral midshaft at a distance of 160 mm from the distal epiphysis in response to shot fracture of the right elbow. Note the terminal snap (arrow) on the posterior surface of the bone.

Plate 8.4: Medical Waste Feature 9, Bilateral Amputation

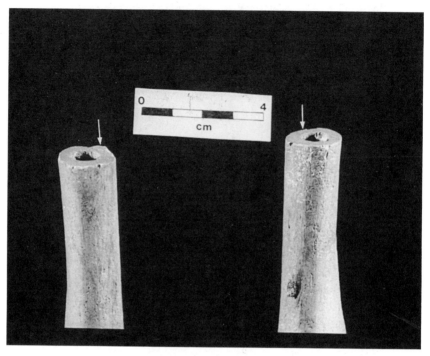

Bilateral amputation of the arms below the midshaft of the humeri at a distance of 129 mm (right) and 131 mm (left) from the distal ephiphyses. Fractures of the left and right ulnae and the left radius revealed injury to both forearms, probably the result of concussive forces from an explosion of multiple projectiles. Note the raised terminal snaps on the posterior surfaces (arrows).

Plate 8.5: Burial 16, Schmorl's Depression

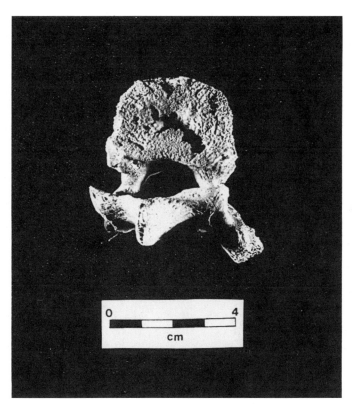

Schmorl's depression in the inferior body of the ninth thoracic vertebra.

Plate 8.6: Burial 16, Vertebral Wedging

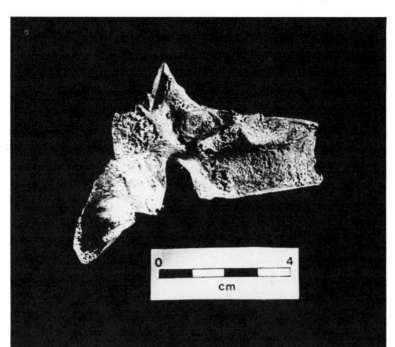

Mild compression fracture and anterior wedging of the ninth thoracic vertebra.

Plate 8.7: Burial 19, Cortical Defect

Right humerus with a cortical defect at the insertion of the pectoralis major muscle.

Plate 8.8: Burial 24, Bilateral Defects

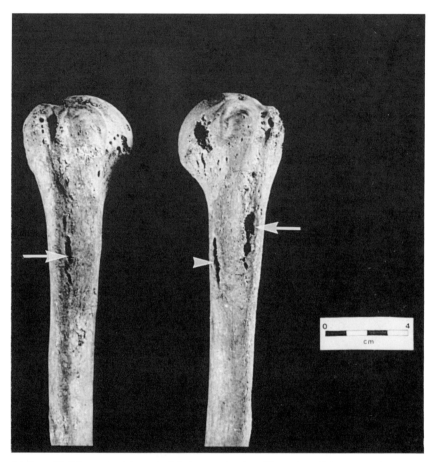

Right and left humeri with cortical defects at the site of insertion of the pectoralis major (arrows) and teres major muscles (arrowhead).

Nine

Dental Pathology

PAUL S. SLEDZIK
PEER H. MOORE-JANSEN

Studying dental remains of historic skeletal populations provides anthropologists, medical historians and epidemiologists with data about dental disease and morphological characteristics of the teeth. These studies may shed light on changes in diet, physical stresses, effects of oral care and types of oral habits. More importantly, this physical evidence can be compared and contrasted to historical records and either corroborated or discounted. Thus, a more complete understanding of the dental health of the population under study can be obtained.

The primary focus of this report is dental health of the Snake Hill soldiers. Diet, disease, socioeconomic background, recruit selection criteria, oral care and other factors affecting dental health are examined. Additional observations on enamel hypoplasia, dental attrition and oral habits are discussed. Historic accounts concerning diet, recruit selection and other factors affecting oral health also will be presented. To aid in the interpretation of dental health among the Snake Hill soldiers, comparisons are made with three contemporaneous military skeletal samples.

Materials and Methods

Dentitions from 25 mandibles and 24 maxillae were analyzed, totalling nearly 600 teeth. Documentary and archaeological evidence indicates that no officers were present in the sample. Prior to their volunteer service, most of the men who served at Snake Hill were farmers or laborers from New York and Pennsylvania. The average age of the sample for this study was 21.6 years, ranging from 18 to 26 years.

In addition to the Snake Hill sample, three contemporaneous military skeletal samples were used for comparison. The National Museum of Health and Medicine, of the Armed Forces Institute of Pathology, maintains a collection of skeletal specimens from soldiers killed or injured during the U.S. Civil War (1862-1865) and Indian Wars of the western U.S. (1867-1899). Forty-nine crania and 10 associated mandibles of Civil War soldiers and 14 crania and eight mandibles from Indian War soldiers were available for study. The Civil War sample ranged in age from 18 to 45 years and averaged 27.1 years. Eight enlisted and two officers were identified as were 18 Confederate and five Union soldiers. Indian War soldiers ranged in age from 20 to 44 years, and averaged 33.6 years. Nine privates and one corporal were identified, as were five infantrymen and four cavalrymen. The third sample consists of 21 soldiers excavated from a Revolutionary War burial ground in Ohio (Sciulli and Gramly 1989). Their average age was 23.5 years, ranging from under 15 years to over 40 years.

Dental caries, commonly known as cavities, are bacterial afflictions affecting the calcified tissue of the teeth. These bacteria, by dissolving areas of inorganic tooth surfaces with bacterial acids, cause disintegration of the organic matrix of the teeth, thus producing pits in the tooth surface. These pits increase in size over time and may, if severe enough, lead to dental abscess. Caries prevalence and severity is largely affected by the chemical composition, texture, preparation and mode of consumption of the diet, particularly carbohydrate intake. Additional factors include tooth morphology, nonalimentary substances (e.g. tobacco), oral hygiene, genetic susceptibility, physical environment and other physiologic and pathologic components (McDonald 1985; Menaker 1980; Powell 1988).

Dental abscesses are usually divided into two types. A periapical abscess is the result of infection, which penetrates the pulp cavity of the tooth, left susceptible by a caries, and affects the alveolar bone at the apex of the tooth. A periodontal abscess is caused by infective foci outside the pulp cavity usually not related to carious lesions. The lesion is observed at the junction of the tooth and the alveolar bone. Nutritional factors have been shown to alter host susceptibility to periodontal disease, which may lead to abscess (Vogel and Alvares 1985).

Antemortem tooth loss can be the result of severe caries, abscess, or tooth extraction. A severe infective process may cause exfoliation of the tooth and, in turn, resorption of the tooth socket. The degree of resorption is directly related to the time since tooth loss.

Dental calculus or tartar is the calcified form of dental plaque, composed of protein, food particles and living and dead bacteria. Certain bacteria present in plaque may lead to caries, although the effect of calculus on dental disease is not clear (Ortner and Putschar 1985; Rosen and Willett 1985).

Dental attrition reflects the erosion of crown enamel due to masticatory stress. Stress may be related to bruxism, foods and other sources such as technological uses. Tooth wear contributes to the reduction of occlusal surface complexity by removing surface morphology of cusps and crenulations. Accordingly, differences in rate of wear is often a key to differences in caries incidence, at least occlusally.

Maxillae and mandibles were analyzed using a standardized data collection form developed by one of the authors (PM-J). Observations of dental pathology were taken on each tooth. Teeth were examined initially for presence, postmortem absence, antemortem absence, congenital absence, partial eruption or uneruption. Each tooth surface (occlusal, buccal, lingual, interproximal and root) was then examined for caries. A four degree code was assigned to each carious lesion: "1" indicates a small pit or fissure; "2" represents a lesion ranging from more than degree "1" to less than half of the tooth surface; "3" indicates destruction of half to not quite all of the tooth surface; and "4" comprises complete destruction of the tooth surface.

Tooth location, type of abscess (periapical or periodontal), and bone resorption and tooth loss due to abscess was also recorded. Pulp exposure from attrition or caries was noted. Calculus was scored on a severity scale. Dental attrition was scored for 26 individuals (21 complete dentitions and five mandibular dentitions) using the system devised by Murphy (1959a; 1959b). Observations on enamel hypoplasias, fillings, artificial wear, and staining were recorded for each individual and the affected teeth noted. Also, certain morphological traits were recorded for each tooth.

Results

Summary statistics for presence and absence of teeth are provided in Table 9.1. As noted, nearly 600 teeth were available for study. Of these more mandibular teeth were available for analysis than maxillary teeth. It was noted that more teeth had been lost before death than lost postmortem.

Dental caries frequency data from Snake Hill are provided in Table 9.2. Nearly 12% of all teeth examined exhibited carious lesions. Maxillary teeth were more prone to incur carious lesions than mandibular teeth. Maxillary incisors, canines, and premolars had higher caries incidences than their mandibular counterparts. In general, mandibular molars exhibited the highest incidence of caries. Mandibular incisors and second premolars showed no evidence of carious lesions. Figure 9.1, a graphic representation of caries incidence by tooth type, indicates that the highest caries rates occurred in posterior teeth.

Incidence of periapical and periodontal abscesses appear in Table 9.3 and Figure 9.2. Dental abscesses are more prevalent in maxillary than mandibular arcades. Mandibular molar sockets exhibit the highest periapical abscess incidence, while maxillary molar sockets exhibited the highest incidence of periodontal abscesses. In general, anterior upper and lower teeth exhibited few, if any, dental abscesses. The total incidences of periodontal and periapical abscesses were nearly equal.

Antemortem tooth loss data are provided in Table 9.4 and Figure 9.3. Antemortem tooth loss occurred in 7.9% of all tooth sockets examined. Nearly one in five mandibular molars were lost before death. Anterior maxillary teeth were more often affected by antemortem tooth loss than anterior mandibular teeth. Mandibular molars exhibited higher antemortem loss incidences than maxillary molars. Mandibular incisors and canines showed no evidence of antemortem tooth loss.

Calculus data, provided in Table 9.5 and Figure 9.4, indicate that 21.4% of all teeth examined showed evidence of calculus deposits (i.e., deposits larger than flecks). All teeth exhibited some degree of calculus. Mandibular teeth were affected more frequently than maxillary teeth. The highest incidences occurred in the mandibular incisors and canines. The lowest incidences were evident on upper and lower third molars.

Mean attrition rates, calculated by side and arch, are shown in Table 9.6. Mandibular dentitions appear uniformly worn for the sample. The slightly greater rate of wear in the right half of the maxillary arch indicates minor asymmetry in maxillary tooth wear. The wear rates also reflect a normal eruption pattern of the molar teeth with the greatest difference being found between first and third molar teeth. Four individuals display moderate to heavy wear with especially noticeable wear of the incisors. Adjacent teeth never differ by more than two stages of two and first molars, and incisors display the most rapid attrition followed by canine teeth.

Additional Observations

Additional dental observations include two individuals with Carabelli's cusp on the first maxillary molars (Burials 14 and 27). This trait is primarily characteristic of European populations, although not exclusively (Dietz

1944). Shovel shaped incisors, a common trait among Asians and American Indians (Dahlberg 1951), were present in one individual (Burial 16). No evidence of dental modification, such as fillings, was observed. One individual (Burial 2) exhibited an occlusal wear pattern of right and left upper and lower canines consistent with facets observed in the dentitions of habitual pipe smokers (Thoma and Goldman 1960).

Hypoplastic enamel lines were observed on the incisors and canines of one individual (Burial 5). These lines were very pronounced (Plate 9.1). Measurements indicate that the stresses causing these defects, possibly disease or nutritional deficiency, occurred while the individual's tooth crowns were forming, between two and four years of age (Goodman and Armelagos 1985).

One interesting skeletal trait was observed in Burial 10. This individual exhibited a Hapsburg jaw: an overly prognathous mandible due more to small dentition rather than a large jaw (Plate 9.2). The presence of this genetically based recessive trait was common in certain royal families that had a high inbreeding rate (Harle 1989; Hart 1971; Loevy and Kowitz 1982). Therefore, the presence of this trait may reflect a rural background with a high inbreeding coefficient.

Discussion

The observed dental disease rates at Snake Hill reflect several aspects of diet and lifestyle of the late eighteenth and early nineteenth century. A large part of the observed degree of dental disease can be explained by diet, but additional factors such as military lifestyle, dental care, age of the soldiers and military recruitment procedures also play a role.

The diet of the general public in the late eighteenth and early nineteenth century consisted largely of salted meat, unprocessed corn meal, and occasionally potatoes, butter, milk, vegetables and fruit. Sugar was consumed in liquid form, such as molasses and maple sugar, rather than the refined granular sugar, which is prevalent today. Rural and urban diets, although differing in proportions, were generally the same (Cummings 1941). The portions of these foods varied depending on local availability, transportation and storage procedures.

Daily military rations at Snake Hill consisted of salt pork, hard bread, a few vegetables, molasses, salt, vinegar and a quantity of rum, whiskey or brandy. A few soldiers were able to supplement their rations with butter, onions, potatoes and prepared foods purchased from local vendors (Whitehorne 1988).

An examination of disease at Snake Hill will provide information on the overall health of the soldiers, which plays a role in the occurrence, prevalence and severity of dental disease. Documentary evidence indicates that the common preantibiotic, high population density diseases such as scurvy, rickets and tuberculosis may have been present at Snake Hill (Noe 1988). Aseptic surgical technique and wound treatment was unknown at this time. Camp hygiene was poor at best, with open latrines and waste areas placed near campsites. Personal and dental hygiene was left to the discretion of the soldier, whose habits usually precluded frequent washing and oral care.

The dental disease data seem to reflect the dietary observations. Caries frequency data indicate that the diet of the Snake Hill soldiers was relatively low in cariogenic agents, especially processed carbohydrates and sugars. The caries rate at Snake Hill (11.9%) is nearly equivalent with average rates in archaeological agricultural groups (e.g., 10.4% seen by Turner [1979] and 11.6% observed by Larsen [1984]), but is substantially lower than those seen in nineteenth century British and modern populations (Corbett and Moore 1976; Hardwick 1960; Turner 1979). In fact, when compared to the three eighteenth and nineteenth century military skeletal samples of equivalent age range (as seen in Figure 9.5), the data reveal that Snake Hill soldiers were experiencing the lowest caries rate of all four samples. The difference between the caries rates of these samples is statistically significant $(p<.001, \chi^2=18.21)$.

The higher caries rate in the Civil War series probably reflects the rapid change in diet that occurred in the mid-nineteenth century (Cummings 1941). The slightly lower caries rate among the Indian War sample may indicate a diet slightly lower in cariogenic foods, although by the latter part of the nineteenth century, the dietary shift to refined carbohydrates and sugars was increasing (Cummings 1941). It may be that, given their positions on western military posts, these men enjoyed fresh meats and local wild plants as a replacement for military rations.

An additional factor in the lower caries rate at Snake Hill may be the consumption of large amounts of salted meats. Moderately low caries rates have been observed in groups with high animal protein and low carbohydrate diets (Leigh 1925). Liquid sugar (e.g., molasses) and unprocessed corn meal has also been shown to cause fewer caries than granular sugar and refined white flour (Gustafsson et al. 1954). On the other hand, an indication of the degree of dental disease in the general population during this period is evident in a report by Alexander Hamilton (1948: 74) who remarked that the dentitions of late eighteenth century northeastern U.S. resident consisted of "rotten teeth and scorbutick gums" and much antemortem loss, "caused by the cold air and their constant diet of salt provisions in the winter."

The low abscess and antemortem loss figures, due in large part to the low caries rate, may reflect the recruit selection process. One document from 1840 indicates that: "Extensive loss of the teeth, particularly the incisors, as they are necessary to mastication, enunciation, and, the incisors especially, to tear cartridges, is a cause for rejection" (Henderson 1840: 16).

As seen in Figure 9.5, abscess and antemortem loss data show a steady increase over time. Due in part to the gradual change in diet, this trend also may reflect the increased use of dentistry in the military. Dental intervention, such as pulling teeth and filling cavities, occurred during the war (Dammann 1984). As more teeth are treated for caries, the chance of them becoming abscessed or pulled increases.

As noted above, the data also may reveal the gradual use of recruit selection procedures, avoiding soldiers with poor oral health and high antemortem loss, and the institution of various types of conscription laws, which allowed wealthier men to bypass the service, forcing poorer men to join in their absence (Lewis 1865; Catton 1985).

Dental attrition, generally slight to moderate in the Snake Hill dentitions, indicates a uniformity in diet and age profile among the sample. The general pattern of wear indicates a moderate rate of attrition reflecting a refined diet. The only evidence of masticatory stress that may indicate influences other than diet is the rapid attrition of central incisor teeth noted in several individuals, possibly due to tearing cartridges.

Conclusions

This brief report has provided general information on the dental health of the Snake Hill soldiers. Comparison with three contemporaneous military skeletal samples has provided a basis for interpreting these data in a temporal context. When compared to men who would go into military service later in the nineteenth century, the Snake Hill soldiers experienced fairly good dental health.

The Snake Hill soldiers, while exhibiting a low incidence of dental caries, also displayed a high incidence of antemortem tooth loss. As a good indicator of diet, the caries rate at Snake Hill suggests that these men were not experiencing a rapid change in the type of foods being consumed. Historical sources recorded that the diet, generally unchanged from that of the soldiers' predecessors, consisted of foods relatively low in cariogenic agents. Examined together, the low caries/high antemortem tooth loss frequencies may indicate that dental extraction was a common method of treating carious teeth. The low incidence of dental abscessing is surprising, given aseptic oral surgery techniques and the poor hygiene of the soldiers. The effect of selecting recruits who had fewer carious, abscessed or missing teeth may reveal itself as lower rates in these categories.

The conclusions of the present investigation into the dental health of the Snake Hill soldiers are tentative. However, until larger data sets become available, this research provided a unique opportunity for interpreting dental disease patterns in an early nineteenth century U.S. military skeletal sample. It is hoped that the excavation, analysis and interpretation of the remains of the Snake Hill soldiers will provide the impetus for future analysis and interpretation of Euroamerican and other historic skeletal samples, thereby providing new insight into the lives of our recent ancestors.

Figure 9.1: Caries Frequency

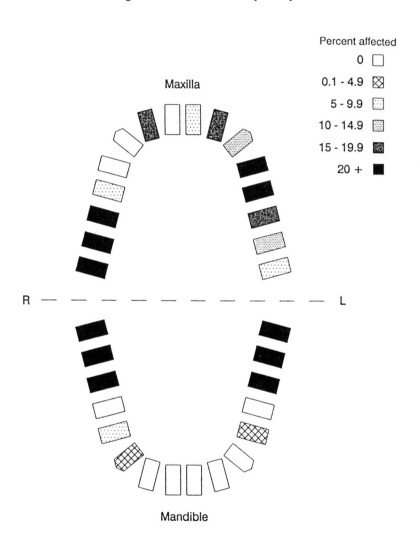

Figure 9.2: Abscess Frequency

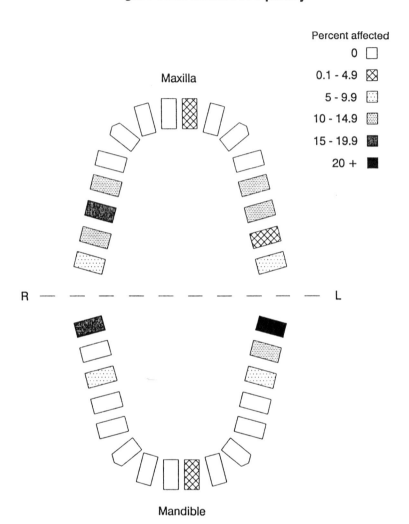

Figure 9.3: Antemortem Loss Frequency

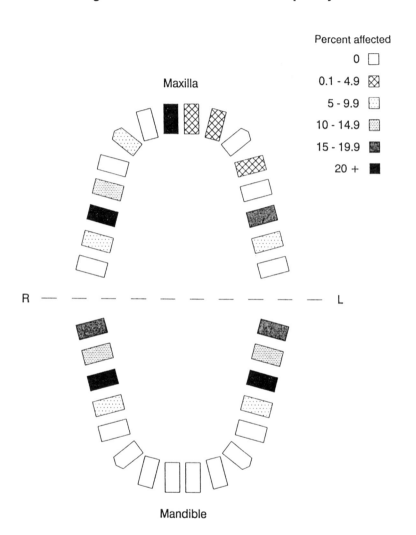

Figure 9.4: Calculus Frequency

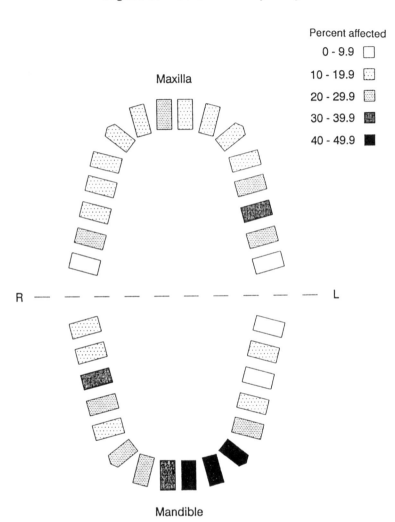

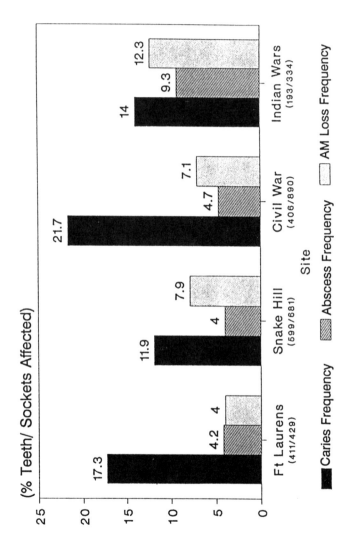

Figure 9.5: Dental Disease (Comparative Data)

Table 9.1: Summary Dental Statistics

	# teeth present	# teeth lost antemortem	# teeth lost postmortem
Maxilla			
I1	32	5	4
I2	37	1	4
C	39	1	1
P1	39	1	1
P2	36	2	2
M1	29	9	0
M2	37	3	0
M3	24	0	2
Total	274	22	14
Mandible			
I1	43	0	4
I2	43	0	4
C	46	0	2
P1	48	0	1
P2	43	4	2
M1	32	16	1
M2	40	6	0
M3	30	6	2
Total	325	32	16
Grand Total	599	54	30

Table 9.2: Frequency Distribution of Carious Permanent Teeth

	# teeth	# carious	%
Maxilla			
I1	32	1	3.1
I2	37	6	16.2
C	39	2	5.1
P1	39	4	10.3
P2	37	6	16.2
M1	29	10	34.5
M2	37	7	18.9
M3	24	4	16.7
Total	274	40	14.6
Mandible			
I1	43	0	0.0
I2	43	0	0.0
C	46	1	2.2
P1	48	3	6.3
P2	43	0	0.0
M1	32	9	28.1
M2	40	11	27.5
M3	30	7	23.3
Total	325	31	9.5
Grand Total	599	71	11.9

Table 9.3: Frequency Distribution of Dental Abscesses

	# tooth sockets	# periapical abscesses	%	# periodontal abscesses	%
Maxilla					
I1	32	1	3.1	0	0.0
I2	37	0	0.0	0	0.0
C	39	0	0.0	0	0.0
P1	39	0	0.0	0	0.0
P2	36	2	5.6	3	8.3
M1	29	1	3.4	3	10.3
M2	37	0	0.0	2	5.4
M3	24	0	0.0	2	8.3
Total	308	4	1.3	10	3.2
Mandible					
I1	43	0	0.0	0	0.0
I2	43	0	0.0	0	0.0
C	46	0	0.0	0	0.0
P1	48	0	0.0	0	0.0
P2	43	0	0.0	0	0.0
M1	32	3	9.4	1	3.1
M2	40	3	7.5	1	2.5
M3	30	3	10.0	2	6.7
Total	373	9	2.4	4	1.1
Grand Total	681	13	1.9	14	2.1

Table 9.4: Frequency of Antemortem Loss

	# tooth sockets	# lost antemortem	%
Maxilla			
I1	32	5	15.6
I2	37	1	2.7
C	39	1	2.6
P1	39	1	2.6
P2	36	2	5.6
M1	29	9	31.0
M2	37	3	8.1
M3	24	0	0.0
Total	308	22	7.1
Mandible			
I1	43	0	0.0
I2	43	0	0.0
C	46	0	0.0
P1	48	0	0.0
P2	43	2	4.7
M1	32	16	50.0
M2	40	6	15.0
M3	30	6	20.0
Total	373	32	8.6
Grand Total	681	54	7.9

Table 9.5: Frequency of Dental Calculus

	# teeth present	# calculus	%
Maxilla			
I1	32	6	18.8
I2	37	6	16.2
C	39	6	15.4
P1	39	6	15.4
P2	37	7	18.9
M1	29	8	27.6
M2	37	9	24.3
M3	24	1	4.2
Total	274	49	17.9
Mandible			
I1	43	16	37.2
I2	43	16	37.2
C	46	16	34.8
P1	48	8	16.7
P2	43	9	20.9
M1	32	6	18.8
M2	40	5	12.5
M3	30	3	10.0
Total	325	79	24.3
Grand Total	599	128	21.4

Table 9.6: Mean Attrition Rates Molar Teeth

Mandible		Maxilla	
Teeth	Rate	Teeth	Rate
LM1/LM2	1.452	LM1/LM2	1.290
LM2/LM3	1.258	LM2/LM3	1.095
LM1/LM3	1.817	LM1/LM3	1.413
RM1/RM2	1.439	RM1/RM2	1.762
RM2/RM3	1.348	RM2/RM3	1.352
RM1/RM3	1.954	RM1/RM3	1.762

Plate 9.1: Burial 5, Enamel Hypoplasias

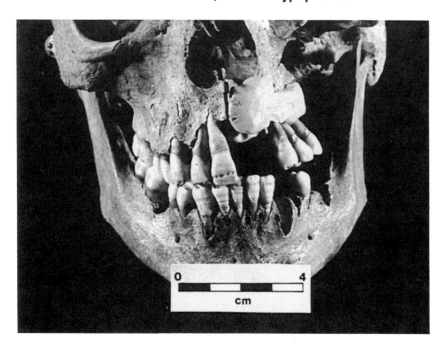

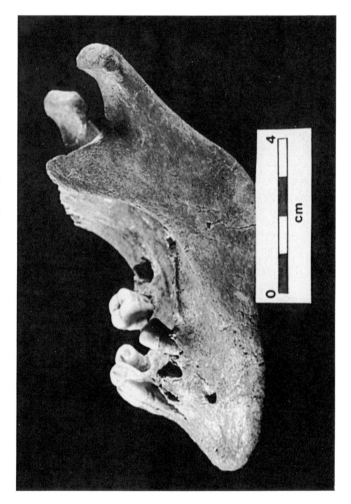

Plate 9.2: Burial 10, Hapsburg Jaw

Ten

Analysis of Stable Isotopes of Carbon and Nitrogen

M. ANNE KATZENBERG

One of the objectives of studying the Snake Hill skeletal remains was to apply a full range of current analytical techniques, in an effort to derive as much information as possible prior to their reinterment. Moreover, identification of the origin of the soldiers constituted one of the principal objectives at the time of initial investigation. The analysis of stable isotopes of carbon and nitrogen can yield relevant information about place of origin. Prehistorians commonly view stable isotope data as useful for reconstructing the diets of prehistoric populations (van der Merwe 1982; DeNiro 1987), but stable isotopes may also be used to reconstruct the place of residence for unidentified human remains (Katzenberg and Krouse 1989). This brief report will describe the variation in carbon and nitrogen stable isotope ratios within a sample of 29 individuals from Snake Hill and will compare the Snake Hill soldiers to native Americans from the Northeast (Schwarcz et al. 1985), and to Europeans (Kennedy, B.V., 1989). This approach addresses the potential for using stable isotopes to aid in the determination of place of residence for unidentified human remains. If the availability of food, and therefore diet, varies geographically, then dietary reconstruction can lead to the deduction of geographic origin.

Background to Stable Isotope Studies

Three isotopes of carbon are found in nature. Approximately 99% of carbon occurs as ^{12}C, 1.1% occurs as ^{13}C, and $10^{-12}\%$ occurs as unstable ^{14}C. The ratio of atoms of ^{13}C to ^{12}C in a sample relative to that ratio in a standard is expressed as $\delta^{13}C$ ‰. The international standard for carbon is a marine fossil

(Belemnitella) from the Peedee geologic formation in South Carolina, referred to as PDB. Because isotopes of an element vary in atomic weight, they react at different rates. Thus, the ratio of ^{13}C to ^{12}C varies from one step to another in chemical reactions. For example, CO_2 in the atmosphere has a $\delta^{13}C$ value of -7 ‰ (Schwarcz 1969). In most temperate zone plant species, the $\delta^{13}C$ value of plant tissues averages -26.5 ‰ (Deines 1980) because the lighter isotope, ^{12}C, is preferentially incorporated during photosynthesis. Other plants, adapted to hot and dry conditions and referred to as C_4 plants, average -12.5 ‰ (Deines 1980) since there is less discrimination against the heavier isotope, ^{13}C. The difference in $\delta^{13}C$ values in plants is retained in human tissues with a shift of approximately +5 ‰ from diet to bone collagen (van der Merwe and Vogel 1978) and +1 ‰ from diet to hair (Tieszen et al. 1983).

Nitrogen isotopes indicate trophic level, and both carbon and nitrogen isotopes may be used to differentiate marine versus terrestrial-based diets (Schoeninger and DeNiro 1984). Individuals consuming legumes have the lowest $\delta^{15}N$ values, followed by terrestrial herbivores, terrestrial carnivores, marine herbivores and marine carnivores. Marine mammals have higher $\delta^{15}N$ values than terrestrial mammals. Human tissues reflect the carbon and nitrogen isotope values of their diets (DeNiro and Epstein 1978; DeNiro 1987). Bone collagen has a slow turnover rate of approximately 10 to 20 years (Stenhouse and Baxter 1979). Its isotope composition thus reflects an individual's general lifetime dietary habits.

In most studies of carbon isotope values in prehistoric populations, results show little variation about the mean values (Table 10.1). Lovell et al. (1986) found little variation in bone isotopic values over 2,000 years at the Gray site in Saskatchewan with one standard deviation of only ±0.3 ‰. A recent study by B.V. Kennedy (1989) of a large number of fifteenth to seventeenth century Europeans, derived from seven different populations, shows minor variation with populations ranging from ±0.2 to 0.4 ‰ for one standard deviation.

Materials and Methods

Rib or other bone fragments from each Snake Hill burial were cleaned ultrasonically, then crushed to a powder. Collagen was extracted following the method described by DeNiro and Epstein (1978). Briefly, the bone mineral is dissolved in 1M hydrochloric acid, humic contaminants are removed by soaking the residue in a weak sodium hydroxide solution. The collagen is then hydrolysed in slightly acidic (pH = 3) hot water (90°C). The remaining solution is reduced, then freeze dried in preparation for analysis by mass spectrometry. Stable nitrogen isotopes were analyzed in the laboratory of Dr. H.P. Schwarcz, Department of Geology, McMaster University. Stable carbon isotopes were analyzed in the laboratory of Dr. H.R. Krouse, Department of Physics, University of Calgary.

Results

With a mean $\delta^{13}C$ value of -15.8 ‰ and a standard deviation of 1.3, results from analysis of the Snake Hill sample show considerably more variation than that reported for most other prehistoric and historic materials (Table 10.1). Historical records indicate that these foot soldiers were drawn from various parts of the northeastern United States. Regional diets varied with respect to staple grains including wheat, rice (both C_3) or maize (C_4). Thus, one would expect less homogeneity in stable isotope values than that seen among prehistoric or early historic samples representing individuals from one settlement. Nitrogen values are similarly dispersed (Figure 10.1).

In the late 1700s, American soldiers may have been American Indians, Americans of European origin and/or recent immigrants from northern Europe. Isotope values from Snake Hill can be compared to those of indigenous North Americans and Europeans for the purpose of determining likely origin. Ideally, contemporaneous populations would be used in such a comparison. However, the data available are from earlier peoples of Europe and North America. These represent people with diets little affected by the exchange of New and Old World cultivated food crops. European grains, wheat, barley and oats, are all C_3 plants while the American cultigen, maize, is C_4. Thus it is not surprising that most of the soldiers, who lived in North America in the late 1700s and early 1800s, show intermediate $\delta^{13}C$ values reflecting reliance on maize, similar to late prehistoric and early historic Ontario Iroquoians characterized by Schwarcz and colleagues (1985) (Figure 10.2). Soldiers who migrated to North America after approximately twelve years of age and died in their late teens or early twenties would reflect a European diet, though some collagen turnover would have occurred.

Figure 10.3 shows $\delta^{13}C$ values ranked in increasing order from top to bottom. European populations reported by B.V. Kennedy (1989) have the most negative values. (Bars represent minimum and maximum $\delta^{13}C$ values for the European samples.) The highest maximum value (least negative) is for the sample from Red Bay, Labrador (rbmax), representing Basque whalers who spent time at sea, in the New World and in Europe. Their $\delta^{13}C$ values are elevated by a high intake of marine foods. The highest maximum value for individuals living mainly in Europe is the sample from the Mary Rose (mrmax), representing a group of British soldiers drawn from many locations throughout England, who died in 1545. Two individuals from Snake Hill, Burials 5 (sh5) and 21 (sh21), are included within the $\delta^{13}C$ range characteristic of Europeans. Kennedy did not report $\delta^{15}N$ values for the European samples so no direct comparison can be made as is done with native Americans in Figure 10.2. Compared to other Snake Hill individuals (Figure 10.1) and to Ontario Iroquoians, Burial 21 has a lower value for $\delta^{15}N$. Burial 5 has the lowest $\delta^{13}C$ value and it is interesting that Lalich and Aufderheide (this volume) found Burial 5 to be particularly high in lead content.

Toward the bottom of the carbon diagram (Figure 10.3) are individual values for Ontario Iroquoians. The most negative values are for individuals from the Cooper Ossuary which dates to circa 1649 and was located along the Grand River in southern Ontario. It is the most recent, and the southernmost of the three Ontario sites included. Snake Hill Burials 20, 1, 28, 25, 29 and 22 fall within the range of the early historic Ontario Iroquoians. Burial 1 has the highest $\delta^{15}N$ value and both Burial 1 and 20 clearly fall within the $\delta^{13}C$ range of native Americans for both carbon and nitrogen (Figure 10.3). Medical Waste Features 22 and 25 and Burials 28 and 29, while heavier than the main cluster for $\delta^{13}C$, fall within the range of other Snake Hill samples for $\delta^{15}N$.

The main cluster of Snake Hill individuals have $\delta^{15}N$ values ranging between 9.6 and 11.8 ‰. Burials 1 and 17 have values of 13.0 and 12.9. A diet high in meat and/or fish and marine foods would explain this. If Burial 1 represents an individual consuming a diet similar to that of native Americans, fish is probably the component which accounts for the high nitrogen value. At the low end of the nitrogen distribution, Burial 21, found with U.S. buttons, may represent a fairly recent European immigrant.

Conclusions

It should not be suggested that an individual is British, or native American, based on stable isotopes alone. However, there is justification in stating that when the diets are similar, place of residence may also be. The interpretation of the isotope results must include other lines of evidence from the skeletal remains. Burial 5, isotopically similar to Europeans, included no buttons characteristic of an American soldier and exhibited dental pathology in the form of hypoplasia of the incisors. Lead content was high and craniometric variables distinguish it from other burials (see other studies in this volume). Burials 1, 4, 20 and 21, all interred in American military garments, fall within the Iroquoian range for both carbon and nitrogen and may have been native American soldiers or non-native soldiers who had depended on a maize or fish dominated diet. Other comparative studies including stature, morphology and pathology, and historical studies have shed further light on these results, as demonstrated elsewhere in this volume.

Figure 10.1: Stable Carbon – Nitrogen Isotope Ratios Plotted for Snake Hill Burials

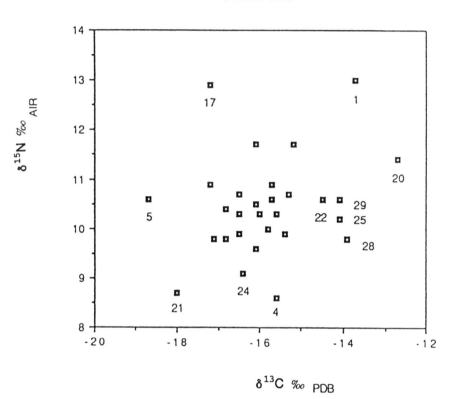

Snake Hill Burials plotted for $\delta^{13}C$ and $\delta^{15}N$ with outliers identified by burial number.

Figure 10.2: Comparisons between Snake Hill Burials and Protohistoric Ontario Iroquoians Using Stable Carbon – Nitrogen Isotope Ratios

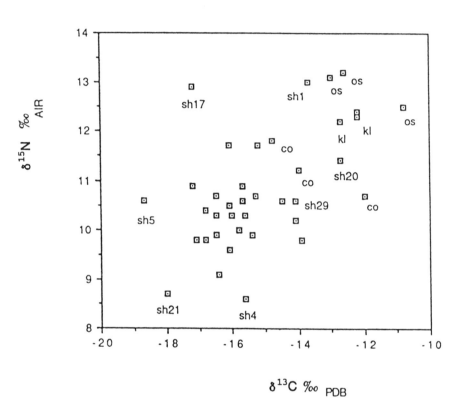

SH = Snake Hill; CO = Cooper Ossuary; OS = Ossossane Ossuary;
KL = Kleinburg Ossuary

Figure 10.3: Stable Carbon Isotope Values for Europeans, Snake Hill Soldiers and Ontario Iroquoians

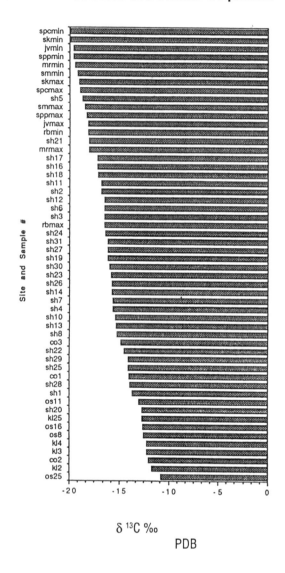

δ ^{13}C ‰

PDB

Europeans are given as minimum and maximum values as reported by B.V. Kennedy (1989) while Snake Hill soldiers and Ontario Iroquois (Schwarcz et al. 1985) values represent individuals.

SH = Snake Hill; CO = Cooper Ossuary; OS = Ossossane Ossuary; KL = Kleinburg Ossuary; all "max" and "min" values = Europeans

Table 10.1: Variation in Carbon Isotope Values in Selected Polulations

Site	Mean	(‰)	s.d.	Ref.
Varden	8	-19.4	0.2	1
Mary Rose	9	-19.1	0.2	2
Saint-Pier	35	-19.0	0.3	2
Gray	50	-17.5	0.3	3
Red Bay	23	-17.2	0.4	2
Miller	5	-13.9	0.9	1
Ball	5	-12.6	1.0	4
Snake Hill	29	-15.8	1.3	5

References

1. Katzenberg et al., in progress
2. B.V. Kennedy, 1989
3. Lovell et al., 1986
4. Schwarcz et al., 1985
5. this study

Eleven   # Lead Exposure

LEANNE LALICH
ARTHUR C. AUFDERHEIDE

In appropriate circumstances the prediction of a variety of human characteristics, including occupation and/or socio-economic status from the lead
content of archaeological skeletal tissue may be useful (Aufderheide et al.
1988). Depending on an individual's occupation or socio-economic status,
lead exposure could come from lead ore processing, use of lead products or
the inhalation or ingestion of lead-contaminated air, foods, or beverages
(Aufderheide et al. 1981; Aufderheide et al. 1985). This is possible because
of the poor ability of the body to excrete absorbed lead, which is then retained and stored primarily in the skeleton (Aufderheide et al. 1981). Con-
tinuous exposure to and absorption of lead results in progressive accumulation of this metal in the bone, the amount of which is a reflection of total
lifetime exposure to lead (Wittmers et al. 1988). Since the natural, unpol-
luted environment is essentially lead-free, the retained bone lead is a reflection of exposure to anthropogenic lead-related activities.

Another application of lead concentration in bone deals with the prediction of health effects due to lead exposure. Clinical symptoms may be determined through a quantitative relationship between bone and blood lead concentrations. Experience with simultaneous bone and blood lead levels in
living individuals has permitted derivation of a mathematical relationship
between these two (Christofferson et al. 1984), which is useful in the prediction of blood level concentrations from analyzed bone lead content values. Calculated blood lead values can then be employed to predict the associated clinical symptoms (Handler et al. 1986).

In the Colonial Era, certain subgroups of the population were exposed to lead in dramatically different ways, and their bone lead content reflected these differences. Wealthy Colonial Americans were exposed to lead in their everyday life, especially in utensils relating to food. Lead-lined containers were used in food storage and preparation, and pewter dishes and flatware were used for eating. On the other hand, black slaves did not have this access to lead, because they were socially and physically separated from their owners. Consequently, lead analysis on the slaves' bones identified substantially lower concentrations than those of their white owners. Therefore, it became evident that lead absorbed and stored in the bones of Colonial Americans correlated with wealth (Aufderheide et al. 1988).

Even the apparent exceptions to this established relationship can be particularly informative. For example, a black female slave might have had domestic duties in the owner's quarters, thus having exposure to lead through sharing in the consumption of the owner's lead-contaminated food and beverages. Although she would not have been wealthy, her bone lead concentration would been elevated, predictive of her unique occupational assignment. In a few cases, whites have been excavated from the slaves' burial grounds with bone lead content at the slaves' level. This might be explained as an indentured servant who died on the plantation while working off his debts (Aufderheide et al. 1981).

Material and Methods

In this case, the skeletal tissues of 27 individuals were tested for lead content. Full cortical thickness samples of bone from the mid-diaphysis of the femur were used. Following mechanical cleaning of these sections, the bones were dried for 24 hours at 110°C, then ashed at 425°C. After the samples were crushed to a fine powder in a mortar, 25 mg of each were then dissolved in 5 mL of nitric acid and diluted with 1 mL of triple distilled water; lanthanum oxide was also added to the solution to suppress matrix effects. The concentration of lead was then determined using the graphite furnace method of atomic absorption spectrometry. Throughout this procedure, all glassware was acid cleaned with nitric acid (Wittmers et al. 1981). In addition, soil samples related to nine of the burials were also available for analysis. They were extracted with nitric acid and their lead content was analyzed in a manner similar to that of the bone samples.

Results

The individual lead concentration values are itemized in Table 11.1 and illustrated in Figure 11.1. The mean lead content of the 27 individuals was 31.3 micrograms per gram ash. These men had values ranging from 7.5 to 113.1. The two high values of 82.9 and 113.1 (Burials 5 and 20, respectively) were considered outliers. The mean age of these soldiers was only 25.5 years. Because the majority of these clustered within the narrow, young adult range between 20 and 35, one would expect only a weakly-demonstrable age relationship to bone lead content. Indeed, a regression line addressing these two variables has such a gentle slope and wide scatter, it is apparent that unique, individualized lead exposure, not age, is the principal determinant.

Discussion

From the concentrations of lead found in the soldiers' skeletal tissue, conclusions about their background may be hypothesized. All but the two outliers have relatively low amounts of lead in their bones, about equal to the levels commonly seen in plantation slaves or modern North American (Aufderheide et al. 1981; Wittmers et al. 1988). From this observation, it can be deduced that this particular group of military recruits came from lower socio-economic levels.

Since certain occupations sometimes account for unusually high values, the increased lead exposure in the two soldiers with very high lead values may reflect permanent military careers. More likely, their youth suggests they may have been from wealthier families or were engaged in some lead-related occupation before entering the military service. Because of their frequently better educational background, officers in hastily recruited Colonial troops were often selected from higher socio-economic families, and the high bone lead content in these two may be signaling this.

In terms of health effects due to lead exposure, most of these individuals were probably exempt from symptoms. The mean calculated blood lead value was 20.9 micrograms per deciliter (Handler et al. 1986), which is within the asymptomatic range (Table 11.2). Such values below 40 are rarely accompanied by clinical symptoms, those between 40 and 80 occasionally, while blood lead levels above 80 micrograms per deciliter demonstrate toxic effects more frequently, depending upon the extent of elevation. A few of the individuals might have experienced nausea or appetite loss, but nothing sufficiently severe to deter them from their duties. Only the two outliers, who may have been from wealthier families than the rest of the soldiers, might have been suffering occasional episodes of muscle weakness, abdominal colic, or partial nerve paralysis form lead poisoning (Hernberg 1980).

An important issue to be addressed when discussing trace elements in skeletal tissue is diagenesis or postmortem change. Under some circumstances, an interred bone may undergo exchange of lead ions with those in the ground water. On occasion this may be of a degree sufficient to obscure the antemortem lead pattern in the buried skeletal tissue (Waldron 1981). Several observations suggest that such diagenetic lead movement, if present at all in this study, is probably not of an order of magnitude to impair appropriate interpretations of the analytical values.

First, the soil lead content is almost uniformly lower than that of the bones. Another point disproving diagenesis in this case relates to the relative burial location of the soldiers. When the lead values were placed on the burial map where each set of bones was found, the outliers were found on opposite sides of the cemetery. The map was also divided into north/south and east/west sections. In each comparison, the mean lead values were similar. Since the individuals with high and low values were evenly distributed, diagenesis doesn't seem to have affected any particular group of bones. In addition, there is no statistically significant correlation between the lead content of the individual bones and that of the soil in which the bones were found.

Conclusions

During the Colonial Era, lead products were a popular symbol of wealth. Constant exposure to this toxic metal, however, causes an increased concentration of lead in the skeletal tissues. Through analyzing bone samples, background information about individuals' socio-economic status can be derived. The majority of the soldiers did not contain excessive amounts of lead in their bones, indicating they probably were recruited from the lower socio-economic segments of the civilian population. The two exceptions to this general pattern conceivably could represent noncommissioned officers selected from well-to-do families. Only the latter two contained enough lead to have put them at risk for intermittent symptoms of lead intoxication.

Partial support for these studies was provided by the National Science Foundation's Research Experiences for Undergraduates site award (Grant No. 8900039), entitled "Training Program in Biosocial Adaptation: Assessment of Paleonutritional Techniques."

Figure 11.1: Scattergram of Bone Lead Concentrations Plotted against Age at Death

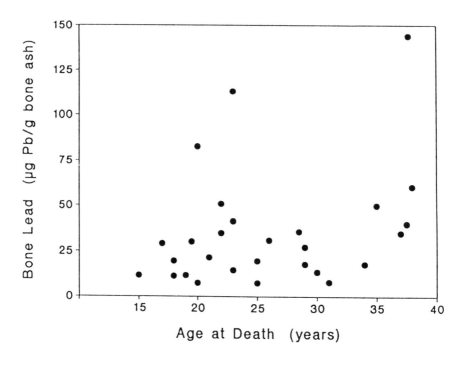

Table 11.1: Bone Lead Concentrations

Estimated Age	Burial Number	Bone Lead μg Pb/g (ash)	Blood Pb μg Pb/dL	Soil Lead μg Pb/g
22-24	1	41.4	30.5	
24-26	2	7.5	5.5	9.8
17-19	3	19.8	28.8	10.5
28-32	4	13.7	8.0	
19-21	5	82.9	69.5	
14-16	6	11.8	13.5	21.8
36-38	7	34.9	16.2	19.6
19-21	8	7.5	6.7	30.9
37-39	10	60.3	26.9	10.5
28-30	11	17.9	10.7	
21-23	12	34.9	26.9	
33-35	13	17.9	9.2	
35-40	14	40.1	18.2	
20-22	15	21.7	17.7	
17-19	16	11.3	10.9	
30-32	17	8.0	4.8	
24-28	18	31.1	20.4	6.0
22-24	19	14.6	11.0	
22-24	20	113.1	82.4	
16-18	21	29.2	29.1	
19-20	23	30.2	25.6	
27-30	24	35.8	22.4	
28-30	26	27.3	16.1	1.5
21-23	27	50.9	39.0	13.5
18-20	28	11.8	10.8	
25+	29	19.8	13.6	
35+	30	49.9	22.6	

Table 11.2: General Relationship of Blood Lead Level to Severity of Three Signs or Symptoms of Lead Intoxication

Organ	Sign or symptom	0-39	40-79	80-119	120-199	Over 200
Intestinal tract	Colic	None	Appetite loss; nausea	Vomiting; constipation; colic	Frequent severe colic	Colic with muscle spasm
Nerves	Palsy	None	None	Weakness in extensor muscles	Marked weakness or paralysis	Extensor muscle paralysis common
Brain	Convulsion	None	None	Occasional	Common	Life threatening; coma

Individuals vary considerably in the correlation between symptoms and blood lead levels. This is a function of age and the fact that blood lead levels fluctuate more rapidly than tissue lead concentrations. Values in this table should be viewed as approximations.

This table reprinted with permission of Duke University Press:

Handler, Jerome et al.
1986   Lead Contact and Poisoning in Barbados. In Slaves: Historical, Chemical and Biological Evidence. *Social Science History* 10:399-425.

Twelve
Oxygen Isotopic Analysis as an Indicator of Place of Origin

HENRY P. SCHWARCZ

LINDA GIBBS

MARTIN KNYF

Introduction

The ratio of the stable isotopes of oxygen, $^{18}O/^{16}O$, varies slightly as a function of the source of the oxygen. For example, a sample of rain from the Arctic will have a lower $^{18}O/^{16}O$ ratio than that of rain from the tropics. Similar variations are found in all natural materials, including human bones and tissues. It is possible to measure these slight variations in isotope ratio and to use them as "fingerprints" to identify the source of the material.

Variations in the $^{18}O/^{16}O$ of bone phosphate have been studied by Luz et al. (1984) and by Luz and Kolodny (1985). These authors found that the $^{18}O/^{16}O$ ratio of bone was principally determined by the isotope ratio in sources of dietary water, through their effect on the $^{18}O/^{16}O$ of body fluid (plasma). It is well known that the $^{18}O/^{16}O$ of meteoric precipitation (rain, snow) varies geographically and, in particular, decreases with increasing distance from the sea, with decreasing temperature, and with increasing elevation. These three effects account for most of the natural variation in $^{18}O/^{16}O$. The result is that the $^{18}O/^{16}O$ in the bone phosphate of any mammal living in North America can be roughly predicted from its geographic location, since the $^{18}O/^{16}O$ ratio of local precipitation on this continent has been mapped (Taylor 1979). However, the precise relation between the $^{18}O/^{16}O$ of local water and that for bone varies for each particular mammalian species (Luz et al. 1990), and is known only approximately for humans.

Nevertheless, we may be able to gain some insight into the place of origin of human skeletal remains from their $^{18}O/^{16}O$ ratio. This paper represents a preliminary attempt to do this, using the Snake Hill burials as a test case. While the results are as yet rather inconclusive, we can make some preliminary statements about place of origin that show the potential value of the method.

Methodology

The samples of bone from Snake Hill consisted of a few milligrams from each of the burials. In addition we have access to archaeological samples of humans of known origin, that is, burials of individuals who were known to have lived and died in the region in which they were found buried. These control samples were provided by Dr. S. Saunders, McMaster University.

The standard method of analysis of oxygen isotopes in phosphate has been described by Tudge (1960). The method requires several days for the preparation of pure bismuth phosphate from each bone sample. At the suggestion of Dr. J.R. O'Neil and P. Koch (University of Michigan) we attempted to bypass this complex and tedious procedure, to arrive at a more direct method of sample preparation.

Samples of bone weighing from 10 to 20 mg were first soaked in concentrated H_2O_2 (hydrogen peroxide) for up to two weeks, until no further reaction (bubbling) was observed. Then the bones were dissolved in nitric acid, and filtered; the insoluble portion was discarded. Bismuth nitrate heated to 80°C was added to the filtrate which was also heated to 80°C until a precipitate of bismuth phosphate formed. This was washed, dried and then vacuum roasted at 450°C. The powder was then reacted at 125°C with bromine pentafluoride (BrF_5), to produce oxygen, which was then converted to carbon dioxide and analysed on a mass spectrometer. The $^{18}O/^{16}O$ ratios are stated in terms of the $\delta^{18}O$ notation, giving the deviation (positive or negative) of the $^{18}O/^{16}O$ ratio from that of a standard SMOW (Standard Mean Ocean Water), in units of per mil (‰). The precision of single analyses is about ±0.5 ‰.

It was found in the course of this study that it was extremely difficult to obtain accurate analyses of phosphate by this means, and we attempted to refine the method in various ways. The present data set is, however, still flawed by problems of analysis, and we expect that in a later publication we shall be able to make a more definitive statement.

Previous work

There are only a few scattered analyses of human teeth and bones in the literature (Luz et al., 1984). These show that $\delta^{18}O$ of phosphate (which we shall call δ_p) is related to that of water, δ_w, by the relation:

$$\delta_p = 0.78 \, \delta_w + 22.7 \qquad (1)$$

If we assume that this is a universal relationship, then we can use it to estimate the origin of humans of a given δ_p based on the local δ_w. Unfortunately, we find that the expected values of δ_p from this equation are significantly higher than those observed in this study. Nevertheless, we note that in central Ontario we observe δ_w values of about -9 ‰ while, near the Gulf of Mexico or on the southeast Atlantic seaboard, δ_w = -3 ‰. The precision of analysis is such that we should be able to resolve major differences in region of origin. The best reported precision for analyses of δ_p is about ±0.1 ‰, i.e., <2% of the expected range in δ_p values.

It is also important to note that the oxygen isotope ratio of bone phosphate is established at the time that the bone is first mineralized (Luz et al. 1984). Subsequently, through the lifetime of the individual, no change in δ_p is expected unless there is significant remodeling of the bone. Any phosphate crystals laid down in bone will preserve their $^{18}O/^{16}O$ ratio even if the body fluid changes in isotopic composition as a result of change in the environment of the host individual. It has also been found that bone phosphate is extremely resistant to isotopic alteration after burial. It should therefore preserve its original $\delta^{18}O$ value in fossil human remains.

Experimental Results and Discussion

The data obtained so far are summarized in Table 12.1A. (Analyses of all the burials are under way, and will be reported later). The total range of the δ_p values is very small, not much larger than the precision of analysis of a single individual. This range is much smaller than the potential range for individuals living in northeastern North America. Thus, these data tend to suggest that all the buried individuals analyzed thus far lived the majority of their lives in the same restricted region.

Conversion of these data to δ_w values using equation (1) gives a value of -13.0±0.3 ‰. Water with this isotopic composition is typical of the subarctic regions of Canada, suggesting that either the correlation obtained by Luz et al. (1984) is inappropriate for this population, or there is a significant error in our estimates of δ_p.

For comparison, in Table 12.1B we present analyses of some individuals from elsewhere in North America. Two southwest Ontario burials give δ_p values of 12.1 ‰, only slightly lower than the Snake Hill average. These data suggest that the relationship given by Luz et al. (1984) is not applicable here, since the calculated δ_w values would be much lower than observed in Southwestern Ontario. Luz et al. (1989) have subsequently shown that local relative humidity also has a large influence on δ_p of bone phosphate of herbivores (e.g., deer). Humidity also may have some influence on human bone phosphate, although humans would be less strongly influenced since, unlike herbivores, most of their water intake is from drinking or from liquid water admixed with foods.

From the map of δ_w values (Figure 12.1), it may be seen that the contours of equal δ_w shift slightly southward as one goes to the east of Ontario, into New England. This is principally the result of higher elevations in the Appalachian region, leading on average to lower $\delta^{18}O$ values for precipitation. The difference between the Snake Hill data and the Southwestern Ontario reference population is in the direction that would be expected if the Snake Hill individuals came from eastern New York, Pennyslvania, or most parts of New England.

A single individual from a cemetery in Antietam, Maryland, gave a δ_p value approximately 0.6 ‰ higher than the Snake Hill data and 1 ‰ higher than Southwestern Ontario. This offset is in the correct sense but not as large as would be expected for a native of this region. Note, however, that the individual was a Civil War casualty who may have lived most of his life elsewhere in the southeastern United States.

Conclusions

Although these data are clearly very preliminary, they show that the $\delta^{18}O$ values of bone phosphate from the Snake Hill individuals are very uniform. This suggests that the members of this group had all spent the major part of their lives living in the same geographical region. Comparison with a limited reference set suggests that the Snake Hill individuals could have originated in the northeastern United States, and that they are somewhat more ^{18}O-enriched than would be expected for natives of Ontario.

Note

This research was supported by a grant from the Natural Sciences and Engineering Research Council to Henry P. Schwarz.

Figure 12.1: Distribution of $^{18}O/^{16}O$ Isotope Values in Atmospheric Precipitation over North America

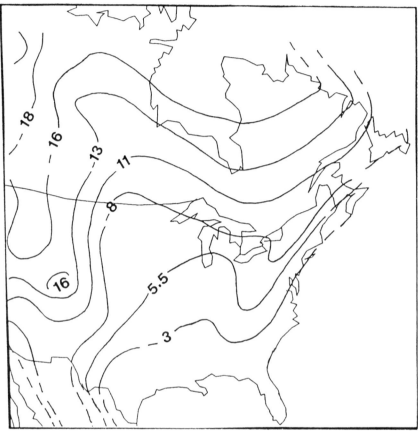

Based on contours of deuterium enrichment from Taylor (1979), and converted to $^{18}O/^{16}O$ isotope values using the equation of Yurtsever and Gat (1981).

Table 12.1: Oxygen Isotope Data for Bone Phosphates

A. Snake Hill Burials

Number	$\delta^{18}O$ (‰, SMOW)
4	12.14
8	12.70
14	12.60
23	12.37
24	12.89
30	12.65
average	12.56±0.26

B. Reference samples

Southwestern Ontario

HB 11	12.15
MB 7	12.17

Antietam, Maryland, USA

ANTIE 4	13.18

Thirteen **Craniometric Variation**

PEER H. MOORE-JANSEN
RICHARD L. JANTZ

Introduction

Anthropologists have a long tradition of seeking insights into human evolution through the study of ancient human remains. However the excavaton and analyses of skeletons of recent human populations yield valuable information as well. Recent skeletal samples offer opportunities to test current analytical approaches, since historical information about health, nutrition and population structure frequently exists. The Snake Hill crania give us the opportunity to extend our knowledge of cranial variation among American populations over the past two centuries. Cranial measurements can give us information about variation and change in the size and shape of the head and face. When there appears to be a directional change over time (presumably non-genetic), we refer to it as a "secular trend." Among human populations there are many examples of a secular trend for increased body size. We know very little, however, about possible secular trends in the size or shape of the face and head. Comparison of measurements taken on Snake Hill crania, compared to those of earlier and later times, may demonstrate such trends.

Materials and Methods

For this comparative analysis, a two-pronged strategy was adopted. The Snake Hill crania were measured using an extensive battery of measurements which we devised. The best, most complete comparative data come from cranial series also measured using the same system, preferably by the same researchers. The numerous measurements in this system can be lumped into three categories: measures of depth, height and width (or forward projection). The various measurements will not be individually described here, since our purpose is to analyze differences in overall shape. The interested reader can find thorough descriptions in Howells (1973). The general orientation of several of our measurements is illustrated in Figure 13.1. A key to the abbreviations is found in Table 13.1.

At present, the series with complete sets of measurements consist of modern forensic cases and of late nineteenth century/early twentieth century crania from the Terry and Todd anatomical collections. They will therefore form our basis for initial comparison. These crania were divided into two samples: an early one consisting of people born prior to 1930 (Terry-Todd) and a more recent one consisting of people born after 1930. This recent group is derived from forensic cases incorporated in the data base at the University of Tennessee, and is here designated as the Tennessee Forensic sample (Table 13.2). The initial strategy was to carry out a comprehensive comparison of Snake Hill crania with the pre- and post-1930 series. The pre-1930 series has an average data of birth of about 1890, post-dating Snake Hill by about 80 years. The average date of birth of the post-1930 series is about 1954, making them nearly 175 years later than Snake Hill.

The second strategy was to compare the Snake Hill crania to a larger number of samples, some of which were more or less contemporary. This comparison relies on data from literary sources, which in turn constrain the number and type of measurements that can be used for comparison. Three samples were identified which could be added to the comparative framework (Table 13.2). These include: the historic Farrington street series, a seventeenth century, probably lower class London cemetery (Hooke 1926); the Nagel series, a New York city cemetery in use during the eighteenth and early nineteenth century (Shapiro 1930); and J.L. Angel's (1976) series of Colonial to Civil war crania, dating from 1675 to 1870. The series compiled by Angel is probably the most heterogenous, with skeletons drawn from populations differing in time and space. There are 10 measurements common to all these samples. The means for each of these measurements are shown in Table 13.3.

Results

The first step was to get a general impression of Snake Hill cranial measurement profiles in relation to our pre- and post-1930 series. To accomplish this, Z-score profiles were used. A Z-score, also known as a standardized value, is the observed value minus the mean value, divided by the standard deviation of the values. Using Z-scores allows us to compare things that differ in their variability. The standardized Z variable will have a mean of zero and a standard deviation of 1. For convenience, measurements of height, width and depth were examined separately. Figure 13.2 shows the depth measurement Z-score profiles comparing Snake Hill to the Terry-Todd and Tennessee Forensic sample. All of these dimensions measure facial projections from basion (the cranial base), or from the transmeatal axis. In all depth dimensions, Snake Hill possesses the smallest values, the Forensic series the largest, and Terry-Todd is intermediate. The temporal arrangement of the samples suggests a secular trend toward increasing facial projection.

Figure 13.3 shows the Z-score profiles for cranial heights. The first three are vault (brain case) heights, the last three are face heights. In all except nasal height, the Tennessee Forensic sample exceeds the Terry-Todd sample. Snake Hill presents a variable pattern for the vault height dimensions. The measurement of basion-bregma (total vault height) is intermediate. The intermediate position is achieved by a low upper vault dimension and a high base height value. The Snake Hill face height dimensions are uniformly and strikingly lower than either of the comparative series.

Figure 13.4 shows the Z-score profiles for the width dimensions. Patterns are not as distinct as they are for depths and heights, but the Terry-Todd sample is slightly wider than the Tennessee Forensic sample. Snake Hill crania are the narrowest in all dimensions but one, maximum frontal breadth.

The next step in the analysis was designed to statistically place the Snake Hill crania in relation to the Terry-Todd and Tennessee Forensic samples. We used these two groups to estimate several discriminant functions. Discriminant analysis is a statistical technique that distinguishes among groups of cases in a manner that incorporates many variables (measurements, in this case), yet controls for relationships among those variables. The results for the best, eight variable model are presented in Table 13.4, which shows the variables that are incorporated and the discriminant coefficients. Variables reflecting vault height, base height, vault breadth, face height and face breadth are all involved. This function correctly classifies 156/166 crania from the groups, making it 94% effective.

Classifying the Snake Hill crania on this function demonstrates the considerable variability found among them. Table 13.5 shows the classification statistics for the five crania. Three crania are found to be more similar to the Forensic sample and two classify with the Terry-Todd sample. Overall, the Snake Hill sample is about equidistant from the two samples, but slightly closer to the recent Forensic one.

With respect to the broader relationships of the Snake Hill sample, statistical population distances were calculated among all of the six samples mentioned earlier. Figure 13.5 shows the intergroup distances arrayed on the first two principal coordinates. These two coordinates account for 82% of the among-group variation. It is apparent that both Snake Hill and Farrington Street are different from each other and from the other samples. The Tennessee Forensic sample is also somewhat distinct. The Nagel, Angel and Terry-Todd samples form a central cluster.

Separation along the first axis is achieved primarily by the face height and vault breadth dimensions, all of which differentiate Snake Hill from the other samples. Separation along the second axis is achieved primarily by vault height (BBH) and base length (BNL). One can discern temporal ordering of the samples along the second principal components axis (PCII). This was further explored by plotting PCII against the median date of each sample and calculating the regression. Figure 13.6 shows the temporal patterning clearly. The regression of PCII on date is statistically significant.

Discussion

Our analysis shows the Snake Hill crania to be different from later crania in a number of respects. They are smaller in most dimensions, indicating a smaller cranium generally. Snake Hill crania also differ from all other samples in breadth and facial height dimensions. The narrow Snake Hill vaults might be partly explained by the fact that they are the crania of very young adults. It has recently been shown that adult face and vault widths increase with age (Moore-Jansen and Jantz 1989). An appropriate age correction might reduce the width difference between Snake Hill and the other series.

The relevance of this work is in exploring the plasticity of the human skeleton through time and looking for changes in skeletal size and shape that appear from one generation to the next – or "secular trends." The secular changes demonstrated by all the samples studied here involve increasing facial projection and increasing vault height. The Snake Hill crania fall into line in this regard. Does the secular change agree with that identified in other studies? Until recently there has been relatively little information available concerning secular changes in cranial size and shape among modern and recent historic populations (Moore-Janson 1989). Smith, Garn and Hunter (1986) report on a two generational study of head dimension in which sons were compared to fathers and daughters to mothers. They identified a clear increase in the anterior-posterior dimension, averaging almost 0.4 standard deviations. They also detected some increase in vault height, and perhaps slight decreases in facial widths.

Our results agree with those of Smith, Garn and Hunter, in that the most convincing direction of secular change is in the anterior-posterior direction, examined here through measurements of cranial depths. We have also documented possible secular change in cranial heights. The study by Smith, Garn and Hunter represents two recent generations. Our results suggest that these secular trends are long term and have continued for the last 200 years.

Figure 13.1: Orientation of Several Cranial Measurements

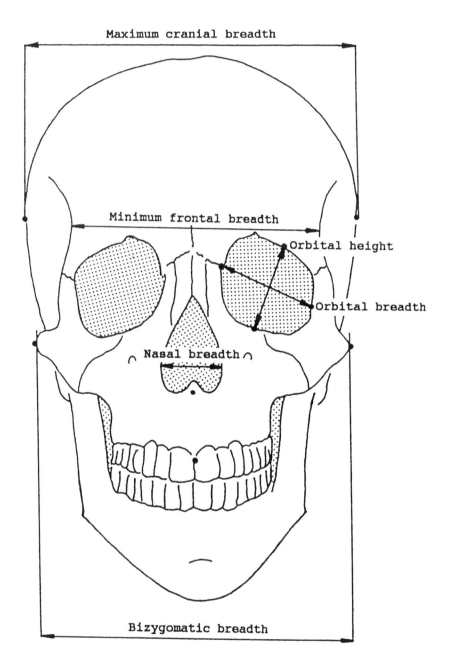

Figure 13.2: Comparison of Z-score Profiles of Male Cranial Depths

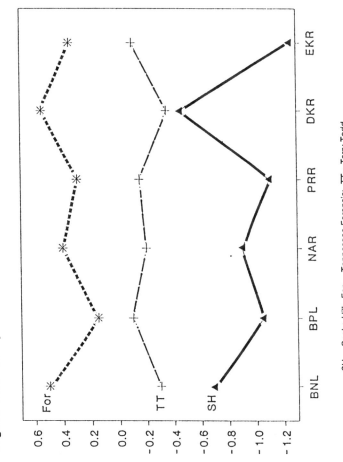

SH = Snake Hill;   For = Tennessee Forensic;   TT= Terry-Todd

BNL = basion-nasion length; BPL = basion-prosthion length; NAR = nasion radius;
PRR = prosthion radius; DKR = dacryon radius; EKR = ectoconchion radius

Figure 13.3: Comparison of Z-score Profiles of Male Cranial Heights

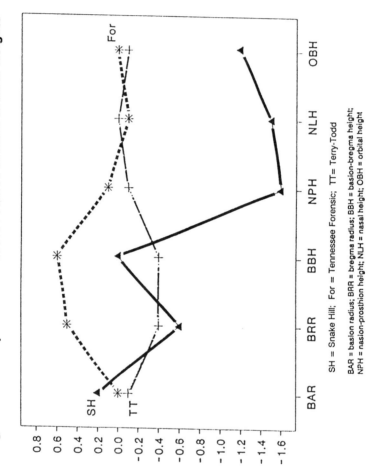

SH = Snake Hill;   For = Tennessee Forensic;   TT= Terry-Todd

BAR = basion radius; BRR = bregma radius; BBH = basion-bregma height;
NPH = nasion-prosthion height; NLH = nasal height; OBH = orbital height

Figure 13.4: Comparison of Z-score Profiles of Male Cranial Breadths

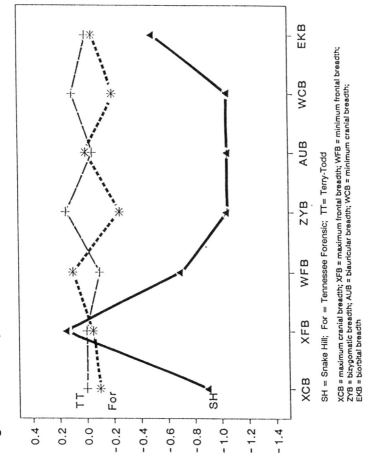

SH = Snake Hill; For = Tennessee Forensic; TT= Terry-Todd

XCB = maximum cranial breadth; XFB = maximum frontal breadth; WFB = minimum frontal breadth;
ZYB = bizygomatic breadth; AUB = biauricular breadth; WCB = minimum cranial breadth;
EKB = biorbital breadth

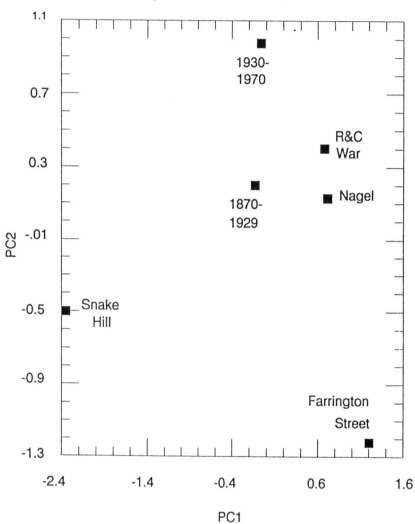

Figure 13.5: PC1 vs PC2

Statistical intergroup population distances arrayed on the first two principal coordinates.

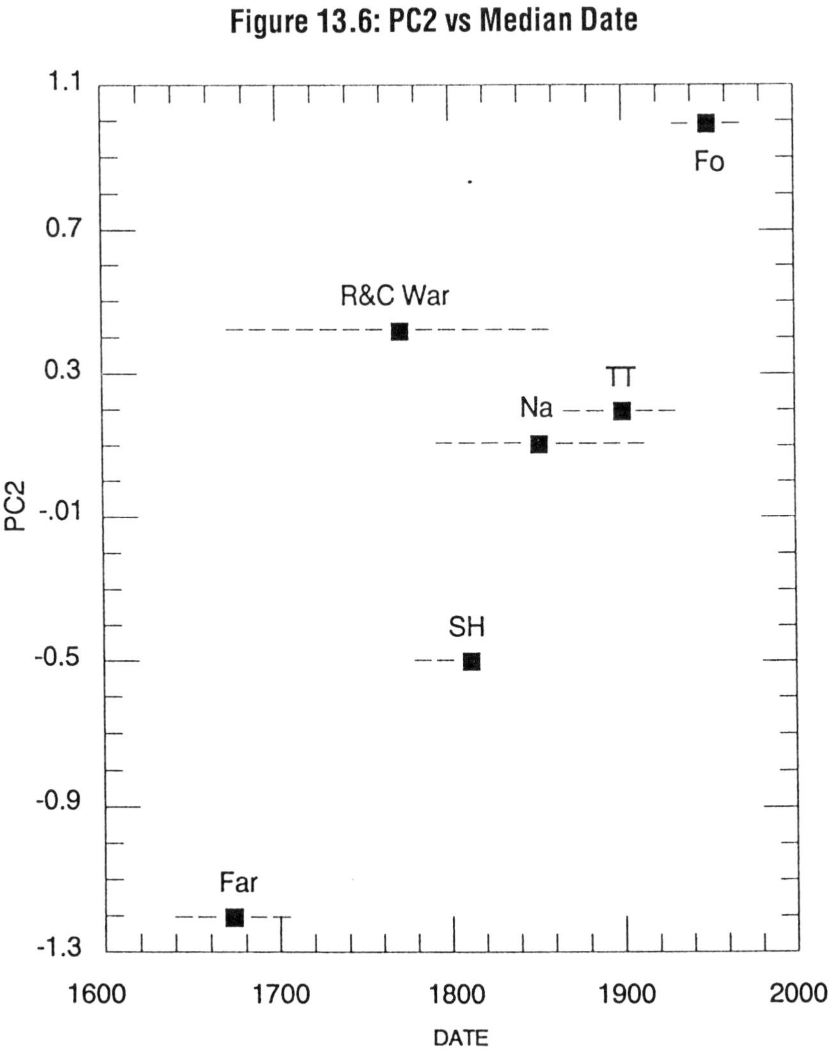

Figure 13.6: PC2 vs Median Date

Plotting of PC2 against the the median date of each sample demonstrating the temporal order of the sites.

SH = Snake Hill; Far = Farrington Street; For = Tennessee Forensic;
Na = Nagel; R & C War = Colonial to Civil War; TT = Terry-Todd

Table 13.1: Key to Measurement Abbreviations
(for Chapter 13 tables and figures)

AUB	biauricular breadth
BAR	basion radius
BBH	basion-bregma height
BNL	basion-nasion length
BPL	basion-prosthion length
BRR	bregma radius
DKR	dacryon radius
DKS	dacryon subtense
EKB	biorbital breadth
EKR	ectoconchion radius
GOL	maximum cranial length
MDH	mastoid height
NAR	nasion radius
NLB	nasal breadth
NLH	nasal height
NPH	nasion-prosthion height
OBB	orbital breadth
OBH	orbital height
PAC	bregma-lambda chord
PRR	prosthion radius
WCB	minimum cranial breadth
WFB	minimum frontal breadth
XCB	maximum cranial breadth
XFB	maximum frontal breadth
ZYB	bizygomatic breadth

Table 13.2: Male Cranial Series Used in This Study

GROUP	N	DATE
Snake Hill	5	1814
Tennessee Forensic	59	1930-1970
Terry-Todd	101	1870-1929
Nagel	ca. 13	1790-1908
Farringdon St.	ca. 100	1675-1879
Colonial to Civil War	ca. 30	1675-1879

Table 13.3: Means for Measurements in Six Cranial Samples

	Terry-Todd	Tennessee Forensic	Snake Hill	Nagel	Farrington Street	Colonial to Civil War
GOL	183	187	185	188	189	187
BNL	101	105	99	102	100	103
BBH	134	141	136	136	130	138
XCB	142	141	137	144	142	142
WCB	97	98	93	98	97	97
BPL	95	97	89	96	94	94
NPH	69	70	63	72	71	72
NLH	53	52	48	52	52	52
NLB	24	24	22	24	25	24
OBH	33	33	31	32	34	35

Table 13.4: Best 8 Measurement Function for Pre- and Post-1930 Samples

BBH	-0.4559
WCB	0.3150
MDH	-0.4249
OBB	-1.6453
EKB	0.4425
DKS	0.7024
PAC	0.1838
BAR	0.3852
CONSTANT	36.1383

Table 13.5: Classification of Snake Hill Crania

	DSQ from			
	Pre-1930	Post-1930	Score	Class
Burial 2	2.432	1.698	-0.367	Post
Burial 5	0.996	14.907	6.955	Pre
Burial 13	5.657	0.235	-2.712	Post
Burial 27	1.849	2.259	0.205	Pre
Burial 28	3.534	0.996	-1.284	Post

Fourteen

The Ox Burial

STEPHEN C. THOMAS

Introduction

Without a well developed supply system, a large scale military campaign such as the Fort Erie operation, would have been impossible. It took an immense effort to keep the armies fed, to keep the weapons firing, and to evacuate the casualties. Animal traction was the energy source upon which land forces of both sides relied. This was as true during the Napoleonic Period as it had been throughout most of military history. Although oxen lack the speed of horses, they possess superior strength and endurance and require less forage. The Snake Hill ox is historically significant because it represented an important component of the military technology of the day. Moreover, it also provides an opportunity to learn about animal husbandry in early nineteenth century North America.

Zooarchaeology, or faunal analysis, is the branch of archaeology that seeks to derive information about past human behaviour and environments from the study of animal remains in archaeological deposits. In contrast to biological anthropology, zooarchaeology deals with a multitude of species, and, consequently, draws on the literature of zoology, paleontology, veterinary medicine, wildlife management and related fields. Anatomical terminology used by faunal analysts reflects this difference in subject matter.

Basic areas of investigation include determination of an animal's age at death, health status, analysis of physical trauma and physical size and shape. The fundamental objective was to ascertain whether the Snake Hill ox was a military draft animal, or simply a farm animal buried by chance near a forgotten military cemetery. During life, the ox's skeleton changed in response to various environmental factors including human culture. From traces of human activities left on the individual bones and from the state of the skeleton as a whole, we were able to reconstruct certain aspects of its life on the American frontier during the Niagara Campaign of 1814 and detemine its manner of death. The species *Bos taurus* continues to change over time under the constraint of culturally determined livestock raising practices. The osteometric data presented here may also help to place the Snake Hill ox within the context of the history of animal husbandry in preindustrial North America.

The ox burial was located by careful monitoring of the mechanical removal of overburden. Excavation procedure was similar to that used for the human burials. The excavated skeleton was removed to the comparative zooarchaeology laboratory of the Department of Anthropology, University of Toronto where it was age, sex, measured and examined for trauma, pathological change and cultural alterations to the bone.

It was necessary to establish the historical context of oxen within the Fort Erie Campaign. This information was assembled by Lieutenant Colonel Joseph Whitehorne from material in the U.S. National Archives in Washington D.C. (NA).

Historical Background

The senior engineer officer of the Fort Erie operation, Lieutenant Colonel William MacRee, requested eight yoke of oxen (16 animals) to aid in the heavy draft work inside the defensive perimeter (between the dock and the fort) and between the fort and the outer works. By approximately 9 August, they had been deployed with the 220 horses already inside the beachhead fortifications (NA, Record Group 94, OAG/QM Accts; Record Group 98, QM File, Left Division). Given the high level of attrition among the American defenders caused by the British bombardment, there must also have been casualties among the livestock. Replacements must have been sent, because near the end of August, a number of chain harnesses for ox teams were purchased for oxen sent to Fort Erie. There is evidence that meeting the military's need for draft animals strained the resources of the thinly populated frontier region. On 10 August, John Hogan, a government purchasing agent, reported acquiring oxen in good health (NA, Record Group 98, Box 134, QM File, General Brown's Left Division; 9th Military District). However, by 19 September, Hogan reported having difficulty obtaining healthy, young oxen, and vouchers for September through November show an increase in day rentals of oxen for work on the U.S. side of the

Niagara River (NA, Record Group 94, Box 45, QM Accts). Because all oxen used within the fortifications were government-owned, the increased demand for rented teams probably reflects a redirection of government-owned oxen to the Fort Erie side of the river.

Animal holding facilities were known to have been established in a relatively safe zone near the hospitals in an effort to ensure the safety of the animals. Whitehorne believes that the oxen may have been kept near the dock area, close to Snake Hill, between revetments which afforded shelter from the British guns deployed near the present-day Peace Bridge. If this is true, the oxen were kept not far from the Snake Hill site itself. As army property, military animals were routinely inspected by the unit Inspector General. On 30 September, Colonel Josiah Snelling, the Inspector General of Brown's Division, reported that the Fort Erie oxen suffered from poor nutrition, neglect and overwork:

> Rarely is forage properly measured, it is dumped on the ground causing ingestion of foreign material as well as waste. The animals cannot graze, are fed too much hay to grain, and are never groomed. Heavy loads, badly balanced, added to the animals' distress. (NA, Record Group 98, vol 406/290—I.G. Order-Letter Book)

Excavation

The ox was buried approximately 16 m northeast of the nearest military graves. The pit that was excavated to accommodate the ox was approximately 3 m long, 1 m deep and slightly over 1 m in breadth. The pit was oriented east to west, parallel to the military graves, and, as with the human interments, the head lay towards the west. The ox lay on its left side, with its back against the south wall in the deepest part of the pit, and its ventral thorax and limbs upslope. The pit contours elevated the carpal area of the anterior left limb slightly above the general level of the rest of the carcass. In consequence, the ox burial was discovered when the gradall hit the distal end of the radius (Plate 14.1).

Preservation was generally good. Breakage of a few of the uppermost elements of the left anterior limb occurred during the removal of topsoil, but horizontal displacement was less than 30 cm. Little postmortem damage had occurred with the exception of some crumbling of the more fragile structures, including horn cores and the ossified costal and scapular cartilages, and minor root damage to the hyoid complex and the mid-cervical vertebrae.

The head was not directed ventrally as it would be in life, but was extended as if it had been stretched while dragging the carcass into the pit by means of a rope tied to the neck or horns. The vertebral column was articulated and the curvature was normal. The pelvis was intact and in normal anatomical position. The tail was represented by less than one third of the caudal vertebrae, and oriented ventrally and to the right. The missing caudal vertebrae are best explained by pre-depositional loss, for the central caudal vertebrae are the size of wine bottle corks, and it is unlikely that they would have been overlooked. Also, no evidence of rodent burrowing was noted near the hiatus in the caudal vertebrae.

All left ribs were present and in normal anatomical position. Right ribs one through seven were also in normal anatomical position. The eighth rib was displaced anterio-laterally, so that its body overlay the seventh rib. While the head of the ninth right rib was articulated, its body had separated completely from that of the eighth rib, and sunk medially, or downwards into the thoracic cavity, suggesting a failure in the ligamentous support between the eighth and ninth ribs. Ribs 10 and 11 were missing completely. The heads of the 12th and 13th ribs articulated with the vertebral column, but their distal ends had been rotated approximately 90 degrees laterally, to a near-vertical position. Their distal halves, which extended well above the rest of the skeleton, had been severed by the blade of the gradall and were not recovered. Both of these ribs had suffered perimortem fractures of the neck, best expressed in the 13th rib. The costal cartilages and sternebrae were well ossified and approximately in normal anatomical position.

The left anterior limb was drawn up to the chest, and the carpus was flexed around a chunk of limestone so that the cannon bone (fused metacarpals three and four) and the phalanges lay approximately parallel to the sternum. Except for the distal radius and some carpal bones which were disturbed when the overburden was removed, most elements were found in their normal articular position. The single exception was a fragment of the scapular cartilage. In oxen, the scapular cartilage is a flat cartilaginous band approximately 2 cm wide, which projects dorsally from the vertebral border of the scapula. It partially ossifies in older individuals, as do costal cartilages in humans. In the Snake Hill ox, the posterior end of the scapular cartilage had been displaced medially and distally, so that it came to rest between the posterior angle of the scapula and the underlying ribs. It seems likely that this was caused by a violent displacement of the thorax relative to the scapula.

No trace of the right anterior leg was found.

The femur of the left posterior limb was extended, and the tibia flexed. All surviving elements were in normal anatomical position, and the patella was high in the patellar groove of the femur. The distal third of the left tibia was missing. One large spiral fracture fragment of the left tibia had come to rest on the posterior side of the knee joint. No traces of the distal tibia or pes were recovered.

The right posterior limb had been disarticulated. The orientation of the limb was reversed; the femoral head lay not far from the posterior margin of the thorax, while the remains of the tibia lay just ventrally to the wing of the right ilium. The limb was turned with the anterior side facing toward the rear. The patella lay close to the distal femur, but had slumped downwards, away from the patellar groove. Only the proximal half of the tibia remained, including the end section and one large and one small spiral fracture fragment. Several other small spiral fracture fragments were recovered from the region between the posterior limbs.

The only artifact associated with the skeleton was a small piece of iron, approximately 17 mm long, which resembled a section of bent nail. It lay just inside posterior edge of the rib cage, on the medial surface of the distal end of the left 13th rib.

Results

A. Age at Death and Sex of the Snake Hill Ox

An age at death exceeding 4.5 years is indicated by the complete maturity of the skeleton. The latest-fusing epiphyses are closed, including the proximal humerus, distal radius, distal femur, iliac crest, and ischial tubercle (Silver 1969:286-287). An age at death somewhat in excess of 10 years is indicated by the condition of the anterior mandibular dentition: the incisors and canines are heavily worn, the teeth are consequently separated, and the dental arch is straightened to a marked degree (Ensminger 1976:916). While this method lacks the precision and accuracy of the age estimation methods based on epiphyseal fusion which are applicable to younger individuals, it can safely be said that the ox was nearing the end of its useful life as a traction animal.

Reconstruction of the thin, fragmented horn cores was incomplete, so it was not possible to apply all aspects of Armitage and Clutton-Brock's sex estimation method based on horn core morphology (1976). However, on the basis of size, cross section, torsion, and angle of attachment, there is a strong indication that the skeletal remains represent a neutered male.

B. Pathological Changes

The advanced age of the ox skeleton is reflected in numerous pathological degenerative changes. There was an advanced degree of alveolar resorption, and most teeth were loose in their sockets (Plate 14.2).

Asymmetric eburnation (pre-mortem polishing caused by destruction of cartilage) seen on the articular facets of the sixth lumbar and first sacral vertebrae indicates severe degenerative arthritis. Other changes of the vertebral body articular surfaces which might be attributable to degenerative arthritis include porous degeneration in nearly all vertebrae, most marked in the lumbar and anterior thoracic regions, and marginal lipping, primarily in the lumbar region. Joint surface irregularities included an 8 mm wide uneven depression in the anterior articular surface of the axis. Elsewhere in the vertebral column there are smaller smooth-sided pits, dimpled areas, and small spur-like projections. Porotic degeneration and other joint surface irregularities were common on costal facets, anterior and posterior articular facets, and the heads and tubercles of ribs. These changes were generally symmetrical. Symmetrical areas of severe porosity were observed on the inner laminar surfaces of lumbar vertebrae four through six.

There was a severe degenerative lesion on the anterior surface of the sagittal ridge of the lateral condyle (capitulum) of the left humerus. The cortical bone had eroded from an area measuring 30mm by 6mm, leaving the underlying cancellous bone exposed. There was no associated eburnation, and edges of the lesion were rounded, indicating that partial healing had occurred. This was the most dramatic pathological change in the appendicular skeleton. It may be attributable to degenerative arthritis. Elsewhere, marginal lipping and areas of apparent porotic resorption had occurred.

C. Bone Measurements

The Snake Hill ox appears to have been significantly smaller in stature than modern cattle. Bone measurements from modern cattle were obtained from specimens in the collections of the Department of Anthropology of the University of Toronto, the Departments of Vertebrate Paleontology and Mammalogy of the Royal Ontario Museum, and the Veterinary College at the University of Guelph. The major long bones of the modern sample averaged approximately 11 to 16% larger than the Snake Hill ox (Table 14.1).

Modern cattle breeding began in Britain during the latter eighteenth century, and was well established by the Napoleonic Period (Ensminger 1976:9–10). Improved cattle were shipped to east coast U.S. commercial centres as early as 1783 (Ensminger 1976:13). Given the estimated age and the time of death of the Snake Hill ox, it was born between 1800 and 1805. It is not known whether developments in breeding had significantly influenced the cattle gene pools in the frontier regions of western New York and Upper Canada by this time. However, the relatively short stature of the Snake Hill ox suggests that it represents an unimproved draft animal which would have been typical during the Colonial Period. More osteometric data from other historic sites are needed to test this suggestion. Documentation of the spread of improved breeds of cattle through early nineteenth century North America is a potential subject for future zooarchaeological research.

D. Physical Trauma at Time of Death

The configuration of the cracks in the necks, and the laterally rotated position of left ribs 12 and 13 indicate that the displacement of these ribs was caused by a powerful force acting radially or laterally on the ribs from inside the anterior abdomen and posterior thorax. This explosive event may also have caused the loss of the 10th and 11th ribs, the apparent disruption of the ligamentous attachment between the eighth and ninth ribs, and the comparatively slighter anterolateral displacement of the eighth rib.

The left tibia had been shattered by a violent perimortem impact on the anterior surface, just proximal of midshaft. The contours of an 11 mm wide gouge and associated crushing on the anterior surface indicate that the principal impact was delivered by a fairly straight-edged object. Several small, proximally directed hinge fractures indicate that the blow was angled slightly towards the knee. Upon reconstruction of the broken pieces, the fracture pattern suggests one or two additional impact points distal to the principal impact. Although the axe was a common butchering tool in the early nineteenth century, it is unlikely that the observed fracture pattern was caused by axe blows. Butchering cuts from axe blows are usually well-defined and typically occur in groups. Furthermore, purposeful disarticulation of the hind leg would be far more likely to involve the knee joint than the massively thick cortex of the tibia midshaft. The tibia had not been chopped through. Rather, it had been smashed by a cluster of one to three very powerful impacts.

The right tibia had also suffered a violent perimortem impact on the anterior surface of the shaft, approximately one or two cm distal of midshaft. The path of impact, as indicated by the position and orientation of negative flake scars, appeared to be through the thick cortex on the medial side of the shaft. The impact shattered the tibia. The similarity of the injuries to both tibias suggests a single, violently powerful event. It is possible that the same event separated the right femur from the acetabulum. The relative position of the right hind leg bones indicates that the surviving portion of the right leg remained attached to the carcass by soft tissue.

It was common practice for soldiers of the period to augment their monotonous field diet with meat from draft animals killed in battle (J. Whitehorne, personal communication). In anticipation that butchering marks would be found, the entire skeleton was inspected carefully, using point source, oblique angle illumination. This technique is effective in locating even very light cut marks in bone. No butcher marks were observed. Since the cleaver, axe and saw figured prominently among the butchering implements of the period, if the right limb had been removed for food, one would expect to find unmistakable traces in the bone. Nevertheless, if intentional butchering is ruled out, it is not readily apparent how the right anterior limb came to be removed. The power equipment which took off the overburden could not possibly have removed all traces of the limb while leaving the anterior right ribs intact.

Discussion and Conclusions

The ox skeleton excavated at Snake Hill appears to represent a neutered male with well-developed muscle attachment areas. The advanced wear of the cheek teeth, the pronounced resorption of the gums, and the degenerative changes observed throughout the postcranial axial skeleton are consistent with an estimated age at death of approximately 10 years. The arthritic changes are consistent with its probable use as a draft animal. Of course, some of the degenerative changes described above may have been caused or accelerated by malnutrition, and from the military records it is known that the oxen were poorly fed.

The injuries sustained by the ox could have been caused by several impact events. However, a single explosion beneath the abdomen of the ox would be the most economical explanation. Perhaps the most satisfactory explanation, which would also account for the small shred of iron inside the posterior thoracic cavity, would be the detonation of an explosive shell beneath the ox's abdomen.

Was the Snake Hill ox a military draft animal from the War of 1812, or just a farm animal which, by chance, came to be buried near a military cemetery? No diagnostic military artifacts were found in close association with the ox remains. Further, while oxen used by the military would normally have been shod, the single remaining hoof bore no iron ox shoe. However, negative artifactual evidence is of limited importance since snaffles, bits and shoes were removed from dead military draft animals by order to the Quartermaster General of the United States Army (J. Whitehorne, personal communication).

The Snake Hill ox is substantially smaller in stature than the twentieth century reference material examined by the author. Although size information cannot be used to date the remains, the relatively small stature of the Snake Hill specimen is consistent with the expectation that improved breeds of cattle had not penetrated as far as the Niagara frontier by 1814. More zooarchaeological research into the history of early breed improvements is needed.

Although no artifacts were found which conclusively demonstrate that the Snake Hill ox was indeed an American military draft animal, such an inference is reasonable. The existence of profound multiple injuries could certainly associate the ox with a military action. In addition, the following contextual facts suggest a link between the American military campaign and the ox: the proximity of the ox burial to the American military graves; the orientation of the ox burial parallel to the American military graves; and the west-facing orientation of the ox within the burial pit, similar to that observed in the American military graves.

The combination of age and physical condition place the ox near the end of its useful life. One might speculate whether the U.S. military had been sold a substandard animal by design. However, records do mention that purchasing agents had difficulty obtaining healthy, young oxen by the middle of September. Frontier farmers would have been reluctant to sell draft animals — their means of production — just when the war had brought a huge market to their doorstep. Rather than duplicity or incompetence on the part of army purchasing agents, the Snake Hill ox may reflect a frontier resource base stretched to the limit. This view would be consistent with the impression given by the forage and grain procurement contracts. The catchment area for the Fort Erie campaign extended from Syracuse, New York to Cleveland, Ohio. However, by the end of August, most of the animal feed was being sent from Ohio (J. Whitehorne, personal communication).

Note

The author wishes to acknowledge Dr. Howard G. Savage for access to the zooarchaeological laboratory facilities and to Bos taurus skeletal specimens at the Department of Anthropology of the University of Toronto. Access to additional Bos taurus skeletal material was provided by Mr. Kevin

Seymore of the Department of Vertebrate Paleontology of the Royal On-
tario Museum, Ms. Wendy Hyluka of the Department of Mammology of the
Royal Ontario Museum, and Ms. Winn Halina of the Veterinary College of
the University of Guelph. Special thanks are extended to Lieutenant Colonel
Joseph Whitehorne for locating the information in the U.S. National Ar-
chives presented above about the procurement, use, care and feeding of
military draft animals.

Table 14.1: Snake Hill Ox Bone Measurements

Measurements (1)	Snake Hill Ox	Comparative Sample			
		Min	Max	Mean	n (2)
Humerus					
Greatest Length (GL)	297	325	339	333	7
Breadth of Distal End (Bd)	87	94	113	99	7
Breadth of Trochlea (Bt)	77	79	99	87	7
Femur					
Greatest Length (GL)	372	392	448	420	5
Greatest Length from Head (GLC)	334	369	403	386	5
Breadth of Proximal End (Bp)	127	141	152	145	5
Breadth of Distal End (Bd)	100	107	119	113	5
Tibia					
Breadth of Proximal End (Bp)	104	112	118	115	6
Metacarpal 3+4					
Greatest Length (GL)	206	213	230	221	6
Greatest Breadth of Proximal End (Bp)	65	67	70	69	6
Smallest Breadth of Shaft (SD)	35	34	40	38	6
Smallest Breadth of Shaft at Midpoint	35	35	40	38	6
Greatest Breadth of Distal End (Bd)	61	65	69	66	6

(1) Most measurements follow von den Driesch (1976), and her standard abbreviations appear in brackets following the measurements which she defined. Calipers and an osteometric board were used, and each measurement was taken three times, the values averaged, and rounded to the nearest whole millimetre.

(2) Values in the number of specimens column indicate the minimum number of individuals represented. If both right and left elements for the same bone of the same individual were present, the measurements for the two were averaged.

Plate 14.1: Ox Burial

Plate 14.2: Left Mandible, Pathological Degeneration

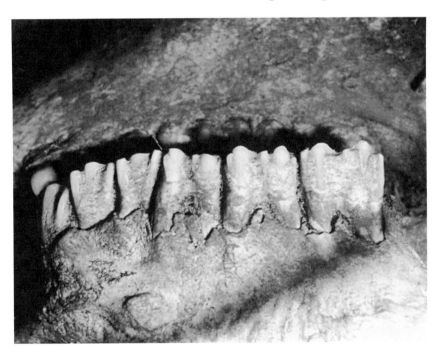

Fifteen	# Conclusions

RONALD F. WILLIAMSON
SUSAN PFEIFFER

In the usual course of events, American casualties and injured British prisoners from Fort Erie were taken to the hospital at Williamsville, New York. However, for 28 or more soldiers, the system failed. The Snake Hill site offered an opportunity to corroborate historical documentation and to contribute new information about life and death on the battlefield. Our first line of evidence was the archaeological context in which the remains were found. Careful examination and interpretation of artifacts and body positions indicated who these people were, and how they came to rest at Snake Hill. Subsequent laboratory analysis shed further light on their origin and death.

The Archaeological Context

Thirty-one archaeological features were documented in the course of eight weeks of intensive fieldwork. Of these, it has been determined that 28 were primary inhumations. The three others, initially designated as burials, contained non-articulated human bone and surgical refuse and were defined as medical waste pits.

The primary burials appear to have been distributed in two groups. However, the full westward extent of the cemetery cannot be delineated due to the presence of the house on the lot immediately to the west of the study area. The presence of more recent historic disturbances (i.e. the construction of early twentieth century cottages and associated services) may have precluded the discovery of burials in the area between the two components. However, the presence of two historic features in that area suggests that this is not the case.

Evidence of binding of the knees and ankles, together with the presence of bandage pins with some individuals, indicates that the men may have received field medical attention prior to their demise. This is consistent with the historic documentation of a field hospital in the vicinity of the study area. It is known that this field hospital (or hospitals) was attached to either the 23d Regiment of Infantry or Porter's Brigade of the New York Militia, or both. The suggestion has been made that two hospitals were situated near each other and may have made use of a single cemetery. If so, there is no indication that the two components reflect segregation of remains.

Indeed, while most of the individuals appear to have been clad in American military-issue garments, their affiliation with regular or militia service is not always readily discernible. It is known that certain militia units were not outfitted in uniforms, but in civilian clothes. It is also possible that militia soldiers were dressed in older uniforms and in mixed civilian and military dress. Burial 3, and perhaps 6, may have been interred wearing old-style uniforms. It is more probable, however, that individuals dressed either partially or entirely in civilian garments belonged to militia units. Three individuals, and a possible fourth, were buried wearing an element of civilian clothing: Burial 8, a civilian cloak; Burial 19, a civilian jacket; Burial 24, civilian trousers; and Burial 12, a civilian jacket, although the plain brass buttons thought to represent the jacket may have been part of some other piece of military equipment. All four of these individuals wore other military outer garments. Given the scope of militia participation in the Fort Erie campaign, an unexpectedly small number of bodies wearing civilian dress were encountered, although many units are known to have worn regular issue.

Since some militia troops wore old-style or mixed uniforms, it is possible that other non-standard issue military dress might be indicative of militia affiliation. The coatee found with Burial 10 had small front-row buttons. This is distinct from the standard coatee which was normally fitted with large buttons. Similarly, the soldier in Burial 13 was dressed in a roundabout fitted with large buttons rather than the standard small ones. Alternatively, this garment may have been a coatee, without the standard collar, cuff and tail buttons.

A total of 270 buttons were associated with burials in the west component while 133 buttons were associated with those in the east (excluding Burial 24). The distribution of buttons characterized by certain designs identifiable to the American military, was not proportionate to the total number of identifiable buttons from each group. For instance, 23 eagle motif buttons were associated with burials in the western component while only three were found with burials in the eastern one, or 17% and 4%, respectively, of identifiable buttons. The "US" motif was also strongly associated with the western group. Twenty-one were found in the west (16%), while only one (1%) was found in the east. Concomitantly, script "I" buttons accounted for 82% of the buttons in the east but only 57% in the west. These distributional asymmetries may suggest more regularity or consistency in uniforms from the eastern component. However, the implications of these data remain unclear. Moreover, there was no obvious evidence that military rank dictated the placement of a soldier in one group or the other since there were no officers found.

Partial uniforms may indicate something about the circumstances of death. Soldiers may not have worn upper garments while on fatigue duty, or when they were off duty. Nine individuals were buried wearing overalls or civilian trousers, but no upper garment (Burials 11, 14, 15, 16, 17, 20, 23, 24 and 26). Garments were likely removed when a soldier entered the field hospital. Burials 2 and 28 were clothed only in shirts with bone buttons and in some cases overalls were removed, probably for purposes of medical treatment. Some of the burials which lacked lower garments, such as 12 and 13, apparently suffered severe trauma to the lower limbs, while others, such as Burial 21, may have been bandaged in the pelvic area. In other cases, the overalls may have been opened to facilitate medical treatment of abdominal or upper leg wounds. It seems most likely that overalls or civilian trousers were opened in the case of Burials 6, 7, 8, 10, 11, 15, 17, 24 and 27. Overalls may have been opened or loosened in other cases, but the evidence was often inconclusive due to the dearth of buttons. In addition, Burial 29 may not have been dressed in a uniform, but a military garment may have been placed over the body.

Amorphous clusters of buttons, usually tightly spaced, were associated with Burials 6, 7, 12 and 24. While it is possible that these groupings were ruined uniform parts which were discarded in burial pits, they were not placed at random, but appear to be associated with the thorax and abdomen. Therefore, these may have been military garment fragments used as wound dressings.

Unfortunately, it was not possible to determine the personal identity of any of the individuals, and in only two cases was regimental affiliation indicated. In Burial 6, nine buttons were identified to the 21st Regiment of Infantry. However, not enough skeletal material remained to make a secure forensic identification based on regimental records. In the case of Burial 7, one button was identified to the 15th Regiment of Infantry. As discussed in Chapter 2 of this volume, outfitting of soldiers was not always well organized. Therefore, the presence of only one button, with discernible regimental designation, in association with this burial, does not constitute a firm foundation upon which to base an identification. Nevertheless, a search of the records of the 15th Regiment of Infantry failed to produce any evidence of a soldier of similar physical description.

One record of interest, in regard to personal identification, was the account of Corporal Robert White, who, according to historian Benson Lossing, was wounded on the night of the 15 August.

> He described what happened in a post-war letter: "Just at twilight as my arms were extended in the act of lifting a vessel on the fire, a 24 pounder came booming over the ramparts and struck off both my arms above the elbows! The blow struck me so numb that at first I could not see. My left arm, as I was subsequently informed, was carried from my body some two rods and struck a man in his back with such force as nearly brought him to the ground. This same shot took off the right arm of another soldier standing not far from me, and passing on to the other side of the encampment, killed three men!" (Lossing 1869, see Whitehorne, this volume)

White was still living in 1867 when he was interviewed by Benson Lossing. This colourful account has some relevance to this study in that White must have been subject to a bilateral amputation, such as the one documented in Medical Waste Feature 9. However, the pattern of wounds in the case of the recovered elements is not consistent with the injury that White sustained. Given that bilateral amputations must have been relatively rare occurrences, the correlation was fully investigated.

The Physical Remains

Throughout all the research described here, we see a pattern of generalizations about the group, juxtaposed against observations about unique individuals. Our conclusions are thus a balance of these perspectives. The soldiers held many characteristics in common, yet each was unique. This is well illustrated in the study of the pathological features of the bones.

Most of the injuries which were documented in the bones reflect the day-to-day life of an American soldier in the Niagara campaign, including the hazards of battle. While the chronic conditions from daily wear and tear were unlikely to have caused death, the battle wounds often constituted trauma severe enough to have done so.

The new battle wounds certainly represent some of the most dramatic features of the Snake Hill burials. At least half of the individuals had sustained traumatic injuries, some of which were thought to have caused death. Indeed, two individuals had died of gunshot wounds to the head, one having been shot directly in the face. The low frequency of infectious conditions indicates a lack of recovery after wounds were sustained. It may also indicate that the "system" was working, in which injured soldiers were removed to American hospitals for recovery. Surgical intervention was indicated by the recovery of eight amputated limbs from a number of medical waste features. While these remains now represent rare and significant scientific specimens, they also represent potent evidence of a time of suffering and carnage.

The day-to-day injuries reflect the sorts of daily hazards faced by the soldiers. While some are the results of acute blows, others reflect chronic overuse. The pattern of disc herniation, wedge-shaped compression of lower vertebrae, separated neural arches and degenerative changes to the surface of the vertebral bodies, reflect chronic trauma to the vertebral column. Habitual lifting and twisting of heavy loads might have caused such changes. Moreover, the presence of cortical excavations at certain sites of muscle attachment provides corroborative evidence of severe wear on the body. These observations, while provisional in nature, appear to constitute direct physical evidence of the daily routine and living conditions of the soldiers and attest to the rigorous training of the American forces by Brigadier General Scott. This apparent correlation between the archival record and the biological evidence has contributed significantly to our understanding of the genesis of these phenomena and has provided direction for future research.

Other analyses of the physical remains contributed to our understanding of the daily routine and life of the soldiers. For example, the dental disease data indicated that the diet of the Snake Hill soldiers was relatively low in cariogenic agents, especially processed carbohydrates and sugars. Once again, our interdisciplinary approach was rewarded by a correlation between the archival record and the biological evidence. Dental analysis also contributed evidence of the soldiers' personal characteristics. Features like pipe stem wear, the "Hapsburg" jaw and poor quality enamel reminded us that each of these men was unique.

The chemical and isotopic analyses expanded our perspective by yielding data concerning the lives of the soldiers, both before and during the war. With respect to the lead content of the bone, two high values were considered outliers. Since certain socio-economic classes or occupations sometimes account for unusually high values, it was argued that the two soldiers, with the high values, may have been from wealthier families or have been engaged in some lead-related occupation before entering the military service. In terms of health effects due to lead exposure, it was concluded that most of the individuals would have been asymptomatic although a few may have experienced nausea or appetite loss. The two outliers, however, might have been suffering occasional episodes of muscle weakness, abdominal colic or partial nerve paralysis.

The analyses of stable isotopes have also proven useful. Because human tissue reflects the dietary contribution of carbon and nitrogen isotopes contributed by certain plant, fish and meat species, the results suggest that at least two of the individuals had been subjected to a European-like diet rich in C_3 plants, unlike the diet of Colonial or native Americans. Alternatively, the diet of others had been nitrogen rich reflecting a high meat and fish diet. Studies of the ratio of the stable isotopes of oxygen in the bone, thought to reflect the source of dietary water, like the archival record, suggest that the soldiers originated from the northeastern United States.

Some comment should be also be made with respect to the age and stature profiles of the recovered individuals. The estimated skeletal ages range from very young adolescent to middle-aged adult – consistent with the sample derived from the archival record – as one can expect, given the inherent imprecision of skeletal age estimation techniques. The Snake Hill group also contains proportionately more tall individuals and consequently has a higher average stature than that of the sample derived from the archival record. The sample may therefore be selectively biased since it is somewhat different from the documented samples of individuals known to have taken part in the siege. Of some interest in this regard, a captain of one of the Pennsylvania companies recorded that he was only interested in "splendidly big fellows." These men were sent straight to Snake Hill on 15 September. It may also be possible that a number of these individuals were from rifle companies, known to have been selected for their height.

Conclusions

Twenty-two of the individuals at Snake Hill were buried wearing, or covered with, American military garments. Historical research and the archaeological analyses confirm that these remains were those of American soldiers. On the basis of archaeological context, it is highly probable that the remaining six individuals were also American. Whether the facility or cemetery was initiated as a result of the battle for Snake Hill on the night of 15 August is not known. It is more likely that the individuals suffered injuries as a result of either camp disease or constant British bombardment of the position.

The fact that there were no soldiers identified as British should not seem surprising. It is recorded that the British killed in the fighting of 15 August were either thrown into the Niagara River or were buried in the mass grave at the Fort. The practice of segregation of British and American dead at War of 1812 cemeteries is also well documented. Moreover, after 15 August, there would not appear to have been an opportunity for British to be buried at this cemetery as action moved further east and inland.

Although five British buttons were found on the site, it can be confidently stated that none represents a burial of a British individual. With the exception of the button recovered from the pocket area of Burial 6, they were associated with body parts only. Two buttons were found with isolated bone fragments in Medical Waste Pit 9 and two buttons with an intrusive lower limb in Burial 17. It is clear that medical waste was disposed of with no regard for nationality — it was merely buried as refuse.

Analysis of the physical remains indicates that the soldiers were generally large young men, from the American northeast. Many, if not all, had spent a physically taxing life as laborers. Their diets were quite variable, but generally adequate. Access to these remains gave researchers a welcome opportunity to test analytical techniques, and to compare remains from a known historical context to those from earlier and later populations.

It is likely that most of these individuals would have wished to be returned to the United States for burial. Indeed, a number of historical narratives include comments that the mortally wounded frequently requested burial on the American side of the river. For example, Alexander McMullen, a private in Colonel Fenton's Regiment of Pennsylvania Volunteers recorded the death of his friend Thomas Poe in the following manner:

Coming to the house at Chippawa, I found Thomas Poe lying on a blanket. He reached his hand to me and told me that he was mortally wounded, that he had but a few moments to live, and told me he wished to be buried on the American side of the river... Carrying him nearly a mile across the plain, in the middle of 26 July, appeared to exhaust what little strength he had left... He shook hands with me for the last time. He said to me in a weak voice: 'Alexander, you will never see me again in this world.' He expired in a few minutes. (Fenton 1814, see Whitehorne, this volume)

On 30 June, 1988 at least some were granted what may have been their last wish. Twenty-eight individuals were repatriated, with full military honours, to the United States where they were transported to the National Cemetery at Bath, New York. Almost two centuries after their tragic passing, the discovery and return of these forgotten soldiers reminded two nations of a distant but shared past.

While this repatriation agreement was without precedent in U.S.–Canadian history, so too were the agreements reached with respect to the ultimate disposition of isolated skeletal elements of scientific interest. The collection was divided between the Academy of Medicine in Toronto and the U.S. Army Medical Museum at the Armed Forces Institute of Pathology in Washington, D.C. Both of these institutions recognized the scientific and historical value of the remains and had requested the collection.

The Snake Hill Site Project focused the attention of an international group of scholars on one small aspect of the War of 1812. In so doing, it stimulated a broad research initiative which, it is hoped, will have far-reaching results.

Arthur C. Aufderheide, M.D.
Department of Pathology &
Laboratory Medicine
University of Minnesota
Duluth School of Medicine
10 University Drive
Duluth, Minnesota
55812-2487

Linda Gibbs, M.A.
Deptartment of Anthropology
McMaster University
Hamilton, Ontario
L8S 4L9

Richard L. Jantz, Ph.D.
Department of Anthropology
The University of Tennessee
252 S. Stadium Hall
Knoxville, Tennessee
37996-0720

M. Anne Katzenberg, Ph.D.
Department of Archaeology
University of Calgary
2500 University Drive N.W.
Calgary, Alberta
T2N 1N4

Martin Knyf
Deptartment of Geology
McMaster University
1280 Main Street West
Hamilton, Ontario
L8S 4M1

Leanne Lalich
Paleobiology Laboratory
University of Minnesota
Duluth School of Medicine
10 University Drive
Duluth, Minnesota
55812-2487

Robert W. Mann, M.A.
Department of Anthropology
National Museum of Natural History
Smithsonian Institution
Washington, D.C.
20560

Marc S. Micozzi, M.D., Ph.D.
Director
National Museum of Health
and Medicine
Armed Forces Institute of Pathology
Washington D.C.
20306-6000

Peer H. Moore-Jansen, Ph.D.
Department of Anthropology
Wichita State University
Box 52
Wichita, Kansas
67208

Sean P. Murphy, M.S.
Department of Anthropology
The University of Tennessee
252 S. Stadium Hall
Knoxville, Tennessee
37996-0720

Adrianne Noe, Ph.D.
Assistant Director
National Museum of Natural History
Smithsonian Institution
Washington, D.C.
20560

Douglas W. Owsley, Ph.D.
Department of Anthropology
National Museum of Natural History
Smithsonian Institution
Washington, D.C.
20560

Susan Pfeiffer, Ph.D.
School of Human Biology
University of Guelph
Guelph, Ontario
NIG 2W1

Shelley R. Saunders, Ph.D.
Department of Anthropology
McMaster University
Hamilton, Ontario
L8S 4L9

Henry P. Schwarcz, Ph.D.
Department of Geology
McMaster University
1280 Main Street West
Hamilton, Ontario
L8S 4M1

Paul S. Sledzik, M.S.
Curator, Anatomical Collections
National Museum of Health
and Medicine
Armed Forces Institute of Pathology
Washington, D.C.
20306-6000

Stephen C. Thomas, M.A.
Archaeological Services Inc.
662 Bathurst Street
Toronto, Ontario
M5S 2R3

Ronald F. Williamson, Ph.D.
Archaeological Services Inc.
662 Bathurst Street
Toronto, Ontario
M5S 2R3

Joseph Whitehorne, Lt. Col. (ret.)
Lord Fairfax Community College
P.O. Box 47
Middletown, Virginia
22645

SNAKE HILL SITE: A WAR OF 1812 CEMETERY
SCIENTIFIC CONSULTING AND TECHNICAL ASSISTANCE TEAM

Project Director: Dr. Ronald F. Williamson (ASI)
Administrative Assistant: Mr. Robert MacDonald (ASI)

Archaeology Section:
Ms. Deborah Steiss (ASI)
Ms. Beverly Garner (ASI)
Mr. Andrew Clish (ASI)
Sgt. Lawrence Llewellyn (AFIP)
Mr. Stephen C. Thomas (ASI)
Ms. Julie MacDonald (ASI)
Mr. Martin Cooper (ASI)
Ms. Anne Wingfield (ASI)

History Section:
Lt. Col. Joseph Whitehorne (USA)
Mr. Rene Chartrand (CPS)
Mr. Patrick Wilder (SHB)
Dr. Adrianne Noe (AFMM)
Mr. David Owen (MTR)
Mr. Tim Shaughnessy (NPC)
Mr. Dennis Carter-Edwards (CPS)
Dr. Charles G. Roland (MU)

Physical Anthropology Section:
Dr. Susan Pfeiffer (UG)
Dr. Douglas W. Owsley (SI)
Dr. Jerry Cybulski (NMC)
Dr. Shelley R. Saunders (MU/ROM)
Mr. Robert W. Mann (SI)
Dr. Peer H. Moore-Jansen (UT)
Dr. Marc S. Micozzi (AFMM)
Mr. Sean P. Murphy (AFMM)
Mr. Paul S. Sledzik (AFMM)

Artifact Conservation & Identification Section:
Ms. Anne MacLaughlin (ROM)
Ms. Julia Fenn (ROM)
Ms. Charlotte Newton (CCI)
Mr. Stephen Poulin (MCC)
Ms. Sandra Lougheed (MCC)
Mr. Rene Chartrand (CPS)
Mr. Patrick Wilder (SHB)
Dr. Donald Brown (THB)
Mr. Donald Kloster (SI)

Institutional Affiliation Key

AFIP	=	Armed Forces Institute of Pathology (U.S.)
AFMM	=	Armed Forces Medical Museum (AFIP)
ASI	=	Archaeological Services Inc.
CCI	=	Canadian Conservation Institute
CPS	=	Parks Service Canada
MCC	=	Ontario Ministry of Culture and Communications
MTR	=	Ontario Ministry of Tourism and Recreation
MU	=	McMaster University
NMC	=	National Museum of Civilization, National Museums of Canada
NPC	=	Niagara Parks Commission
ROM	=	Royal Ontario Museum
SHB	=	Sackets Harbor Battlefield State Historic Site (N.Y.)
SI	=	Smithsonian Institution (U.S.)
THB	=	Toronto Historical Board
UG	=	University of Guelph
USA	=	United States Army
UT	=	University of Tennessee

The U.S. Military Button Assemblage from Snake Hill

Buttons Listed by Burial Using the Albert Type Code System

The most detailed catalogue of uniform buttons used by the United States military has been compiled by Alphaeus Albert. In his system, buttons are classified according to branching hierarchical alphanumeric type codes. Albert regularly appended a "V" to a code to indicate a small-diameter variant of a defined type. The analytical team has added four more modifying characters to Albert's original system. A question mark after a code indicates a probable identification which cannot be confirmed because an important design element is indistinct. For example, in several cases the number of points of a star determine the specific type code, but detail of this size has been obscured by corrosion. However, if it appears that an indistinct design element could take one of two forms, both code letters are given, separated by a slash. Ellipsis points are used to indicate the complete omission of one character or element from a type code. Finally, a plus sign was appended to a type code when a button varied from the closest of Albert's defined types, and the variation appeared to be significant enough so that it might warrant a new type code.

Catalogue Number	Motif	Albert Code	Page Reference,	Remarks
01-01	Script "I"	GI36D2?	(Albert 1975:20)	Similar design but the major loops of "I" do not touch. Perpendicular "I".
01-06	Script "I"	GI36D1?	(Albert 1975:21)	The major loops almost touch one another. Perpendicular "I".
01-09	Script "I"	GI36D2?	(Albert 1975:21)	The major loops do not touch.Perpendicular "I".
01-18	Script "I"	GI36D2?	(Albert 1975:21)	The major loops touch.
01-19	Script "I"	GI36D2?	(Albert 1975:21)	The major loops almost touch. Perpendicular "I". The embellishments are more pronounced.
03-01	Eagle	GI41B	(Albert 1975:23)	
03-09	Eagle	GI41B	(Albert 1975:23)	
03-10	Eagle	GI46?	(Albert 1975:23-24)	Stars around periphery are obscured. "US" in the oval.
03-24	Eagle	GI41B	(Albert 1975:23)	
03-27	Eagle	GI45+	(Albert 1975:23-24)	Motif variant: Similar to Albert's GI45, except that area inside oval is blank, and profile of left wing is more incurvate.
04-06	Script "I"	GI36BV?	(Albert 1975:21)	The "I" is not perpendicular. Unembellished. Upper loop is very small. Slightly obscured star may have six points.
04-14	"US"	GI30A	(Albert 1975:18)	Motif variant: The first perpendicular of the letter "U" is just as narrow as the second. In Albert, the first is wider.
04-17	"US"	GI30AV	(Albert 1975:18)	
04-19	"US"	GI30AV	(Albert 1975:18)	
06-01A	Eagle	GI53R21DP	(Albert 1975:29-30)	
06-01B	Eagle	GI53R21DP	(Albert 1975:29-30)	Numeral "1" of the regimental number "21" is partly visible.

Catalogue Number	Motif	Albert Code	Page Reference, Remarks
06-02	Eagle	GI53R21DP	(Albert 1975:29-30) Parts of the regimental numerals "21" are visible.
06-05	Eagle	GI53R21DP	(Albert 1975:29-30) "21" and small upper case "R" inside oval.
06-09	Eagle	GI53R21DP	(Albert 1975:29-30) "21 R" in oval. The lettering "ANTRY" encloses the left side.
06-11	Eagle	GI53R21DP	(Albert 1975:29-30)
06-15	Eagle	GI46A?	(Albert 1975:23-24) Encircling stars and the contents of the oval are obscured.
06-19	Eagle	GI53R21DP	(Albert 1975:29-30)
06-20	Eagle	GI53R21DP	(Albert 1975:30)
06-21	Eagle	GI46A	(Albert 1975:23-24) Not all encircling stars described in Albert are visible.
06-25	Eagle	GI53R21DP	(Albert 1975:29-30)
06-26	Eagle	GI53R21DP	(Albert 1975:29-30)
06-28	Eagle	GI53R21DP	(Albert 1975:29-30)
06-29	Eagle	GI53R21DP	(Albert 1975:29-30)
06-30	Eagle	GI53R21DP	(Albert 1975:29-30) Particularly good specimen.
07-02	Script "I"	GI36D1	(Albert 1975:21)
07-05	Script "I"	GI36D1	(Albert 1975:21) Perpendicular "I".
07-07	Script "I"	GI36D1	(Albert 1975:21)
07-11	Script "I"	GI36D1	(Albert 1975:21) Perpendicular "I".
07-16	Script "I"	GI36DI	(Albert 1975:21) Perpendicular "I". The best example in Burial 16.
07-22	Script "I"	GI36DI	(Albert 1975:21) Perpendicular "I".
07-30	Script "I"	GI34R15	(Albert 1975:20) Perpendicular "I".

Catalogue Number	Motif	Albert Code	Page Reference,	Remarks
07-31	Script "I"	GI36C?	(Albert 1975:21)	Perpendicular "I". The upper loops are very wide. The upper and bottom loops touch.
07-32	Script "I"	GI36D1	(Albert 1975:21)	Perpendicular "I".
07-44	Script "I"	GI36D2?	(Albert 1975:21)	Perpendicular "I". The upper loops are very wide. May also be GI36D3.
08-02	"US"	GI30AV	(Albert 1975:18)	
08-03	"US"	GI30A	(Albert 1975:18)	
08-04	"US"	GI30AV	(Albert 1975:18)	
08-07	Script "I"	GI36B	(Albert 1975:21)	Very ornate. "I" not perpendicular.
08-10	Script "I"	GI36B	(Albert 1975:21)	Very ornate, the "I" is slanted. One of the best examples of this type.
08-14	Script "I"	GI36A3V	(Albert 1975:21)	Prime point of star is down. Perpendicular "I". Few embellishments. Narrow upper loop touches the bottom loop.
08-15	Script "I"	GI36A...V	(Albert 1975:21)	Similar to 0814 but design is more obscured.
08-16	Script "I"	GI36B	(Albert 1975:21)	Very ornate "I" is slanted.
08-20	Script "I"	GI36BV	(Albert 1975:21)	Small version of 0810 and 0811.
08-22	"US"	GI30AV	(Albert 1975:18)	
08-23	"US"	GI30AV	(Albert 1975:18)	
09-01	Eagle	GI53R6B+	(Albert 1975:27)	Same as Albert's GI53R6B, except for back mark: "BEST PLATED", and two olive branches encircling.
09-02	Eagle	RF3A1V+	(Albert 1975:75-76)	Small version of Albert's RF3A1. Also, has no back mark.
09-04	Script "A"	AY38A1	(Albert 1975:50-51)	Design variant: Slight variation in execution of letter "A".

Catalogue Number	Motif	Albert Code	Page Reference, Remarks
09-06	Script "RA"	AY33A	(Albert 1975:50)
09-07	Script "RA"	AY33AV+	(Albert 1975:50) Similar to Albert's AY33A, except for small size.
09-12	Eagle	GI32R1C+	(Albert 1975:19, Supplement section, page 10) Design variant: Differs from description in that device is encircled by raised ring at edge. No back mark.
10-01	Script "I"	GI36D2V?	(Albert 1975:21) Perpendicular "I". The upper and lower loops do not touch. No visible star.
10-03	Script "I"	GI36A3V	(Albert 1975:21) Perpendicular "I". The upper and lower loops touch. Indistinct pentagonal shape inside oval may represent star, prime point down.
10-04	Script "I"	GI36A...V	(Albert 1975:21) Perpendicular "I". The upper and lower loops do not touch. The oval is compressed top to bottom, enclosing very indistinct star.
10-05	Script "I"	GI36A...V	(Albert 1975:21) Perpendicular "I". The upper and lower loops do not touch. The oval, compressed top to bottom, encloses indistinct star.
10-07	Script "I"	GI36A...V	(Albert 1975:21) Perpendicular "I". The upper and lower loops do not touch. The oval is compressed top to bottom, encloses an indistinct star.
10-09	Script "I"	GI36BV	(Albert 1975:21) Perpendicular "I". Upper and lower loops touch. Oval, compressed top to bottom, contains a six pointed star.
10-10	Script "I"	GI36A...V	(Albert 1975:21) Perpendicular "I". Upper and lower loops do not touch. Oval is compressed top to bottom, may enclose very indistinct shape.
10-11	Script "I"	GI36A...V	(Albert 1975:21) Perpendicular "I". Upper an lower loops touch. Oval, not compressed, enclosing an indistinct star, probably five pointed, prime point down.

Catalogue Number	Motif	Albert Code	Page Reference, Remarks
10-12	Script "I"	GI36A...V	(Albert 1975:21) Perpendicular "I". Upper and lower loops do not touch. Oval compressed top to bottom, encloses indistinct shape, probably a star.
10-18	Script "I"	GI36A...V	(Albert 1975:21) Probable perpendicular "I". The upper and lower loops do not touch. Compressed oval with probable eight pointed star.
10-24	Script "I"	GI36A...V	(Albert 1975:21) Perpendicular "I". Upper and lower loops may touch. Oval is not compressed.
11-03	"US"	GI30A	(Albert 1975:18)
11-04	"US"	GI30A	(Albert 1975:18)
11-05	"US"	GI30A	(Albert 1975:18)
17-03	Script "I"	GI36A3	(Albert 1975:21) The prime point of mullet is down.
18-02	Eagle	GI46A?	(Albert 1975:23-24) Little of design present. Excurvate profile of left wing, & notch between right wing suggest a variant of Albert's GI46.
18-03	Eagle	GI46A?	(Albert 1975:23-24) Very little of design remains. Excurvate profile of left wing indicates possible variant of Albert's GI46A.
21-02	Script "I"	GI36AL3	(Albert 1975:21) Perpendicular "I". Upper and lower loops do not touch. Upper swirl is more widely flared than shown by Albert. Prime point of mullet down.
21-12	Script "I"	GI36A3	(Albert 1975:21) Prime point of star is down. Perpendicular "I". Proximity of upper and lower loops obscured. Flourish on upper loop wider than shown by Albert.
21-15	Script "I"	GI36A3	(Albert 1975:21) Prime point of mullet is down. Perpendicular "I". The upper and lower loops almost touch. Top flourish is larger than shown in Albert.

Catalogue Number	Motif	Albert Code	Page Reference, Remarks
21-16	Script "I"	GI36A3	(Albert 1975:21) Prime point of mullet is down. Perpendicular "I". The upper and lower loop almost touch, but upper flourish is obscured.
21-17	Script "I"	GI36...V	(Albert 1975:21) Perpendicular "I". The upper and lower loops touch.
21-18	Script "I"	GI36A2	(Albert 1975:21) Perpendicular "I". Prime point of mullet is up. The upper and lower loops almost touch.
21-21	Script "I"	GI36A3	(Albert 1975:21) Prime point of mullet is down. Perpendicular "I". The upper and lower loops touch.
21-22	Script "I"	GI36A2	(Albert 1975:21) The prime point of mullet is up. The contact between upper and lower loops of "I" is obscured.
21-24	Script "I"	GI36A3	(Albert 1975:21) Prime point of star is down. Perpendicular "I". The upper and lower loops touch. The flourish on upper loop is larger than shown in Albert.
21-26	Script "I"	GI36A3	(Albert 1975:21) Prime point of mullet is up. Perpendicular "I". The proximity of the upper and lower loops is obscured.
21-31	Script "I"	GI36A...	(Albert 1975:21) Perpendicular "I". The upper and lower loops almost touch. The region of the oval is obscured.
21-34	Script "I"	GI36A3	(Albert 1975:21) Prime point of mullet is down. Perpendicular "I". The upper and lower loops almost touch.
22-01	Script "I"	GI36A3V	(Albert 1975:21) Prime point of star is down. Perpendicular "I". The upper and lower loops touch.
23-03	"US"	GI30A	(Albert 1975:18) The height of the letters is greater than shown in Albert.
23-04	"US"	GI30A	(Albert 1975:18) Design variant: The height of the letters is greater than shown in Albert.
23-05	"US"	GI30A	(Albert 1975:18) Design variant: The height of the letters is greater than shown in Albert.

Catalogue Number	Motif	Albert Code	Page Reference, Remarks
23-06	"US"	GI30A	(Albert 1975:18) Design variant: The height of the letters is greater than shown in Albert.
23-07	"US"	GI30A	(Albert 1975:18) Design variant: The height of the letters is greater than shown in Albert.
23-08	"US"	GI3OA	(Albert 1975:18) Design variant: The height of the lettering is greater than shown in Albert.
24-09	Script "I"	GI36B/C?	(Albert 1975:21) The script "I" is very faint. There are more than five star points.
24-10	Script "I"	GI36A3V	(Albert 1975:21) Perpendicular "I". The upper and lower loops do not touch.
26-01	"US"	GI30BV	(Albert 1975:18) Design variant: In place of six pointed star there is a dot, even with base of letters. Size of the letters is larger than Albert's GI30BV.
27-01	Script "I"	GI36CV?	(Albert 1975:21) Perpendicular "I". Upper and lower loops do not touch. Lines of "I" are strong, simple. Number of star points uncertain, but more than 5.
27-02A	Script "I"	GI36C?	(Albert 1975:21) Perpendicular I. Stem and lower loop are bold and simple. The number of star points is greater than five.
27-02B	Script "I"	GI36C?	(Albert 1975:21) The "I" is slightly slanted. The stem and lower loop are bold and simple. The image of star is unclear.
27-03	Script "I"	GI36C?	(Albert 1975:21) Perpendicular I. Stem and lower loop are bold and simple. The image of star is unclear.
27-04	Script "I"	GI36CV?	(Albert 1975:21) Perpendicular "I". Stem and lower loop are bold and simple. The image of star is very faint.
27-05	Script "I"	GI36C?	(Albert 1975:21) Perpendicular I. Stem and lower loop are bold and simple. The image of the star is obscured.
27-06	Script "I"	GI36CV?	(Albert 1975:21) The "I" is on a slight slant. Upper and lower loops do not touch. Stem and lower loop are bold and simple. Number of star points uncertain.

Catalogue Number	Motif	Albert Code	Page Reference, Remarks
27-07	Script "I"	GI36CV?	(Albert 1975:21) The "I" is slightly slanted. The stem and lower loop are bold and simple. Star only partially present, but has more than five points.
27-08	Script "I"	GI36C?	(Albert 1975:21) Perpendicular I. Stem and lower loop are bold and simple. Image of the star is very faint.
27-09	Script "I"	GI36CV?	(Albert 1975:21) Perpendicular "I". Upper and lower loops do not touch. Stem and lower loops are bold and simple. Image of the star is very faint.
27-10	Script "I"	GI36CV?	(Albert 1975:21) Perpendicular "I". The stem and lower loop are bold and simple. Details of the star are obscured.
27-11	Script "I"	GI36CV?	(Albert 1975:21) Perpendicular "I". Stem and lower loop are bold and simple. Details of the star are obscured.
27-12	Script "I"	GI36CV?	(Albert 1975:21) Perpendicular "I". The upper and lower loops do not touch. The stem and lower loop are bold and simple. Details of the star are very faint.
27-13	Script "I"	GI36CV?	(Albert 1975:21) Perpendicular "I". The stem and lower loop are bold and simple. Upper & lower loops do not touch. Details of star are vague.
27-14	Script "I"	GI36C	(Albert 1975:21) Perpendicular I. Upper & lower loops do not touch. Stem & lower loop bold & simple. Eight pointed star.
27-15	Script "I"	GI36C	(Albert 1975:21) Slightly slanted "I". Stem and lower loop bold & simple. Eight pointed star.
27-17	Script "I"	GI36C?	(Albert 1975:21) Slightly slanted "I". Stem &lower loop are bold and simple. Details of star are unclear.
27-18	Script "I"	GI36C?	(Albert 1975:21) Perpendicular I. Stem and loop are bold and simple. The star has eight points.

Catalogue Number	Motif	Albert Code	Page Reference, Remarks
27-19	Script "I"	GI36C?	(Albert 1975:21) Perpendicular I. The upper and lower loops do not touch. Details of star are obscured.
27-24	Script "I"	GI36C?	(Albert 1975:21) Perpendicular I. Stem & lower loop are strong & simple. Star has six or eight points.
27-28	Script "I"	GI36C?	(Albert 1975:21) Perpendicular I. The stem and lower loop are bold and simple. Details of star are obscured.
27-29	Script "I"	GI36CV?	(Albert 1975:21) Perpendicular I. Upper and lower loops do not touch. Details of the star are obscured.
27-31	Script "I"	GI36C	(Albert 1975:21) Perpendicular I. Stem and lower loop are bold and simple. The star has eight points.
27-34	Script "I"	GI36C?	(Albert 1975:21) Perpendicular I. Stem and lower loop are bold and simple. The star is obscured.
27-37	Script "I"	GI36C?	(Albert 1975:21) The "I" is on a slight slant. Stem and lower loop are bold and simple. Details of star are obscured.
27-38	Script "I"	GI36C?	(Albert 1975:21) Perpendicular I. Stem and lower loop are bold and simple. Upper and lower loops do not touch. The number of star points is greater than five.
29-32	Script "I"	GI36A2	(Albert 1975:21) Perpendicular I. The upper and lower loops touch.
29-38	Eagle	GI45A	(Albert 1975:23-24) Fits description, but the number of stars cannot be distinguished.

Plates

Plate 1:
Burial 1,
Button 1

Plate 2:
Burial 1,
Button 19

Plate 3:
Burial 2,
Button 2

Plate 4:
Feature 9,
Recovered Fabric

Plate 5:
Burial 3,
Button 24

Plate 6:
Burial 3,
Button 1

Plate 7:
Burial 4,
Button 6

Plate 8:
Burial 4,
Button 14

Plate 9:
Burial 4,
Button 17

Plate 10:
Burial 4,
Button 13

Plate 11:
Burial 6,
Button 5

Plate 12:
Burial 6,
Button 12

Plate 13:
Burial 6,
Button 30

Plate 14:
Burial 6,
Button 9

Plate 15:
Burial 7,
Button 16

Plate 16:
Burial 7,
Button 30

Plate 17:
Burial 7,
Button 47

Plate 18:
Burial 8,
Button 1b

Plate 19:
Burial 8,
Button 20

Plate 20:
Burial 8,
Large Civilian Button

Plate 21:
Feature 9,
Button 1

Plate 22:
Feature 9,
Button 5

Plate 23:
Burial 9,
Button 6

Plate 24:
Feature 9,
Button 2

Plate 25:
Feature 9,
Button 7

Plate 26:
Feature 9,
Button 4

Plate 27:
Burial 10,
Button 16

Plate 28:
Burial 10,
Button 18

Plate 29:
Burial 11,
Button 6

Plate 30:
Burial 13,
Button 2

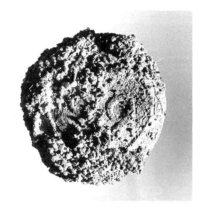

Plate 31:
Burial 17,
Button 11

Plate 32:
Burial 21,
Button 34

Plate 33:
Burial 21,
Button 21

Plate 34:
Burial 24,
Button 1

Plate 35:
Burial 29,
Button 38

Plate 36:
Burial 29,
Button 32

Plate 37:
Burial 26,
Button 1

Plate 38:
Burial 27,
Button 12

Plate 39:
Burial 19,
Button 3

Button Assemblage Summary

Burial 1 Button Assemblage
Listing by Nationality, Motif and Unit Device

Catalogue Number	Nationality	Button Motif	Regimental Device
01-06	American	Script "I"	Obscured
01-09	American	Script "I"	Obscured
01-10	American	Script "I"	Obscured
01-17	American	Script "I"	Obscured
01-18	American	Script "I"	Obscured
01-01	American	Script "I"	None
01-02A	American	Script "I"	None
01-04	American	Script "I"	None
01-05B	American	Script "I"	None
01-08A	American	Script "I"	None
01-19	American	Script "I"	None
01-03	American	Eagle	Star
01-05A	—	Obscured	None
01-02B	—	U/I	None
01-07	—	U/I	None
01-08B	—	U/I	None
01-11	—	U/I	None
01-12	—	U/I	None
01-13	—	U/I	None
01-14	—	U/I	None
01-15	—	U/I	None
01-16	—	U/I	None
01-20	—	U/I	None

Totals:	British	0
	American	12
	Not Identified	11
		====

23

Burial 2 Button Assemblage
Listing by Nationality, Motif and Unit Device

Catalogue Number	Nationality	Button Motif	Regimental Device
02-01	—	Plain (bone)	None
02-02	—	Plain (bone)	None
Totals:	British	0	
	American	0	
	Not Identified	2	
		====	
		2	

Burial 3 Button Assemblage
Listing by Nationality, Motif and Unit Device

Catalogue Number	Nationality	Button Motif	Regimental Device
03-01	American	Eagle	Star
03-09	American	Eagle	Star
03-24	American	Eagle	Star
03-10	American	Eagle	"US"
03-27	American	Eagle	Obscured
03-25A	—	Plain	None
03-25B	—	Plain	None
03-31	—	Plain	None
03-32	—	Plain	None
03-02	—	Obscured	None
03-04	—	Obscured	None
03-07	—	Obscured	None
03-11	—	Obscured	None
03-23	—	Obscured	None
03-26	—	Obscured	None
03-28	—	Obscured	None
03-03	—	U/I	None
03-05	—	U/I	None
03-06	—	U/I	None
03-08	—	U/I	None
03-12	—	U/I	None
03-13	—	U/I	None
03-14	—	U/I	None
03-15	—	U/I	None
03-16	—	U/I	None
03-17	—	U/I	None
03-18	—	U/I	None
03-19	—	U/I	None
03-20	—	U/I	None
03-21	—	U/I	None
03-22	—	U/I	None
03-29	—	U/I	None
03-30	—	U/I	None

Totals:	British	0
	American	5
	Not Identified	28
		====
		33

Burial 4 Button Assemblage
Listing by Nationality, Motif and Unit Device

Catalogue Number	Nationality	Button Motif	Regimental Device
04-05	American	Script "I"	Mullet
04-04	American	Script "I"	Star
04-06	American	Script "I"	Star
04-01	American	Script "I"	Obscured
04-02	American	Script "I"	Obscured
04-03	American	Script "I"	Obscured
04-11	American	Script "I"	Obscured
04-14	American	"US"	None
04-17	American	"US"	None
04-19	American	"US"	None
04-20	American	"US"	None
04-09	American	Plain: depressed centre	None
04-10	American	Plain: depressed centre	None
04-12	American	Plain: depressed centre	None
04-13	American	Plain: depressed centre	None
04-15A	American	Plain: depressed centre	None
04-16	American	Plain: depressed centre	None
04-18	American	Plain: depressed centre	None
04-21	American	Plain: depressed centre	None
04-15B	—	Obscured	None
04-07	—	U/I	None
04-08	—	U/I	None

Totals:	British	0
	American	19
	Not Identified	3
		====
		22

Burial 6 Button Assemblage
Listing by Nationality, Motif and Unit Device

Catalogue Number	Nationality	Button Motif	Regimental Device
06-12	British	Other: circled "104"	"104"
06-07	American	Eagle	"21"
06-11	American	Eagle	"21"
06-19	American	Eagle	"21"
06-05	American	Eagle	"21R"
06-09	American	Eagle	"21R"
06-25	American	Eagle	"21R"
06-26	American	Eagle	"21R"
06-28	American	Eagle	"21R"
06-29	American	Eagle	"21R"
06-21	American	Eagle	"US"
06-02	American	Eagle	Obscured
06-15	American	Eagle	Obscured
06-20	American	Eagle	Obscured
06-30	American	Eagle	Obscured
06-01A	American	Eagle	None
06-01B	American	Eagle	None
06-10	American	Plain: depressed centre	None
06-13	American	Plain: depressed centre	None
06-23	American	Plain: depressed centre	None
06-27	American	Plain: depressed centre	None
06-32	American	Plain: depressed centre	None
06-34	American	Plain: depressed centre	None
06-03	—	Obscured	None
06-08	—	Obscured	None
06-14	—	Obscured	None
06-16	—	Obscured	None
06-17	—	Obscured	None
06-18	—	Obscured	None
06-22	—	Obscured	None
06-33	—	Obscured	None
06-35	—	Obscured	None
06-36	—	Obscured	None
06-37	—	Obscured	None
06-39	—	Obscured	None
06-04	—	U/I	None
06-06	—	U/I	None
06-24	—	U/I	None
06-31	—	U/I	None
06-38	—	U/I	None
06-40	—	U/I	None

Totals:	British	1
	American	22
	Not Identified	18
		====
		41

Burial 7 Button Assemblage
Listing by Nationality, Motif and Unit Device

Catalogue Number	Nationality	Button Motif	Regimental Device
07-30	American	Script "I"	"15"
07-02	American	Script "I"	Obscured
07-05	American	Script "I"	Obscured
07-07	American	Script "I"	Obscured
07-11	American	Script "I"	Obscured
07-16	American	Script "I"	Obscured
07-22	American	Script "I"	Obscured
07-31	American	Script "I"	Obscured
07-32	American	Script "I"	Obscured
07-44	American	Script "I"	Obscured
07-12	American	Script "I"	None
07-17	American	Script "I"	None
07-20	American	Script "I"	None
07-21	American	Script "I"	None
07-33	American	Script "I"	None
07-34	American	Script "I"	None
07-37	American	Script "I"	None
07-40B	American	Script "I"	None
07-45	American	Script "I"	None
07-47	—	Plain (bone)	None
07-01	—	Obscured	None
07-18A	—	Obscured	None
07-18B	—	Obscured	None
07-46	—	Obscured	None
07-03	—	U/I	None
07-04	—	U/I	None
07-06A	—	U/I	None
07-06B	—	U/I	None
07-08	—	U/I	None
07-09	—	U/I	None
07-10	—	U/I	None
07-13	—	U/I	None
07-14	—	U/I	None
07-15	—	U/I	None
07-19	—	U/I	None
07-23	—	U/I	None
07-24	—	U/I	None
07-25	—	U/I	None
07-26	—	U/I	None
07-28	—	U/I	None
07-29	—	U/I	None
07-35	—	U/I	None
07-36	—	U/I	None
07-38	—	U/I	None
07-39	—	U/I	None
07-40A	—	U/I	None

Burial 7 Button Assemblage
Listing by Nationality, Motif and Unit Device (continued)

07-41	—	U/I	None
07-42	—	U/I	None
07-43	—	U/I	None

Totals:	British	0
	American	19
	Not Identified	30
		====
		49

Burial 8 Button Assemblage
Listing by Nationality, Motif and Unit Device

Catalogue Number	Nationality	Button Motif	Regimental Device
08-01B	American	Script "I"	Star
08-10	American	Script "I"	Star
08-14	American	Script "I"	Star
08-15	American	Script "I"	Star
08-16	American	Script "I"	Star
08-20	American	Script "I"	Star
08-05	American	Script "I"	Obscured
08-07	American	Script "I"	Obscured
08-08	American	Script "I"	Obscured
08-09	American	Script "I"	Obscured
08-13	American	Script "I"	Obscured
08-12	American	Script "I"	None
08-01A	American	"US"	None
08-02	American	"US"	None
08-03	American	"US"	None
08-04	American	"US"	None
08-22	American	"US"	None
08-23	American	"US"	None
08-17	—	Plain (bone)	None
08-18	—	Plain (bone)	None
08-11	—	Obscured	None
08-06	—	U/I	None
08-19	—	U/I	None
08-21	—	U/I	None

Totals:	British	0
	American	18
	Not Identified	6
		====
		24

Feature 9 (Medical Refuse Pit) Button Assemblage
Listing by Nationality, Motif and Unit Device

Catalogue Number	Nationality	Button Motif	Regimental Device
09-05	British	Other: 3 cannon	None
09-08	British	Other: 3 cannon	None
09-12	American	Eagle	"1.Rt."
09-01	American	Eagle	"6RFGT"
09-02	American	Eagle	"R"
09-06	American	Script "RA"	"2"
09-07	American	Script "RA"	"2"
09-04	American	Other: script "A"	"3"
09-03	—	Plain	None
09-09	—	Plain	None
09-10	—	Plain	None
09-11	—	Plain	None
09-13	—	Plain	None

Totals:	British	2
	American	6
	Not Identified	5
		====
		13

Burial 10 Button Assemblage
Listing by Nationality, Motif and Unit Device

Catalogue Number	Nationality	Button Motif	Regimental Device
10-02	American	Script "I"	Star
10-03	American	Script "I"	Star
10-04	American	Script "I"	Star
10-05	American	Script "I"	Star
10-07	American	Script "I"	Star
10-09	American	Script "I"	Star
10-11	American	Script "I"	Star
10-12	American	Script "I"	Star
10-16	American	Script "I"	Star
10-17	American	Script "I"	Star
10-18	American	Script "I"	Star
10-24	American	Script "I"	Star
10-26	American	Script "I"	Star
10-01	American	Script "I"	Obscured
10-15	American	Script "I"	Obscured
10-19	American	Script "I"	Obscured
10-21	American	Script "I"	Obscured
10-22	American	Script "I"	Obscured
10-23	American	Script "I"	Obscured
10-28	American	Script "I"	Obscured
10-10	American	Script "I"	None
10-13	American	Script "I"	None
10-27	American	Script "I"	None
10-14	—	Obscured	None
10-06	—	U/I	None
10-08	—	U/I	None
10-20	—	U/I	None
10-25	—	U/I	None

Totals:		
	British	0
	American	23
	Not Identified	5
		====
		28

Burial 11 Button Assemblage
Listing by Nationality, Motif and Unit Device

Catalogue Number	Nationality	Button Motif	Regimental Device
11-03	American	"US"	None
11-04	American	"US"	None
11-05	American	"US"	None
11-06	American	"US"	None
11-01	—	Plain (bone)	None
11-02	—	Plain (bone)	None
Totals:	British	0	
	American	4	
	Not Identified	2	
		====	
		6	

Burial 12 Button Assemblage
Listing by Nationality, Motif and Unit Device

Catalogue Number	Nationality	Button Motif	Regimental Device
12-01B	American	Script "I"	None
12-02	—	Plain	None
12-01A	—	U/I	None
12-03	—	U/I	None
12-04	—	U/I	None
Totals:	British	0	
	American	1	
	Not Identified	4	
		====	
		5	

Burial 13 Button Assemblage
Listing by Nationality, Motif and Unit Device

Catalogue Number	Nationality	Button Motif	Regimental Device
13-04	American	Script "I"	Obscured
13-05	American	Script "I"	Obscured
13-03	American	Script "I"	None
13-01	—	Other: floral (cuff link)	None
13-02	—	Other: floral (cuff link)	None
13-06	—	Obscured	None
13-07	—	U/I	None
Totals:	British	0	
	American	3	
	Not Identified	4	
		====	
		7	

Burial 14 Button Assemblage
Listing by Nationality, Motif and Unit Device

Catalogue Number	Nationality	Button Motif	Regimental Device
14-05	American	Eagle	Obscured
14-04	American	"US"	None
14-06	American	Plain: depressed centre	None
14-01	—	Plain (bone)	None
14-02	—	U/I	None
14-03	—	U/I	None
14-07	—	U/I	None
Totals:	British	0	
	American	3	
	Not Identified	4	
		====	
		7	

Burial 15 Button Assemblage
Listing by Nationality, Motif and Unit Device

Catalogue Number	Nationality	Button Motif	Regimental Device
15-01	American	Script "I"	None
15-05	American	Script "I"	None
15-07	American	Script "I"	None
15-02	—	U/I	None
15-03	—	U/I	None
15-06	—	U/I	None
Totals:	British	0	
	American	3	
	Not Identified	3	
		====	
		6	

Burial 16 Button Assemblage
Listing by Nationality, Motif and Unit Device

Catalogue Number	Nationality	Button Motif	Regimental Device
16-01	American	Plain: depressed centre	None
16-02	American	Plain: depressed centre	None
16-03	American	Plain: depressed centre	None
16-04	American	Plain: depressed centre	None
16-05	American	Plain: depressed centre	None
16-06	American	Plain: depressed centre	None
16-07	American	Plain: depressed centre	None
16-10	American	Plain: depressed centre	None
16-08	—	U/I	None
16-09	—	U/I	None
Totals:	British	0	
	American	8	
	Not Identified	2	
		====	
		10	

Burial 17 Button Assemblage
Listing by Nationality, Motif and Unit Device

Catalogue Number	Nationality	Button Motif	Regimental Device
17-11	British	Other: circled 89	"89"
17-12	British	Other: circled 89	"89"
17-03	American	Script "I"	Mullet
17-07	—	Plain	None
17-02	—	Obscured	None
17-04	—	Obscured	None
17-01	—	U/I	None
17-05	—	U/I	None
17-06	—	U/I	None
17-08	—	U/I	None
17-09	—	U/I	None
17-10	—	U/I	None

Totals:	British	2 (in secondary inclusion)
	American	1
	Not Identified	9 (including 2 in secondary inclusion)
		====
		12

Burial 18 Button Assemblage
Listing by Nationality, Motif and Unit Device

Catalogue Number	Nationality	Button Motif	Regimental Device
18-09	American	Script "I"	None
18-03	American	Eagle	Obscured
18-02	American	Eagle	None
18-07	—	Obscured	None
18-01	—	U/I	None
18-04	—	U/I	None
18-05	—	U/I	None
18-06	—	U/I	None
18-08	—	U/I	None
18-10	—	U/I	None

Totals:	British	0
	American	3
	Not Identified	7
		====
		10

Burial 19 Button Assemblage
Listing by Nationality, Motif and Unit Device

Catalogue Number	Nationality	Button Motif	Regimental Device
19-02	—	Other: flowers	None
19-03	—	Other: flowers	None
19-04	—	Other: flowers	None
19-01	—	Plain (bone)	None
Totals:	British	0	
	American	0	
	Not Identified	4	
		====	
		4	

Burial 20 Button Assemblage
Listing by Nationality, Motif and Unit Device

Catalogue Number	Nationality	Button Motif	Regimental Device
20-03	American	Script "I"	Star
20-01	—	U/I	None
20-02	—	U/I	None
20-04	—	U/I	None
20-05	—	U/I	None
20-06	—	U/I	None
Totals:	British	0	
	American	1	
	Not Identified	5	
		====	
		6	

Burial 21 Button Assemblage
Listing by Nationality, Motif and Unit Device

Catalogue Number	Nationality	Button Motif	Regimental Device
21-02	American	Script "I"	Mullet
21-15	American	Script "I"	Mullet
21-16	American	Script "I"	Mullet
21-18	American	Script "I"	Mullet
21-21	American	Script "I"	Mullet
21-22	American	Script "I"	Mullet
21-26	American	Script "I"	Mullet
21-34	American	Script "I"	Mullet
21-12	American	Script "I"	Star
21-24	American	Script "I"	Star
21-07A	American	Script "I"	Obscured
21-14	American	Script "I"	Obscured
21-17	American	Script "I"	Obscured
21-23	American	Script "I"	Obscured
21-31	American	Script "I"	Obscured
21-32	American	Script "I"	Obscured
21-33	American	Script "I"	Obscured
21-03	American	Script "I"	None
21-04	American	Script "I"	None
21-07B	American	Script "I"	None
21-28	American	Obscured	Star
21-01	—	Obscured	None
21-06	—	Obscured	None
21-05	—	U/I	None
21-07C	—	U/I	None
21-08	—	U/I	None
21-09	—	U/I	None
21-10	—	U/I	None
21-11	—	U/I	None
21-13	—	U/I	None
21-19	—	U/I	None
21-20	—	U/I	None
21-25	—	U/I	None
21-27	—	U/I	None
21-29	—	U/I	None
21-30	—	U/I	None

Totals:	British	0
	American	21
	Not Identified	15
		====
		36

Feature 22 (Medical Waste Pit) Button Assemblage
Listing by Nationality, Motif and Unit Device

Catalogue Number	Nationality	Button Motif	Regimental Device
22-01	American	Script "I"	Star
22-06	American	Plain: depressed centre	None
22-02	—	U/I	None
22-03	—	U/I	None
22-04	—	U/I	None
22-05	—	U/I	None
22-07	—	U/I	None
22-08	—	U/I	None
Totals:	British	0	
	American	2	
	Not Identified	6	
		====	
		8	

Burial 23 Button Assemblage
Listing by Nationality, Motif and Unit Device

Catalogue Number	Nationality	Button Motif	Regimental Device
23-03	American	"US"	None
23-04	American	"US"	None
23-05	American	"US"	None
23-06	American	"US"	None
23-07	American	"US"	None
23-08	American	"US"	None
23-01	—	Plain (bone)	None
23-02	—	Plain (bone)	None
Totals:	British	0	
	American	6	
	Not Identified	2	
		====	
		8	

Burial 24 Button Assemblage
Listing by Nationality, Motif and Unit Device

Catalogue Number	Nationality	Button Motif	Regimental Device
24-09	American	Script "I"	Star
24-10	American	Script "I"	Star
24-08	American	Script "I"	None
24-01	—	Plain (bone)	None
24-02	—	Plain (bone)	None
24-03	—	Plain (bone)	None
24-04	—	Plain (bone)	None
24-06A	—	Plain (bone)	None
24-05	—	U/I	None
24-06B	—	U/I	None
24-07	—	U/I	None
Totals:	British	0	
	American	3	
	Not Identified	8	
		====	
		11	

Burial 26 Button Assemblage
Listing by Nationality, Motif and Unit Device

Catalogue Number	Nationality	Button Motif	Regimental Device
26-01	American	"US"	None
Totals:	British	0	
	American	1	
	Not Identified	0	
		====	
		1	

Burial 27 Button Assemblage
Listing by Nationality, Motif and Unit Device

Catalogue Number	Nationality	Button Motif	Regimental Device
27-01	American	Script "I"	Star
27-02A	American	Script "I"	Star
27-02B	American	Script "I"	Star
27-03	American	Script "I"	Star
27-04	American	Script "I"	Star
27-06	American	Script "I"	Star
27-07	American	Script "I"	Star
27-08	American	Script "I"	Star
27-09	American	Script "I"	Star
27-10	American	Script "I"	Star
27-11	American	Script "I"	Star
27-12	American	Script "I"	Star
27-13	American	Script "I"	Star
27-14	American	Script "I"	Star
27-15	American	Script "I"	Star
27-17	American	Script "I"	Star
27-18	American	Script "I"	Star
27-19	American	Script "I"	Star
27-24	American	Script "I"	Star
27-26	American	Script "I"	Star
27-28	American	Script "I"	Star
27-29	American	Script "I"	Star
27-31	American	Script "I"	Star
27-32	American	Script "I"	Star
27-34	American	Script "I"	Star
27-37	American	Script "I"	Star
27-38	American	Script "I"	Star
27-05	American	Script "I"	Obscured
27-16	American	Script "I"	Obscured
27-21	American	Script "I"	Obscured
27-22	American	Script "I"	Obscured
27-23	American	Script "I"	Obscured
27-20	American	Plain	Star
27-35	—	Other: machined bone	None
27-30	—	Plain	None
27-33	—	Plain	None
27-40	—	Plain	None
27-25	—	Obscured	None
27-27	—	U/I	None
27-36	—	U/I	None
27-39	—	U/I	None

Totals:			
	British	0	
	American	33	
	Not Identified	8	
		====	
		41	

Burial 28 Button Assemblage
Listing by Nationality, Motif and Unit Device

Catalogue Number	Nationality	Button Motif	Regimental Device
28-01	—	Plain (bone)	None
Totals:	British	0	
	American	0	
	Not Identified	1	
		====	
		1	

Burial 29 Button Assemblage
Listing by Nationality, Motif and Unit Device

Catalogue Number	Nationality	Button Motif	Regimental Device
29-32	American	Script "I"	Mullet
29-38	American	Eagle	"US"
29-35	—	Obscured	None
29-01	—	U/I	None
29-06	—	U/I	None
29-18	—	U/I	None
29-20	—	U/I	None
29-21	—	U/I	None
29-23	—	U/I	None
29-24	—	U/I	None
29-25	—	U/I	None
29-26	—	U/I	None
29-27	—	U/I	None
29-28	—	U/I	None
29-29	—	U/I	None
29-30	—	U/I	None
29-31	—	U/I	None
29-33	—	U/I	None
29-34	—	U/I	None
29-36	—	U/I	None
29-37	—	U/I	None
Totals:	British	0	
	American	2	
	Not Identified	19	
		====	
		21	

Feature H2 Button Assemblage
Listing by Nationality, Motif and Unit Device

Catalogue Number	Nationality	Button Motif	Regimental Device
H2-01	American	Script "I"	Star
H2-02	American	"US"	None
H2-03	—	U/I	None
Totals:	British	0	
	American	2	
	Not Identified	1	
		====	
		3	
Site-Wide Totals:	British	5	
	American	221	
	Not Identified	212	
		=====	
		438	

Catalogue

Cat. Number	Material	Shape, Attachment	Size, Portion	Motif, Unit Device, Design Features	Location Information
				BURIAL 01	
01-01:	Pewter	Round, Flat Shank	20.0mm 100%	AMERICAN, SCRIPT I motif. Excellent condition. Flat rim.	LEFT THORAX. Side of body. Shank up. Four cm left of lower thorax, between ribcage & distal left humerus.
01-02A:	Pewter	Round, Flat Shank	------ 70%	AMERICAN, SCRIPT I motif. Good condition. May have different type of Script I motif than button 1. Large button.	RIGHT NECK. Over body. Shank up. In cluster on right side of neck with buttons 2B & 9, in the badly disturbed neck area.
01-02B:	Pewter	------ ----	------ 5%	Motif obscured or absent. Poor condition. Just a sliver.	RIGHT NECK. Over body. In cluster on right side of neck with buttons 2A & 9. Area was badly disturbed early in exhumation, so this item may be part of 2A.
01-03:	Pewter	Round, Convex Shank	23.0mm 50%	AMERICAN, EAGLE motif, unit device is a STAR. Good condition. Lower half of large convex eagle button. Associated with metal fragments.	MIDLINE THORAX. Over body. Shank up. On top of lower thoracic vertebra. Cranialmost in vertical linear series (3, 4, 6, 7) in midline of lower thorax & upper waist.
01-04:	Pewter	Round, Flat Shank	20.0mm 80%	AMERICAN, SCRIPT I motif. Good condition.	MIDLINE THORAX. Over body. Shank up. About 1 cm right of T12 and L1. Third down in vertical linear series (3, 4, 6, 7) in midline of lower thorax & upper waist.
01-05A:	Pewter	Round, Flat Shank	------ 40%	OBSCURED motif. Good condition.	RIGHT WAIST. Over body. In close association with 5B, in upper right waist area.
01-05B:	Pewter	Round, Flat Shank	------ 50%	AMERICAN, SCRIPT I motif. Good condition. One piece cast. Large button.	RIGHT WAIST. Over body. In close association with 5A, in upper right waist area.

Cat. Number	Material	Shape, Attachment	Size, Portion Features	Motif, Unit Device, Design	Location Information
01-06:	Pewter	Round, Flat Shank	21.0mm 80%	AMERICAN, SCRIPT I motif, unit device obscured. One piece cast. Good condition.	MIDLINE THORAX. Over body. Shank down. About 1 cm right of a lower thoracic vertebra. Second down vertical linear series (3, 4, 6, 7) in midline of lower thorax & waist.
01-07:	Pewter	Round, Flat ----	------ 20%	Motif obscured or absent. Poor condition. Small button.	MIDLINE WAIST. Over body. Touching right side of L2. Caudalmost in vertical linear series (3, 4, 6, 7) in midline of lower thorax & upper waist.
01-08A:	Pewter	Round, Flat Shank	------ 80%	AMERICAN, SCRIPT I motif. Good condition. Large button.	RIGHT THORAX. Over body. Shank up. Cranialmost in vertical linear series (8, 12, 13) just lateral to lower right thorax. Touching lower right rib. Analogous in location to 1.
01-08B:	Pewter	----- Flat Shank	------ 40%	Motif obscured or absent. Poor condition. Large button.	THORAX. Exact location unknown, but was recovered with rib fragment, so must be from thorax region.
01-09:	Pewter	Round, Flat Shank	20.3mm 90%	AMERICAN, SCRIPT I motif, unit device obscured. One piece cast. Flat rim.	RIGHT NECK. With buttons 2A & 2B, in cluster at right of neck.
01-10:	Pewter	Round, Flat Shank	------ 60%	AMERICAN, SCRIPT I motif, unit device obscured. Poor condition. Large button.	LEFT WRIST. Over body. Shank down. In left wrist area.
01-11:	Pewter	---- ----	------ 5%	Motif obscured or absent. Poor condition.	RIGHT WRIST (PELVIS). Over body. In area of right wrist, overlying central right ilium.
01-12:	Pewter	----- Flat Shank	14.4mm 40%	Motif obscured or absent. Poor condition.	RIGHT THORAX. Over body. Shank down. Just lateral of lower right thorax. Caudalmost in linear vertical series (8, 12, 13).

Cat. Number	Material	Shape, Attachment	Size, Portion Features	Motif, Unit Device, Design Features	Location Information
01-13:	Pewter	----- Flat Shank	------ 50%	Motif obscured or absent. Poor condition. Large button.	RIGHT THORAX. Over body. Shank down. Just lateral of lower right thorax. Central in vertical linear series (8, 12, 13).
01-14:	Pewter	----- ----	------ 10%	Motif obscured or absent. Poor condition. Just slivers and very small fragments.	LEFT THORAX. Over body. Overlying left ribs & 5 cm left of T10. Possibly associated with 15.
01-15:	Pewter	----- Flat Shank	------ 40%	Motif obscured or absent. Poor condition. Large button.	LEFT THORAX. Over body. Shank up. In left thorax, even with T10. Possibly associated with 14.
01-16:	Pewter	----- -----	------ 5%	Motif obscured or absent. Poor condition.	MIDLINE THORAX. In lower thorax, near T9.
01-17:	Pewter	Round, Flat Shank	20.7mm 80%	AMERICAN, SCRIPT I motif, unit device obscured. Excellent condition. One piece cast.	Location not available. No provenience data.
01-18:	Pewter	Round, Flat Shank	19.9mm 100%	AMERICAN, SCRIPT I motif, unit device obscured. Excellent condition. One piece cast. Flat rim.	Location not available. No provenience data.
01-19:	Pewter	Round, Flat Shank	20.5mm 90%	AMERICAN, SCRIPT I motif. Excellent condition. One piece cast.	THORAX. Thorax area. Specific location not available.
01-20:	Pewter	----- Flat Shank	------ 30%	Motif obscured or absent. Poor condition. Large button.	PELVIS. Lower pelvic area. Specific location not available.

Cat. Number	Material	Shape, Attachment	Size, Portion	Motif, Unit Device, Design Features	Location Information
::::::::::::::::: BURIAL 02 :::::::::::::::::				
02-01:	Bone	Round, Flat 1-Hole	12.8mm 100%	PLAIN (BONE) motif. Excellent condition. Has saw marks. Possible worn area on rim.	LEFT WRIST. Over body. Centred over distal left forearm.
02-02:	Bone	Round, Flat 1-Hole	12.6mm 100%	PLAIN (BONE) motif. Excellent condition. Has saw marks. Appears worn on one edge.	WAIST. Under body. Beneath L4.
::::::::::::::::: BURIAL 03 :::::::::::::::::				
03-01:	Pewter	Round, Convex Shank	22.1mm 100%	AMERICAN, EAGLE motif, unit device is a STAR. Excellent condition. "UNITED STATES INFANTRY" encircles eagle facing left. Red corroded pinch base shank.	LEFT WRIST. Over body. Shank down. On top of distal left radius and ulna. Central in cluster around distal left forearm (1, 2, 3, 4).
03-02:	Pewter	Round, Convex Shank	22.0mm 100%	OBSCURED motif. Good condition. Red corrosion on pinch base shank. "...STAR..." around edge. Probably eagle button.	LEFT WRIST. Under body. Shank down. Just lateral to left ulna & button 1, in cluster around distal left forearm (1, 2, 3, 4). Shank slightly angled towards arm.
03-03:	Pewter	Round, Convex Shank	22.8mm 30%	Motif obscured or absent. Poor condition. Central area missing, but over 50% of rim is present.	LEFT WRIST (PELVIS). Over body. On medial side of, & shank touching, distal left radius. In cluster around distal left forearm (1, 2, 3, 4). Just proximal of 4.
03-04:	Pewter	Round, Convex Shank	22.6mm 90%	OBSCURED motif. Good condition. Unidentified substance adhered to back. Pinch base shank.	LEFT WRIST (PELVIS). Over body. Shank up. Just medial to left radius in cluster around distal left forearm (1, 2, 3, 4). Just prox of 3. Shank up & slightly angled towards 3.

Cat. Number	Material	Shape, Attachment	Size, Portion	Motif, Unit Device, Design Features	Location Information
03-05:	Pewter	----- ----	----- 10%	Motif obscured or absent. Poor condition.	LEFT WAIST. Over body. In left waist area. Caudalmost in vertical linear series (5, 6, 7, 8, 24) in left thorax-waist region.
03-06:	Pewter	----- ----	----- 10%	Motif obscured or absent. Poor condition.	LEFT THORAX. Over body. In lower left thorax or waist area. In vertical linear series (5, 6, 7, 8, 24) in left trunk region.
03-07:	Pewter	Round, Shank	Convex 23.4mm 60%	OBSCURED motif. Good condition. Material adhered to back. Red corrosion in shank area.	LEFT THORAX. Over body. Shank up. In central left thorax area. Third up in vertical linear series (5, 6, 7, 8, 24) in left trunk region.
03-08:	Pewter	----- Shank	Convex ----- 0%	Motif obscured or absent. Poor condition. Field diameter = 25 mm. Highly fragmented.	LEFT THORAX. Over body. In upper left thorax beneath disturbed rib. Very close to 24 in vertical linear series (5, 6, 7, 8, 24) in left trunk region.
03-09:	Pewter	Round, Shank	Convex 21.8mm 100%	AMERICAN, EAGLE motif, unit device is a STAR. Excellent cond. "UNITED STATES INFANTRY" with eagle facing left. Red corrosion, fabric, on pinch base shank.	LEFT THORAX. Over body. Shank up. Proximalmost in tight cluster (9, 10, 11) between left central humerus & ribs.
03-10:	Pewter	Round, Shank	Flat 14.5mm 100%	AMERICAN, EAGLE motif, unit device is US. Excellent condition. One piece cast.	LEFT THORAX. Over body. Shank up. Part of tight cluster (9, 10, 11) between left central humerus & ribs. Caudalmost & smallest item of cluster.
03-11:	Pewter	Round, Shank	Convex 22.6mm 80%	OBSCURED motif. Good condition. Recovered in cast. Red corrosion on pinch base shank.	LEFT THORAX. Over body. Shank up. Part of tight cluster (9, 10, 11) between left central humerus & ribs. Touching medial side of humerus opposite 23.

Cat. Number	Material	Shape, Attachment	Size, Portion	Motif, Unit Device, Design Features	Location Information
03-12:	Pewter	----- -----	------ 5%	Motif obscured or absent. Poor condition - just crumbs.	RIGHT NECK. Side of body. Furthest right at latero-posterior side of left-turned skull, in tight neck cluster (12, 21, 22, 26, 27, 28, 29).
03-13:	Pewter	------ Shank	------ 10%	Motif obscured or absent. Poor cond. Large button - 6 x 4 cm size reduced to powder. Located at laterocranial end of organic material.	RIGHT THORAX. Over body. Shank up. Upper right thorax near shoulder. Removed from block. Associated w 19 & 20. Not mapped.
03-14:	Pewter	----- -----	------ 10%	Motif obscured or absent. Poor condition.	RIGHT THORAX. Over body. Cranialmost in vertical linear series (14, 15, 16) in right thorax area.
03-15:	Pewter	----- -----	------ 0%	Motif obscured or absent. Poor condition. Highly fragmented.	RIGHT THORAX. Over body. Middle button in vertical linear series (14, 15, 16) in right thorax area.
03-16:	Pewter	----- -----	------ 5%	Motif obscured or absent. Poor condition.	RIGHT THORAX. Over body. Caudalmost in vertical linear series (14, 15, 16) in right thorax. Series could have continued caudad into area of poor preservation.
03-17:	Pewter	----- -----	------ 30%	Motif obscured or absent. Poor cond. Just grains. Field-estimated diameter = 25mm. Copper staining with preserved fabric or leather.	RIGHT PELVIS (WRIST L). Over body. Shank down. Found overlying right ilium in area of distal left hand, in dense cluster (17, 18, 30, 31, 32).
03-18:	Pewter	Convex -----	------ 10%	Motif obscured or absent. Poor condition. Found in area of copper staining & preserved fabric or leather.	RIGHT PELVIS. Over body. Caudolateralmost in cluster (17, 18, 30, 31, 32) in area of left hand & right ilium.

Cat. Number	Material	Shape, Attachment	Size, Portion	Motif, Unit Device, Design Features	Location Information
03-19:	Pewter	----- Shank	------ 10%	Motif obscured or absent. Poor condition. Just powder. Located proximo-laterally to unidentified organic material, possibly leather.	RIGHT THORAX. Over body. Right lateral edge of central thorax, & touching 20. Removed from block. Associated with organic material & 13, 20.
03-20:	Pewter	----- Shank	------ 10%	Motif obscured or absent. Poor condition. Just powder. Located lateral to organic material, possibly leather.	RIGHT THORAX. Over body. Right margin of central thorax, just lateral of 19. Removed from excavated block. Associated with organic material & 13, 19.
03-21:	Pewter	Round, Shank	------ 70%	Motif obscured or absent. Poor condition. Removed in cast. Estimated diameter in cast = 25.0 mm.	NECK. Side of body. Shank up. On right lateroposterior side of left-turned skull. In tight neck cluster (12, 21, 22, 26, 27, 28, 29) in neck region.
03-22:	Pewter	Round, Shank	------ 60%	Motif obscured or absent. Poor condition. Removed in cast. Field measurement = 25 mm, approximately.	NECK. Side of body. Next to lateroposterior side of left-turned skull. Almost touching 21, in dense neck cluster (12, 21, 22, 26, 27, 28, 29).
03-23:	Pewter	Round, Shank	23.0mm 90%	OBSCURED motif. Good condition. Removed in cast.	LEFT ARM. Side of body. Shank up. One cm lateral of left central humerus, opposite 11, & possibly related to cluster (9, 10, 11) between ribcage & humerus.
03-24:	Pewter	Round, Shank	22.1mm 100%	AMERICAN, EAGLE motif, unit device is a STAR. Excellent cond. Recovered in cast. "UNITED STATES INFANTRY" encircling left-facing eagle. Red stained shank.	LEFT THORAX. Over body. Shank up. In upper left thorax. Cranialmost in vertical linear series (5, 6, 7, 8, 24) in left trunk region.

Cat. Number	Material	Shape, Attachment	Size, Portion	Motif, Unit Device, Design Features	Location Information
03-25A:	Copper Alloy	Round, Flat Shank	14.6mm 100%	PLAIN motif. Excellent condition. Recovered early in sequence. Soldered ring shank inside 5 mm raised circle.	RIGHT ARM (WAIST, R). Over body. Overlying & near distal right forearm. Face in contact with face of 25B.
03-25B:	Copper Alloy	Round, Flat Shank	14.5mm 100%	PLAIN motif. Excellent condition. Soldered ring shank inside 5 mm raised circle.	RIGHT WRIST (WAIST). Over body. Overlying & near the distal right radius and ulna. Face in contact with face of 25A.
03-26:	Pewter	Round, Convex Shank	22.8mm 80%	OBSCURED motif. Good condition. Recovered early in sequence. Pinch base shank.	NECK. Over body. Near angle of right mandible, in neck cluster (12, 22, 26, 27, 28, 29).
03-27:	Pewter	Round, Convex Shank	16.2mm 100%	AMERICAN, EAGLE motif, unit device obscured. Excellent condition. No red stain on shank.	NECK. Under body. Shank up. Taken from block removed with skull. Part of dense neck cluster (12, 21, 22, 26, & 27, 28, 29). Beneath 28 & 29.
03-28:	Pewter	Round, Convex Shank	21.8mm 100%	OBSCURED motif. Excellent condition.	NECK. Under body. Shank up. Taken from block removed with skull. Part of dense cluster behind neck (12, 21, 22, 27, 28, 29). Overlying 27.
03-29:	Pewter	Round, Convex Shank	----- 20%	Motif obscured or absent. Poor condition, just crumbs.	NECK. Under body. Shank up. Taken from block removed with skull. In basicranial area. Part of dense neck cluster (12, 21, 22, 26, 27, 28, 29). Overlying 27.
03-30:	Pewter	---- Shank	------ 30%	Motif obscured or absent. Poor condition. Just small fragments.	RIGHT PELVIS. Over body. On central right ilium, right of central sacrum. Beneath 32, 3 cm caudolateral of 31, near 17 & 18. Beneath left hand elements. Not mapped.

Cat. Number	Material	Shape, Attachment	Size, Portion	Motif, Unit Device, Design Features	Location Information
03-31:	Copper Alloy	Round, Flat Shank	16.0mm 90%	PLAIN motif. Excellent condition. Associated with over- & underlying organic material.	RIGHT PELVIS (WRIST, L). Over body. Shank up. Beneath left hand elements, near cranial border of right ilium close to sacrum. About 3 cm craniomedial of 30 & 32, near 17 & 18.
03-32:	Copper Alloy	Round, Flat Shank	20.5mm 100%	PLAIN motif. Excellent condition. Associated with over- & underlying preserved organic material.	RIGHT PELVIS. Over body. Shank up. Beneath 30 on the central right ilium, lateral of central sacrum, 3 cm caudolateral of 31. In cluster with 17 & 18.

BURIAL 04

Cat. Number	Material	Shape, Attachment	Size, Portion	Motif, Unit Device, Design Features	Location Information
04-01:	Pewter	Round, Flat Shank	16.7mm 100%	AMERICAN, SCRIPT I motif, unit device obscured. Excellent condition. One piece cast. Flat rim, front edge slightly rounded, back edge sharp.	RIGHT THORAX. Over body. Shank down. Just caudomedial of right shoulder. Cranialmost in vertical linear series (1, 2, 3, 4, 5, 6, 7, 11) in right thorax area.
04-02:	Pewter	Round, Flat Shank	16.4mm 100%	AMERICAN, SCRIPT I motif, unit device obscured. Excellent condition. One piece cast. Flat rim, front edge rounded, back edge sharp.	RIGHT THORAX. Over body. Shank down. 3 cm caudolateral of proximal clavicle. Second down in vertical linear series (1, 2, 3, 4, 5, 6, 7, 11) in right thorax area.
04-03:	Pewter	Round, Flat Shank	16.6mm 100%	AMERICAN, SCRIPT I motif, unit device obscured. Excellent condition. One piece cast. Flat rim, front edge rounded, back edge sharp.	RIGHT THORAX. Over body. Shank down. Third from top in right central thorax. Right central thorax. Third from top in vertical linear series (1, 2, 3, 4, 5, 6, 7, 11) in right thorax area.

Cat. Number	Material	Shape, Attachment	Size, Portion	Motif, Unit Device, Design Features	Location Information
04-04:	Pewter	Round, Flat Shank	16.5mm 100%	AMERICAN, SCRIPT I motif, unit device is a STAR. Excellent condition. One piece cast. Flat rim, front edge rounded, back edge sharp.	RIGHT THORAX. Over body. Shank down. Fourth from top in vertical linear series (1, 2, 3, 4, 5, 6, 7, 11) in right thorax area.
04-05:	Pewter	Round, Flat Shank	16.3mm 100%	AMERICAN, SCRIPT I motif, unit device is MULLET. Excellent condition. One piece cast. Flat rim, front edge rounded, back edge sharp.	RIGHT THORAX. Over body. Shank down. Right central thorax. Fifth down in vertical linear series (1, 2, 3, 4, 5, 6, 7, 11) in right thorax area.
04-06:	Pewter	Round, Flat Shank	16.7mm 100%	AMERICAN, SCRIPT I motif, unit device is a STAR. Excellent condition. One piece cast. Flat rim, front edge rounded, back edge sharp.	RIGHT THORAX. Over body. Shank down. Lower right thorax. Sixth down in vertical linear series (1, 2, 3, 4, 5, 6, 7, 11) in right thorax area.
04-07:	Pewter	----- ----	------ 20%	Motif obscured or absent. Poor condition. Just crumbs.	RIGHT THORAX. Over body. Lower right thorax, about even with T11. Out of line with, but possibly related to, vertical linear series 1-6 & 11.
04-08:	Pewter	Round, ----	------ 0%	Motif obscured or absent. Specimen not available for analysis.	RIGHT WAIST (ARM, R). Over body. Shank down. Upper right waist area, partly beneath 9. In vertical cluster (8, 9, 10) at right side of waist.
04-09:	Pewter	Round, Flat 4-Hole	18.2mm 100%	AMERICAN, PLAIN: DEPRESSED CENTRE motif. Excellent condition.	RIGHT WAIST (THORAX, R). Over body. Shank down. Upper right waist, overlying 8. In vertical cluster (8, 9, 10) at right side of waist.

Cat. Number	Material	Shape, Attachment	Size, Portion	Motif, Unit Device, Design Features	Location Information
04-10:	Pewter	Round, Flat 4-Hole	18.0mm 100%	AMERICAN, PLAIN: DEPRESSED CENTRE motif. Excellent condition.	RIGHT WAIST. Over body. Shank up. Right central waist. Caudalmost in cluster (8, 9, 10) at right side of waist. In line with 13 (and possibly 12) in midline, and 17 on left.
04-11:	Pewter	Round, Flat Shank	16.4mm 100%	AMERICAN, SCRIPT I motif, unit device obscured. Excellent condition. One piece cast. Flat rim, front edge rounded, back edge sharp.	RIGHT THORAX. Over body. Shank up. Lower right thorax. Caudalmost in vertical linear series (1, 2, 3, 4, 5, 6, 7, 11) in right thorax area.
04-12:	Pewter	Round, Flat 4-Hole	18.1mm 100%	AMERICAN, PLAIN: DEPRESSED CENTRE motif. Excellent condition. Depressed centre encircled by slightly raised ridge.	MIDLINE WAIST. Over body. Shank down. On right side of L3. Third down in vertical linear series (12, 13, 14, 20) in waist midline.
04-13:	Pewter	Round, Flat 4-Hole	18.1mm 100%	AMERICAN, PLAIN: DEPRESSED CENTRE motif. Excellent condition.	MIDLINE WAIST. Over body. Shank down. On top of L2. Second down in vertical linear series (12, 13, 14, 20) in waist midline. In line with 16 on L & 10 on R.
04-14:	Pewter	Round, Flat Shank	20.6mm 100%	AMERICAN, US motif. Excellent condition. One piece cast.	MIDLINE WAIST. Over body. Shank down. On top of L1. Cranialmost in vertical linear series (21, 13, 14, 20) in waist midline. Same style as 20.
04-15A:	Pewter	Round, Flat 4-Hole	18.5mm 100%	AMERICAN, PLAIN: DEPRESSED CENTRE motif. Excellent condition.	LEFT THORAX (WAIST, L). Over body. Shank down. Lower left thorax, or upper left waist. Overlying 15B. Directly cranial of 16. Roughly even with 8 & 9 on the right side of waist.

Cat. Number	Material	Shape, Attachment	Size, Portion Features	Motif, Unit Device, Design Features	Location Information
04-15B:	Pewter	----- Flat Shank	------ 20%	OBSCURED motif. Poor condition.	LEFT THORAX (WAIST, L). Over body. Lower central thorax, beneath 15A. Directly cranial of 16. In line with 14 medially, and 8 & 9 on the right side of waist.
04-16:	Pewter	Round, Flat 4-Hole	17.9mm 100%	AMERICAN, PLAIN: DEPRESSED CENTRE motif. Excellent condition.	LEFT WAIST. Over body. Shank down. Central left waist. Directly caudal to 15. Horizontally in line with 13 (and poss 12) in the waist midline, and 10 on the right of waist.
04-17:	Pewter	Round, Flat Shank	14.0mm 100%	AMERICAN, US motif. Excellent condition. One piece cast. Enlarged shank base. Flat rim, both edges sharp.	LEFT WAIST. Side of body. At left of waist & 4 cm medial of proximal left radius. Corresponds to 19 at right of waist. Directly caudal of 18.
04-18:	Pewter	Round, Flat 4-Hole	18.1mm 100%	AMERICAN, PLAIN: DEPRESSED CENTRE motif. Excellent condition.	LEFT THORAX (ARM, L). Shank down. Between lower left thorax & distal condyle of left humerus. Even with, & may correspond to, 21 beneath lower right thorax.
04-19:	Pewter	Round, Flat Shank	14.0mm 100%	AMERICAN, US motif. Excellent condition. Shank missing. Flat rim, both edges sharp.	RIGHT THORAX (ARM, R). Side of body. Outside ribcage at right of thorax or waist. About 5 cm caudomedial of the head of the right radius. May correspond to 17 at left of waist.
04-20:	Pewter	Round, Flat Shank	20.6mm 100%	AMERICAN, US motif. Excellent condition. One piece cast.	MIDLINE WAIST. Side of body. Shank down. Beside L5. Caudalmost in vertical linear series (12, 13, 14, 20) in waist midline. Same style as 14.
04-21:	Pewter	Round, Flat 4-Hole	18.1mm 100%	AMERICAN, PLAIN: DEPRESSED CENTRE motif. Excellent condition.	RIGHT THORAX. Under body. Beneath ninth right rib. Even with, and may correspond to, number 18 lateral of lower left thorax.

Cat. Number	Material	Shape, Attachment	Size, Portion	Motif, Unit Device, Design Features	Location Information
				BURIAL 06	
06-01A:	Pewter	Round, Convex Shank	20.4mm 60%	AMERICAN, EAGLE motif. Good condition. Eagle faces left. Red corrosion on shank.	RIGHT ARM. Over body. Five mm lateral of central right ulna, shank towards ulna. Part of cluster (1A, 2, 3, 5) loosely clustered around central right forearm.
06-01B:	Pewter	Round, Convex Shank	20.9mm 100%	AMERICAN, EAGLE motif. Excellent condition. Eagle faces left. Red stain at base of broken shank.	Location not available. No provenience data.
06-02:	Pewter	Round, Convex Shank	21.5mm 100%	AMERICAN, EAGLE motif, unit device obscured. Excellent condition. Eagle faces left. Small amount of red corrosion around shank.	RIGHT ARM. Over body. Shank down. Between central right radius & ulna. At centre of cluster (1A, 2, 3, 5) loosely clustered around central right forearm.
06-03:	Copper Alloy	Round, Convex Shank	22.1mm 80%	OBSCURED motif. Good condition. Small amount of red staining on shank.	RIGHT ARM (WAIST, R). Over body. Just lateral of central left ulna, & 15 mm distal of 1A. In loose cluster (1A, 2, 3, 5) around central right forearm. Shank towards ulna.
06-04:	Pewter	----- Flat Shank	----- 30%	Motif obscured or absent. Poor condition. Copper staining on shank.	RIGHT ARM (WAIST, R). Over body. Just medial of proximal right radius. At right side of loose cluster (4, 10, 13, 23, 27, 32, 34, 38) in lower thorax - waist area.
06-05:	Pewter	Round, Convex Shank	21.4mm 100%	AMERICAN, EAGLE motif, unit device is 21R. Excellent condition. Eagle faces left. Red corrosion on shank.	RIGHT ARM (WAIST, R). Over body. Shank up. One cm medial of right radius midshaft, 2 cm distal of button 4, just cranial of right iliac crest. In loose cluster (1, 2, 3, 5).

Cat. Number	Material	Shape, Attachment	Size, Portion	Motif, Unit Device, Design Features	Location Information
06-06:	Pewter	----- Shank	------ 20%	Motif obscured or absent. Poor condition.	RIGHT ARM (THORAX, R). Over body. On top of humerus, three fourths down shaft. Lateralmost in tight cluster (6, 7, 8, 9, 11, 33) in central upper arm-chest area.
06-07:	Pewter	Round, Shank	Convex 22.3mm 100%	AMERICAN, EAGLE motif, unit device is 21. Excellent condition. Eagle faces left. Design partly obscured. Red corroded shank.	RIGHT THORAX (ARM, R). Over body. Shank down. Cranialmost in tight cluster (6, 7, 8, 9, 11, 33) between central upper arm & chest.
06-08:	Pewter	Round, Shank	Convex 21.6mm 100%	OBSCURED motif. Excellent condition. Eagle faces left. A little red corrosion in shank area.	RIGHT THORAX (ARM, R). Over body. Shank down. Medialmost in tight cluster (6, 7, 8, 9, 11, 33) between central upper arm & chest. Touching rib. Overlying button 11.
06-09:	Pewter	Round, Shank	Convex 20.2mm 95%	AMERICAN, EAGLE motif, unit device is 21R. Excellent condition. Eagle faces left. Red corroded shank.	RIGHT THORAX (ARM, R). Over body. Shank up. Part of tight cluster (6, 7, 8, 9 11, 33) between central upper arm & chest.
06-10:	Pewter	Round, 4-Hole	Flat 18.4mm 100%	AMERICAN, PLAIN: DEPRESSED CENTRE motif. Good condition.	RIGHT THORAX (ARM, R). Over body. Shank up. At right side of loose cluster (4, 10, 13, 23, 27, 32, 34, 38) in the lower thorax - waist area.
06-11:	Pewter	Round, Shank	Convex 21.4mm 100%	AMERICAN, EAGLE motif, unit device is 21. Excellent condition. Eagle faces left. Red corrosion on shank.	RIGHT THORAX (ARM, R). Over body. Shank up. Underneath button 8. Part of tight cluster (6, 7, 8, 9, 11, 33) between central upper arm & chest.

Cat. Number	Material	Shape, Attachment	Size, Portion	Motif, Unit Device, Design Features	Location Information
06-12:	Pewter	Round, Flat Shank	21.0mm 100%	BRITISH, OTHER: CIRCLED 104 motif, unit device is 104. Excellent cond. "NEW BRUNSWICK REGIMENT" on garter encircles "104". Red shank. Back mark: "...ENT GARDEN".	RIGHT THORAX (WAIST, R). Over body. Shank down. Lower right thorax, possibly related to 23. Isolated caudal to, but in line with, vertical line (14, 15, 16, 17) just right of chest midline.
06-13:	Pewter	Round, Flat 4-Hole	17.8mm 100%	AMERICAN, PLAIN: DEPRESSED CENTRE motif. Excellent condition. Raised ridges encircle both depressed centre and outer edge of button.	RIGHT THORAX. Over body. Shank down. In lower right thorax. Part of loose cluster (4, 10, 13, 23, 27, 32, 34, 38) in the lower thorax – waist area.
06-14:	Pewter	Round, Flat Shank	14.4mm 100%	OBSCURED motif. Excellent condition. Motif may be eagle, facing left, but design is heavily encrusted.	RIGHT THORAX. Over body. Shank down. On sternum. Caudalmost in vertical linear series (14, 15, 16, 17) very slightly to the right of chest midline.
06-15:	Pewter	Round, Flat Shank	14.9mm 100%	AMERICAN, EAGLE motif, unit device obscured. Excellent condition. Heavily encrusted. Eagle faces left.	RIGHT THORAX. Over body. Shank down. On sternum. Third down in vertical linear series (14, 15, 16, 17) very slightly to the right of chest midline.
06-16:	Pewter	Round, Flat Shank	15.0mm 90%	OBSCURED motif. Good condition.	RIGHT THORAX. Over body. Shank down. On sternum. Second down in vertical linear series (14, 15, 16, 17) very slightly to the right of chest midline.
06-17:	Pewter	Round, Flat Shank	15.5mm 80%	OBSCURED motif. Good condition. One piece cast.	MIDLINE THORAX. Over body. Shank up. On manubrium between ribs 1 & 2. Cranialmost button in vertical series (14, 15, 16, 17) just right of chest midline.

Cat. Number	Material	Shape, Attachment	Size, Portion	Motif, Unit Device, Design Features	Location Information
06-18:	Pewter	Round, Shank	Convex 22.0mm 100%	OBSCURED motif. Good condition. Red corrosion on shank.	LEFT THORAX. Over body. Shank down. Third down in vertical linear series (18, 19, 20, 22, 36, 37) to left of chest midline.
06-19:	Pewter	Round, Shank	Convex 22.2mm 100%	AMERICAN, EAGLE motif, unit device is 21. Excellent condition. Eagle faces left. A little red corrosion in shank area.	LEFT THORAX. Over body. Shank down. Fourth down in vertical linear series (18, 19, 20, 22, 36, 37) to left of chest midline.
06-20:	Pewter	Round, Shank	Convex 21.7mm 100%	AMERICAN, EAGLE motif, unit device obscured. Excellent condition. Eagle faces left. Very small amount of red corrosion on shank.	LEFT THORAX. Over body. Shank down. Fifth down in vertical linear series (18, 19, 20, 22, 36, 37) to left of chest midline.
06-21:	Pewter	Round, Shank	Flat 14.2mm 100%	AMERICAN, EAGLE motif, unit device is US. Excellent condition. Eagle faces left. One piece cast, bulge at base of shank. Similar to 18-02.	LEFT THORAX. Over body. Shank up. Lower left thorax near manubrium. In line with series (8-37) to left of chest midline, but, unlike others of that series, small & flat.
06-22:	Pewter	Round, Shank	Convex 21.0mm 90%	OBSCURED motif. Good condition. A little red corrosion in shank area.	LEFT THORAX. Over body. Shank up. Caudalmost in vertical series (18, 19, 20, 22, 36, 37) to left of chest midline.
06-23:	Pewter	Round, 4-Hole	Flat 17.9mm 100%	AMERICAN, PLAIN: DEPRESSED CENTRE motif. Excellent condition. Raised ridge encircles depressed centre.	LEFT WAIST. Over body. Shank down. Two cm left of L2. Part of loose cluster (4, 10, 13, 23, 27, 32, 34, 38) in the lower thorax - waist area.
06-24:	Pewter	----- Shank	Convex ----- 40%	Motif obscured or absent. Poor condition. Large button.	LEFT THORAX. Over body. Shank up. Lower left thorax. Medialmost in loose cluster (24, 25, 26, 30, 35) between left elbow & chest.

Cat. Number	Material	Shape, Attachment	Size, Portion	Motif, Unit Device, Design Features	Location Information
06-25:	Pewter	Round, Convex Shank	20.6mm 100%	AMERICAN, EAGLE motif, unit device is 21R. Excellent condition. Eagle faces left. Red corrosion in shank area.	LEFT THORAX (ARM, L). Over body. Shank up. Cranialmost in loose cluster (24, 25, 26, 30, 35) between left elbow & chest. Very close to 26.
06-26:	Pewter	Round, Convex Shank	21.0mm 90%	AMERICAN, EAGLE motif, unit device is 21R. Good condition. Eagle faces left. Little red corrosion in shank area.	LEFT THORAX (ARM, L). Over body. Shank up. Beneath button 25. At cranial end of loose cluster (24, 25, 26, 30, 35) between left elbow & chest.
06-27:	Pewter	Round, Flat 4-Hole	18.0mm 100%	AMERICAN, PLAIN: DEPRESSED CENTRE motif. Excellent condition. Raised ridge encircles depressed centre.	LEFT WAIST (ARM, L). Over body. At left of loose cluster (4, 10, 13, 23, 27, 32, 34, 38) in the lower thorax - waist area. Top facing towards body. Paired with button 30.
06-28:	Pewter	Round, Convex Shank	20.5mm 100%	AMERICAN, EAGLE motif, unit device is 21R. Excellent condition. Eagle faces left. Large area of red corrosion on shank.	LEFT ARM. Over body. Shank up. Medial side of central forearm. Possibly related to 29 in same area.
06-29:	Pewter	Round, Convex Shank	20.3mm 100%	AMERICAN, EAGLE motif, unit device is 21R. Excellent condition. Eagle faces left. First unit numeral mostly obscured. Red corroded shank.	LEFT ARM. Over body. Lateral side of left forearm. Possibly related to 28 in same area. Shank oriented towards radius.
06-30:	Pewter	Round, Convex Shank	20.7mm 100%	AMERICAN, EAGLE motif, unit device obscured. Excellent condition. Eagle facing left encircled by "REGIMENT OF INFANTRY". Red corrosion on shank.	LEFT WAIST (ARM, L). Over body. Shank down. Left waist area, below button 27. Close to caudal edge of loose cluster (24, 25, 26, 30, 35) between left elbow & chest.

Cat. Number	Material	Shape, Attachment	Size, Portion	Motif, Unit Device, Design Features	Location Information
06-31:	Pewter	Round, Convex Shank	22.5mm 100%	Motif obscured or absent. Excellent condition. Face almost covered with coarse woven fabric. Red stain on shank.	MIDLINE THORAX. Over body. Shank down. Lower thorax. Out from T10 & overlying ribs. Possibly related to vertical linear series of large convex buttons 22-37. Not mapped.
06-32:	Pewter	Round, Flat 4-Hole	18.7mm 100%	AMERICAN, PLAIN: DEPRESSED CENTRE motif. Excellent condition. Red stain on face suggests contact with button 31.	MIDLINE THORAX. Over body. Shank down. Lower thorax. Overlying ribs & lateral of T10. In loose cluster (4, 10, 13, 23, 27, 32, 34, 38) in the lower thorax – waist area.
06-33:	Pewter	Round, Convex Shank	21.2mm 100%	OBSCURED motif. Excellent condition. Fabric adhering to back.	RIGHT THORAX (ARM, R). Over body. Shank up. Just lateral of central right thorax, between chest & central humerus, in tight cluster (6, 7, 8, 9, 11, 33).
06-34:	Pewter	Round, Flat 4-Hole	17.7mm 100%	AMERICAN, PLAIN: DEPRESSED CENTRE motif. Excellent condition.	LEFT THORAX (ARM, L). Over body. Shank up. Just medial to left elbow. On right of loose cluster (4, 10, 13, 23, 27, 32, 34, 38) in the lower thorax – waist area.
06-35:	Pewter	Round, Convex Shank	22.3mm 100%	OBSCURED motif. Good condition. Very little red stain on shank.	LEFT THORAX (ARM, L). Over body. Shank down. At centre of loose cluster (24, 25, 26, 30, 35) between left elbow & chest.
06-36:	Pewter	Round, Convex Shank	20.6mm 90%	OBSCURED motif. Good condition. Red corrosion in shank area.	MIDLINE THORAX. Over body. Beneath manubrium & overlying vetebrae & ribs. Cranialmost in vertical linear series (18, 19, 20, 22, 36, 37) at left of thorax.
06-37:	Pewter	Round, Convex Shank	20.8mm 100%	OBSCURED motif. Excellent condition. Red corrosion in shank area.	MIDLINE THORAX. Over body. Shank up. Second down in vertical series (18, 19, 20, 22, 36, 37) to left of chest midline.

Cat. Number	Material	Shape, Attachment	Size, Portion	Motif, Unit Device, Design Features	Location Information
06-38:	Pewter	Round, Flat Shank	15.3mm 80%	Motif obscured or absent. Good condition. Disk elongated by numerous parallel cracks. Some red staining on back.	MIDLINE THORAX. Over body. In lower thorax, touching T11. In loose cluster (4, 10, 13, 23, 27, 32, 34, 38) in the lower thorax - waist area.
06-39:	Pewter	Round, Convex Shank	22.8mm 90%	OBSCURED motif. Good condition. Coarse woven fabric adhering to face. Slight red stain on back.	RIGHT THORAX. Under body. Shank up. Beside & beneath right ribs. Not mapped.
06-40:	Pewter	Round, Convex Shank	----- 50%	Motif obscured or absent. Poor condition. Red staining on shank. Large button.	LEFT THORAX. Left of T10.

::::::::::::::::::::::::::::::::: BURIAL 07 :::::::::::::::::::::::::::::::::

Cat. Number	Material	Shape, Attachment	Size, Portion	Motif, Unit Device, Design Features	Location Information
07-01:	Pewter	Round, Flat Shank	22.0mm 90%	OBSCURED motif. Good condition. One piece cast.	RIGHT PELVIS. Shank up. Three cm lateral of femoral head. Caudalmost of vertical series (1, 20, 21) from right hip up to lower right waist (30).
07-02:	Pewter	Round, Flat Shank	20.0mm 70%	AMERICAN, SCRIPT I motif, unit device obscured. Good condition. Measurement approximate due to attrition. Only part of regimental oval present.	RIGHT PELVIS (WRIST, R). Over body. On right ilium next to sacro-iliac joint. Shank towards right arm. Possibly corresponds to 25 on left ilium, or may be a left cuff button.
07-03:	Pewter	----- Flat Shank	----- 40%	Motif obscured or absent. Poor condition. Large button.	MIDLINE THORAX (WAIST, M). Over body. Caudalmost in vertical linear series (3, 5, 7, 11, 12) in midline of chest to upper waist. Disk face oriented towards T12.

Cat. Number	Material	Shape, Attachment	Size, Portion	Motif, Unit Device, Design Features	Location Information
07-04:	Pewter	----- Flat Shank	------ 20%	Motif obscured or absent. Poor condition. One piece cast. Small button.	LEFT THORAX. Over body. Lower left thorax. Caudalmost in vertical linear series (4, 6A, 6B, 8) over left of mid-thorax. Shank facing up and laterally.
07-05:	Pewter	Round, Flat Shank	19.8mm 80%	AMERICAN, SCRIPT I motif, unit device obscured. Good condition.	MIDLINE THORAX. Over body. Fourth down in vertical linear series (3, 5, 7, 11, 12) in thorax midline. On right side of T9 & T10. Shank oriented towards cranium.
07-06A:	Pewter	----- Flat Shank	------ 10%	Motif obscured or absent. Poor condition. Small button.	LEFT THORAX. Over body. Central thorax, slightly to left of midline, even with 5. Found with 6B in vertical linear series (4, 6A, 6B, 8) over left thorax.
07-06B:	Pewter	----- Flat Shank	------ 10%	Motif obscured or absent. Poor condition. One piece cast. Small button.	LEFT THORAX. Over body. Central thorax slightly to left of midline, even with 5. Found with 6A in vertical linear series (4, 6A, 6B, 8) over left thorax.
07-07:	Pewter	Round, Flat Shank	20.8mm 70%	AMERICAN, SCRIPT I motif, unit device obscured. Good condition.	MIDLINE THORAX. Over body. Shank down. On T7. Third down in vertical linear series (3, 5, 7, 11, 12) in midline of thorax & waist.
07-08:	Pewter	----- Flat Shank	------ 10%	Motif obscured or absent. Poor condition. Unusually small shank for this burial, so button is probably small.	LEFT THORAX. Over body. Shank down. Over central thorax, just left of vertebrae, even with 7. Cranialmost in vertical linear series (4, 6A, 6B, 8) of small & probably small buttons.
07-09:	Pewter	----- Flat Shank	------ 40%	Motif obscured or absent. Poor condition. One piece cast. Large button.	LEFT THORAX. Over body. Central left thorax. Possibly related to 26 and 39.

Cat. Number	Material	Shape, Attachment	Size, Portion	Motif, Unit Device, Design Features	Location Information
07-10:	Pewter	----- -----	----- 10%	Motif obscured or absent. Poor condition.	RIGHT THORAX (ARM, R). Shank down. Caudalmost in tight, somewhat vertical cluster (10, 23, 34, 35, 36, 37) between central thorax & right humerus.
07-11:	Pewter	Round, Flat Shank	20.3mm 100%	AMERICAN, SCRIPT I motif, unit device obscured. Excellent condition. One piece cast. Flat rim, sharp edges.	MIDLINE THORAX. Over body. Shank down. Imbedded in sternum. Second down in vertical linear series (3, 5, 7, 11, 12) in midline of thorax & waist.
07-12:	Pewter	----- Flat Shank	------ 30%	AMERICAN, SCRIPT I motif. Poor condition. One piece cast. Large button.	MIDLINE THORAX. Over body. Shank down. Imbedded in manubrium. Cranialmost in vertical linear series (3, 5, 7, 11, 12) in midline of thorax & waist.
07-13:	Pewter	----- Shank	------ 30%	Motif obscured or absent. Poor condition. Large button.	RIGHT NECK. Over body. Above 18. These are the medialmost in tight cluster (13, 14, 15, 16, 17, 18A, 18B, 46) at right of neck. Shank oriented laterally.
07-14:	Pewter	----- -----	------ 10%	Motif obscured or absent. Poor condition. Highly fragmented.	RIGHT NECK. Side of body. Part of tight cluster (13, 14, 15, 16, 17, 18A, 18B, 46) at right of neck, beside base of skull.
07-15:	Pewter	----- -----	------ 10%	Motif obscured or absent. Poor condition. Highly fragmented.	RIGHT NECK. Side of body. Closest to skull in tight cluster (13, 14, 15, 16, 17, 18A, 18B, 46) at right of neck, beside base of skull.
07-16:	Pewter	Round, Flat Shank	20.4mm 90%	AMERICAN, SCRIPT I motif, unit device obscured. Excellent condition. One piece cast.	RIGHT NECK. Part of tight cluster (13, 14, 15, 16, 17, 18A, 18B, 46) at right of neck, beside base of skull.

Cat. Number	Material	Shape, Attachment	Size, Portion	Motif, Unit Device, Design Features	Location Information
07-17:	Pewter	----- Flat Shank	------ 30%	AMERICAN, SCRIPT I motif. Poor condition. Large button.	RIGHT NECK. Side of body. Lateralmost in tight cluster (13, 14, 15, 16, 17, 18A, 18B, 46) at right of neck, beside base of skull.
07-18A:	Pewter	----- Flat Shank	------ 10%	OBSCURED motif. Poor condition. Possible Script I motif. One piece cast.	RIGHT NECK. Side of body. Overlying button 13. In tight cluster (13, 14, 15, 16, 17, 18A, 18B, 46) at right of neck, beside base of skull.
07-18B:	Pewter	----- Flat Shank	------ 10%	OBSCURED motif. Poor condition. One piece cast. Small button.	RIGHT NECK. Side of body. Underneath button 13. In tight cluster (13, 14, 15, 16, 17, 18A, 18B, 46) at right of neck, beside base of skull.
07-19:	Pewter	----- ----	------ 10%	Motif obscured or absent. Poor condition.	LEFT THORAX. Under body. Shank down. Part of tight cluster (19, 28, 29) beneath in upper left thorax.
07-20:	Pewter	Round, Flat Shank	22.2mm 60%	AMERICAN, SCRIPT I motif. Good condition. Large button.	RIGHT PELVIS. Side of body. Touching lateral right ilium. Third down in vertical series lateral of right hip & waist (1, 20, 21, 30). Shank towards iliac crest.
07-21:	Pewter	Round, Flat Shank	19.6mm 60%	AMERICAN, SCRIPT I motif. Good condition. Measurement approximate due to edge attrition.	RIGHT PELVIS. Side of body. Second down in vertical linear series lateral of right hip & waist (1, 20, 21, 30). Shank towards iliac crest.
07-22:	Pewter	Round, Flat Shank	20.5mm 90%	AMERICAN, SCRIPT I motif, unit device obscured. Excellent condition. Surface preservation good. One piece cast.	RIGHT THORAX. Over body. Overlying right 11th rib at lower right corner of thorax. Top slants medially. May correspond to 38 in lower left thorax.

Cat. Number	Material	Shape, Attachment	Size, Portion	Motif, Unit Device, Design Features	Location Information
07-23:	----	----	0%	Motif obscured or absent. Specimen not available for analysis.	RIGHT THORAX. Under body. Shank down. Beneath lateral border of right scapula. Medialmost in tight cluster (10, 23, 34, 35, 36, 37) between central thorax & right humerus.
07-24:	Pewter	----- Shank	10%	Motif obscured or absent. Poor condition. Just shank. One piece cast.	MIDLINE WAIST. Under body. Shank up. Beneath spinous process of L3. May be related to 38 beneath lower left thorax.
07-25:	Pewter	Flat Shank	10%	Motif obscured or absent. Poor condition. One piece cast.	LEFT PELVIS. Over body. On lateral side of left ilium. Possibly corresponds to 2 on right ilium. Shank oriented laterally.
07-26:	Pewter	Flat Shank	50%	Motif obscured or absent. Poor condition. Piece of tightly woven fabric adhering to undetermined side. Large button.	LEFT THORAX. Side of body. Shank down. Lateral of left thorax, about even with caudal border of scapula & medial to left humerus. Possibly related to 9 and 39.
07-28:	Pewter	Round, Flat Shank	40%	Motif obscured or absent. Poor condition. One piece cast. Large button.	LEFT THORAX. Under body. Shank up. Part of tight cluster (19, 28, 29) beneath upper left thorax.
07-29:	Pewter	Round, Flat Shank	40%	Motif obscured or absent. Large button.	LEFT THORAX. Under body. Shank down. Part of tight cluster (19, 28, 29) beneath upper left thorax.
07-30:	Pewter	Round, Flat Shank	21.0mm 80%	AMERICAN, SCRIPT I motif, unit device is 15. Excellent condition. One piece cast. May be silver plated.	RIGHT WAIST. Lower right waist area. Cranialmost in vertical linear series lateral of right hip & waist (1, 20, 21, 30).

Cat. Number	Material	Shape, Attachment	Size, Portion	Motif, Unit Device, Design Features	Location Information
07-31:	Pewter	Round, Flat Shank	21.0mm 80%	AMERICAN, SCRIPT I motif, unit device obscured. Good condition.	RIGHT ARM. Over body. Shank up. Just lateral of distal right humerus, & 1 cm proximal of 33. In cluster (31, 32, 33) associated with distal right humerus.
07-32:	Pewter	Round, Flat Shank	21.0mm 80%	AMERICAN, SCRIPT I motif, unit device obscured. Good condition.	RIGHT ARM. Over body. Shank up. One cm medial of distal right humerus. In cluster (31, 32, 33) associated with distal right humerus.
07-33:	Pewter	Round, Flat Shank	------ 70%	AMERICAN, SCRIPT I motif. Poor condition. Large button.	RIGHT ARM. Over body. Shank down. Just lateral of distal right humerus. In cluster (31, 32, 33), 1 cm distal of 31. Disk face slightly angled towards midline.
07-34:	Pewter	----- Flat Shank	------ 40%	AMERICAN, SCRIPT I motif. Poor condition. Large button.	RIGHT SHOULDER (THORAX, R). Under body. Shank down. Cranialmost in tight cluster (10, 23, 34, 35, 36, 37) between central thorax & right humerus. Just lateral of 23.
07-35:	Pewter	----- Shank	------ 20%	Motif obscured or absent. Poor condition. Just crumbs and a shank base.	RIGHT THORAX. Under body. Shank down. In tight vertical cluster (10, 23, 34, 35, 36, 37) between central thorax & right humerus. Lateral of 23.
07-36:	Pewter	----- ----	------ 20%	Motif obscured or absent. Poor condition. Just crumbs.	RIGHT THORAX. Side of body. In tight vertical cluster (10, 23, 34, 35, 36, 37) between central thorax & right humerus. Shank oriented towards humerus.
07-37:	Pewter	Round, Flat Shank	20.9mm 90%	AMERICAN, SCRIPT I motif. Good condition but fragmented. One piece cast. Large button.	RIGHT THORAX. Side of body. Shank up. In tight vertical cluster (10, 23, 34, 35, 36, 37) between thorax & right humerus. Lateral to 34 & 35.

Cat. Number	Material	Shape, Attachment	Size, Portion	Motif, Unit Device, Design Features	Location Information
07-38:	Pewter	----- Flat Shank	------ 70%	Motif obscured or absent. Poor condition. Large button.	LEFT THORAX. Under body. Shank up. Lower left corner of lower thorax. Beneath distal end of left sixth rib. May be related to 22 in lower right thorax, and to 24 beneath L3.
07-39:	Pewter	----- Flat ----	------ 10%	Motif obscured or absent. Poor condition.	LEFT SHOULDER (THORAX, L). Over body. Shank down. Upper left corner of thorax, close to neck of left scapula. Possibly related to 9 and 26.
07-40A:	Pewter	----- Flat Shank	------ 40%	Motif obscured or absent. Poor condition. Large button.	LEFT ARM. Part of loose cluster centred on the middle of the left forearm (40A, 40B, 41, 42, 43).
07-40B:	Pewter	Round, Flat Shank	------ 70%	AMERICAN, SCRIPT I motif. Poor condition. Probably a large sized button.	LEFT ARM. Over body. Shank down. Just medial of left radius midshaft. In loose cluster centred on left forearm (40A, 40B, 41, 42, 43).
07-41:	Pewter	----- Shank	------ 30%	Motif obscured or absent. Poor condition.	LEFT ARM. Over body. Just lateral of left ulna midshaft, just proximal of 42. In loose cluster centred on left forearm (40A, 40B, 41, 42, 43).
07-42:	Pewter	----- Flat Shank	------ 30%	Motif obscured or absent. Poor condition. Large button.	LEFT ARM. Over body. Just lateral of left ulna midshaft, & just distal of 41. In loose cluster centred on left forearm (40A, 40B, 41, 42, 43).
07-43:	Pewter	----- Shank	------ 20%	Motif obscured or absent. Poor condition.	LEFT ARM. Side of body. Lateral of left elbow, between right ribs 6 & 7 of Burial 12. Shank oriented medially, towards arm. In loose cluster (40A, 40B, 41, 42, 43).

Cat. Number	Material	Shape, Attachment	Size, Portion	Motif, Unit Device, Design Features	Location Information
07-44:	Pewter	Round, Flat Shank	------ 80%	AMERICAN, SCRIPT I motif, unit device obscured. Good condition. Only upper part of oval present. Removed from excavated block. Large button.	RIGHT WRIST (PELVIS, M). In right wrist area.
07-45:	Pewter	Round, Flat Shank	------ 70%	AMERICAN, SCRIPT I motif. Good condition. Removed from excavated block. Large button.	RIGHT WRIST (PELVIS, M). In right wrist area.
07-46:	Pewter	Round, Flat Shank	------ 40%	OBSCURED motif. Poor condition. Removed from excavated block. Small button.	NECK. Under body. Beneath skull. Associated with tight cluster (13, 14, 15, 16, 17, 18A, 18B, 46) at right of neck, beside base of skull.
07-47:	Bone	Round, Flat 1-Hole	10.1mm 100%	PLAIN (BONE) motif. Excellent condition. Slightly polished.	RIGHT NECK. Under body. Right side of neck. Removed from excavated block.

::::::::::::::::::::: BURIAL .08 :::::::::::::::::::::

Cat. Number	Material	Shape, Attachment	Size, Portion	Motif, Unit Device, Design Features	Location Information
08-01A:	Pewter	Round, Flat Shank	14.2mm 100%	AMERICAN, US motif. Excellent condition. Large shank for small button. One piece cast. Rim flat, edges sharp.	MIDLINE POSTPELVIC. Under body. Shank down. Touching right femur at distal 1/3 point. Caudal of 2, even with 3. Lower right in square-shaped cluster (1A, 2, 3, 4) between proximal femora.
08-01B:	Pewter	Round, Flat Shank	20.5mm 100%	AMERICAN, SCRIPT I motif, unit device is a STAR. Excellent cond. No dot in star. Little corrosion, one of best. One piece cast, sharp flat edge, silver plated.	MIDLINE WAIST (WRIST, L). Over body. Lower waist, 2 cm left of lower lumbars. Close to & cranial of left metacarpals. Caudal of 7 & medial of 5.

Cat. Number	Material	Shape, Attachment	Size, Portion	Motif, Unit Device, Design Features	Location Information
08-02:	Pewter	Round, Flat Shank	14.1mm 100%	AMERICAN, US motif. Excellent condition. One piece cast. Large shank for small disk. Rim flat, edges sharp.	MIDLINE POSTPELVIC. Under body. Shank down. Just caudal of right ischium. Cranial of 1A, even with 11 & 4. Upper right in roughly square-shaped cluster (1A, 2, 3, 4) between prox femora.
08-03:	Pewter	Round, Flat Shank	20.9mm 100%	AMERICAN, US motif. Good condition. One piece cast.	MIDLINE POSTPELVIC. Under body. Shank down. Caudal of 4, even with 1A. Lower left in roughly square-shaped cluster (1A, 2, 3, 4) between proximal femora. Top of motif towards midline.
08-04:	Pewter	Round, Flat Shank	20.7mm 100%	AMERICAN, US motif. Excellent condition. One piece cast. Possibly large button.	MIDLINE POSTPELVIC. Under body. Shank down. Just caudal of left ischium. Cranial of 3, even with 2 and 11. Upper left in roughly square-shaped cluster (1A, 2, 3, 4) between proximal femora.
08-05:	Pewter	Round, Flat Shank	25.0mm 80%	AMERICAN, SCRIPT I motif, unit device obscured. Poor condition. One piece cast.	LEFT WRIST (WAIST, L). Over body. Shank down. Lower left waist, & touching distal left radius on medial side. Just distal of 6 along radial shaft.
08-06:	Pewter	----- ----	------ 5%	Motif obscured or absent. Poor condition. Highly fragmented.	LEFT ARM (WAIST, L). At left side of waist, 1 cm medial of midshaft of left radius. Proximal of number 5, even with & lateral to number 7.
08-07:	Pewter	Round, Flat Shank	24.8mm 100%	AMERICAN, SCRIPT I motif, unit device obscured. Excellent condition. Silver plated. One piece cast, sharp flat edges.	MIDLINE WAIST. Over body. Shank down. Central waist, slightly to left of L4. Cranial of 1B and even with 6 on the left.

Cat. Number	Material	Shape, Attachment	Size, Portion	Motif, Unit Device, Design Features	Location Information
08-08:	Pewter	Round, Flat Shank	15.0mm 100%	AMERICAN, SCRIPT I motif, unit device obscured. Excellent condition. One piece cast.	MIDLINE WAIST. Over body. Shank down. Just to right of L1 & L2. Fifth down in vertical linear series (8, 9, 12, 14, 15, 16) in midline of thorax and waist.
08-09:	Pewter	Round, Flat Shank	14.8mm 100%	AMERICAN, SCRIPT I motif, unit device obscured. Excellent condition. One piece cast.	MIDLINE WAIST. Over body. Shank down. Just to right of L1 & L2. Caudalmost in vertical linear series (8, 9, 12, 14, 15, 16) in midline of thorax & waist.
08-10:	Pewter	Round, Flat Shank	20.6mm 100%	AMERICAN, SCRIPT I motif, unit device is a STAR. Excellent condition. Silver plated, flat edge. Script "I" has bold flourishes. One piece cast.	MIDLINE WAIST. Over body. Shank down. Touching right side of L3. May be related to other large waist area buttons, especially 7 and 1B.
08-11:	Pewter	Round, Flat Shank	14.3mm 100%	OBSCURED motif. Excellent condition. One piece cast. The shank is large in relation to the button size.	LEFT POSTPELVIC. Under body. Shank up. Beneath lateral side of left femur just distal of greater trochanter. Approximately even with 2 & 4, and may be related to 22 & 23.
08-12:	Pewter	Round, Flat Shank	15.3mm 100%	AMERICAN, SCRIPT I motif. Good condition. Probably one piece cast.	MIDLINE THORAX. Over body. Shank down. On top of T11. Fourth down in vertical linear series (8, 9, 12, 14, 15, 16) in midline of thorax & waist.
08-13:	Pewter	Round, Flat Shank	14.7mm 100%	AMERICAN, SCRIPT I motif, unit device obscured. Excellent condition. One piece cast.	LEFT THORAX. Over body. Shank up. At right margin of central thorax, on 4th rib. Even with gap in thorax midline series (8, 9, 12, 14, 15, 16) & appropriate size for that series.

Cat. Number	Material	Shape, Attachment	Size, Portion	Motif, Unit Device, Design Features	Location Information
08-14:	Pewter	Round, Flat Shank	14.9mm 100%	AMERICAN, SCRIPT I motif, unit device is a STAR. Excellent condition. One piece cast.	MIDLINE THORAX. Over body. Shank down. On lower part of manubrium. Third down in vertical linear series (8, 9, 12, 14, 15, 16) in midline of thorax & waist.
08-15:	Pewter	Round, Flat Shank	14.6mm 100%	AMERICAN, SCRIPT I motif, unit device is a STAR. Excellent condition. One piece cast.	MIDLINE THORAX. Over body. Shank down. On upper manubrium. Second down in vertical linear series (8, 9, 12, 14, 15, 16) in midline of thorax & waist.
08-16:	Pewter	Round, Flat Shank	14.9mm 100%	AMERICAN, SCRIPT I motif, unit device is a STAR. Excellent condition. One piece construction. Silver plated. Part of rim flat, part rounded.	MIDLINE THORAX. Over body. Shank down. One cm right of upper thoracic vertebrae. Cranialmost in vertical linear series (8, 9, 12, 14, 15, 16) in thorax midline.
08-17:	Bone	Round, Flat 1-Hole	9.3mm 100%	PLAIN (BONE) motif. Excellent condition.	MIDLINE THORAX. Over body. Two cm to left of upper thoracics, & probably related to other bone button, number 18. Even with 16.
08-18:	Bone	Round, Flat 1-Hole	9.1mm 100%	PLAIN (BONE) motif. Excellent condition. Warped.	MIDLINE THORAX (NECK, M). Under body. Beneath body in area of T1 & C7. Probably related to the other bone button, number 17.
08-19:	Pewter	Round, Flat Shank	------ 70%	Motif obscured or absent. Poor condition. One piece cast. Large sized button.	RIGHT ARM. Under body. Shank up. Beneath right forearm, one-fourth down ulnar shaft. May equate to 6 near midshaft of left forearm.

Cat. Number	Material	Shape, Attachment	Size, Portion	Motif, Unit Device, Design Features	Location Information
08-20:	Pewter	Round, Flat Shank	15.5mm 100%	AMERICAN, SCRIPT I motif, unit device is a STAR. Excellent cond. One piece cast. Ornate Script I. Six pointed star, no dot. Slight convexity. Silver plated.	RIGHT PELVIS. Under body. Beneath right pelvis. Possibly related to other small buttons 1A & 2 caudal of pelvis. Shank medially oriented.
08-21:	Pewter	Round, Flat Shank	------ 70%	Motif obscured or absent. Good condition. One piece cast. Flat rim. Silver plated. Two pieces: estimated diameter = 21.8mm.	LEFT WAIST (ARM, R). Under body. Just cranial of left pelvis. Possibly related to 1B, 5, & 7 on right.
08-22:	Pewter	Round, Flat Shank	14.4mm 100%	AMERICAN, US motif. Excellent condition. One piece cast. Large shank for small disk. Flat rim.	POSTPELVIC. Over body. Associated with proximal end of unspecified femur. Possibly related to 2, 4, 11, and 23, all close to or over proximal femora. Not mapped.
08-23:	Pewter	Round, Flat Shank	14.2mm 100%	AMERICAN, US motif. Excellent condition. One piece cast. Large shank for small disk. Flat rim.	POSTPELVIC. Over body. Associated with proximal end of unspecified femur. Poss related to 2, 4, 11, & 22, all near to or over proximal femora. Not mapped.

Cat. Number	Material	Shape, Attachment	Size, Portion	Motif, Unit Device, Design Features	Location Information

:::::::::::::::::::::::::::::::::::: BURIAL 09 ::::::::::::::::::::::::::::::::::::

Cat. Number	Material	Shape, Attachment	Size, Portion	Motif, Unit Device, Design Features	Location Information
09-01:	Copper	Round, Flat Shank	24.2mm 100%	AMERICAN, EAGLE motif, unit device is 6RFGT. Excellent condition. Left facing eagle, wings extended, with shield, arrow, & olive branch. One piece cast.	NOT ASSOCIATED WITH BODY. Not in burial context. Motif: "U S A" over "E PLURIBUS UNUM" scroll above eagle. Backmark: "BEST PLATED" & wreath of 2 branches around edge.
09-02:	Copper	Round, Flat Shank	14.8mm 100%	AMERICAN, EAGLE motif, unit device is R. Excellent cond. Eagle facing right with arrows, olive branch, & shield. Soldered omega shank w adhered fabric.	NOT ASSOCIATED WITH BODY. Not in burial context. Motif: Eagle has flexed wings. Within inverted triangle on shield over breast is an "R".
09-03:	Silver	Round, Flat Shank	19.4mm 100%	PLAIN motif. Excellent condition. Pinch based shank with large amount of fabric adhering. Copper stained.	NOT ASSOCIATED WITH BODY. Not in burial context.
09-04:	Copper	Round, Flat Shank	14.1mm 100%	AMERICAN, OTHER: SCRIPT A motif, unit device is 3. Excellent condition. Motif: script "A" & regimental "3" for 3rd artillery. Soldered omega shank.	NOT ASSOCIATED WITH BODY. Not in burial context.
09-05:	Copper	Round, Convex Shank	20.8mm 100%	BRITISH, OTHER: 3 CANNON motif. Excellent condition. Motif: shield with 3 cannons. Soldered ring shank.	NOT ASSOCIATED WITH BODY. Not in burial context.
09-06:	Copper	Round, Flat Shank	20.3mm 100%	AMERICAN, SCRIPT RA motif, unit device is 2. Excellent condition. Soldered omega shank.	NOT ASSOCIATED WITH BODY. Not in burial context.

Cat. Number	Material	Shape, Attachment	Size, Portion	Motif, Unit Device, Design Features	Location Information
09-07:	Copper	Round, Flat Shank	15.0mm 100%	AMERICAN, SCRIPT RA motif, unit device is 2. Excellent condition. Soldered omega shank.	NOT ASSOCIATED WITH BODY. Not in burial context.
09-08:	Copper	Round, Convex Shank	20.8mm 100%	BRITISH, OTHER: 3 CANNON motif. Excellent condition. Shield & 3 cannon motif. Unidentified material, poss organic adhering to much of back.	NOT ASSOCIATED WITH BODY. Not in burial context.
09-09:	Copper	Round, Convex Shank	13.4mm 100%	PLAIN motif. Excellent condition. Fabric adhering to much of back.	NOT ASSOCIATED WITH BODY. Not in burial context.
09-10:	Silver	Round, Flat Shank	19.9mm 70%	PLAIN motif. Excellent condition. Copper stained. Pinched base shank.	NOT ASSOCIATED WITH BODY. Not in burial context.
09-11:	Copper	Round, Flat Shank	20.7mm 100%	PLAIN motif. Excellent condition. Fabric in shank. Pinched base shank.	NOT ASSOCIATED WITH BODY. Not in burial context.
09-12:	Pewter	Round, Flat Shank	20.4mm 50%	AMERICAN, EAGLE motif, unit device is 1.Rt. Good condition. Eagle faces right. One piece cast. In "1.Rt." the "t" is superscribed over period.	NOT ASSOCIATED WITH BODY. Not in burial context.
09-13:	Pewter	Round, Flat Shank	15.0mm 100%	PLAIN motif. Excellent condition. Red corrosion on shank.	NOT ASSOCIATED WITH BODY. Not in burial context.

Cat. Number	Material	Shape, Attachment	Size, Portion	Motif, Unit Device, Design Features	Location Information

▓▓▓▓▓▓▓▓▓▓▓▓▓▓▓▓▓ BURIAL 10 ▓▓▓▓▓▓▓▓▓▓▓▓▓▓▓▓▓

Cat. Number	Material	Shape, Attachment	Size, Portion	Motif, Unit Device, Design Features	Location Information
10-01:	Pewter	Round, Flat Shank	14.9mm 100%	AMERICAN, SCRIPT I motif, unit device obscured. Excellent condition. One piece cast. Flat rim.	RIGHT NECK. Side of body. Shank down. Touching button 2. In loose cluster (1, 2, 3) to right of neck.
10-02:	Pewter	Round, Flat Shank	14.4mm 100%	AMERICAN, SCRIPT I motif, unit device is a STAR. Excellent condition. One piece. Flat rim.	RIGHT NECK. Side of body. Shank up. Touching button 1. In loose cluster (1, 2, 3) to right of neck.
10-03:	Pewter	Round, Flat Shank	14.4mm 100%	AMERICAN, SCRIPT I motif, unit device is a STAR. Excellent condition. One piece cast.	RIGHT NECK (SHOULDER, R). Side of body. Shank down. Just touching distal right clavicle. Caudalmost in loose cluster (1, 2, 3) to right of neck.
10-04:	Pewter	Round, Flat Shank	14.5mm 100%	AMERICAN, SCRIPT I motif, unit device is a STAR. Excellent condition. One piece cast. Silver plated.	MIDLINE THORAX. Over body. Shank down. Upper thorax between clavicles. Cranialmost in vertical linear series (4, 5, 6, 8, 9, 10, 13, 14, 22) in thorax - waist midline.
10-05:	Pewter	Round, Flat Shank	14.5mm 100%	AMERICAN, SCRIPT I motif, unit device is a STAR. Excellent condition. One piece cast. Flat rim.	MIDLINE THORAX. Over body. Shank down. Upper thorax. Just cranial of 6. Second down in vertical linear series (4, 5, 6, 8, 9, 10, 13, 14, 22) in thorax - waist midline.
10-06:	Pewter	----- Flat Shank	------ 30%	Motif obscured or absent. Poor condition. One piece cast. Small sized button. Possible Script I motif.	MIDLINE THORAX. Over body. Shank down. Upper thorax. Just caudal of 5. Third down in vertical linear series (4, 5, 6, 8, 9, 10, 13, 14, 22) in thorax - waist midline.
10-07:	Pewter	Round, Flat Shank	15.1mm 100%	AMERICAN, SCRIPT I motif, unit device is a STAR. Excellent condition. One piece cast. Flat rim.	RIGHT THORAX. Over body. Shank down. Just to right of midline in central thorax. Closest to 6 & 8 in midline series (4-14, 22).

Cat. Number	Material	Shape, Attachment	Size, Portion	Motif, Unit Device, Design Features	Location Information
10-08:	Pewter	----- Flat Shank	------ 30%	Motif obscured or absent. Good condition. One piece cast. Small button.	MIDLINE THORAX. Over body. Shank down. Central thorax. Fourth down in vertical linear series (4, 5, 6, 8, 9, 10, 13, 14, 22) in thorax - waist midline.
10-09:	Pewter	Round, Flat Shank	16.0mm 70%	AMERICAN, SCRIPT I motif, unit device is a STAR. Good condition. One piece cast. Flat rim.	MIDLINE THORAX. Over body. Shank down. Central thorax. Fifth down in vertical linear series (4, 5, 6, 8, 9, 10, 13, 14, 22) in thorax - waist midline.
10-10:	Pewter	Round, Flat Shank	------ 50%	AMERICAN, SCRIPT I motif. Good condition. One piece cast. Flat rim. Small button.	MIDLINE THORAX. Over body. Lower thorax. With 22, sixth down in vertical linear series (4, 5, 6, 8, 9, 10, 13, 14, 22) in thorax - waist midline.
10-11:	Pewter	Round, Flat Shank	14.5mm 100%	AMERICAN, SCRIPT I motif, unit device is a STAR. Excellent condition. One piece cast. Flat rim.	RIGHT THORAX. Over body. Shank down. With 12, in lower right corner of thorax. Possibly also associated with 17.
10-12:	Pewter	Round, Flat Shank	14.6mm 100%	AMERICAN, SCRIPT I motif, unit device is a STAR. Excellent condition. One piece cast. Flat rim.	RIGHT THORAX. Over body. Shank up. With 11 in extreme lower right thorax. Possibly also associated with 17. Face down on right eleventh rib. Loop of shank parallel to eleventh rib.
10-13:	Pewter	Round, Flat Shank	15.7mm 70%	AMERICAN, SCRIPT I motif. Good condition.	MIDLINE THORAX. Over body. Shank down. On L2. Second from bottom in vertical linear series (4, 5, 6, 8, 9, 10, 13, 14, 22) in thorax - waist midline.
10-14:	Pewter	Round, Flat Shank	14.5mm 90%	OBSCURED motif. Excellent condition.	MIDLINE THORAX. Over body. Shank down. On L3. Caudalmost in vertical linear series (4, 5, 6, 8, 9, 10, 13, 14, 22) in thorax - waist midline.

Cat. Number	Material	Shape, Attachment	Size, Portion	Motif, Unit Device, Design Features	Location Information
10-15:	Pewter	Round, Flat Shank	20.8mm 80%	AMERICAN, SCRIPT I motif, unit device obscured. Good condition. Bold Script I. One piece cast.	MIDLINE WAIST (PELVIS). Over body. Shank down. Touching right side of L4, just cranial of 16. In loose cluster (15, 16, 17, 20, 25, 26) is waist area.
10-16:	Pewter	Round, Flat Shank	20.5mm 90%	AMERICAN, SCRIPT I motif, unit device is a STAR. Excellent condition. Silver plated, with flat, sharp edge. Ornate Script I. One piece cast.	MIDLINE WAIST (PELVIS). Over body. Shank down. Touching right side of L5, just caudal of 15. In loose cluster (15, 16, 17, 20, 25, 26) is waist area. Only large Script I button from Burial 10.
10-17:	Pewter	Round, Flat Shank	15.1mm 100%	AMERICAN, SCRIPT I motif, unit device is a STAR. Excellent condition. One piece cast.	RIGHT ARM. Side of body. Shank up. One cm medial of central right forearm. Possibly related to loose waist area cluster, or linear series beneath right forearm. Near musket tool.
10-18:	Pewter	Round, Flat Shank	14.7mm 100%	AMERICAN, SCRIPT I motif, unit device is a STAR. Excellent condition. One piece cast. Associated with gunflints. Design is off centre. Flat rim.	RIGHT ARM. Side of body. Shank up. Right forearm, 1 cm medial of radius, 5 cm medial of elbow. Shank loop perpendicular to radius. Position corresponds with 19 on left.
10-19:	Pewter	Round, Flat Shank	15.3mm 100%	AMERICAN, SCRIPT I motif, unit device obscured. Excellent condition. One piece cast. In association with spoon. Flat rim.	LEFT ARM. Under body. Shank up. Left forearm, 3 cm medial of proximal radius, 7 cm medial of elbow. Shank loop parallel to radius. Position corresponds with 18 near right elbow.
10-20:	Pewter	Round, Flat Shank	------ 30%	Motif obscured or absent. Poor condition. In 14-15 mm size range. One piece cast. Small size.	MIDLINE WAIST. Over body. On top of distal end of the left transverse process of L4. In loose cluster (15, 16, 17, 20, 25, 26) is waist area.

Cat. Number	Material	Shape, Attachment	Size, Portion	Motif, Unit Device, Design Features	Location Information
10-21:	Pewter	Round, Flat Shank	14.6mm 100%	AMERICAN, SCRIPT I motif, unit device obscured. Excellent condition. One piece cast. Flat rim.	RIGHT ARM (PELVIS, R). Under body. Shank up. Near wrist on right iliac crest. Distalmost in linear series (21, 23, 24) beneath right forearm.
10-22:	Pewter	Round, Flat Shank	14.4mm 100%	AMERICAN, SCRIPT I motif, unit device obscured. Design is off centre. Star may have 6 or 8 points. Heavily encrusted.	MIDLINE THORAX. Over body. Lower thorax. With 10, sixth down in vert linear series (4, 5, 6, 8, 9, 10, 13, 14, 22) in thorax-waist midline. Shank towards side.
10-23:	Pewter	Round, Flat Shank	14.6mm 100%	AMERICAN, SCRIPT I motif, unit device obscured. Excellent condition. One piece cast. Flat rim. Heavily encrusted.	RIGHT ARM (WAIST, R). Under body. Shank down. Just cranial of iliac crest. At centre of linear series (21, 23, 24) beneath right forearm.
10-24:	Pewter	Round, Flat Shank	14.5mm 100%	AMERICAN, SCRIPT I motif, unit device is a STAR. Excellent condition. One piece cast.	RIGHT ARM (WAIST, R). Under body. Shank up. Near midpoint of forearm, & proximalmost in linear series (21, 23, 24) beneath right forearm. Only one in series with shank down.
10-25:	Pewter	----- ----	------- 10%	Motif obscured or absent. Poor condition, just sliver present.	MIDLINE THORAX. Under body. Beneath T12. In loose cluster (15, 16, 17, 20, 25, 26) is waist area.
10-26:	Pewter	Round, Flat Shank	14.9mm 100%	AMERICAN, SCRIPT I motif, unit device is a STAR. Good condition. Star in oval may have 6 or 8 points. One piece cast.	THORAX. Under body. Lower thorax. Lateral to end 10th rib, side unspecified. Poss part of waist cluster or may correspond to 11 & 12, lower right thorax. Not mapped.
10-27:	Pewter	Round, Flat Shank	14.5mm 100%	AMERICAN, SCRIPT I motif. Excellent condition. One piece cast. Flat rim.	LEFT NECK. Under body. Even with C3 & C4, left of neck, cranial of left scapula, and lateral of number 28.

Cat. Number	Material	Shape, Attachment	Size, Portion	Motif, Unit Device, Design Features	Location Information
10-28:	Pewter	Round, Flat Shank	14.5mm 100%	AMERICAN, SCRIPT I motif, unit device obscured. Excellent condition. One piece cast. Flat rim.	LEFT NECK. Under body. Shank down. Even with C3 & C4, left of neck, and medial to 27.

BURIAL 11

Cat. Number	Material	Shape, Attachment	Size, Portion	Motif, Unit Device, Design Features	Location Information
11-01:	Bone	Round, Flat 1-Hole	12.8mm 100%	PLAIN (BONE) motif. Excellent condition.	MIDLINE THORAX (NECK, M). Over body. Upper thorax close to base of neck. Just to right of vertebrae, at head of first rib. Associated with number 2.
11-02:	Bone	Round, Flat 1-Hole	12.8mm 100%	PLAIN (BONE) motif. Excellent condition.	MIDLINE THORAX. Over body. Upper central thorax in midline, at head of second rib. Associated with number 1.
11-03:	Pewter	Round, Flat Shank	20.9mm 100%	AMERICAN, US motif. Excellent condition. One piece cast. Flat rim.	RIGHT POSTPELVIC. Side of body. Shank down. Five cm lateral of proximal right femur. Approximately in line with 4 in centre & 5 to the left.
11-04:	Pewter	Round, Flat Shank	20.9mm 100%	AMERICAN, US motif. Excellent condition. One piece cast.	MIDLINE POSTPELVIC. Under body. Shank up. Midway between proximal ends of left & right femora. In line with 3 on right & 5 on left.
11-05:	Pewter	Round, Flat Shank	20.2mm 100%	AMERICAN, US motif. Excellent condition. One piece cast. Bevelled rim. Excellent specimen.	LEFT POSTPELVIC. Under body. Shank up. Five cm left of proximal left femur. In line with 3 on right & 4 in centre.
11-06:	Pewter	Round, Flat Shank	19.7mm 100%	AMERICAN, US motif. Excellent condition. One piece cast.	Association is ambiguous. Found north of grave shaft in disturbed context.

Cat. Number	Material	Shape, Attachment	Size, Portion	Motif, Unit Device, Design Features	Location Information
13-02:	Copper Alloy	Oval, Flat Shank	17.4mm 100%	OTHER: FLORAL (CUFF LINK) motif. Excellent condition. Civilian cuff link: flower motif, zigzag border. Associated with large organic object.	LEFT ARM (PELVIS, L). Under body. Shank down. Beneath centre of left forearm. Associated with, & just distal of 1.
13-03:	Pewter	Round, Flat Shank	------ 60%	AMERICAN, SCRIPT I motif. Poor condition. Large button.	LEFT THORAX. Over body. Shank down. Lateral edge of lower left thorax, overlying rib fragment.
13-04:	Pewter	Round, Flat Shank	20.6mm 100%	AMERICAN, SCRIPT I motif, unit device obscured. Good condition. Elaborate, wide curved Script I. One piece cast. Silver plated.	MIDLINE WAIST (THORAX). Over body. Shank down. In midline, on L3 or L2. Caudalmost in vertical linear series (4, 5, 6) in central torso area.
13-05:	Pewter	Round, Flat Shank	20.5mm 100%	AMERICAN, SCRIPT I motif, unit device obscured. Good condition. More elaborate type Script I. One piece cast. Flat sharp edge.	MIDLINE THORAX. Over body. Shank down. Lower thorax or upper waist, on L1 or T12. Second down in vertical linear series (4, 5, 6) in central torso area.
13-06:	Pewter	Round, Flat Shank	------ 100%	OBSCURED motif. Poor condition. One piece cast. Large button.	RIGHT THORAX. Over body. Shank down. Central right thorax. About even with and 4 cm medial of number 7. Cranialmost in vertical linear series (4, 5, 6) in central torso area.
13-07:	Pewter	Round, Flat ----	------ 20%	Motif obscured or absent. Poor condition. Large button.	RIGHT THORAX. Over body. Shank up. Right edge of central thorax. Even with & 4 cm to right of 6. May be laterally displaced continuation of linear series (4, 5, 6) in midline.

BURIAL 14

Cat. Number	Material	Shape, Attachment	Size, Portion	Motif, Unit Device, Design Features	Location Information
14-01:	Bone	Round, Flat 1-Hole	12.2mm 90%	PLAIN (BONE) motif. Excellent condition, although more deteriorated than most bone buttons.	MIDLINE THORAX. Over body. Top of thorax in midline, touching left side of manubrium.
14-02:	Pewter	----- ----	------ 20%	Motif obscured or absent. Poor condition. Just crumbs.	MIDLINE WAIST (THORAX, M). Over body. Centre of upper waist, touching right side of L1. In possible relationship with 3.
14-03:	Pewter	Round, Flat Shank	20.1mm 100%	Motif obscured or absent. Good condition. Removed in cast.	MIDLINE WAIST (PELVIS, M). Over body. Shank down. Very close to & at lower left of L5, above level of ilium. In possible vertical relationship with 2.
14-04:	Pewter	Round, Flat Shank	------ 60%	AMERICAN, US motif. Good condition. One piece cast. Large button.	RIGHT WRIST (PELVIS, L). Under body. Beneath lunate bone of right wrist, overlying left wrist. (Right hand, not mapped, was beneath left radius & ulna, & overlying the left ilium.)
14-05:	Pewter	Round, Convex Shank	20.5mm 70%	AMERICAN, EAGLE motif, unit device obscured. Good condition. Red stain in shank area. Most of regimental oval present. Encrusted.	Location not available. No provenience data. Found above skeleton prior to exhumation, & not mapped.
14-06:	Pewter	Round, Flat 4-Hole	19.5mm 100%	AMERICAN, PLAIN: DEPRESSED CENTRE motif. Excellent condition. Narrow raised ring encircles depressed centre.	Location not available. No provenience data. Found above skeleton prior to exhumation, & not mapped.
14-07:	Pewter	----- Flat Shank	------ 30%	Motif obscured or absent. Poor condition. Red stain on shank. Possibly a small button.	Location not available. No provenience data. Found above skeleton prior to exhumation, & not mapped.

Cat. Number	Material	Shape, Attachment	Size, Portion	Motif, Unit Device, Design Features	Location Information
				░░░ BURIAL 15 ░░░	
15-01:	Pewter	Round, Flat Shank	------ 50%	AMERICAN, SCRIPT I motif. Good condition. One piece cast. Large button.	LEFT ARM. Shank down. Even with lower thorax, & 30 cm to left of midline. About where elbow would be if the left hand were on the left hip.
15-02:	Pewter	----- Flat Shank	------ 25%	Motif obscured or absent. Poor condition. One piece cast.	RIGHT ARM (PELVIS, R). Over body. Shank down. Between radius & ulna. Third distalmost in linear series (3, 2, 6, 5) along right forearm.
15-03:	Pewter	----- Flat Shank	------ 60%	Motif obscured or absent. Poor condition. One piece cast. Large button.	RIGHT ARM (PELVIS, R). Over body. Shank down. Between radius & ulna. Near wrist & distalmost in linear series (3, 2, 6, 5) along right forearm.
15-05:	Pewter	Round, Flat Shank	15.3mm 70%	AMERICAN, SCRIPT I motif. Good condition. One piece cast.	RIGHT ARM. Shank down. Just lateral of ulna, about fourth down shaft. Proximalmost in linear series (3, 2, 6, 5) along right forearm.
15-06:	Pewter	Round, Flat Shank	20.6mm 90%	Motif obscured or absent. Good condition. One piece cast. Large button.	RIGHT ARM (WAIST, R). Just lateral of ulna. Second down in linear series (3, 2, 6, 5) along right forearm.
15-07:	Pewter	Round, Flat Shank	------ 60%	AMERICAN, SCRIPT I motif. Good condition. One piece cast. Large button.	MIDLINE WAIST. Shank up. Close to right side of central L3.
				░░░ BURIAL 16 ░░░	
16-01:	Pewter	Round, Flat 4-Hole	18.6mm 100%	AMERICAN, PLAIN: DEPRESSED CENTRE motif. Excellent condition. Associated with organic material.	LEFT PELVIS. Under body. Lateral of left ilium & cranial of femoral neck. Furthest left in loose horizontal cluster (1, 2, 3, 4, 5, 6, 7, 10) across pelvic area.

Cat. Number	Material	Shape, Attachment	Size, Portion	Motif, Unit Device, Design Features	Location Information
16-02:	Pewter	Round, Convex 4-Hole	18.5mm 100%	AMERICAN, PLAIN: DEPRESSED CENTRE motif. Excellent condition.	LEFT PELVIS. Over body. Shank down. Overlying left acetabulum in loose horizontal cluster (1, 2, 3, 4, 5, 6, 7, 10) across pelvic area. Close to & cranial of number 3.
16-03:	Pewter	Round, Flat 4-Hole	18.2mm 100%	AMERICAN, PLAIN: DEPRESSED CENTRE motif. Excellent condition.	LEFT PELVIS. Over body. Shank down. Overlying acetabulum in loose horizontal cluster (1, 2, 3, 4, 5, 6, 7, 10) across pelvic area. Caudal of 2.
16-04:	Pewter	Round, Flat 4-Hole	18.0mm 100%	AMERICAN, PLAIN: DEPRESSED CENTRE motif. Excellent condition.	MIDLINE PELVIS. Over body. Cranial to pubic symphysis in loose horizontal cluster (1, 2, 3, 4, 5, 6, 7, 10) across pelvic area.
16-05:	Pewter	Round, Flat 4-Hole	18.2mm 100%	AMERICAN, PLAIN: DEPRESSED CENTRE motif. Excellent condition.	RIGHT PELVIS. Over body. Shank down. Overlying right acetabulum in loose horizontal cluster (1, 2, 3, 4, 5, 6, 7, 10) across pelvic area.
16-06:	Pewter	Round, Flat 4-Hole	18.8mm 100%	AMERICAN, PLAIN: DEPRESSED CENTRE motif. Excellent condition. Fabric adhered to much of top.	RIGHT PELVIS. Over body. Shank down. On lateral edge of right ilium near acetabulum, in loose cluster (1, 2, 3, 4, 5, 6, 7, 10) across pelvic area. Cranial to number 7.
16-07:	Pewter	Round, Flat 4-Hole	18.4mm 100%	AMERICAN, PLAIN: DEPRESSED CENTRE motif. Excellent condition.	RIGHT PELVIS. Under body. Beneath right ilium (acetabulum) in loose horizontal cluster (1, 2, 3, 4, 5, 6, 7, 10) across pelvic area. Caudal to number 6.
16-08:	Pewter	----- -----	----- 10%	Motif obscured or absent. Poor condition. Just small fragments.	LEFT THORAX (ARM, L). Just lateral of left edge of lower thorax, between chest & humerus, & caudal of 9.

Cat. Number	Material	Shape, Attachment	Size, Portion	Motif, Unit Device, Design Features	Location Information
16-09:	Pewter	---- ----	------ 5%	Motif obscured or absent. Poor condition. Just a small fragment. Possibly a four-hole button with raised ring around depressed centre.	LEFT THORAX. Just lateral of left edge of central thorax, between chest and humerus, & cranial of 8.
16-10:	Pewter	Round, Flat 4-Hole	18.4mm 100%	AMERICAN, PLAIN: DEPRESSED CENTRE motif. Excellent condition. Associated with organic material.	LEFT WRIST (PELVIS, R). Over body. Shank down. In photo, overlying the knuckle area of left hand. May be associated with loose cluster (1, 2, 3, 4, 5, 6, 7, 10) in pelvic area.

BURIAL 17

Cat. Number	Material	Shape, Attachment	Size, Portion	Motif, Unit Device, Design Features	Location Information
17-01:	Pewter	---- ----	------ 5%	Motif obscured or absent. Poor condition. Just very small fragments.	MIDLINE WAIST. Over body. At left side of L1. Cranialmost in vertical linear series (1, 2, 6).
17-02:	Pewter	Round, Flat Shank	22.4mm 50%	OBSCURED motif. Good - poor condition. Large button.	MIDLINE WAIST (ARM, R). Over body. Shank down. At left side of L2 & 2 cm medial of right radius. In vertical linear series (1, 2, 6), or possibly associated with right forearm.
17-03:	Pewter	Round, Flat Shank	20.3mm 80%	AMERICAN, SCRIPT I motif, unit device is MULLET. Excellent condition. Prominent mullet in regimental oval. One piece cast.	LEFT THORAX. Side of body. About 5 cm medial of left elbow, between lower left thorax & arm. Possibly analogous to 9 on other side of proximal forearm.
17-04:	Pewter	Round, Flat Shank	15.0mm 90%	OBSCURED motif. Excellent condition. Red corrosion on shank.	LEFT POSTPELVIC. With button 5, in ankle area of extra left tibia & foot secondarily interred above Burial 17. About 18 mm lateral of left ilium of Burial 17.

Cat. Number	Material	Shape, Attachment	Size, Portion	Motif, Unit Device, Design Features	Location Information
17-05:	Pewter	Round, Flat Shank	------ 30%	Motif obscured or absent. Poor condition. Associated with wood-like object.	LEFT POSTPELVIC. With button 4, in ankle area of extra left tibia & foot secondarily interred above Burial 17. About 18 cm lateral of left ilium of Burial 17.
17-06:	Pewter	----- ----	------ 5%	Motif obscured or absent. Poor condition. Just granules remain.	MIDLINE WAIST (ARM, R). Over body. On left side of L3 & L4, & between right radius & ulna. Caudalmost in vertical linear series (1, 2, 6) or possibly associated with right forearm.
17-07:	Copper Alloy	Round, Flat Shank	19.8mm 100%	PLAIN motif. Excellent condition. Cloth adhering both sides, & may have been cloth covered. Organic material on shank.	LEFT ARM. Side of body. Lateral of proximal end of left ulna. Possibly associated with 3. Shank oriented towards ulna.
17-08:	Pewter	----- Shank	------ 50%	Motif obscured or absent. Poor condition. Cracked & crumbling. Large button.	LEFT WRIST (PELVIS, L). Side of body. At angle between crossed arms: lateral side of right wrist, medial of left wrist, & overlying crest of left ilium.
17-09:	Pewter	Round, Flat Shank	15.8mm 80%	Motif obscured or absent. Excellent condition. One piece cast.	RIGHT ARM (WAIST, R). Between right ulna and right iliac crest, 3 cm lateral of proximal ulna. About 2 cm proximal along ulna from 10.
17-10:	Pewter	Round, Flat Shank	------ 70%	Motif obscured or absent. Poor condition. Large button.	RIGHT ARM (WAIST, R). Between right ulna and iliac crest. Three cm lateral of proximal ulna, and 2 cm distal of number 9 along ulna. Just cranial of right iliac crest.

Cat. Number	Material	Shape, Attachment	Size, Portion	Motif, Unit Device, Design Features	Location Information
17-11:	Pewter	Round, Convex Shank	14.0mm 100%	BRITISH, OTHER: CIRCLED 89 motif, unit device is 89. Excellent condition. British motif: circle enclosing "89". Red corroded shaft.	LEFT WRIST (PELVIS, L). Over body. Encountered above area of both wrists and left abdomen.
17-12:	Pewter	Round, Convex Shank	14.2mm 90%	BRITISH, OTHER: CIRCLED 89 motif, unit device is 89. Excellent condition. Semi-obscured British 89th regiment motif – only back of "9" visible. Red corroded shank.	LEFT WRIST (PELVIS, L). Over body. Encountered above area of both wrists & left abdomen.

Cat. Number	Material	Shape, Attachment	Size, Portion	Motif, Unit Device, Design Features	Location Information
18-01:	Pewter	----- Flat Shank	------ 20%	Motif obscured or absent. Poor condition. Just granules.	MIDLINE THORAX. Over body. Shank down. About 2 or 3 cm right of upper thoracic vertebrae. Cranialmost in vertical linear series (1, 2, 3, 4) in thorax midline.
18-02:	Pewter	----- Flat Shank	------ 40%	AMERICAN, EAGLE motif. Good condition. One piece cast. Motif is similar to number 21 of Burial 06. Small button.	MIDLINE THORAX. Over body. Shank down. Upon an upper thoracic vertebra. Second from top in vertical linear series (1, 2, 3, 4) in thorax midline.
18-03:	Pewter	Round, Flat Shank	14.9mm 80%	AMERICAN, EAGLE motif, unit device obscured. Good condition. Partly imbedded in thoracic vertebra.	MIDLINE THORAX. Over body. Shank down. Third from top in vertical linear series (1, 2, 3, 4) in midline of thorax.

Cat. Number	Material	Shape, Attachment	Size, Portion	Motif, Unit Device, Design Features	Location Information
18-04:	Pewter	----- Flat Shank	------ 30%	Motif obscured or absent. Large Poor condition. button.	MIDLINE THORAX (WRIST, L). Over body. Shank down. Upon a central thoracic vertebra. Caudalmost in vertical linear series (1, 2, 3, 4). Series may continue in waist area with 7 & 8.
18-05:	Pewter	----- ----	------ 5%	Motif obscured or absent. Poor condition. Just granules.	RIGHT WRIST. Over body. Overlying right forearm, between distal right radius & ulna. Three cm distal of button 6.
18-06:	Pewter	----- ----	------ 10%	Motif obscured or absent. Poor condition. Just small fragments.	RIGHT THORAX (WRIST, L/R). Over body. Overlying right forearm, between central radius & ulna. Three cm proximal of button 5.
18-07:	Pewter	----- Flat Shank	------ 30%	OBSCURED motif. Poor condition. One piece cast. Small button.	RIGHT WAIST (THORAX, R). Shank down. Lower right thorax/upper waist. With 6 & 8, possibly part of vertical linear series (1, 2, 3, 4) slightly to right of midline.
18-08:	Pewter	----- Shank	------ 20%	Motif obscured or absent. One piece cast.	RIGHT WAIST. Upper right waist. With 7 & 8, possibly part of vertical linear series (1, 2, 3, 4) slightly to right of midline. Shank to right side of body.
18-09:	Pewter	Round, Flat Shank	20.1mm 90%	AMERICAN, SCRIPT I motif. Good condition. One piece cast.	RIGHT PELVIS. Over body. About 5 cm lateral of left ilium. Shank oriented medially, towards body.
18-10:	Pewter	----- Shank	------ 20%	Motif obscured or absent. Poor condition. Just fragments.	MIDLINE PELVIS. Overlying sacrum. Roughly even with button 9 to the left.

Cat. Number	Material Shape, Attachment	Size, Portion	Motif, Unit Device, Design Features	Location Information

19-01:	Bone	Round, Flat 1-Hole	17.7mm 100%	PLAIN (BONE) motif. Excellent condition. Unusually large for one-hole bone button.	RIGHT THORAX. Over body. Lower right thorax, very close to midline, between ribs 11 & 12. Position is unusual for one-hole bone button.
19-02:	Copper Alloy	Round, Flat Shank	15.7mm 100%	OTHER: FLOWERS motif. Excellent condition. Soldered shank. Civilian motif: flowers in basket within circle.	RIGHT ARM. Over body. Shank down. Cranialmost of 3 buttons adhering to piece of wood overlying right humerus.
19-03:	Copper Alloy	Round, Flat Shank	15.6mm 100%	OTHER: FLOWERS motif. Excellent condition. Soldered shank. Civilian motif: flowers in basket within circle. Fabric adhered to back.	RIGHT ARM. Over body. Shank down. One of 3 buttons adhering to piece of wood overlying right humerus.
19-04:	Copper Alloy	Round, Flat Shank	15.5mm 100%	OTHER: FLOWERS motif. Excellent condition. Soldered shank. Civilian motif: flowers in basket within circle.	RIGHT ARM. Over body. Shank down. Caudalmost of 3 buttons adhering to piece of wood overlying right humerus.

20-01:	Pewter	----- Flat Shank	------ 30%	Motif obscured or absent. Poor condition. Large button.	RIGHT ARM (WAIST). Over body. Shank down. Two cm medial of right radius at midshaft, & 2 cm proximal of button 2. Also 5 cm right of L3.
20-02:	Pewter	----- Flat Shank	------ 30%	Motif obscured or absent. Poor condition.	RIGHT ARM (WAIST, M). Over body. Three cm medial of right radius, & 2 cm distal of button 1. Also in central waist area, about 2 cm right of L3.

Cat. Number	Material	Shape, Attachment	Size, Portion	Motif, Unit Device, Design Features	Location Information
20-03:	Pewter	Round, Flat Shank	16.9mm 100%	AMERICAN, SCRIPT I motif, unit device is a STAR. Excellent condition. Heavily encrusted with cemented sand. One piece cast.	LEFT ARM. Under body. Just lateral of proximal left ulna, and about 3 cm proximal of button 4.
20-04:	Pewter	Round, Flat Shank	------ 70%	Motif obscured or absent. Good condition. Heavily encrusted with cemented sand. Large button.	LEFT ARM. Under body. Just lateral of left ulna at midshaft. About 3 cm distal of button 3.
20-05:	Pewter	----- Shank	------ 30%	Motif obscured or absent. Poor condition.	MIDLINE WAIST. Under body. Beneath L4. In loose cluster with buttons 1 & 2.
20-06:	Pewter	----- Shank	------ 30%	Motif obscured or absent. Poor condition. Just small fragments.	Location not available. Shank up. Probably beneath body. Not mapped.

▒▒▒▒▒▒▒▒▒▒▒▒▒▒▒▒▒▒▒▒▒ BURIAL 21 ▒▒▒▒▒▒▒▒▒▒▒▒▒▒▒▒▒▒▒▒▒

Cat. Number	Material	Shape, Attachment	Size, Portion	Motif, Unit Device, Design Features	Location Information
21-01:	Pewter	Round, Flat Shank	21.1mm 100%	OBSCURED motif. Excellent condition. Tightly woven fabric adhering to front & back. One piece cast. Flat rim.	LEFT SHOULDER. Side of body. Shank down. Approximately 10 cm lateral of left shoulder, in loose cluster (1, 2, 13).
21-02:	Pewter	Round, Flat Shank	21.0mm 100%	AMERICAN, SCRIPT I motif, unit device is MULLET. Excellent condition. Rim is flat, sharp edged. One piece cast.	LEFT SHOULDER. Side of body. Shank down. Approximately 10 cm lateral of left shoulder, in loose cluster (1, 2, 13).
21-03:	Pewter	Round, Flat Shank	21.3mm 100%	AMERICAN, SCRIPT I motif. Excellent condition. Flat, sharp edge. One piece cast.	LEFT ARM. Side of body. Just medial of left radius at midshaft.

Cat. Number	Material	Shape, Attachment	Size, Portion	Motif, Unit Device, Design Features	Location Information
21-04:	Pewter	Round, Flat Shank	22.1mm 100%	AMERICAN, SCRIPT I motif. Good condition. Heavily encrusted with cemented sand.	RIGHT SHOULDER (THORAX, R). Side of body. Shank down. About 4 cm caudal of head of right humerus. Cranialmost in vertical cluster (4, 5, 6, 7A-C, 8, 9, 19) between right humerus & ribcage.
21-05:	Pewter	----- Flat Shank	24.9mm 70%	Motif obscured or absent. Good condition. Heavily encrusted with cemented sand.	RIGHT THORAX. Side of body. Third down in vertical cluster (4, 5, 6, 7A, 7B, 7C, 8, 9, 19) between right humerus & ribcage. Shank towards right arm.
21-06:	Pewter	Round, Flat Shank	21.4mm 100%	OBSCURED motif. Good condition. Heavily encrusted with cemented sand. One piece cast. Shank eccentrically placed.	RIGHT THORAX. Side of body. Just lateral of central ribcage. Fourth down in vertical cluster (4, 5, 6, 7A, 7B, 7C, 8, 9, 19) between right humerus & ribcage.
21-07A:	Pewter	Round, Flat Shank	20.8mm 100%	AMERICAN, SCRIPT I motif, unit device obscured. Excellent condition. Large clump of fabric adhering. Edge is flat & sharp.	RIGHT THORAX. Side of body. Lateral of central thorax, middle of cluster (4, 5, 6, 7, 8, 9, 19) between right humerus & thorax. 7A-C bunched, diff orientations.
21-07B:	Pewter	Round, Flat Shank	21.9mm 80%	AMERICAN, SCRIPT I motif. Good condition. Large clump of fabric adhering. Heavily encrusted with cemented sand.	RIGHT THORAX. Side of body. At centre of linear series (4, 19, 5, 6, 7A-C, 8, 9, 19) at lateral edge of right thorax. 7A-C bunched, dissimilar orientations.
21-07C:	Pewter	Round, Flat Shank	------ 80%	Motif obscured or absent. Good cond. Encrusted w/ cemented sand. Shank eccentrically placed. Large button. Parallel cracks deform disk.	RIGHT THORAX. Side of body. At centre of linear series (4, 19, 5, 6, 7A-C, 8, 9, 19) at lateral edge of right thorax. 7A-C bunched, dissimilar orientations.

Cat. Number	Material	Shape, Attachment	Size, Portion	Motif, Unit Device, Design Features	Location Information
21-08:	Pewter	Round, Flat Shank	22.2mm 100%	Motif obscured or absent. Good condition. Heavily encrusted with cemented sand.	RIGHT THORAX. Side of body. Lateral of lower right thorax. Second up in roughly linear series (4, 5, 6, 7A, 7B, 7C, 8, 9, 19) between ribcage and humerus.
21-09:	Pewter	Round, Flat Shank	------ 100%	Motif obscured or absent. Good condition. Heavily encrusted with cemented sand. Large button. Disk elongated by many parallel cracks.	RIGHT THORAX. Side of body. Even with right elbow. Caudalmost in roughly linear series (4, 5, 6, 7A, 7B, 7C, 8, 9, 19) between right humerus & thorax.
21-10:	Pewter	Round, Flat Shank	22.3mm 100%	Motif obscured or absent. Good - poor condition. Heavily corroded, encrusted with cemented sand. Disk elongated by many parallel cracks.	RIGHT ARM. Over body. Overlying interosseous space between proximal radius & ulna. In loose cluster (10, 11, 12) at proximal right forearm. About 1 cm proximal of 11.
21-11:	Pewter	----- Flat Shank	------ 80%	Motif obscured or absent. Poor condition. Badly fragmented. Heavily encrusted with cemented sand. Large button.	RIGHT ARM. Just medial of proximal right radius. In loose cluster (10, 11, 12) at proximal right forearm. About 1 cm distal of 10.
21-12:	Pewter	Round, Flat Shank	20.7mm 100%	AMERICAN, SCRIPT I motif, unit device is a STAR. Excellent condition. Flat, sharp edge. One piece cast.	RIGHT ARM. Under body. Shank down. Even with 11 in loose cluster (10, 11, 12) at upper central portion of right forearm. Partly beneath ulna, shank oriented down.
21-13:	Pewter	Round, Flat Shank	------ 80%	Motif obscured or absent. Poor condition. Large button.	LEFT SHOULDER. Side of body. About 5 cm lateral of left shoulder, in loose cluster (1, 2, 13). Midway between shoulder & 1 and 2.

Cat. Number	Material	Shape, Attachment	Size, Portion	Motif, Unit Device, Design Features	Location Information
21-14:	Pewter	Round, Flat Shank	21.9mm 80%	AMERICAN, SCRIPT I motif, unit device obscured. Good condition. Heavily encrusted with cemented sand.	RIGHT NECK. Just to right of cervicals. In loose 18-button series (14-18, 20, 22-28, 30-34) spanning shoulder-neck area.
21-15:	Pewter	Round, Flat Shank	21.5mm 100%	AMERICAN, SCRIPT I motif, unit device is MULLET. Excellent condition. Rim is flat, sharp edged. One piece cast.	RIGHT THORAX. At angle of right first rib. In loose 18-button series (14-18, 20, 22-28, 30-34) spanning shoulder-neck area.
21-16:	Pewter	Round, Flat Shank.	23.1mm 100%	AMERICAN, SCRIPT I motif, unit device is MULLET. Excellent condition. Organic material associated with both sides. One piece cast.	RIGHT THORAX. At midshaft of right clavicle. In loose 18-button series (14-18, 20, 22-28, 30-34) spanning shoulder-neck area.
21-17:	Pewter	Round, Flat Shank	15.6mm 100%	AMERICAN, SCRIPT I motif, unit device obscured. Excellent condition. One piece cast. Heavily encrusted with cemented sand.	RIGHT SHOULDER. Next to distal end of right clavicle. In loose 18-button series (14-18, 20, 22-28, 30-34) spanning shoulder-neck area.
21-18:	Pewter	Round, Flat Shank	20.1mm 100%	AMERICAN, SCRIPT I motif, unit device is MULLET. Excellent condition. Organic material adhering to back. Flat, sharp edge. One piece cast.	RIGHT SHOULDER. Under body. Beneath head of right humerus. Part of loose 18-button series (14-18, 20, 22-28, 30-34) spanning shoulder-neck area.
21-19:	Pewter	----- Flat Shank	24.0mm 60%	Motif obscured or absent. Good condition. Heavily encrusted with cemented sand. One piece cast.	RIGHT THORAX. Side of body. Shank down. Just lateral of upper thorax & right scapula. Second down in linear series (4, 5, 6, 7A-C, 8, 9, 19) between thorax & humerus.

Cat. Number	Material	Shape, Attachment	Size, Portion	Motif, Unit Device, Design Features	Location Information
21-20:	Pewter	Round, Flat Shank	------ 80%	Motif obscured or absent. Good condition. Associated with large amount of organic material. Large button.	MIDLINE NECK. Under body. Beneath C7. In loose 18-button series (14-18, 20, 22-28, 30-34) spanning shoulder-neck area.
21-21:	Pewter	Round, Flat Shank	20.3mm 100%	AMERICAN, SCRIPT I motif, unit device is MULLET. Excellent condition. Rim is flat, sharp edged. One piece cast.	Location not available. Under body. Beneath burial.
21-22:	Pewter	Round, Flat Shank	21.4mm 100%	AMERICAN, SCRIPT I motif, unit device is MULLET. Excellent condition. Flat, sharp edge. Associated with 2 metal objects.	LEFT NECK. Side of body. Shank down. Cranial of 23 & to left of neck. In loose 18-button series (14-18, 20, 22-28, 30-34) spanning shoulder-neck area.
21-23:	Pewter	Round, Flat Shank	22.0mm 100%	AMERICAN, SCRIPT I motif, unit device obscured. Excellent condition. Associated with fabric. One piece cast.	LEFT NECK. Side of body. Shank down. To left of neck & caudal of 22. In loose 18-button series (14-18, 20, 22-28, 30-34) spanning shoulder-neck area.
21-24:	Pewter	Round, Flat Shank	22.2mm 100%	AMERICAN, SCRIPT I motif, unit device is a STAR. Good condition. Associated with organic material. Heavily encrusted with sand. One piece cast.	LEFT THORAX. Side of body. Shank down. Cranial of left shoulder & overlying 25. In loose 18-button series (14-18, 20, 22-28, 30-34) spanning shoulder-neck area.
21-25:	Pewter	Round, Flat Shank	------ 80%	Motif obscured or absent. Good condition. Large button. Organic material on back. Encrusted w cemented sand. Disk deformed by parallel cracks.	LEFT THORAX. Side of body. Shank up. Cranial to left shoulder & beneath 24. In loose 18-button series (14-18, 20, 22-28, 30-34) spanning shoulder-neck area.

Cat. Number	Material	Shape, Attachment	Size, Portion	Motif, Unit Device, Design Features	Location Information
21-26:	Pewter	Round, Flat Shank	21.4mm 90%	AMERICAN, SCRIPT I motif, unit device is MULLET. Good condition. Organic material on front & back.	LEFT SHOULDER. Side of body. Shank down. Left lateralmost in loose 18-button cluster (14-18, 20, 22-28, 30-34) spanning shoulder-neck area.
21-27:	Pewter	----- Flat Shank	------ 70%	Motif obscured or absent. Good condition. Associated with organic material. Large button.	LEFT SHOULDER. Over body. With (28, 30, 31) overlying proximal end of left humerus. Probably related to shoulder & neck series (14-18, 20, 22-28, 30-34).
21-28:	Pewter	Round, Flat ----	15.8mm 50%	AMERICAN, OBSCURED motif, unit device is a STAR. Poor condition. Organic material on one side.	LEFT SHOULDER. Over body. With (27, 30, 31) overlying proximal left humerus. Probably related to shoulder & neck series (14-18, 20, 22-28, 30-34).
21-29:	Pewter	----- Shank	------ 30%	Motif obscured or absent. Poor condition. Large button.	Exact location unavailable. From left side of body.
21-30:	Pewter	Round, Flat Shank	21.7mm 100%	Motif obscured or absent. Poor condition. With organic material. Disk elongated by numerous parallel cracks.	LEFT ARM. Over body. With (27, 28, 31) overlying proximal left humerus. Probably associated with shoulder-neck series (14-18, 20, 22-28, 30-34).
21-31:	Pewter	Round, Flat Shank	20.4mm 100%	AMERICAN, SCRIPT I motif, unit device obscured. Excellent condition. Flat, sharp edges. One piece cast.	LEFT ARM. Over body. Probably from proximal left humerus area, & associated with (27, 28, 30) in shoulder-neck series (14-18, 20, 22-28, 30-34).
21-32:	Pewter	Round, Flat Shank	22.0mm 100%	AMERICAN, SCRIPT I motif, unit device obscured. Excellent condition. One piece cast.	NECK, GENERAL AREA. Removed from excavated block with skull. Shank oriented towards shoulder. Part of 18-button cluster (14-18, 20, 22-28, 30-34).

Cat. Number	Material	Shape, Attachment	Size, Portion	Motif, Unit Device, Design Features	Location Information
21-33:	Pewter	Round, Flat Shank	20.7mm 100%	AMERICAN, SCRIPT I motif, unit device obscured. Excellent condition. One piece cast.	LEFT NECK, GENERAL AREA. Shank down. Removed from excavated block with skull. Part of 18-button cluster (14-18, 20, 22-28, 30-34) spanning shoulders. Shank oriented down.
21-34:	Pewter	Round, Flat Shank	20.2mm 100%	AMERICAN, SCRIPT I motif, unit device is MULLET. Excellent condition. One piece cast. Flat rim.	LEFT NECK, GENERAL AREA. Under body. Part of loose 18-button cluster (14-18, 20, 22-28, 30-34) spanning shoulder-neck area. Removed from excavated block with skull.

BURIAL 22

Cat. Number	Material	Shape, Attachment	Size, Portion	Motif, Unit Device, Design Features	Location Information
22-01:	Pewter	Round, Flat Shank	17.1mm 100%	AMERICAN, SCRIPT I motif, unit device is a STAR. Good condition. One piece cast.	NOT ASSOCIATED WITH BODY. Not in burial context.
22-02:	Pewter	----- Flat Shank	------ 40%	Motif obscured or absent. Poor condition. Large button.	NOT ASSOCIATED WITH BODY. Not in burial context.
22-03:	Pewter	Round, Flat Shank	------ 90%	Motif obscured or absent. Poor condition. Large button.	NOT ASSOCIATED WITH BODY. Not in burial context.
22-04:	Pewter	----- Flat Shank	------ 30%	Motif obscured or absent. Poor condition.	NOT ASSOCIATED WITH BODY. Not in burial context.
22-05:	Pewter	----- Shank	------ 20%	Motif obscured or absent. Poor condition.	NOT ASSOCIATED WITH BODY. Not in context.
22-06:	Pewter	Round, Flat 4-Hole	19.3mm 100%	AMERICAN, PLAIN: DEPRESSED CENTRE motif. Excellent condition. Thread adhering to back.	NOT ASSOCIATED WITH BODY. Not in burial context.

Cat. Number	Material	Shape, Attachment	Size, Portion	Motif, Unit Device, Design Features	Location Information
22-07:	Pewter	---- ----	------ 5%	Motif obscured or absent. Poor condition. Just 2 very small fragments.	NOT ASSOCIATED WITH BODY. Not in burial context.
22-08:	Pewter	Round, Flat Shank	.21.6mm 70%	Motif obscured or absent. Poor condition.	NOT ASSOCIATED WITH BODY. Not in burial context.

BURIAL 23

Cat. Number	Material	Shape, Attachment	Size, Portion	Motif, Unit Device, Design Features	Location Information
23-01:	Bone	Round, Flat 1-Hole	11.6mm 100%	PLAIN (BONE) motif. Excellent condition.	MIDLINE NECK. Side of body. Touching right cranial portion of C7, & just cranial of number 2.
23-02:	Bone	Round, Flat 1-Hole	11.5mm 100%	PLAIN (BONE) motif. Excellent condition.	MIDLINE NECK. Side of body. Touching C7 at caudal right side.
23-03:	Pewter	Round, Flat Shank	18.4mm 100%	AMERICAN, US motif. Excellent condition. One piece cast. Fabric impression on the front.	MIDLINE PELVIS. Over body. Shank down. On centre of first sacral segment. In loose cluster (3, 4, 5, 6, 7, 8) in central & left pelvic area.
23-04:	Pewter	Round, Flat Shank	18.3mm 100%	AMERICAN, US motif. Excellent condition. One piece cast.	LEFT PELVIS. Over body. Shank down. About even with 3, straddling sacro-iliac joint. In loose cluster (3, 4, 5, 6, 7, 8) in central & left pelvic area.
23-05:	Pewter	Round, Flat Shank	19.9mm 100%	AMERICAN, US motif. Excellent condition. One piece cast.	LEFT PELVIS. Over body. Shank up. On craniolateral edge of left ilium. Roughly in line with 3 & 4, and cranial to 6. In loose cluster (3-8) in central & left pelvic area.
23-06:	Pewter	Round, Flat Shank	19.9mm 100%	AMERICAN, US motif. Excellent condition. Heavily encrusted.	LEFT PELVIS. Over body. Shank down. At lateral edge of ilium, caudal to 5. In loose cluster (3, 4, 5, 6, 7, 8) in central & left pelvic area.

Cat. Number	Material	Shape, Attachment	Size, Portion	Motif, Unit Device, Design Features	Location Information
23-07:	Pewter	Round, Flat Shank	19.9mm 100%	AMERICAN, US motif. Excellent condition. One piece cast.	MIDLINE PELVIS. Over body. With 8, in midline of pelvic cavity. Just caudal of sacrum. In loose cluster (3-8) in central & left pelvic area. Shank oriented caudad.
23-08:	Pewter	Round, Flat Shank	18.5mm 100%	AMERICAN, US motif. Excellent condition. One piece cast.	MIDLINE PELVIS. Over body. Shank up. With 7, within pelvic cavity in midline. Caudal of fifth sacral element. In loose cluster (3-8) in central & left pelvic area. Shank up.

BURIAL 24

Cat. Number	Material	Shape, Attachment	Size, Portion	Motif, Unit Device, Design Features	Location Information
24-01:	Bone	Round, Flat 1-Hole	16.4mm 100%	PLAIN (BONE) motif. Excellent condition.	MIDLINE POSTPELVIC. Side of body. Just medial of distal right fibula. In loose cluster (1, 2, 3, 6A) centred on distal tibias.
24-02:	Bone	Round, Flat 1-Hole	16.3mm 100%	PLAIN (BONE) motif. Excellent condition.	MIDLINE POSTPELVIC. Side of body. Two cm medial of right tibia. To left of 1 and cranial of 3, in loose cluster (1, 2, 3, 6A) centred on distal tibias.
24-03:	Bone	Round, Flat 2-Hole	16.6mm 100%	PLAIN (BONE) motif. Excellent condition. False circular cut, slightly off centre, probable manufacturing error in cutting blank.	MIDLINE POSTPELVIC. Side of body. Just medial of distal condyle of right tibia. Caudal of button 2, in loose cluster (1, 2, 3, 6A) centred on distal tibias.
24-04:	Bone	Round, Flat 1-Hole	16.2mm 80%	PLAIN (BONE) motif. Good condition, some attrition on opposing sides.	MIDLINE POSTPELVIC. Between distal femora, medial of & cranial to, right knee. Probably associated with loose cluster (1, 2, 3, 6A) centred on distal tibias.

Cat. Number	Material	Shape, Attachment	Size, Portion	Motif, Unit Device, Design Features	Location Information
24-05:	Pewter	Round, Flat Shank	------ 50%	Motif obscured or absent. Poor condition. Large button.	RIGHT WAIST. Over body. Shank up. Upper right waist area, roughly even with L2. In loose cluster (5, 6B, 7, 8, 9, 10) in area of right waist & upper right forearm.
24-06A:	Bone	Round, Flat 1-Hole	15.5mm 100%	PLAIN (BONE) motif. Good condition.	RIGHT POSTPELVIC. Under body. Beneath distal right tibia, in line with buttons 1 & 2. In loose cluster (1, 2, 3, 6A) centred on distal tibias.
24-06B:	Pewter	----- Flat Shank	------ 50%	Motif obscured or absent. Poor condition.	RIGHT ARM (WAIST, R). Just lateral of proximal right radius. In loose cluster (5, 6B, 7, 8, 9, 10) in area of right waist & upper right forearm.
24-07:	Pewter	----- Flat Shank	------ 20%	Motif obscured or absent. Poor condition.	RIGHT ARM. Shank up. Three cm lateral of proximal right radius. In loose cluster (5, 6B, 7, 8, 9, 10) in area of right waist & upper right forearm.
24-08:	Pewter	Round, Flat Shank	15.7mm 60%	AMERICAN, SCRIPT I motif. Good condition. Unit device area appears worn smooth. One piece cast. Disk elongated by many parallel cracks.	RIGHT ARM (WAIST, R). Over body. Shank down. Two cm medial of midshaft of right radius. In loose cluster (5, 6B, 7, 8, 9, 10) in area of right waist & upper right forearm.
24-09:	Pewter	Round, Flat Shank	15.2mm 80%	AMERICAN, SCRIPT I motif, unit device is a STAR. Good condition. Front edge of rim rounded, back edge sharp, giving slightly bevelled effect.	RIGHT ARM. Under body. Shank up. Beneath neck of right radius. In loose cluster (5, 6B, 7, 8, 9, 10) in area of right waist & upper right forearm.
24-10:	Pewter	Round, Flat Shank	14.5mm 80%	AMERICAN, SCRIPT I motif, unit device is a STAR. Excellent condition. Base of shank enlarged.	RIGHT ARM. Over body. Shank down. In crook of right elbow. In loose cluster (5, 6B, 7, 8, 9, 10) in area of right waist & upper right forearm.

Cat. Number	Material	Shape, Attachment	Size, Portion	Motif, Unit Device, Design Features	Location Information

| 26-01: | Pewter | Round, Flat Shank | 14.3mm 100% | AMERICAN, US motif. Excellent condition. One piece cast. | RIGHT ARM (PELVIS, MID). Side of body. Shank up. About 2 cm lateral of right ulna, about two thirds down ulnar shaft, and overlying right wing of sacrum (S1). |

27-01:	Pewter	Round, Flat Shank	16.6mm 100%	AMERICAN, SCRIPT I motif, unit device is a STAR. Excellent condition. Regimental device is star, not mullet. One piece cast.	RIGHT NECK. Side of body. In tight cluster (1, 2A, 2B) between back of skull and right shoulder. Near 28, 29, & 31 in neck midline area.
27-02A:	Pewter	Round, Flat Shank	21.0mm 100%	AMERICAN, SCRIPT I motif, unit device is a STAR. Excellent condition. One piece cast.	RIGHT NECK. Side of body. In tight cluster (1, 2A, 2B) between back of skull and right shoulder. Near 28, 29, & 31 in neck midline area.
27-02B:	Pewter	Round, Flat Shank	20.6mm 100%	AMERICAN, SCRIPT I motif, unit device is a STAR. Excellent condition. Regimental device is star, not mullet. One piece cast.	RIGHT NECK. Side of body. In tight cluster (1, 2A, 2B) between back of skull and right shoulder.
27-03:	Pewter	Round, Flat Shank	20.6mm 100%	AMERICAN, SCRIPT I motif, unit device is a STAR. Excellent condition. Regimental device is star, not mullet. One piece cast.	RIGHT THORAX. Over body. Shank up. Three cm medial of humeral head. Cranialmost in vertical series of large buttons (3, 5, 8) at right of midline, upper thorax.
27-04:	Pewter	Round, Flat Shank	16.8mm 100%	AMERICAN, SCRIPT I motif, unit device is a STAR. Excellent condition. One piece cast.	MIDLINE THORAX. Over body. Shank up. Upper thorax, midline. Cranialmost in vertical linear series of small buttons (4, 6, 7, 9-13) near torso midline. Shank slants to skull.

Cat. Number	Material	Shape, Attachment	Size, Portion	Motif, Unit Device, Design Features	Location Information
27-05:	Pewter	Round, Flat Shank	20.2mm 100%	AMERICAN, SCRIPT I motif, unit device obscured. Excellent condition. One piece cast.	RIGHT THORAX. Over body. Second down in vertical linear series of large buttons (3, 5, 8) right of midline, upper thorax. Shank slanted up to sternum.
27-06:	Pewter	Round, Flat Shank	16.7mm 100%	AMERICAN, SCRIPT I motif, unit device is a STAR. Excellent condition. Regimental device is star, not mullet. One piece cast.	MIDLINE THORAX. Over body. Upper thorax midline. Second down in vertical linear series of small buttons (4, 6, 7, 9, 10, 11, 12, 13) near midline, down trunk.
27-07:	Pewter	Round, Flat Shank	16.8mm 100%	AMERICAN, SCRIPT I motif, unit device is a STAR. Excellent condition. One piece cast.	MIDLINE THORAX. Over body. Central thorax. Third down in vertical linear series of small buttons (4, 6, 7, 9, 10, 11, 12, 13) near midline, down trunk.
27-08:	Pewter	Round, Flat Shank	20.7mm 100%	AMERICAN, SCRIPT I motif, unit device is a STAR. Excellent condition. Regimental device is star, not mullet.	MIDLINE THORAX. Over body. Shank down. On sternum. Caudalmost in vertical series of large buttons (3, 5, 8) at right of midline, upper thorax.
27-09:	Pewter	Round, Flat Shank	16.8mm 100%	AMERICAN, SCRIPT I motif, unit device is a STAR. Excellent condition. Regimental device is star, not mullet. One piece cast.	MIDLINE THORAX. Over body. Shank down. Central thorax. Fourth down in vertical linear series of small buttons (4, 6, 7, 9, 10, 11, 12, 13) near midline, down trunk.
27-10:	Pewter	Round, Flat Shank	16.5mm 100%	AMERICAN, SCRIPT I motif, unit device is a STAR. Excellent condition. One piece cast.	LEFT THORAX. Over body. Shank down. Central left thorax. Fifth down in vertical linear series of small buttons (4, 6, 7, 9, 10, 11, 12, 13) near midline, down trunk.

Cat. Number	Material	Shape, Attachment	Size, Portion	Motif, Unit Device, Design Features	Location Information
27-11:	Pewter	Round, Flat Shank	16.8mm 100%	AMERICAN, SCRIPT I motif, unit device is a STAR. Excellent condition. One piece cast.	LEFT THORAX. Over body. Shank down. Lower left thorax. Sixth down in vertical linear series of small buttons (4, 6, 7, 9, 10, 11, 12, 13) near midline, down trunk.
27-12:	Pewter	Round, Flat Shank	16.8mm 100%	AMERICAN, SCRIPT I motif, unit device is a STAR. Excellent condition. Star in oval is very faint. One piece cast.	LEFT WAIST. Over body. Shank down. In upper left waist area. Seventh down in vertical linear series of small buttons (4, 6, 7, 9, 10, 11, 12, 13) near midline, down torso.
27-13:	Pewter	Round, Flat Shank	17.3mm 100%	AMERICAN, SCRIPT I motif, unit device is a STAR. Excellent condition. One piece cast.	LEFT WAIST. Over body. Shank down. In upper waist, just left of midline. Caudalmost in vertical linear series of small buttons (4, 6, 7, 9, 10, 11, 12, 13) near torso midline.
27-14:	Pewter	Round, Flat Shank	19.8mm 100%	AMERICAN, SCRIPT I motif, unit device is a STAR. Excellent condition. Regimental device is star, not mullet. One piece cast.	RIGHT ARM (WAIST, M). Over body. Over centre of right radius. Proximalmost in loose cluster of brass buttons (14, 15, 30, 40) centred on distal right forearm & wrist.
27-15:	Pewter	Round, Flat Shank	20.0mm 100%	AMERICAN, SCRIPT I motif, unit device is a STAR. Excellent condition. Regimental device is star, not mullet. One piece cast.	RIGHT ARM. Over body. Shank down. Overlying right radius & ulna, proximal of wrist. In loose brass button cluster (14, 15, 30, 40) centred distal half of right forearm & wrist.
27-16:	Pewter	Round, Flat Shank	20.4mm 100%	AMERICAN, SCRIPT I motif, unit device obscured. Excellent condition. One piece cast.	RIGHT ARM (WAIST, M). Under body. Shank down. Beneath 15 & distal forearm. In loose cluster (14, 15, 16, 17, 30, 40) centred around distal half of right forearm & wrist.

Cat. Number	Material	Shape, Attachment	Size, Portion	Motif, Unit Device, Design Features	Location Information
27-17:	Pewter	Round, Flat Shank	20.7mm 100%	AMERICAN, SCRIPT I motif, unit device is a STAR. Excellent condition. One piece cast.	RIGHT ARM (WAIST, M). Under body. Beneath 14. In loose cluster (14, 15, 16, 17, 30, 40) centred around distal half of right forearm & wrist.
27-18:	Pewter	Round, Flat Shank	20.0mm 100%	AMERICAN, SCRIPT I motif, unit device is a STAR. Excellent condition. One piece cast.	RIGHT ARM. On lateral side of right humerus midshaft. Distalmost in linear series (18, 23, 33, 34) on lateral side, proximal 2/3rds of right humerus.
27-19:	Pewter	Round, Flat Shank	20.7mm 100%	AMERICAN, SCRIPT I motif, unit device is a STAR. Excellent condition. Regimental device is star, not mullet. One piece cast.	LEFT THORAX. Side of body. Shank down. Lateralmost in tight cluster (19, 38, 39) in lower left thorax, about 1 cm lateral of ribcage.
27-20:	Pewter	Round, Flat Shank	20.4mm 100%	AMERICAN, PLAIN motif, unit device is a STAR. Excellent condition. Face unobscured and plain, no major motif, only star inside oval. One piece cast.	LEFT ARM. Side of body. On medial side of left radius, about one third down shaft. In loose cluster (20, 21, 22, 32) centred around left forearm.
27-21:	Pewter	Round, Flat Shank	20.4mm 100%	AMERICAN, SCRIPT I motif, unit device obscured. Excellent condition. Heavily encrusted with cemented sand. One piece cast.	LEFT ARM. Side of body. Shank down. Lateral of left ulna, about one third down shaft. In loose cluster (20, 21, 22, 32) centred around left forearm.
27-22:	Pewter	Round, Flat Shank	16.2mm 100%	AMERICAN, SCRIPT I motif, unit device obscured. Excellent condition. Bevelled rim. One piece cast.	LEFT ARM. Side of body. About 2 cm lateral of distal left ulna. In loose cluster (20, 21, 22, 32) centred around left forearm.

Cat. Number	Material	Shape, Attachment	Size, Portion	Motif, Unit Device, Design Features	Location Information
27-23:	Pewter	Round, Flat Shank	20.8mm 100%	AMERICAN, SCRIPT I motif, unit device obscured. Excellent condition.	RIGHT ARM. Under body. Beneath right humerus, proximal of 18. Second up in linear series (18, 23, 33, 34) on lateral side of proximal 2/3rds of right humerus.
27-24:	Pewter	Round, Flat Shank	20.2mm 100%	AMERICAN, SCRIPT I motif, unit device is a STAR. Excellent condition. Regimental device is star, not mullet. One piece cast.	RIGHT PELVIS. Under body. Half beneath crest of right ilium. Cranialmost in vertical linear series (24, 25, 26) at lateral edge of right ilium.
27-25:	Pewter	Round, Flat Shank	22.5mm 80%	OBSCURED motif. Good condition.	RIGHT PELVIS. Under body. Beneath lateral edge of crest of right ilium. In vertical linear series (24, 25, 26) at lateral edge of right ilium.
27-26:	Pewter	Round, Flat Shank	16.0mm 100%	AMERICAN, SCRIPT I motif, unit device is a STAR. Excellent condition. Possible bevelled edge. Regimental device probably not mullet. One piece cast.	RIGHT PELVIS. Under body. Partly beneath crest of right ilium. Caudalmost in vertical linear series (24, 25, 26) at lateral edge of right ilium.
27-27:	Pewter	----- Flat Shank	----- 20%	Motif obscured or absent. Poor condition.	RIGHT ARM (THORAX, R). In crook of right elbow, near button 36. Position is analogous to 20 on left side. Associated with dense cluster of buckshot.
27-28:	Pewter	Round, Flat Shank	20.5mm 100%	AMERICAN, SCRIPT I motif, unit device is a STAR. Excellent condition. Regimental device is star, not mullet. One piece cast.	MIDLINE NECK. Under body. Shank down. Beneath central cervical vertebra. In loose cluster (28, 29, 31) centred on upper neck.

Cat. Number	Material	Shape, Attachment	Size, Portion	Motif, Unit Device, Design Features	Location Information
27-29:	Pewter	Round, Flat Shank	16.8mm 100%	AMERICAN, SCRIPT I motif, unit device is a STAR. Excellent condition. Regimental device is star, not mullet. One piece cast.	MIDLINE NECK. Under body. Touching right side of upper cervicals. In loose cluster (28, 29, 31) centred on upper neck. Craniomedial of 28.
27-30:	Copper Alloy	Round, Flat Shank	15.0mm 100%	PLAIN motif. Excellent condition. Organic material on back.	RIGHT ARM. Over body. Shank down. With 40, overlying right wrist beneath left hand. In loose brass button cluster (14, 15, 30, 40) centred on distal half of right forearm & wrist.
27-31:	Pewter	Round, Flat Shank	20.0mm 100%	AMERICAN, SCRIPT I motif, unit device is a STAR. Excellent condition. One piece cast.	MIDLINE NECK. Under body. On left side of upper cervicals, opposite buttons 28 & 29. In loose cluster (28, 29, 31) centred on upper neck.
27-32:	Pewter	Round, Flat Shank	20.2mm 100%	AMERICAN, SCRIPT I motif, unit device is a STAR. Excellent condition. Heavily encrusted in cemented sand. One piece cast.	LEFT ARM. Under body. Shank down. Beneath distal end of left radius. In loose cluster (20, 21, 22, 32) centred around left forearm.
27-33:	Pewter	Round, Flat Shank	19.9mm 100%	PLAIN motif. Excellent cond. Plant material, grass stem or wood splinter, adheres to front. Only 25% of front is visible.	RIGHT ARM. Under body. Beneath neck of right humerus. With 34, proximalmost in linear series (18, 23, 33, 34) on lateral side of the proximal 2/3rds of right humerus.
27-34:	Pewter	Round, Flat Shank	20.0mm 100%	AMERICAN, SCRIPT I motif, unit device is a STAR. Excellent condition. Associated with organic material. One piece cast.	RIGHT ARM. Under body. Beneath neck of right humerus. With 33, proximalmost in linear series (18, 23, 33, 34) on lateral side of proximal 2/3rds of right humerus.

Cat. Number	Material	Shape, Attachment	Size, Portion	Motif, Unit Device, Design Features	Location Information
27-35:	Bone	Round, Flat 4-Hole	15.3mm 90%	OTHER: MACHINED BONE motif. Good condition. Machined: rounded raised ring encircles depressed central area in which are 4 perforations.	LEFT SHOULDER. Under body. Just cranial of head of left humerus & glenoid of scapula.
27-36:	Pewter	Round, Flat Shank	------ 80%	Motif obscured or absent. Good - poor condition. Estimated diameter, based on reconstruction, = 24.9 mm.	RIGHT THORAX. Under body. At lower right corner of thorax near button 27. Corresponds to cluster (19, 38, 39) in lower left thorax. Near dense cluster of buckshot.
27-37:	Pewter	Round, Flat Shank	20.1mm 100%	AMERICAN, SCRIPT I motif, unit device is a STAR. Excellent condition. One piece cast.	LEFT ARM. Under body. Shank up. Beneath left arm, shank up. Not mapped.
27-38:	Pewter	Round, Flat Shank	20.7mm 100%	AMERICAN, SCRIPT I motif, unit device is a STAR. Good condition. One piece cast.	LEFT THORAX. Under body. Beneath rib at lower left edge of ribcage. Caudalmost in tight cluster (19, 38, 39) in lower left thorax.
27-39:	Pewter	Round, Flat Shank	20.6mm 100%	Motif obscured or absent. Excellent condition. Fabric adhering to top. One piece cast.	LEFT THORAX. Under body. Beneath ribs at lower left edge of ribcage. Cranialmost in tight cluster (19, 38, 39) in lower left thorax.
27-40:	Copper Alloy	Round, Flat Shank	15.0mm 100%	PLAIN motif. Excellent condition. Very slightly convex. Organic material on back obscures shank.	WRIST. Over body. With 30 above right hand & beneath left hand. In loose brass button cluster (14, 15, 30, 40) in area of distal right forearm & wrist.

Cat. Number	Material	Shape, Attachment	Size, Portion	Motif, Unit Device, Design Features	Location Information

BURIAL 28

Cat. Number	Material	Shape, Attachment	Size, Portion	Motif, Unit Device, Design Features	Location Information
28-01:	Bone	Round, Flat 1-Hole	10.9mm 100%	PLAIN (BONE) motif. Excellent condition.	RIGHT ARM (WAIST, R). Under body. About 2 cm medial of right radius midshaft. About 3 cm craniolateral of right iliac crest.

BURIAL 29

Cat. Number	Material	Shape, Attachment	Size, Portion	Motif, Unit Device, Design Features	Location Information
29-01:	Pewter	----- -----	----- 10%	Motif obscured or absent. Poor condition. May include material from another button (field number 2). Just small fragments.	RIGHT ARM. Over body. Just medial of right elbow. A positive find locus with 1 or 2 items, in vertical linear series (1, 20, 21) between thorax and right humerus.
29-06:	Pewter	----- -----	----- 10%	Motif obscured or absent. Poor condition. Just a small flat fragment.	RIGHT WAIST. Over body. Right central waist area. Isolated caudolaterally from cluster (18, 24, 25, 26, 36, 37) in area of lower right thorax and upper right waist.
29-18:	Pewter	----- -----	----- 10%	Motif obscured or absent. Poor condition. Just small granules.	MIDLINE THORAX. Over body. Thorax - waist area near midline. Medialmost of loose cluster (18, 24, 25, 26, 36, 37) in area of lower right thorax and upper right waist.
29-20:	Pewter	----- -----	----- 10%	Motif obscured or absent. Poor condition. Probably includes material from another button (field number 2). Just granules.	RIGHT ARM (THORAX, R). Over body. Four cm medial of distal humerus. Second down in vertical linear cluster (1, 20, 21) between lower thorax & lower right humerus.
29-21:	Pewter	----- Flat Shank	----- 30%	Motif obscured or absent. Poor condition. Large button.	RIGHT ARM (THORAX,R). Shank down. Cranialmost in vertical linear cluster (1, 20, 21) between lower thorax & lower right humerus. Just caudal of find locus 22, a buckle.

Cat. Number	Material	Shape, Attachment	Size, Portion	Motif, Unit Device, Design Features	Location Information
29-23:	Pewter	----- -----	----- 5%	Motif obscured or absent. Find location may include another button (field number 5). Very small granules.	RIGHT THORAX (WAIST, R). Over body. At right of thorax-waist area. Isolated caudolaterally from cluster (18, 24, 25, 26, 36, 37) in area of lower right thorax and upper right waist.
29-24:	Pewter	----- -----	----- 5%	Motif obscured or absent. Poor condition. May include material from another button (field number 17). Just granular fragments.	MIDLINE THORAX. Over body. Shank down. Lower thorax or upper waist, close to midline. In loose cluster (18, 24, 25, 26, 36, 37) in area of lower right thorax and upper right waist.
29-25:	Pewter	----- Flat	----- 10%	Motif obscured or absent. Poor condition. This location may include remains of another button (field number 10). Just small granules.	MIDLINE THORAX. Over body. In midline, 1 cm right of xiphoid process. In loose cluster (18, 24, 25, 26, 36, 37) in area of lower right thorax and upper right waist.
29-26:	Pewter	----- -----	----- 10%	Motif obscured or absent. Poor condition. Just granular fragments.	RIGHT THORAX. Lower right waist, just medial of 37. In loose cluster (18, 24, 25, 26, 36, 37) in area of lower right thorax and upper right waist.
29-27:	Pewter	----- -----	----- 10%	Motif obscured or absent. Poor condition. Just tiny fragments.	LEFT THORAX. Lower left of thorax, roughly even with xiphoid. Caudalmost in vertical linear cluster (27, 28, 29) at left side of central thorax.
29-28:	Pewter	----- -----	----- 10%	Motif obscured or absent. Poor condition.	LEFT THORAX. Left edge, central thorax. Second down in vertical linear cluster (27, 28, 29) at left side of central thorax, even with left humerus midshaft.

Cat. Number	Material	Shape, Attachment	Size, Portion	Motif, Unit Device, Design Features	Location Information
29-29:	Pewter	----- -----	------ 10%	Motif obscured or absent. Poor condition. Just small fragments.	LEFT THORAX. Left edge, central thorax. Cranialmost in vertical linear cluster (27, 28, 29) at left side of central thorax. Even with left humerus midshaft.
29-30:	Pewter	----- -----	------ 10%	Motif obscured or absent. Poor condition. Just small fragments.	LEFT WAIST. With 32, caudalmost in vertical series (30-35) between the lower thorax and the distal left humerus & elbow.
29-31:	Pewter	----- -----	------ 10%	Motif obscured or absent. Poor condition. Just small fragments.	LEFT WAIST (ARM, L). Between left elbow and lower thorax. Fourth down in vertical series (30-35) between the lower thorax and the distal left humerus & elbow.
29-32:	Pewter	Round, Flat Shank	20.6mm 80%	AMERICAN, SCRIPT I motif, unit device is MULLET. Good condition. One piece cast.	LEFT WAIST (ARM, L). Shank down. With 30, caudalmost in vertical series (30-35) between the lower thorax and the distal left humerus & elbow.
29-33:	Pewter	----- -----	------ 10%	Motif obscured or absent. Poor condition.	LEFT ARM (THORAX, L). Two cm from medial side of distal condyle of left humerus. Third down in vertical series (30-35) between lower thorax and distal left humerus.
29-34:	Pewter	----- -----	------ 10%	Motif obscured or absent. Poor condition.	LEFT ARM (THORAX, L). Three cm medial of left humerus. Second down in vertical series (30-35) between the lower thorax and the distal left humerus & elbow.
29-35:	Pewter	Round, Flat Shank	14.6mm 50%	OBSCURED motif. Poor condition. Button in 2 pieces, measurement approximate.	LEFT ARM (THORAX, L). Shank down. One cm medial of humerus midshaft. Cranialmost vertical series (30-35) between the lower thorax and distal left humerus and elbow.

Cat. Number	Material	Shape, Attachment	Size, Portion	Motif, Unit Device, Design Features	Location Information
29-36:	Pewter	----- Flat Shank	------ 30%	Motif obscured or absent. Poor condition. Large button.	RIGHT THORAX. Under body. In lower right thorax, caudolateral of 26 & 37. In loose cluster (18, 24, 25, 26, 36, 37) in area of lower right thorax and upper right waist.
29-37:	Pewter	----- -----	------ 5%	Motif obscured or absent. Poor condition. Just granular fragments.	RIGHT THORAX. In lower right thorax. Cranialmost in loose cluster (18, 24, 25, 26, 36, 37) in area of lower right thorax and upper right waist.
29-38:	Pewter	Round, Convex Shank	20.1mm 90%	EAGLE motif, unit device is US. Excellent condition. Eagle faces left. Red stain on shank.	RIGHT POSTPELVIC. Over body. Shank down. Five cm lateral of right tibia midshaft. Probably an accidental inclusion, not related to the primary interment.

::::::::::::::::: HISTORIC FEATURE 02 :::::::::::::::::

Cat. Number	Material	Shape, Attachment	Size, Portion	Motif, Unit Device, Design Features	Location Information
H2-01:	Pewter	Round, Flat Shank	20.4mm 100%	AMERICAN, SCRIPT I motif, unit device is a STAR. Excellent condition. One piece cast. Design eccentrically placed.	NOT ASSOCIATED WITH BODY. Not in burial context. One of three buttons loosely associated with human skeletal fragments & teeth in "Historic Feature 2".
H2-02:	Pewter	Round, Flat Shank	20.4mm 100%	AMERICAN, US motif. Excellent condition. One piece cast. Shank ring flattened prior to recent break.	NOT ASSOCIATED WITH BODY. Not in burial context. One of three buttons loosely associated with human skeletal fragments & teeth in "Historic Feature 2".
H2-03:	Pewter	----- ----- Flat	------ 60%	Motif obscured or absent. Poor condition. 3 small pewter fragments.	NOT ASSOCIATED WITH BODY. Not in burial context. One of three buttons loosely associated with human skeletal fragments & teeth in "Historic Feature 2".

References

A. Books & Dissertations

Ashburn, P.M.
1929   *History of the Medical Department of the United States Army.*
              Boston: Houghton, Mifflin.

Auchinleck, G.
1972   *A History of the War Between Great Britain and the United States of*
              America During the Years 1812, 1813, and 1814. London: Arms &
              Armor Press (repr. 1855 ed.).

Babcock, L.L.
1899   *The Siege of Fort Erie, An Episode of the War of 1812.* Buffalo:
              Peter Paul Book Co.

Baylies, N.
1890   *Eleazer Wheelock Ripley and the War of 1812.* Des Moines:
              Brewster & Co.

Bingham, R.H.
1927   *The Cradle of the Queen City.* Buffalo: Buffalo Hist. Soc.

Bingham, R.
1939   *Address at Opening of Restored Fort Erie, 6 July 1939.* Fort Erie
              Public Library.

Brannan, J., ed.
1823   *Official Letters of the Military and Naval-Officers of the U.S.*
              During the War with Great Britain. Washington.

Brown, F.R.
1919   *History of the 9th U.S. Infantry 1799–1909.* Chicago: R.R.
              Donnelly.

Brown, H.E.
1873   *The Medical Department of the United States Army from 1775 to*
              1783. Washington: Surgeon General's Office.

Callan, J.F.
1863   *The Military Laws of the United States Relating to the Army,*
              Volunteers, Militia, and to Bounty Lands and Persons, From the
              Foundation of the Government to the Year 1863. Philadelphia:
              George W. Childs.

Clarke, W.P.
1909   *Official History of the Militia and National Guard of the State of*
              Pennsylvania. 3 vols. Philadelphia.

Court Martial
1816   *Proceedings of a GCM, Held at Ft Independence, (Boston Harbor)*
               for the Trial of Major Charles K. Gardner... Preferred Against Him
               by M.Gen Ripley. Boston: n.p.

Crosswell, D.
1957   American Invasion of the Niagara Frontier. Unpublished M.A.
               thesis. Milwaukee: University of Wisconsin.

Cruickshank, E.A., ed.
1907   *Documentary History of the Campaign Upon the Niagara Frontier.*
               9 vols. Welland, Ontario.
1920   *Documents Relating to the Invasion of the Niagara Peninsula by the*
               United States Army Commanded by General Jacob Brown in July
               and August 1814. Niagara-on-the-Lake: Niagara Hist. Soc., Publ.
               #33.

Cruickshank, E.A.
1930   *The Old Fort at Fort Erie.* Welland: Tribune-Telegraph Press.

Cullum, G.W., ed.
1879   *Campaign of the War of 1812.* New York: James Miller, Publ.

DeVernon, G.
1817   *A Treatise on the Science of War and Fortification.* 2 vols. New
               York: J. Seymour.

Douglass, D.B.
1969   *The American Voyager; The Journal of David Bates Douglass,* ed.
               by Sidney W. Jackman and John F. Freeman. Marquette, Michigan:
               Northern Michigan Univ. Press.

Douglas, J.
1819   *Medical Topography of Upper Canada.* London: Burgess and Hill.

Dunlop, W.
1905   *Recollections of the American War 1813–1814.* Toronto: Historical
               Publ. Co.

Dunlop, W.
1967   *Tiger Dunlop's Upper Canada....* Toronto: McClelland & Stewart.

Elliot, C.W.
1937   *Winfield Scott, The Soldier and the Man.* New York: Macmillan Co.

[Fenton, J.]
1814   *Journal of the Military Tour by the Pennsylvania Troops and Militia*
               under the Command of Col. James Fenton, to the Frontiers of
               Pennsylvania and New York. Carlisle, Pennsylvania: George Kline.

[Anonymous]
1867   *Forest Lawn: Its History, Dedications, Progress,... Names of Lot*
               Holders, etc. Buffalo: Thomas, Howard & Johnson.

Gillett, M.C.
1981   *The Army Medical Department, 1775–1818.* Washington: Army
               Center of Military History.

Goodhue, J.F.
1861   *History of the Town of Shoreham, Vermont....* Middlebury, Ver-
               mont: A.H. Copeland.

Graves, D.E.
1982   Joseph Willcocks and the Canadian Volunteers: An Account of
               Political Disaffection in Upper Canada During the War of 1812.
               Unpublished M.A. thesis. Ottawa: Carleton University.

Hampton, C.E.
1909   *The Twenty First's Trophy of Niagara.* Fort Logan.

Hastings, H., ed.
1898   *Public Papers of Daniel D. Tompkins, Governor of New York, 1807–1817.* 3 vols. New York & Albany: Wynkoop, Hallenbeck, Crawford Co.

Hill, H.W.
1923   *Municipality of Buffalo, New York; a History 1720–1923.* 4 vols. New York: Lewis Publishing Co., Vol. 1, 115–58.

Hough, F.B.
1854   *A History of Jefferson County in the State of New York....* Albany: Joel Munsell.

Irving, L. H.
1908   *Officers of the British Forces in Canada During the War of 1812–15.* Welland, Ontario.

Izard, G.
1816   *Official Correspondence with the Department of War Relative to the Military Operations of the American Army Under the Command of Major General Izard on the Northern Frontier of the United States in the Years 1814, 1815.* Philadelphia: Thomas Dobson.

Jenkins, J.S.
1849   *The Generals of the Last War with Great Britain.* Auburn: Derby, Miller & Co.

Johnson, C.
1876   *Centennial History of Erie County....* Buffalo: Mathews & Warren.

Ketchum, W.
1865   *Authentic and Comprehensive History of Buffalo.* Buffalo: Rockwell, Baker & Hill.

Kieffer, C.L.
1979   *Maligned General: The Biography of Thomas Sidney Jesup.* San Rafael, California: Presidio Press.

Kimball, J.
1969   Strategy on the Northern Frontier, 1814. Unpublished Ph.D. thesis. Baton Rouge: Louisiana State University.

Kropf, R.C.
1957   *Notes on Surgeons of the Indian Wars and [the] War of 1812.* Mimeo. Columbus, Ohio: Anthony Wayne Parkway Brd.

Landon, H.F.
1954   *Bugles on the Border: The Story of the War in Northern New York.* Watertown, New York: Watertown Daily Times.

Linn, J.B., and W.H. Egle
1956   *Muster Rolls of Pennsylvania Volunteers in the War of 1812.* Baltimore: Genealogical Publishing Co. (repr. 1890 ed.).

Lossing, B.J.
1869   *Pictorial Field Book of the War of 1812.* New York: Harper.

Lundy's Lane Historical Society
1919   *The Centennial Celebration of the Battle of Lundy's Lane July 25th 1914.* Niagara Falls.

Mahon, J.K.
1972   *The War of 1812.* Gainesville: University of Florida Press.

Mann, J.
1816   *Medical Sketches of the Campaigns of 1812, 13, 14....* Dedham, Massachusetts: H. Mann & Co.

Marquis, T.G.
   1930   *Battlefields of 1814*. Toronto: Ryerson.
Mason, P.P., ed.
   1973   *After Tippecanoe: Some Aspects of the War of 1812*. Westport,
                 Connecticut: Greenwood Press (repr. 1963 ed.).
McCauley, I.H.
   1876   *Historical Sketch of Franklin County*. Chambersburg.
McRee, W.
   1834   *Memoir of Colonel William McRee, USE*. Wilmington, North
                 Carolina.
Michigan Daughters of the War of 1812
   1964   *What So Proudly We Hailed*. Ann Arbor.
Nead, B.M.
   1900   *Waynesboro, the History of a Settlement in Franklin Co.*
                 Harrisburg: Harrisburg Publ. Co.
Peterson, C.S.
   1955   *Known Dead During the War of 1812*. Mimeo. Baltimore.
Porter, P.A.
   ND 1915   *American Niagara Frontier in War of 1812....*
Pratt, J.
   1935–37   *The War of 1812*. Vol. 5 in Alexander Flick, ed., *History of the
                 State of New York*. New York.
Raddall, T.H.
   1957   *The Path of Destiny*. New York: Popular Library.
Ripley, E.W.
   1815   *Facts Relative to the Campaign on the Niagara in 1814*. Boston:
                 Patriot Office.
Schneider, D.H.
   1976   The Training and Organization of General Winfield Scott's Brigade
                 and the Life of the Regular Soldiers in It. Unpublished M.A. thesis.
                 University of Florida.
Schweitzer, G.K.
   1983   *War of 1812 Genealogy*. Knoxville, Tennessee: privately published.
Scott, W.S.
   1864   *Memoirs of Lt. Gen. Scott, LLD*. 2 vols. New York: Sheldon & Co.
Silver, J.W.
   1949   *Edmund P. Gaines, 1777–1849; Frontier General*. Baton Rouge:
                 Louisiana State University.
[Anonymous]
   1842   *Sketch of the Life of General Nathan Towson, US Army*.
                 Baltimore: N. Hickman.
Stanley, G.F.G.
   1983   *The War of 1812, Land Operations*. Toronto: Macmillan of Canada
                 in collaboration with the National Museum of Man, National
                 Museums of Canada.
Starke, E.
   1879   *History of Cayuga County, New York*. Syracuse: D. Mason & Co.
Stone, W.L.
   1841   *The Life and Times of Red Jacket*. New York: Wiley, Putnam.
Treat, J.
   1815   *The Vindication of Captain Joseph Treat, Late of the 21st Regiment,
                 US Infantry*. Philadelphia: n.p.

U.S. Army, Adjutant General's Office
1969   *Index of Awards of Claims of the Soldiers of the War of 1812.*
Baltimore: Genealogical Publishing Co.

U.S. Congress
1832–61   *American State Papers: Documents, Legislative and Executive of the Congress of the U.S., Class V Military Affairs, Class IX Claims.* Washington D.C.: Gales & Seaton.

U.S. Congress
1883   *United States Pensioners, War of 1812, Mexican and Civil War.* Washington, D.C.: Government Printing Office.

U.S. Senate
Document 100, 16 Cong, 2d sess, 1820–1821, "Statement of the Number of Militia from Each State ... During the War of 1812."

U.S. War Department
1886   *Subject Index, 1809–1860, General Orders, AGD, Subject Index of the WDGO's 1 Jan 1809 to 31 Dec 1860.* Washington, D.C.: Government Printing Office.

Watmough, J.G.
1835   *A Brief Sketch of the Services of John G. Watmough ... When an Officer in the United States Army.* Philadelphia: n.p.

Way, R.L.
1938   Defenses of the Niagara Frontier. Unpublished M.A. thesis. Kingston: Queen's University.

White, L.D.
1959   *The Jeffersonians: A Study in Administrative History, 1801–1829.* New York: Macmillan Co.

White, P.C.T.
1812   *A Nation on Trial: America and the War of 1812.* New York.

White, S.
1830   *A History of American Troops ... under General Gaines, Brown, Scott and Porter.* Baltimore: privately published (repr. 1896, George P. Humphrey, Rochester, N.Y.).

Wilkinson, J.
1816   *Memoirs of My Own Times.* 3 vols. Philadelphia: Abraham Small.

Wilner, M.M.
1931   *Niagara Frontier: A Narrative and Documentary History.* 5 vols. Chicago: S.J. Clarke Publishing Co.

Zaslow, M., and W.B. Turner, eds.
1964   *The Defended Border: Upper Canada and the War of 1812.* Toronto: Macmillan.

B. Articles
Anderson, F.J.
1944   Medical Practices During the War of 1812. *Bulletin of the History of Medicine* 16:261–75.

Ashburn, P.M.
1930   American Army Hospitals of the Revolution and War of 1812. *Bulletin of Johns Hopkins Hospital* 46:47–60.

Assault on Fort Erie, or, Two Ways of Telling a Story
1834   *Littell's Museum of Foreign Literature* 43:427–35.

Ayars, C.W.
1922   Some Notes on the Medical Service of the Army, 1812–1839. *Military Surgeon* 50:505–24.

Babcock, J.L., ed.
1963   Campaign of 1814 on the Niagara Frontier. *Niagara Frontier* 10
                   (4): 121–78.
Babcock, L.L.
1909   The Siege of Ft Erie. *Proceedings of the New York State Historical
                   Association* 7.
BECHSP-*Buffalo & Erie County Historical Society Publications*
Bingham, R.W., ed.
1947   Niagara Frontier Miscellany. *BECHSP* 34.
Biographical Sketch of Major Thomas Biddle
1832   *Hazard's Register of Pennsylvania* 10 (8): 121–28 (Aug. 25).
Biography of Colonel Jacob Hindman.
1816   *Portico* 3:38–52.
Bird, W.A.
1902   The Sortie from fort Erie. *BECHSP* 5: 95–98.
Brady, W.T.
1949   The 22d Regiment in the War of 1812. *Western Pennsylvania
                   Historical Magazine* 32:56–60.
Brooke, St. G.T.
1904   The Brooke Family in Virginia. *Virginia Magazine of History and
                   Biography* 11:445–47 (George Mercer Brooke).
1905   The Brooke Family in Virginia. *Virginia Magazine of History and
                   Biography* 12:102–103 (George Mercer Brooke).
1906   The Brooke Family in Virginia. *Virginia Magazine of History and
                   Biography* 13 (George Mercer Brooke).
1907   The Brooke Family in Virginia. *Virginia Magazine of History and
                   Biography* 14 (George Mercer Brooke).
Colquhoun, A.H.
1926   The Career of Joseph Willcocks. *Canadian Historical Review* 7
                   (Dec.): 287–93.
Crombie, J.N.
1967   The 22d U.S. Infantry: A Forgotten Regiment in a Forgotten War,
                   Western Pennsylvania Historical Magazine 60:133–47, 221–31.
Crombie, J.N.
1968   The Papers of Daniel McFarland. *Western Pennsylvania Historical
                   Magazine* 61:101–25.
Cruickshank, E.
1905   The Siege of Fort Erie, August 1st – September 23d 1814. *Lundy's
                   Lane Historical Society Publications*. Welland: Tribune Office.
Doan, D.
1970   The Enigmatic Moody Bedel. *Historical New Hampshire* 25
                   (3): 27–36.
Dorsheimer, W.
1879   Buffalo During the War of 1812. *BECHSP* 1:185–98.
Douglas, R.A.
1963   Weapons of the War of 1812. *Michigan History* 47:321–26.
[Douglass, D.B.]
1964   An Original Narrative of the Niagara Campagn of 1814, ed. by John
                   T. Horton. *Niagara Frontier* 2 (1): 1–36.

Duncan, L.L.
   1932   Sketches of the Medical Service in the War of 1812. *Military Surgeon* 81:436–40, 539–42.
   1932   Sketches of the Medical Service in the War of 1812. *Military Surgeon* 82:48–56.

Einstein, L., ed.
   1926   Recollections of the War of 1812 by George Hay, Eighth Marquess of Tweeddale. *American Historical Review* 32.

Ferguson, A.J.
   1983   Militia Medicine in New York, 1812. *Military Collector and Historian* 35 (4): 167–68.

Forman, S.
   1945   The U.S. Military Philosophical Society, 1802–1803. *William & Mary Quarterly*, 3d ser., 2 (July): 273–85.

Frederiksen, J.C., ed.
   1984   Chronicle of Valor: The Journal of a Pennsylvania Officer in the War of 1812. *Western Pennsylvania Historical Magazine* 67 (3): 243–84.

Graves, D.E.
   1979   The Canadian Volunteers, 1813–1815. *Military Collector and Historian* 31:112–17.

Green, E.
   1912   Some Graves in Lundy's Lane. *Niagara Historical Society Publications,* no. 22.

Green, E.
   1927   New Light on the Battle of Chippawa. *Welland County Historical Society Papers and Records,* Vol. 3. Welland: Welland Publishing Co.

Guelzo, C.
   1959   Fort Erie: High Point of a Low War. *Military Review* 38 (10).

Hager, F.E.
   1931   Thomas Sidney Jesup. *Quartermaster Review* 11:14–47.

Hall, A.
   1902   Militia Service of 1812–1814 as shown by the Correspondence of M. Gen Amos Hall. *BECHSP* 5:26–62.

Hall, J.A.
   1831   Biographical Sketch of Major Thomas Biddle. *Illinois Monthly Magazine* 1:549–61.

[Hanks, J.]
   1960   A Drummer Boy in the War of 1812: The Memoir of Jarvis Frary Hanks, ed. by Lester Smith. *Niagara Frontier* 7.

Harris, S.D.
   1920   Service of Capt. Samuel D. Harris: A Sketch of His Military Career ... 2d Light Dragoons..... *BECHSP* 24:327–42.

Hitsman, J. M.
   1962   The War of 1812 in Canada. *History Today* 12 (9): 632–39 (Sept.).

Hodge, W.
   1879   Buffalo Cemeteries. *BECHSP* 1:49–75.

Holley, G.W.
   1881   The Sortie from Fort Erie. *Magazine of American History* 6:401–13.

Homer, W.E.
1853   Surgical Sketches: A Military Hospital at Buffalo, New York, in the Year 1814. *Medical Examiner and Record of Medical Science* 9:1–25, 69–85.

Howe, E.D.
1906   Recollections of a Pioneer Printer. *BECHSP* 9:375–406.
1919   Life of General Ely S. Parker. *BECHSP* 13.

Jay, W., comp.
1849   Table of the Killed and Wounded in the War of 1812. *Collections of the New York Historical Society*, 2d ser., 2:447–66.

Kerley, R.L.
1977   The Militia System and the State Militias in the War of 1812. *Indiana Magazine of History* 73 (2): 102–24.

Kimball, J.
1968   The Battle of Chippawa: Infantry Tactics in the War of 1812. *Military Affairs* 32:169–86.

Kochan, J.L.
1981   22d US Infantry Regiment, 1812–1813. *Military Collector and Historian* 33:164–65.

Livingstone, J.
1854   General Nathan Towson. *Sketches of Eminent Americans*, 381–422. New York: Craighead.

Longslow, R.
1902   A Niagara Falls Tourist of ... 1817. *BECHSP* 5:110–24.

Martin, J.D.
1960   The Regiment DeWatteville: Its Settlement and Services in Upper Canada. *Ontario Historical Society Papers and Records* 62:17–30.

McGinnis, G.
1940   The Part That Buffalo, New York, Played in the War of 1812. *Military Surgeon* 86:393–95.

McKee, M.
1917   Services of Supply in the War of 1812. *Quartermaster Review* 6:45–55.

[Norton, J.P.]
1965   Jacob Peter Norton, A Yankee on the Niagara Frontier in 1814, ed. by Daniel R. Porter. *Niagara Frontier* 12.

O'Reilly, I.M.
1902   A Hero of Ft. Erie. *BECHSP* 5:63–93.

Parker, A.C.
1916   The Senecas in the War of 1812. *New York State Historical Association Proceedings* 15:78–90.

Phalen, J.M.
1940   Surgeon James Mann's Observations on Battlefield Amputations. *Military Surgeon* 87:463–66.

Riddell, W.R.
1930   Benajah Mallory, Traitor. *Ontario Historical Society Papers and Records* 26:435–49.

Ripley, E.W.
1815   Biographical Memoirs of Major General Ripley. *Port Folio* 25:108–36.

Salisbury, H.
    1906   A Guardsman of Buffalo ... a Participant in the War of 1812.
                    BECHSP 9:311–70.
Sawyer, B.G.
    1851   The War of 1812 and Biographical Sketches. In Abby M.
                    Hemenway, ed., *Vermont Historical Gazeteer* 1:574–81.
Severance, F.
    1902   Papers Relating to the War of 1812 on the Niagara Frontier.
                    BECHSP 5:98–109.
    1903a   The Story of Cpt Jasper Parrish, captive.... *BECHSP* 6:527–
                    38.
    1903b   Personal Recollections of Cpts Jones & Parrish. *BECHSP*
                    6:539–46.
    1922   William Hodge Papers. *BECHSP* 26:169–314.
The Siege of Fort Erie
    1840   *United States Military Magazine* 2:65–73.
Smith, C. C.
    1891   Memoirs of Colonel Thomas Aspinwall. *Massachusetts Historical
                    Society Proceedings* 3:30–38.
Sortie from Fort Erie.
    1840   *United States Military Magazine* 1 (12).
Stacy, C.P., ed.
    1956   Upper Canada at War 1814: Captain Armstrong Reports. *Ontario
                    History* 47.
Steppler, G.A.
    1979   Logistics on the Canadian Frontier, 1812–1814. *Military Collector
                    and Historian* 31:8–10
Tuttle, M.M.
    1905   William Allen Trimble. *Ohio Archaeological and Historical
                    Society Journal* 14:225–46.
Wainwright, N.B.
    1980   The Life and Death of Major Thomas Biddle. *Pennsylvania
                    Magazine of History and Biography* 104:326–44.
Walker, J.E.
    1945   A Soldier's Diary for 1814. *Pennsylvania History* 12:292–303.
Wyman, H.C.
    1907   Remarks on the Surgery of the War of 1812. *Physician and Surgeon*
                    29:203–9.

C. Archival Sources

Tulane University, Tilton Library, New Orleans, Louisiana
    —   Materials on New York militia affairs by Asa B. Sizer.
Massachusetts Historical Society, Boston, Massachusetts
    —   1812 Collection, including letters of Jacob Brown concerning
                    various Niagara campaigns.
American Antiquarian Society, Worcester, Massachusetts
    —   2 letters by Sergeant Hector Shields, 25th Infantry in regard to the
                    Battle of Chippawa.
University of Michigan, Clements Library, Ann Arbor, Michigan
    —   Collection of Jacob Brown and Winfield Scott on the Niagara
                    Campaign (60 items in regard to Niagara 1814).

—   Accounts of the Battles of Stoney Creek and Fort Erie in John Kearnsey Memoirs, Lucus D. Lyon Papers.

—   Papers of Surgeon William H. Wilson on the Northern Frontier.

Minnesota Historical Society, St. Paul, Minnesota

—   2 orderly books by Lt. Lawrence Taliaferro, 1st Infantry.

Missouri Historical Society, St. Louis, Missouri

—   Small collection 1st and 17th Infantry muster rolls.

—   Memoirs of Cpt. Louis Bissell, 1st Infantry, including his role in the Fort Erie sortie.

—   Correspondence of Col. Jacob Kingsbury, 1st Infantry.

Dartmouth College, Baker Library, Hanover, New Hampshire

—   John W. Weeks correspondence in regard to Chippawa and Lundy's Lane.

New Hampshire Historical Society, Concord, New Hampshire

—   Papers re 11th Infantry and 2d Dragoons, including muster rolls and supply requisitions.

—   Letters of Cpt. John McNeil, 11th Infantry.

—   Letters of Col. Moody Bedel, 11th Infantry.

New Jersey Historical Society, Newark, New Jersey

—   Muster rolls of New York and Pennsylvania militias.

Buffalo & Erie County Historical Society, Buffalo, New York

—   Peter Porter Papers.

—   A.C. Goodyear Collections, including Chippawa, Fort Erie.

—   Jarvis Hanks, Memoir.

St. Lawrence University Museum, Canton, New York

—   Orderly Book kept at Fort Erie.

Cornell University Library, Ithaca, New York

—   John G. Camp Papers (QM during Niagara Campaign).

Geneva Historical Society, Geneva, New York

—   Papers of General Hugh Dobbins, New York Militia.

New York Historical Society, New York, New York

—   14 letters of Richard Goodell, 23d Infantry.

—   47 pieces by Cpt. John McNeil, 11th Infantry.

—   Diary of Col. G. McFeely, 25th Infantry.

—   Orderly book of 25th Infantry.

—   John M. O'Connor Papers – muster rolls, reports Fort Erie 1814 (60 items).

New York State Library, Albany, New York

—   Letters of Thomas S. Jesup, 25th Infantry.

—   Paddick Papers on 1814 Niagara Campaign.

Oneida Historical Society, Utica, New York

—   Col. Nathan Williams' correspondence with Jacob Brown.

University of Rochester Library, Rochester, New York

—   32 letters of Nathanial Rochester in regard to militia affairs.

United States Military Academy, West Point, New York

—   13 letters of Col. James Miller, 21st Infantry.

United States Army Military History Institute, Carlisle Barracks, Pennsylvania

—   Diary of Amasa Ford, 23d Infantry, in regard to 1814 Niagara Campaign (copy).

—   Letter, Thomas Jesup to Maj.William McDonald.

—   Stuart Goldman Collection.

Pennsylvania History and Museum Commission, Harrisburg, Pennsylvania
— John Witherow Journal on the 1814 Niagara Campaign.
— 5th Pennsylvania Infantry (Simon Snyder Papers).
Pennsylvania Historical Society, Philadelphia, Pennsylvania
— #998 Pennsylvania Volunteers in War of 1812 and Civil War.
Vermont Historical Society, Monpelier, Vermont
— David Crawford and John McNeil, 11th Infantry, papers.
Library of Congress, Washington, D.C.
— Jacob Brown Correspondence.
— Thomas S. Jesup on Niagara Campaign.
— Amasa Troubridge on Battles of York, Fort George & Fort Erie.
— Letters of Cpt. John McNeil, 11th Infantry.
— Military reports, rosters and correspondence of Col.
      Jacob Kingsbury, 1st Infantry.
— E.P. Gaines Papers.

National Archives, Washington, D.C.
1. Microfilm
Office of the Adjutant General
   M602   Index to Compiled Service Records of Volunteer Soldiers
                Who Served During The War of 1812.
   M233   Register of Enlistments in the U.S. Army, 1798–1914.
   M566   Letters Received, 1805–1821.
   M565   Letters Sent, 1800–1890.
   M711   Register of Letters Sent, 1812–1889.
Office of the Secretary of War
   M220   Reports to Congress.
   M221   Records, Main Series, 1801–1870.
   M222   Letters Received, 1789–1861.
   M127   Letters Sent to the President, 1800–1863.
   M6   Letters Sent concerning Military Affairs.
   M370   Misc Letters Sent, 1800–1809.
   M22   Register of Letters Received, Main Series, 1800–1870.
   M7   Confidential Letters Sent.
Veterans Administration
   M313   Index to War of 1812 Pension Application Files.
Bureau of Land Management
   M848   War of 1812 Military Bounty Land Warrants, 1815–1858.
Miscellaneous
   M41   Peter B. Porter Papers.
2. Documents
   RG 15 –   Veterans Administration
                War of 1812 Pension Application Files.
                Post Revolutionary War Series of Bounty Land Applications.
   RG 49 –   Bureau of Land Management
                Entries 13–18 Bounty Land Warrants 1812–1855.
   RG 92 –   Office of the Quartermaster General
                Entry 225, Consolidated Correspondence File
                   "Medical," "Batavia," "Brady."
                Entry 562, QM Cemeteries.
                Entry 563, QM Cemeteries.

RG 94 –   Records of the Adjutant General's Office
Entry 53, Muster Rolls of Regular Army
Organizations 1784–Oct. 31, 1912.
Entry 55, Muster Rolls of Volunteer Organizations War of 1812.
Entry 71, Returns of Killed and Wounded in Battles
or Engagements with Indians, British and
Mexicans, 1790–1848 (Eaton's Compendium).
Entry 85, Register of Returns and General
Information Relating to the Army.
Entry 89, Register of Enlistments 1798–1914.
Entry 91, Regular Army Enlistment Papers.
Entry 95, Certificates of Disability 1812–1899.
Entry 125, Miscellaneous Records 1812–1815.
Entry 126, Index to Miscellaneous Records 1812–1815.
Entry 407, QM Accounts and Returns.
Entries 309, 312, 320, 321, 323, Commissioned Officers.
Entry 510, Compiled Service Records.

RG 98 –   Records of US Army Commands, 1784–1821
Entries 35–40, Headquarters and 1st Div. (Right
Wing) 1813–15, 9th Mil. Dist.
Entries 41–51, 2d Div. (Left Wing), 1812–15,
9th Mil. Dist.
Entries 52–60, Miscellaneous Records, 9th Mil Dist.
Entry 78, Records of Bvt MGEN E.P. Gaines, 1814–19.
Entries 96, 97, 99, 1st Infantry Books.
Entry 102, CPT Fanning's Co., 2d Arty, Co. Book.
Entry 104, CPT Williams' Co., 2d Arty, Co. Book.
Entry 105, CPT Fanning's Co., 2d Arty, Clothing Book.
Entry 114, CPT Fanning's Co., 2d Arty, Clothing Book.
Entries 199–207, 11th Infantry Co. Books.
Entries 233–40, 21st Infantry Co. Books.
Entries 241–47, 22d Infantry Co. Books.
Entries 252–59, 25th Infantry Co. Books.
Entries 367–71, 1st Rifles Co. Books.

RG 99 –   Office of the Paymaster General, 1799–1912
Entry 1, Letters Sent 1814.
Entry 7, Letters Received 1814.

RG 153 –   Office of the Judge Advocate General
Court Martial Case Files 1814–1815.

RG 156 –   Records of the Chief of Ordnance
Entry 3, Correspondence.

RG 159 –   Records of the Inspector General of the Army
Entry 1, Inspection Reports 1814–1836, 1842.

Wisconsin Historical Society, Madison, Wisconsin
—   Correspondence by Cpt. John Symmes, 1st Infantry ... Lundy's
Lane and Fort Erie.
—   Letters of Cpt. William Armstrong, 1st Rifles in regard to
Fort Erie.
—   Diary of Jacob Norton in regard to Izard's activities 1814.

Adams, T.R.
1972–76   The Medical and Political Activities of Dr. James Tilton. *Annual Report of the John Carter Brown Library* (Brown University and the Colonial Society of Massachusetts, Providence, Rhode Island) 7:30–32.

Akerly, S.
1817   Medical Topography of the Military Positions in the Third United States Military District: Together with a Summary Report on the Diseases of the Army.... *Medical Repository*, 2d ser. 3.

Anderson, F.J.
1944   Medical Practices During the War of 1812. *Bulletin of the History of Medicine* 16:261–75.

Aries, P.
1974   *Western Attitudes Toward Death: From the Middle Ages to the Present*. Translated by Patricia M. Ranum. Baltimore: Johns Hopkins University Press.

Aries, P., et al.
1975   *Death in America*. Edited, with an introduction by David E. Stannard. Philadelphia: University of Pennsylvania Press.

Ashburn, P.M.
1929   *A History of the Medical Department of the United States Army*. Boston: Houghton Mifflin Co.
1930   American Army Hospitals of the Revolution and the War of 1812. *Bulletin of the Johns Hopkins Hospital* 46:47–60.

Babcock, L.L.
1899   *The Siege of Fort Erie, An Episode of the War of 1812*. Buffalo, New York: Peter Paul Book Co.
1927   *The War of 1812 on the Niagara Frontier*. Buffalo, New York: Buffalo Historical Society.

Barton, W.P.C.
1817   *A Treatise Containing a Plan for the Internal Organization and Government of Marine Hospitals in the United States; Together with Observations on Military and Flying Hospitals, and a Scheme for Amending and Systematizing the Medical Department of the Navy*. 2d ed. Philadelphia.

Bayne-Jones, S.
1968   *The Evolution of Preventive Medicine in the United States Army,*
              1607–1939. Washington: Government Printing Office.
Bell, C., Sir.
1807–09   *A System of Operative Surgery, Founded on the Basis of Anatomy.* 2
              vols. London: Longman.
1812   *A System of Operative Surgery, Founded on the Basis of Anatomy.* 2
              vols. 1st American edition. Hartford: Hale and Hosmer.
1814   *A System of Operative Surgery, Founded on the Basis of Anatomy.*
              2d ed. London: Longman.
1816   *A System of Operative Surgery, Founded on the Basis of Anatomy.* 2
              vols. 2d American ed., from the last London ed. Hartford: George
              Goodwin and Sons.
Bendann, E.
1930   *Death Customs.* London: Kegan Paul.
Bernard, H.Y.
1979   *The Law of Death and the Disposal of the Dead.* Dobbs
              Ferry, New York: Oceana Publications.
Bick, E.M.
1957   French Influences on Early American Medicine and Surgery.
              Journal of the Mount Sinai Hospital 24:499–509.
Billroth, T.
1931–32   Historical Studies on the Nature and Treatment of Gunshot Wounds
              from the Fifteenth Century to the Present Time. Translated by C.P.
              Rhoads. *Yale Journal of Biology and Medicine* 4:3–36, 119–48,
              225–57.
Binford, L.R.
1971   Mortuary Practices: Their Study and Their Potential. In James A.
              Brown, ed., Approaches to the Social Dimensions of Mortuary
              Practices. *American Antiquity* 36:6–29.
Brennan, R.L.
1951   *The Law Governing Cemetery Rules and Regulations.* Los Angeles:
              Interment Association of California.
Brown, H.E.
1873   *The Medical Department of the United States Army from 1775 to*
              1873. Washington: The Surgeon General's Office.
Chevalier, T.
1806   *Treatise on Gunshot Wounds.* 3d ed. London: Samuel Bagster.
Church of England, Liturgical Commission.
1967   The Burial of the Dead and Commemoration of the Faithful
              Departed. *The Report of the Church of England Liturgical Commis-*
              sion to the Archbishop of Canterbury and York as amended
              and accepted by the Convocations on 11 October 1966. London:
              S. P. C. K.
Coffin, M.M.
1976   *Death in Early America.* New York: Thomas Nelson, Inc.
Cruikshank, E.A.
1893   *The Battle of Lundy's Lane.* Welland, Ontario: Lundy's Lane
              Historical Society.
1971   *Documentary History of the Campaign Upon the Niagara Frontier.*
              4 vols. Arno Press and the New York Times, reprint of the 1896–
              1908 edition.

Cullum, G.W., ed.
    1879   *Campaigns of the War of 1812–1815*. New York: Miller.

Cutbush, E.
    1808   *Observations on the Means of Preserving the Health of Soldiers and Sailors; and on the Duties of the Medical Departments of the Army and Navy: With Remarks on Hospitals and their Internal Arrange ments*. Philadelphia: Fry and Kammerer.

Douglas, J.
    1985   *Medical Topography of Upper Canada*. London: Burgess and Hill, 1819. Republished, with an introduction by Charles G. Roland. Canton, Massachusetts: Watson Publishing International.

Duffy, J.
    1953   *Epidemics in Colonial America*. Baton Rouge: Louisiana State University Press.

Duncan, L.
             Sketches of the Medical Service in the War of 1812. *Military Surgeon* 71 (1932): 436–40, 539–42; 72 (1932): 48–56; 73 (1933): 144–50, 241–46, 324–29.

Dunlop, W.
    1908   *Recollections of the War of 1812*. Toronto: Toronto Historical Publications.

Ewell, J.
    1817   *The Medical Companion: Treating, According to the Most Successful Practice, I. The Diseases Common to Warm Climates and on Ship Board; II. Common Cases in Surgery, as Fractures, Dislocations &c; III. The Complaints Peculiar to Women and Children, With a Dispensatory and Glossary....* 3d ed. Philadelphia.

Favrot, A.
    1868   *Funerailles et Sepultures: Histoire des Inhumations Chez les peuples Anciens et Modernes*. Paris: Librairie Internationale.

Gillett, M.C.
    1981   *The Army Medical Department, 1775–1818*. Washington: Center of Military History.

Gooch, B.
    1767   *A Practical Treatise on Wounds and Other Chirurgical Subjects; to Which is Prefixed a Short Historical Account of the Rise and Progress of Surgery and Anatomy, Addressed to Young Surgeons.* 2 vols. Norwich: W. Chase.

Guthrie, G.
    1815   *On Gun Shot Wounds of the Extremities, Requiring the Different Operations of Amputation with their After-Treatment*. London.

Habenstein, R.W., and W.M. Lamers
    1955   *The History of American Funeral Directing*. Milwaukee: Bulfin Printers.
    1960   *Funeral Customs the World Over*. Milwaukee: Bulfin Printers, Inc.

Hanks, J.F.
             Diary of Jarvis Frary Hanks, 1831–42. Buffalo and Erie County Historical Society, Buffalo, New York. Entry A00-263.

Harrah, Barbara K., and D.F. Harrah
    1976   *Funeral Service: A Bibliography of Literature on its Past, Present, and Future*. Metuchen, New Jersey: Scarecrow Press.

Horner, W.E.
1853   Surgical Sketches: A Military Hospital in Buffalo, 1814. *Medical Examiner and Record of Medical Science* 9:1–25, 69–85.

Hosack, D.
1815   *Observations on the Laws Governing the Communication of Contagious Diseases and the Means of Arresting Their Progress.* New York: Van Winkle and Wiley.

Huntington, R.
1979   *Celebrations of Death: The Anthropology of Mortuary Ritual.* Cambridge: Cambridge University Press.

Huntt, H.
1818   An Abstract Account of the Diseases Which Prevailed Among the Soldiers, Received into the General Hospital at Burlington, Vermont, During the Summer and Autumn of 1814. *Medical Recorder* 1:176–79.

Jackson, P.E.
1936   *The Law of Cadavers and of Burials and Burial Places.* New York: Prentice Hall.

Jones, B.M.
1967   *Design for Death.* New York: Bobbs-Merrill.
Jones, J.
1775   *Treatment of Wounds and Fractures.* New York: John Holt.
Kerin, C.A.
1941   *The Privation of Christian Burial: An Historical Synopsis and Commentary.* Washington: Catholic University of America Publications.

Kroeber, A.L.
1927   Disposal of the Dead. *American Anthropologist* 29:308–15.
Lagarde, L.A.
1914   *Gunshot Injuries, How They are Inflicted, Their Complications and Treatment.* New York: William Wood.

Lee, R.P.
1929   *Burial Customs.* Minneapolis: The ARYA Co.
Mann, J.
1813   *Rules and Regulations for the Hospital Department of the United States Army.* Albany: J. Buel.
1815–16   Health Police of an Army and Military Hospitals with Rules and Regulations for the Medical Department. MS, National Library of Medicine, Bethesda, Maryland.
1816   *Medical Sketches of the Campaigns of 1812, 13, 14. To Which are Added, Surgical Cases, Observations of Military Hospitals; and Flying Hospitals Attached to a Moving Army. Also, an Appendix Comprising a Dissertation on Dysentery: Which Obtained the Boylstonian Prize Medal for the Year 1806, and Observations on the Winter Epidemic of 1815–16. Denominated Peripneumonia Notha; as it Appeared at Sharon and Rochester, State of Massachusetts.* Dedham, Massachusetts.

Mitchell, S.C.
1801   Internment of the Dead in Cities. *Medical Repository* 4:94.
Osborne, B.S.
1974   The Cemeteries of the Midland District of Upper Canada. *Pioneer America* 6:46–55.

O'Shea, J.M.
1984   *Mortuary Variability: An Archaeological Investigation.* Orlando: Academic Press.

Perley, S.
1896   *Mortuary Law.* Boston: George B. Read.

Phalen, J.M.
1940   Surgeon James Mann's Observations on Battlefield Amputations. *Military Surgeon* 87:463–66.

Puckle, B.S.
1926   *Funeral Customs, Their Origin and Development.* London: T. Werner Laurie, Ltd.

Roland, C.G.
1980   War Amputations in Upper Canada. *Archivaria* 10:73–84.
1983   Medical Aspects of the War in the West in 1812. In K.G. Pryke and L.L. Kulisek, eds., *The Western District: Papers from the Western District Conference.* Windsor, Ontario.

Russell D., M.R.
1982   *The Law of Burial, Cremation and Exhumation.* 5th ed. London: Shaw and Sons.

Smith, H. P., ed.
1884   *History of the City of Buffalo and Erie County.* 2 vols. Syracuse, New York: D. Mason and Co.

Stewart, T.D.
1979   *Essentials of Forensic Anthropology.* Springfield, Illinois: Charles C. Thomas.

Street, A.L.H.
1924   *American Funeral Law.* Chicago: Trade Periodical Co.

Stueve, T.F.H.
1984   *Mortuary Law.* 7th rev. ed. Cincinnati, Ohio: Cincinnati Foundation for Mortuary Education.

Tegg, W.
1876   *The Last Act; Being the Funeral Rites of Nations and Individuals.* London: William Tegg and Co.

Thomas, R.
1815   *The Modern Practice of Physic: Exhibiting the Characters, Causes, Symptoms, Prognostic, Morbid Appearances, and Improved Method of Treating the Diseases of All Climates.* 3d American ed. New York: Collin and Co.

Tilton, J.
1813   *Economical Observations on Military Hospitals and the Prevention and Cure of Diseases Incident to an Army. In Three Parts: Addressed I. To Ministers of State and Legislatures, II. To Commanding Officers, III. To the Medical Staff.* Wilmington, Delaware: J. Wilson.

Townsend, J.
1887   *A Catalog of Some Books Relating to the Disposal of Bodies and Perpetuating the Memories of the Dead.* New York: privately published.

Troubridge, A.W.
            Ac 1556. Personal Papers in the Manuscript Division, Library of Congress, Washington, D.C.

1838   Gunshot Wounds. *The Boston Medical and Surgical Journal* 14:341–47.

Wangensteen, O.H., J. Smith, and S.D. Wangensteen
1967   Some Highlights on the History of Amputation Reflecting Lessons in Wound Healing. *Bulletin of the History of Medicine* 41:97–131.

Wangensteen, O.H., and S.D. Wangensteen
1971   Successful Pre-Listerian Antiseptic Management of Compound Fracture: Crowther (1802), Larrey (1824), and Bennion (ca. 1840). *Surgery* 69:881–24.

White, T.C.
1898   *Our County and Its People, A Descriptive Work on Erie County, New York.* Boston: Boston History Co.

Wilner, M.M.
1931   *Niagara Frontier: A Narrative and Documentary History.* 5 vols. New York: S. J. Clarke Publishing Co.

Albert, A. H.
    1975   *Record of American Uniform and Historical Buttons.*
        Hightstown, New Jersey: Boyertown Publishing Company.

Angel, J.L.
    1966   Porotic Hyperostosis, Anemias, Malarias, and Marshes in the
        Prehistoric Eastern Mediterranean. *Science* 153:760–63.

    1967   Porotic Hyperostosis or Osteoporosis Symmetrica. In *Diseases in
        Antiquity: A Survey of the Diseases Injuries and Surgery of Early
        Populations.* D. Brothwell and A.T. Sandison, eds., pp. 378–89.
        Springfield: Charles C. Thomas.

    1976   Colonial to Modern Skeletal Change in the U.S.A. Am. J. Phys.
        Anth. 45:723–36.

    1978   Porotic Hyperostosis in the Eastern Mediterranean. *Medical College
        of Virginia Quarterly* 14 (1): 10–16.

    1985   The Forensic Anthropologist's Examination. Pathologist 39 (5): 1–
        8.

Archaeological Services Incorporated
    1988   *The Snake Hill Site: a War of 1812 American Cemetery.* Vol. 1.
        R. Williamson, ed. Unpublished manuscript.

Armitage, P.L., and J. Clutton-Brock
    1976   A System for Classification and Description of the Horn Cores of
        Cattle from Archaeological Sites. *J. of Archaeological Science*
        3:329–48

Aufderheide, A.C., F.D. Neiman, L.E. Wittmers, and G. Rapp
    1981   Lead in Bone.II. Skeletal Lead Content as an Indicator of Lifetime
        Lead Ingestion and the Social Correlates in an Archaeological
        Population. *Am. J. of Phys. Anth.* 55: 497–501.

    1988   Anthropologican Applications of Skeletal Lead Analysis. *American
        Anthropologist* 90:932–36.

Aufderheide, A.C., J.L. Angel, J.O. Delley, A.C. Outlaw, M.A. Outlaw, G. Rapp, and
L.E. Wittmers
    1985   Lead in Bone III. Prediction of Social Correlates from Skeletal Lead
        Content in Four Colonial American Populations (Catoctin Furnace,
        College Landing, Governor's Land and Irene Mound). *Am. J. of
        Phys. Anth.* 66 (4): 353, 361.

Bass, W.M.
    1971   *Human Osteology: A Laboratory and Field Manual.* Second
        Edition. Columbia, Missouri: Missouri Arch. Soc.

Batts, M.
1939   Rupture of the Nucleus Pulposus: An Anatomical Study. *J. of Bone and Joint Surgery* 21:121–26.

Brower, A.C.
1977   Cortical Defect of the Humerus at the Insertion of the Pectoralis Major. *Am. J. of Roentgenology* 128:677–78.

Bufkin, W.J.
1971   The Avulsive Cortical Irregularity. *Am. J. of Roentgenology* 112:487–92.

Caldwell, N.W.
1955   The Enlisted Soldier at the Frontier Post, 1790–1814. *Mid-America* 37:195-204.

Catton, B.
1985   *The Civil War*. New York: American Heritage Press, Inc.

Christofferson, J.O., A. Schutz, L. Ahlgren, B. Haeger-Aronsen, S. Mattson, and S. Skerfving
1984   Lead in Finger-bone Analyzed *in vivo* in Active and Retired Lead Workers. *Am. J. of Industrial Medicine* 6:447–57.

Coffman, E.M.
1986   *The Old Army: A Portrait of the American Army in Peacetime, 1784–1898*. New York: Oxford University Press.

Collins, D.H.
1949   *Pathology of Articular and Spinal Diseases*. London: Edward Arnold.

Corbett, M.E., and W.J. Moore
1976   Distribution of Dental Caries in Ancient British Populations. IV. The 19th Century. *Caries Research* 10 (6): 401–14.

Cummings, R.O.
1941   *The American and His Food. A History of Food Habits in the United States*. Chicago: University of Chicago Press.

Cybulski, J.S.
n.d.   The Human Skeletons of Courtine Saint-Louis-Bastion des Ursulines, Quebec City. Final Report prepared for the Canadian Parks Service, Quebec Region, August 31, 1988.

Dahlberg, A.A.
1951   The Dentition of the American Indian. In *The Physical Anthropology of the American Indian*. W.S. Laughlin, ed., pp. 138–76. New York: Viking Fund.

Dammann, G.E.
1984   Dental Care during the Civil War. *Illinois Dental Journal* 53 (1): 12–17.

Deines, P.
1980   The Isotopic Composition of Reduced Organic Carbon. In *Handbook of Environmental Isotope Geochemistry*. P. Fritz and J.C. Fontes, eds., pp. 329–406. Elsevier.

DeNiro, M.J.
1987   Stable Isotopy and Archaeology. *American Scientist* 75:182–91.

DeNiro, M.J., and S. Epstein
1978   Influence of Diet on the Distribution of Nitrogen Isotopes in Animals. *Geochimica et Cosmochimica Acta* 45:341–51.

Dietz, V.H.
1944   Common Dental Morphotrophic Factor, Carabelli Cusp. *J. of the Am. Dental Association* 31:635–89.

Driesch, A. von den
    1976   *A Guide to the Measurement of Animal Bones from Archaeological Sites*. Peabody Museum Bulletin 1, Peabody Museum of Archaeology and Ethnology, Harvard University, Cambridge, Massachusetts.

El-Najjar, M.Y., B. Loxoff, and D.J. Ryan
    1975   The Paleoepidemiology of Porotic Hyperostosis in the American Southwest, radiological and ecological considerations. *Am. J. of Roentgenology* 125:918–24.

Ensminger, M. E.
    1976   *Beef Cattle Science*. 5th ed. Interstate Printers & Publishers, Danville, Illinois.

Fredricksen, J.C.
    1985   *Free Trade and Sailor's Rights: A Bibliography of the War of 1812*. Westport, Connecticut: Greenwood Press.

Gillett, M.C.
    1981   *The Army Medical Department 1775–1818*. United States Army Center of Military History, Washington, D.C.

Goodman, A.H., and G.J. Armelagos
    1985   Factors Affecting the Distribution of Enamel Hypoplasias within the Human Permanent Dentition. *Am. J. Phys. Anth.* 68:479–93.

Gray, H.
    1959   *Anatomy of the Human Body*. Lea & Febiger, Philadelphia, Pennsylvania.

Gustafsson, B.E., et al.
    1954   The Vipeholm Caries Study. The Effect of Different Levels of Carbohydrate Intake on Caries Activity in 436 Individuals Observed for Five Years. *Acta Odontologica Scandinavica* 11:232–364.

Hamilton, A.
    1948   *Gentleman's Progress: The Itinerarium of Dr. Alexander Hamilton, 1744*. Edited with an introduction by Carl Bridenbaugh. Chapel Hill: University of North Carolina Press.

Handler, J.S., A.C. Aufderheide, R.S. Corruccini, E.M. Brandon, and L.E. Wittmers Jr.
    1986   Lead Contact and Poisons in Barbados Slaves: Historical, Chemical, and Biological Evidence. *Social Science History* 10 (4):399–425.

Hardwick, J.L.
    1960   The Incidence and Distribution of Caries Throughout the Ages in Relation to the Englishman's Diet. *British Dental Journal* 108 (1): 9–17.

Harle, F.
    1989   The Mandibular Prognathism of the Spanish Hapsburgs. *Bulletin of the History of Dentistry* 37:87–94.

Hart, G.D.
    1971   The Habsburg Jaw. *Canadian Medical Association Journal* 104:601–3.

    1981   Anemia in Ancient Times. *Blood Cells* 7:485–89.

Henderson, T.
    1840   *Hints for the Medical Examination of Recruits for the Army*. Philadelphia: Haswell, Barrington, and Haswell.

Hernberg, S.
    1980   Biochemical and Clinical Effects and Responses as Indicated by Blood Concentration. In *Lead Toxicity*. R.L. Singhal and J.A. Thomas, eds., 367–96. Baltimore: Urban and Schwarzenberg.

Hilton, R.C., J. Ball, and R.T. Benn
   1976   Vertebral End-plate Lesions (Schmorl's nodes) in the Dorsolumbar Spine. *Annals of the Rheumatic Diseases* 35:127–32.

Hooke, B.G.E.
   1926   A Third Study of the English Skull, with Special Reference to the Farrington Street Crania. *Biometrika* 18:1–55.

Howells, W.W.
   1973   *Cranial Variation in Man: A Study by Multivariate Analysis of Patterns of Difference among Recent Human Populations.* Papers of the Peabody Museum, Vol. 67, Cambridge, Mass.

Iscan, M.Y., S.R. Loth, and R.K. Wright
   1984   Age Estimation from the Rib by Phase Analysis: White Males. *J. of Forensic Sciences* 29:1094–1104.

Jantz, R.L., and P.H. Moore-Jansen
   1988   *Data Base for Forensic Anthropology: Structure, Content and Analysis.* Report of Investigations, No. 47, Dept. of Anthropology, University of Tennessee, Knoxville, Tennessee.

Katz, D., and J.M. Suchey
   1986   Age Determination of the Male Os Pubis. *Am. J. Physical Anthropology* 69:427–35.

Katzenberg, M.A., and R.H. Krouse
   1989   Application of Stable Isotope Variation in Human Tissues to Problems in Identification. *Canadian Society of Forensic Sciences Journal* 22:7–19.

Katzenberg, M.A., H.P. Schwarcz, and F.J. Melbye
   n.d.   In progress: Further Analyses of Stable Isotopes in Southern Ontario Prehistory.

Kelley, J.O., and J.L. Angel
   1983   The Workers of Catoctin Furnace. *Maryland Archeology* 19 (1): 1–17.

Kennedy, B.V.
   1989   Variation in $\delta^{13}C$ Values of Post-Medieval Europeans. Unpublished Ph.D. dissertation. Department of Archaeology, University of Calgary.

Kennedy, K.R.
   1989   Skeletal Markers of Occupational Stress. In *Reconstruction of Life From the Skeleton.* M.Y. Iscan and K.R. Kennedy, eds., pp. 129–60. New York: Alan R. Liss.

Kobayashi, K.
   1967   Trend in the Length of Life Based on Human Skeletons from Prehistoric to Modern Times in Japan. *J. Fac. Sci. Univ. Tokyo* 3:107–62.

Krogman, W.M., and M.Y. Iscan
   1987   *The Human Skeleton in Forensic Medicine.* Springfield, Illinois: Charles C. Thomas.

Lallo, J.W., G.J. Armelagos, and R.P. Mensforth
   1977   The role of diet, disease and physiology in the origin of porotic hyperostosis. *Human Biology* 49 (3): 471–83.

Lanyon, L.E., W.G.J. Hampson, A.E. Goodship, and J.S. Shah
   1975   Bone Deformation Recorded *in Vivo* from Strain Gauges Attached to the Human Tibial Shaft. *Acta Orthopaedica Scandinavia* 46:256–68.

Larsen, C.S.
  1984   Health and Disease in Prehistoric Georgia: The Transition to
                Agriculture. In *Paleopathology at the Origins of Agriculture*. M.N.
                Cohen and G.J. Armelagos, eds., pp. 367–92. New York: Academic
                Press.
Leigh, R.W.
  1925   Dental pathology of Indian tribes in varied environmental and food
                conditions. *Am. J. Phys. Anth.* 8:179–99.
Lewis, J.R.
  1865   Exemption from military service on account of loss of teeth.
                American Dental Association Transactions, July 1865, 164–69.
Loevy, H.T., and A. Kowitz
  1982   The Habsburgs and the "Habsburg Jaw." *Bulletin of the History of
                Dentistry* 30:19–23.
Lovejoy, C.O., A.H. Burstein, and K.G. Heiple
  1976   The Biomechanical Analysis of Bone Strength: a Method and Its
                Application to Platycnemia. *Am. J. Phys. Anth.* 44:489–506.
Lovejoy, C.O., R.S. Meindl, T.R. Pryzbeck, and R.P. Mensforth
  1985   Chronological Metamorphosis of the Auricular Surface of the Ilium:
                A New Method for the Determination of Adult Skeletal Age at
                Death. *Am. J. Phys. Anth.* 68:15–28.
Lovell, N.C., D.E. Nelson, and H.P. Schwarcz
  1986   Carbon Isotope Ratios in Palaeodiet: Lack of Age or Sex Effect.
                Archaeometry 28 (1): 51–55.
Lovell, N.C.
  1989   Test of Phenice's Technique for Determining Sex from the Os
                Pubis. *Am. J. Phys. Anth.* 79:117–20.
Luz, B., and Y. Kolodny
  1985   Oxygen Isotope Variations in Phosphate of Biogenic Apatites. IV
                Mammal teeth and bones. *Earth Planet. Sci. Lett.* 75:29–36.
Luz, B., Y. Kolodny, and M. Horowitz
  1984   Fractionation of Oxygen Isotopes Between Mammalian Bone-
                phosphate and Environmental Drinking Water. *Geochimica et
                Cosmochimica* Acta 48:1689–93.
Luz, B., A. Cormie, and H.P. Schwarcz
  1989   Oxygen Isotope Variations in Phosphate of Deer Bones. Submitted
                to *Geochimica et Cosmochimica Acta*.
Luz, B., A. Cormie, and H.P. Schwarcz
  1990   Oxygen Isotope Variation in Phosphate of Deer Bones. *Geochimica
                et Cosmochimica Acta* 54 (6): 1723–28.
McDonald, J.L.
  1985   Cariogenicity of Foods. In *Nutrition in Oral Health and Disease*.
                R.L. Pollack and E. Kravitz, eds., pp. 320–45. Philadelphia: Lea and
                Febiger.
McKern, T., and T.D. Stewart
  1957   *Skeletal Age Changes in Young American Males*. Technical Report
                EP-45, Headquarters Quartermaster Research and Development
                Command. Natick, Quartermaster Research and Development
                Center Environmental Protection Research Division.

Mann, R.W., and S.P. Murphy
1990   *Regional Atlas of Bone Disease: A Guide to Pathologic and Normal Variation in the Human Skeleton*. Springfield, Charles C. Thomas.

Meindl, R.S., and C.O. Lovejoy
1985   Ectocranial Suture Closure: A Revised Method for the Determination of Skeletal Age at Death Based on the Lateral-anterior Sutures. *Am. J. Phys. Anth.* 68:57–66.

Menaker, L., ed.
1980   *The Biologic Basis of Dental Caries*. New York: Harper and Row.

Mensforth, R.P., C.O. Lovejoy, J.W. Lallo, and G.J. Armelagos
1978   The Role of Constitutional Factors, Diet, and Infectious Disease in the Etiology of Porotic Hyperostosis and Periosteal Reactions in Prehistoric Infants and Children. *Medical Anthropology* 2 (Winter), part 2.

Merbs, C.F.
1983   *Patterns of Activity-Induced Pathology in a Canadian Inuit Population*. National Museum of Man, Mercury Series, Archaeological Survey of Canada Paper No. 119. Ottawa: National Museums of Canada.

Moore-Jansen, P.H.
1989   *A Multivariate Craniometric Analysis of Secular Change and Variation among Recent North American Populations*. Ph.D. Dissertation, University of Tennessee. Ann Arbor, Michigan: University Microfilms Incorporated

Moore-Jansen, P.H., and R.L. Jantz
1989   Effects of Age On Sex Determination In Crania. Paper presented at the 41st Annual Meeting of the American Academy of Forensic Sciences, Physical Anthropology Section, Las Vegas.

Murphy, T.
1959a   The Changing Pattern of Dentine Exposure in Human Tooth Attrition. *Am. J. Phys. Anth.* 17:167–78.
1959b   Gradients of Dentine Exposure in Human Molar Teeth Attrition. *Am. J. Phys. Anth.* 17:179–86.

Noe, A.
1988   The Snake Hill Site: a War of 1812 American Cemetery. Vol. 1. Unpublished manuscript.

Ortner, D.J., and W.G.J. Putschar
1985   *Identification of Pathological Conditions in Human Skeletal Remains*. 2d ed. Smithsonian Contributions to Anthropology No. 28.

Owsley, D.W., C.E. Orser, R.W. Mann, P.H. Moore-Jansen, and R.L. Montgomery
1987   Demography and Pathology of an Urban Slave Population from New Orleans. *Am. J. Phys. Anth.* 74:185–97.

Pfeiffer, S.
1989   Characterization of Archaeological Bone Decomposition in a Sample of Known Length of Interment. *Am. J. Phys. Anth.* 78:283.

Phenice, T.W.
1969   A Newly Developed Visual Method of Sexing the Os Pubis. *Am. J. Phys. Anth.* 30:297–302.

Powell, M.L.
1988   *Status and Health in Prehistory*. Washington: Smithsonian Institution Press.

Resnick, D., and G. Greenway
  1982   Distal Femoral Cortical Defects, Irregularities, and Excavations.
                Radiology 143 (2): 345–54.
Rosen, S., and N.P. Willett
  1985   Nutrient Requirements, Regulation, and Interdependence of
                Microbes in the Dental Plaque. In *Nutrition in Oral Health and
                Disease*. R.L. Pollack and E. Kravitz, eds., pp. 119–27. Philadel-
                phia: Lea and Febiger.
Ruff, C.B.
  1987   Sexual Dimorphism in Human Lower Limb Bone Structure:
                Relationship to Subsistence Strategy and Sexual Division of Labor.
                J. of Human Evolution 16:391–416.
Ruff, C.B., and W.C. Hayes
  1983   Cross-sectional Geometry of Pecos Pueblo Femora and Tibiae – a
                Biomechanical Investigation: Method and General Patterns of
                Variation. *Am. J. Phys. Anth*. 60:359–81.
Saluja, G.K., M.B. Fitzpatrick, and J. Cross
  1986   Schmorl's Nodes (Intravertebral Herniations of Intervertebral Disc
                Tissue) in Two Historic British Populations. *J. of Anatomy* 145:87–
                96.
Schmorl, G., and H. Junghanns
  1971   *The Human Spine in Health and Disease*. 2d ed. New York: Grune
                and Stratton.
Schoeninger, M.J., and M.J. DeNiro
  1984   Nitrogen and Carbon Isotopic Composition of Bone Collagen from
                Marine and Terrestrial Animals. *Geochimica et Cosmochimica Acta*
                48:625–39
Schwarcz, H.P.
  1969   The Stable Isotopes of Carbon. *In Handbook of Geochemistry*. K.H.
                Wedepohl, ed., Chapter 6B. Berlin: Springer-Verlag.
Schwarcz, H.P., F.J. Melbye, M.A. Katzenberg, and M. Knyf
  1985   Stable Isotopes in Human Skeletons of Southern Ontario: Recon-
                structing Paleodiet. *J. of Archaeological Science* 12:187–206.
Sciulli, P.W., and R.M. Gramly
  1989   Analysis of the Fort Laurens Skeletal Sample. *Am. J. Phys. Anth.*
                80 (1): 11–24.
Sebes, J.
  1989   Personal communication, University of Tennessee School of
                Medicine, Memphis.
Shapiro, H.L.
  1930   Old New Yorkers. A Series of Cranial from the Nagel Burial
                Ground, New York City. *Am. J. Phys. Anth*. 14:379–404.
Silver, I. A.
  1969   The Ageing of Domestic Animals. In *Science in Archaeology*. D.
                Brothwell and E. Higgs, eds., pp. 281–302. London: Thames and
                Hudson.
Smith, B.H., S.M. Garn, and W.S. Hunter
  1986   Secular Trends in Face Size. *Angle Orthodontist* 56:196–204.
Steegmann, A.T., Jr.
  1985   18th Century British Military Stature: Growth Cessation, Selective
                Recruiting, Secular Trends, Nutrition at Birth, Cold and
                Occupation. *Human Biology* 57:77–96.

1986   Skeletal Stature Compared to Archival Stature in Mid-Eighteenth Century America: Fort William Henry. *Am. J. Phys. Anth.* 71:431–36.

Steegmann, A.T., Jr., and P.A. Haseley
1988   Stature Variation in the British American Colonies: French and Indian War Record, 1755–1763. *Am. J. Phys. Anth.* 75:413–22.

Steinbock, R.T.
1976   *Paleopathological Diagnosis and Interpretation.* Springfield: Charles C. Thomas.

Stenhouse, M.J., and M.S. Baxter
1979   The Uptake of Bomb ^{14}C in Humans. In *Radiocarbon Dating.* R. Berger and H. Suess, eds., pp. 324–41. Berkeley: University of California Press.

Stuart-Macadam, P.
1985   Porotic Hyperostosis: Representative of Childhood Condition. *Am. J. Phys. Anth.* 66:391–98.

Taylor, H.P.
1979   Oxygen and Hydrogen Isotope Relationships in Hydrothermal Mineral Deposits. In *Geochemistry of Hydrothermal Ore Deposits.* H.L. Barnes, ed., pp. 236–77. New York: Wiley Interscience.

Thoma, K.H., and H.M. Goldman
1960   *Oral Pathology.* St Louis: C.V. Mosby.

Tieszen, L.L., T.W. Boutton, K.G. Tesdahl, and N.A. Slade
1983   Fractionation and Turnover of Stable Carbon Isotopes in Animal Tissues: Implications for δ^{13}C Analysis of Diet. *Oecologia* 57:32–37.

Trotter, M., and G.C. Gleser
1958   A Re-evaluation of Estimation of Stature Based on Measurements of Stature Taken During Life and of Long Bones After Death. *Am. J. Phys. Anth.* 16:79–123.

Tudge, A.P.
1960   A Method of Analysis of Oxygen Isotopes in Othophosphates: Its Use in Measurements of Paleotemperatures. *Geochimica et Cosmochimica Acta* 18:81–93.

Turner, C.G. II
1979   Dental Anthropological Indications of Agriculture among the Jomon People of Central Japan. *Am. J. Phys. Anth.* 51:619–36.

van der Merwe, N.J.
1982   Carbon Isotopes, Photosynthesis, and Archaeology. *American Scientist* 70:596–606.

van der Merwe, N.J., and J.C. Vogel
1978 ^{13}C Content of Human Collagen as a Measure of Prehistoric Diet in Woodland North America. *Nature* 276:815–16.

Vogel, R.I., and O.F. Alvares
1985   Nutrition and Periodontal Disease. In *Nutrition in Oral Health and Disease.* R.L. Pollack and E. Kravitz, eds., pp. 136–50. Philadelphia: Lea and Febiger.

Wachter, K.W., and J. Trussell
1982   Estimating Historical Heights. *J. of the American Statistical Association* 77:279–93.

Waldron, H.A.
1981   Postmortem Absorption of Lead by the Skeleton. *Am. J. Phys. Anth.*
                55:395–98.
Whitehorne, J.W.A.
1988   U.S. Operations. In the Snake Hill Site: a War of 1812 American
                Cemetery. Vol. I. R. Williamson, ed., pp. 15–47. Unpublished
                manuscript.
Williamson, R., ed.
1988   The Snake Hill Site: a War of 1812 American Cemetery. Unpub-
                lished manuscript.
Wittmers, L.E., A. Alich, and A.C. Aufderheide
1981   Lead in Bone. I. Direct Analysis for Lead in Milligram Quantities of
                Bone Ash Aby Graphite Furnace Atomic Absorption Spectroscopy.
                Am. J. of Clinical Pathology 75 (1): 80–85.
Wittmers, L.E., A.C. Aufderheide, J. Wallgren, G. Rapp, and A. Alich
1988   Lead in Bone IV. Distribution of Lead in the Human Skeleton.
                Archives of Environmmental Health 43 (67): 381–91.
Yurtsever, Y., and J.R. Gat
1981   Atmospheric Waters. In *Stable Isotope Hydrology: Deuterium and
                Oxygen -18 in the Water Cycle.* Vienna: International Atomic
                Energy Agency.